The Other Belfast
An Irish Youth

By John Sidney Rickerby
with Mark Rickerby

ACKNOWLEDGEMENTS

A million thank you's to:

Mark, my son, for his determination to travel to the furthest corners of my memory, excavate these old stories, and help bring them into the world.

My wife Rosaleen, who heard me say *"I'm going to write a book"* several hundred times over the years and patiently encouraged me every time.

Our editor, Suzanne Egle, who gave us the fresh perspective we both needed and went above and beyond what was expected of her, throwing herself heart and soul into the task. A better editor does not exist. She can be reached at writersue25@yahoo.com

Our friend Sally Robinson, daughter of "Buck" Alec Robinson, for helping us depict her legendary father accurately.

Darren Shaw, Alfie McKee's grandson, for sharing stories about and photos of the eccentric and lovable "Uncle Alfie."

Finally, my parents, relatives and old friends, who left such an indelible mark upon my soul, I always knew I would have to write a book about them. It took over fifty years but I finally did it. I only wish I could thank you all in person. What I would give to see your smiling eyes again.

For my dear Rosaleen. They say fortune favors the bold. It's true. And I thank heaven every day that I was bold enough to say hello to you almost sixty years ago.

You are, and have always been, my fortune.

CONTENTS

"Belfast is like an ugly child; you love it the most."
(Steven Rae)

FOREWORD

If my father were asked to tell every story and joke that he knows, every member of the audience would expire of old age before he ran out. He has filled my head with so many wild and colorful tales over the years, I thought it was a great idea when he told me he wanted to finish writing his memoir. For four decades, he had scribbled his memories of his youth in Belfast in notebooks, which were yellowed with time and languishing in ancient boxes in his garage. I volunteered to find them and help patch them together. It has been a monumental task, mainly because the notebooks were only the tip of the proverbial iceberg. Just when I thought the book was finished, he would tell me another story that the book couldn't possibly do without.

It's no mystery what happens to things we don't appreciate. Eventually, we lose them. Some things in life are bound to be lost whether we appreciate them or not, but some can be saved if we are willing to make the effort, until they too are swallowed by time forever. The young traditionally turn a deaf ear to older people; the very people they can learn the most from. It's yet another way that youth is wasted on the young; an ancient paradox.

There's an old saying: "When an elderly person dies, it's like a vast library burning to the ground." The older the person, the more epic the tale. Conquering ourselves can make just as compelling a story as conquering a foreign power. Exploring our own spirits can be every bit as perilous and full of discovery as exploring the world outside ourselves. It has been said that artistic expression is simply the desire to capture the beauty and drama of life and put it into a more permanent and lasting form. The things in life most in danger of being taken for granted are those we perceive to be perennial. As Longfellow observed, *"If Spring came but once in a century, instead of once a year, or burst forth with the sound of an earthquake, and not in silence, what wonder and expectation there would be in all hearts to behold the miraculous change!"* And so it is with everything.

When I was a boy, I saw a Disney movie called *Darby O'Gill and the Little People.* Darby was an old man and my dad was young then so I didn't make the connection between him and Darby, the charming, old tale-spinner, but I do now. Like Darby, he never runs out of stories to tell, tells them with great aplomb, and doesn't mind "gilding the lily" once in a while for dramatic effect. As an old writer's saying goes, *"Never let the truth ruin a good story."* In his spoken tales, anything can happen, but this book is the gospel truth. It is his life, after all, and as he put it, he wants to make sure he "gets it right."

As a child, my father's stories were as natural a part of life to me as the seasons. At Los Angeles pubs and weekend parties with "the Irish crowd", he could always be found entertaining his friends, who would nod with understanding at the old ways his stories celebrated. Non-Irish people were usually present as well, and I was always impressed by the way he could enchant even them, the uninitiated. The tales he spun usually ended on a humorous note and as I sat playing with friends somewhere in the distance, I came to recognize the group's eruption of laughter as the end of one of his jokes or stories.

He is also a tenor and has entertained the same crowd for decades. At weddings, funerals, or any other event, someone will inevitably say, "Get Rickerby up for a song." I watched him sing Danny Boy a hundred times growing up, some obscure ballad from the old country that would cause everyone's eyes to well with tears, or a raucous, bawdy, tavern song that would get them all up dancing, and was always amazed by his ability to make people feel more emotion than they otherwise might have. I'm sure witnessing that wonderful, magical power was what made me want to become an artist.

Still, my Irish heritage held no great allure for me as a child. I was born and raised in Los Angeles, and it was the California lifestyle I identified with - the beach, surfing, the glittery and false world of Hollywood. Belfast was as obscure to me as the Himalayas, and I had no desire to bring it closer.

But it wasn't just my own lack of interest that prevented me from embracing my heritage. As I was growing up in the 1970's, my parents and I were constantly angered by news stories coming out of Ireland with sickening regularity of yet another bombing or shooting. All my life, the house would fall silent during these reports, and I could feel my parents' dismay permeate the house, which had been light and cheerful moments before. This ritual was repeated dozens of times over the years, and it left its marks on my heart. The longer the conflict dragged on, the more anger I felt toward the Irish people responsible for such acts and for their apparent unwillingness or inability to settle their differences without violence.

It's easy for me to condemn them because I had never been immersed in "the troubles." Hate is a learned emotion. Like many civil wars around the world rooted in ancient grievances, intolerance is passed along from parent to child like a hereditary disease. Everyone has a story to tell about who did what to whom, even if it's just something they heard about and didn't experience themselves. Hatred becomes so entrenched over time that the only solution to the stubborn conflicts constantly raging in the world's hot zones might be to take every newborn child to some remote island for a hundred years or so, tell them nothing about where they're from, let the hatred and resentment die off with the people left behind, then bring them back and repopulate the place. Obviously, that is completely impossible, so we're all stuck with ourselves as much as we're stuck with whomever we consider to be "the enemy."

My father has had a long-standing correspondence with the British Consulate and has appeared on numerous radio and talk shows since the early 1970's discussing the situation in Northern Ireland. He has also contributed many articles to the *Los Angeles Times* on the subject. When I was about ten years old, I stumbled upon a pamphlet hidden at the bottom of a drawer. It contained graphic photos of the aftermath of an IRA (Irish Republican Army) bombing. One of the photos looked like a charred tree branch on a metal gurney.

The caption below it read, "This is what the IRA did to a six year-old girl." Only then did I make out the shape of a small body, which had curled into the fetal position as the fire sucked all the moisture out. I stared at that photo in horrified fascination until I felt the impulse to vomit. It was my first introduction to barbarity, and I couldn't believe human beings were capable of doing such things to each other. My resilient young mind was able to bury the image somehow, and I went on with my childhood. But the image was never really gone, and like most Americans, I began to associate Ireland with terrorism.

It was only through exposure to my parents' kindly Irish friends, both Protestant and Catholic, meeting the warm-hearted people of Ireland during trips back to "the old country," and watching movies like *The Quiet Man* that I was made aware of another Ireland. It may have been a romanticized version, as *Darby O'Gill and the Little People* was, but this world has always required romanticizing and probably always will.

My father wrote a poem in 1972 which helped teach me that although the people of Ireland have their differences and too often live up to the pugnacious, hot-tempered, hard-drinking stereotype they're famous for, they are for the most part very kind-hearted and decent, north or south. I suspect the same is true of people anywhere. As a taxi driver in Belfast told me during my last visit there in 2002, *"The Irish get along with everyone, except each other."*

This is my father's poem.

ULSTER

There are those who say that Ulster
is a place of hate and pain.
But many who have left it
would still go back again.
The strangers do not see
behind the bombs and flames and smoke
And fail to see the character
of the kindly Ulster folk.
But we have memories of the days
when we were young and gay,
Of carefree romps through Ormeau Park
or over Cave Hill's Bray.
The Saturdays at Windsor,
the Sundays by the sea,
The bathing belles at Pickie,
the sands at Donaghadee.
Our best suit pressed and ready
and we were Plaza-bound
But first a stop at Mooney's
and pints bought all around.

The Sunday morning papers,
the bacon and dip bread,
Then a dander to the castle
where all the scores are read.
Back to work on Monday,
the weekend's tales are told
While the oldsters smile and chuckle
as our youthful tales unfold.
A new girl in the office,
she's a quare wee bit o' stuff.
Is she going strong, you wonder,
as you act so big and tough.
Those were the days; there is no doubt,
as my memory wanders back.
That is what we all recall,
not the rifle's crack.
Will it ever be the same, you ask.
Will today's kids ever know
The simple life we all enjoyed
a long, long time ago.

In 1972, Bill Cunningham, a good friend of my father's, heard about a woman in Belfast named Mary Peters, who was trying to raise funds to build a racetrack for troubled children. He and my father wanted to help her, so they contacted James Young, who was Belfast's most famous and well-loved comedian at the time. He was loved by Protestants and Catholics alike because he picked on both of them equally. They asked Jimmy if he would be willing to come to Hollywood and perform at the Ebell Theater to raise funds for the project. He accepted the offer whole-heartedly, saying it was a lifelong dream of his to perform in Hollywood. He and his manager, Jack Hudson, stayed with our family for a week. My father secured the booking at the Wilshire Ebell Theater and advertised Jimmy's performance. The theater sold out almost overnight. Jimmy's act was three hours long, the longest stand-up comedy routine in the history of the Ebell Theater. The stage manager, who had worked there for over forty years, said he had never heard laughter like that in his entire life.

Toward the end of his trip, we all went to Disneyland. I sat beside Jimmy on the *It's a Small World* ride, which was his favorite ride of the day. When he was leaving for Belfast the next morning, he said to me, "The best thing I can wish for you is that you'll grow up to be exactly like your father."

I remember James as a gentle-spirited and eloquent man. Sadly, he died of a heart attack a few years later. However, even today, almost everyone in Belfast remembers him, even those who were born after he died, and the Irish refer to him affectionately as "Our Jimmy".

The author (right) with Belfast comedian James Young (left), and his manager, Jack Hudson.

Despite meeting the crown prince of Irish comedy, I continued to ignore my Irish heritage. After all, that was their world, not mine. My parents took me to Irish fairs every summer as a child, and though I felt oddly at home there (Joseph Campbell called it "recognizing one's tribe"), I couldn't stand the music, the dancing looked silly to me, the food was awful, and I just wanted to go home and play baseball in the street with my friends. I remained stubbornly Californian, but my parents never seemed to mind. My father would just laugh when I complained about the Irish music he played in the car during long trips and would give the universal parental response, *"When you have your own car, you can pick the music."* This open antagonism only caused me to further deny their culture. Then came the onslaught of adolescence and the conformity to peers that it demanded. My attitude did not improve.

As the years passed, I met the parents of many American friends and couldn't help noticing, as awful as it sounds, how inanimate their homes seemed to be compared to my own. There was little and often none of the laughter, singing, storytelling, sharing of poems, endless jokes and incessant ribbing that went on in my house. Being young, I even took their bored demeanors personally at times. It wasn't until many years later that I finally realized that their parents were actually just boring in comparison. There were exceptions, of course, and maybe I just had the bad luck of crossing paths with a lot of dullards. Whatever the case, I finally stopped taking my own parents and all their wonderful quirks for granted. I began to realize how lucky I was to have been raised in an atmosphere bursting with so much humor, music, and whimsy - traits the Irish are famous for the world over. Until then, I had mistakenly assumed such qualities to be commonplace.

So what did I do after this epiphany? Relish every moment with my parents? Record their stories for posterity? Tell them every day how lucky I felt to be their son? No. I wasn't much different from most young people so I let many more years pass before making any grand demonstrations of my esteem for them, or making any permanent record of the tales they told. However, this time, it was not due to lack of appreciation on my part. It was ordinary, old-fashioned denial. I was in my mid-twenties before the full breadth of what I had in them finally dawned on me.

I had found my father's tattered notebooks in a box years earlier and thought about encouraging him to finish his memoir, but on a subconscious level I felt that if I did I would be acknowledging the fact that the stories would someday end; that my parents would not always be with me. That thought made me too uncomfortable, so like most of us do, I lived as if we were all immortal, as if death only existed for other people, as if my parents would be with me forever. Though I had begun to toy with the idea of being a writer, I all but ignored the greatest sources of inspiration and the deepest wellsprings of experience in my life. Many more years would pass before the old notebooks would be rescued from the dusty garage.

Then tragedy struck. My older brother and only sibling, who had been battling a heroin addiction for over ten years, died suddenly of an overdose at the age of thirty-seven just when we all thought he was finally getting his life together. For years since we became aware of his problem, we feared it might happen and did everything in our power to prevent it. The last ditch effort he made to stay clean toward the end of his life had raised our hopes for him higher than they had ever been. When he died, my parents and I were utterly devastated.

I was not a complete stranger to death. I had lost all of my grandparents by that time except for my maternal grandmother. However, their deaths were an abstraction to me because they all lived in Ireland, and I had only met them briefly on two short trips there. When they died, I felt sadness but mostly for my parents' sake. A robbery victim had also died in my arms on a Los Angeles street, and I had lost a close friend to leukemia. But my brother's death hit me over the head with everything I had been denying for so long - that life most certainly does not go on forever, that death will come for all of us eventually, and that we must celebrate the people we love in every way possible while they are alive. As the poet Andrew Marvell wrote,

The grave's a fine and private place
but none I think do there embrace.

Several years ago, I was talking with a friend, who is also the son of Belfast immigrants. My parents and his met in Canada when they were young and have been friends ever since. His father and mine were dancing together (or "acting the eejit" as they would say in Ireland.) During a break in the laughter, he said to me, *"Do you realize that if we don't marry Irish girls, the whole Irish thing is over? Once our parents are gone, that's it. It all dies with them. They're part of a world that doesn't exist anymore."* I nodded in agreement, and as I watched our fathers carrying on, it struck me how true his words were. I had already let so much slip past. I vowed again silently to myself that I would not let the folklore of my parents' lives die. I would help my father finish his book, this book, once and for all.

I didn't run off to the Emerald Isle to find an Irish girl to marry. I married for love, not background (though I have taught my wife how to do a passable Irish accent and sing "The Unicorn" by The Irish Rovers.) So my way of preserving the magical world I was given is the book you are now holding in your hands – tales of a simpler time in an infinitely less perilous world. As my father said with a cracking voice in his eulogy at my brother's memorial service to all of his friends gathered in the small church, every one of them heartbroken along with us, *"There are evils in the modern world we never dreamed of as kids back in Ireland."*

There are, and my heart is heavy with them. This world has become a minefield of dangers not only to the body but to the mind and spirit as well. So as well as a record, this book is also an escape. It was an escape during a difficult time for my father and I to work on it together. I hope it will be an escape for you to read it.

I'm not sure what drove my father to write these stories down over the years. His great love is singing, not writing. But my guess is it was plain, old homesickness. He left Belfast at the age of twenty-four and could not afford to return until he was thirty-five. Those eleven years were a struggle, especially with two boys to feed. He had quit school at fourteen to support his family so he had no fancy degrees to flash at potential employers. That kind of pressure can give rise to a lot of fond reminiscing. Most of the stories are in their original form. Others were gleaned more recently during conversations, some of which I secretly recorded so that his natural storytelling abilities would not be impeded. Others are new to me as well; stories he held onto until someone expressed the proper interest in hearing them. This book is forty years in the making, and the old stories are finally seeing the light of day.

I wish that I'd had the same desire to read them when I was a teenager and my father and I seemed to be at odds about everything. It surely would have helped me understand him more and resent him less. This project has taught me how little I really knew about him. It has also made me wonder how many other people there are who don't know their loved ones as well as they imagine they do, and how many other dusty memoirs are decomposing in drawers or boxes all over the world. There are things that just don't come up in conversation that can be told to an old journal when the kids are asleep and the world is quiet.

We often don't understand the behavior of our family members, or anyone else for that matter, because we don't know the whole story. Understanding another is like putting together a jigsaw puzzle. If there are pieces missing, the whole picture never becomes clear and we continue to be baffled by their surface behavior. Finding the missing pieces and completing the picture of my father's life has been one of the most rewarding adventures of my own, and it has increased my love and compassion for him immensely.

One word of warning: My father can be a bit, well, gross. He loves to shock people. A few chapters are both gross and shocking. In assisting my father with this book, I entertained the idea of leaving them out but changed my mind, for to do so would be to leave the portrait unfinished. The kind of person who would be offended is exactly the kind of person my father directs this kind of humor at like little bombs. The fact is, he enjoys it and feels they deserve it for taking life and themselves too seriously.

So, these are the tales of a little town called Belfast in the first half of the twentieth century, a time and place less sophisticated but also far less treacherous than the world I find myself in today, the world that took my brother and almost destroyed the spirits of my mother and father. However, the most common adjective placed before the expression *Irish spirit* is "irrepressible", and since my brother died I have been given the grandest demonstration of this that anyone ever could. During the first year or so after his death, I didn't think my parents or I would ever recover or that any of us would ever laugh or smile again. It just didn't seem possible. Anyone who has ever lost a loved one, particularly a child, will know what I mean. But I have seen my parents' spirits rise again, even through this, in spite of this. Not even the loss of their first-born son can suppress forever the beauty and vibrancy of their souls, and it shouldn't. We do no honor to those we have lost by lying down and dying next to them.

So, from the devastation of that horror, the humor has risen again, and the stories are being told once more, as irrepressible as ever, always one more just when I think I must have heard them all. And my parents have begun to sing again.

Much has been written and said about the tenacity of the Irish, how they conquer everything with a joke or a song. For instance, an Irish wake is a happy occasion, not a somber one, a party meant to celebrate the life of the departed. To a stranger, it appears to be madness, singing in the midst of such pain, but it is the singing that saves them from madness. The stories, the laughter and the singing are what have preserved and upheld the spirit of the Irish race through wars, famines, persecution, and all the other woes which have befallen that lyrical and tragic land. Likewise, my parents and I will go on living, as we must, and we'll honor the good that there was in my brother's life the same way the Irish always have, with a humorous tale told with an open heart and a tear sparkling in the eye.

So come with me now, friend, to a simpler day
Just for a moment, 'fore you're back in the fray.
There are just a few people I'd like you to meet
Over that hill there and down the next street.
You might recognize them as family because
Half the world's Irish - and half wishes it was!

Mark Rickerby © 2008

CHAPTER 1

THE UNDYING SUPPORT OF FAMILY

"Love is an ideal thing, marriage a real thing; a confusion of the real with the ideal never goes unpunished."
~ Johann Wolfgang Von Goethe

My parents, Jack and Elsie Rickerby

The Ireland my parents were born into was going through tremendous upheaval over the issue of Home Rule. The movement for Irish Independence had gained momentum in the latter half of the 19th century and it seemed that Irish freedom from Britain was imminent. During this tumultuous time, my father's family lived in County Wexford in southern Ireland. They had moved there from the north of England during one of the 17th century plantations engineered by England.

The patriarch of the family had ten sons and worked as a groomsman on the estate of an Anglo-Irish landowner. This trade apparently did not agree with him because he suffered multiple hernias one morning while carrying a newborn pony from a pasture to the estate barn. Shortly thereafter, not fully recovered from his last injury, a horse kicked him squarely in the jaw. Perhaps due to the severity of this injury, he contracted cancer of the mouth and suffered a slow and miserable death. It was a difficult time for Protestants in a society dominated by Roman Catholics. With the head of the clan gone, friendly neighbors suggested it would be better if the family moved away. Some moved north to Ulster and the rest scattered around the world.

My father, Jack Rickerby, was among those who moved north with his mother and father to Dungannon in County Tyrone. He moved to Belfast in his late teens where he met and married my mother, Elsie McKee. The relationship met with opposition right from the start. Upon meeting Elsie's new love, her father declared with finality that he was "an empty man." Elsie's mother, a haughty and imperious English woman from London, was also unimpressed by her daughter's choice and made no bones about it. My father was not special in this regard, however, for she approved of almost no one. My Aunt Flo, who married my mother's brother, Alfie, told me that her mother thought Alfie was too good for her, too, and that she had attempted to halt her marriage as well. My mother had married in haste to escape her own mother's overbearing personality.

Probably in reaction to the in-laws condemnation of their son, my father's family condemned Elsie in return, accusing her of being a "put on" - someone overly impressed with herself for no apparent reason. When I was a child, my paternal grandmother, Tilly Reid, would often tell me how irresponsible my mother was, especially when it came to money. *"Fools and their money are easily parted!"* she would say, accentuating her point by blowing into her hand and winking at me. And my Uncle Alfie, never one to mince words, simplified the entire matter by stating, *"All the Rickerby's are nuts. Elsie is the only one with any common sense."*

The marriage went ahead despite this mountain of opposition and each family reluctantly resigned themselves to it. Unrelenting, the two families stood on opposite sides of the church during the wedding, barely acknowledging each other.

Disapproving in-laws have always been the stuff of fairy tales and Shakespearean dramas. However, in fairy tales, the couple usually overcomes all odds and lives happily ever after. In fact, the in-laws unwittingly contribute to the union they hope to destroy, unaware that their hard-headed attitudes only create a sense of destiny and purpose in the young lovers, strengthening their desire for each other and their resolve to be together. I wish I could say my parents proved them all wrong in the fairy tale tradition but that, sadly, was not the case. Though their love may have burned hot at first, it extinguished itself quickly as the realities of life and the collective weight of their condemning families bore down on them. The two families merely tolerated each other and my parents were left to face life alone.

CHAPTER 2

THE GREATER DEPRESSION

"Being unwanted, unloved, uncared for, forgotten by everybody, I think that is a much greater hunger, a much greater poverty than the person who has nothing to eat."
~ Mother Teresa

My father, Jack Rickerby, got a job as a shunter at the Great Northern Railway on Great Victoria Street in Central Belfast, but there was nothing "great" about it. It was a dirty and dangerous job joining and separating boxcars. Needless to say, one does not want to get a hand stuck between the hitches of two train cars. My father was not a large man, but his arms were very muscular because of his occupation. I remember admiring them when I was a child and hoping to have arms as strong as his one day.

Despite the physical demands of his job, the pay was less than average, and he would often work extra hours to make ends meet. My mother, rather than praising him for working longer hours, constantly complained over the inadequacy of his pay, oblivious to the fact that their money problems had more to do with her poor management of his income than the amount. Others in similar positions seemed to manage quite well, but we were always hand to mouth.

Shortly after I was born on May 11, 1933, the Great Depression hit and my father was laid off. My parents were forced to give up their rented home and live with their families again. This was a severe blow to my father's ego and completed the destruction of any self-esteem he might have had. Living with her parents again with my father unemployed gave her family the opportunity to turn her against him even more. When they were back together, she complained more than ever about his lack of success. She even started to repeat her father's words during their arguments - "My father was right, y'ar an empty man!" I remember crying for my father. Even as a child, I knew that was a terrible thing to say to anyone.

My mother's parents now felt they had bona-fide proof of what they had always believed – that my father could not sustain a family. In turn, his family blamed my mother for squandering his income. Truth be told, she was probably more to blame. My father was just one more of thousands who were being laid off at that time, but she had no excuse for overspending. This cemented the bad feelings between the two clans even further. With all their finer qualities, the Irish are the worst for holding grudges.

My father got his job at the railway back after a few months, and he and my mother were able to get a place of their own again, a small rented flat. He soon became a guard, or conductor as the job is called in America, and his wages increased. But rather than being happy for him, my mother continued to complain about money. She would overspend on unnecessary items and leave herself short on essential ones. Any raises in pay my father achieved would be met with greater spending on her part.

The Great Depression was a perfect name for that time, economically and emotionally. Joseph Campbell once wrote that people aren't really interested in the "meaning" of life. What they really want is to feel that they are living their lives completely and passionately. This is why people jump out of perfectly good airplanes. Human beings are not designed to endure an endless chain of monotonous, identical, ordinary days. They want to feel alive. So, like my ma, they will often spend what little money they have, or spend money they don't have if credit is available, on frivolous things that make them happy in the moment, and throw all common sense right out the window.

Great Northern Railway Station, Great Victoria Street

My da napping after a hard day's work.

CHAPTER 3

A NEW START

"We cannot really love anybody with whom we never laugh."
~ Agnes Repplier

It was a cold spring morning when an aging black taxi picked us all up at our rented flat, labored across town and up a steep hill, coughed irritably, and grinded to a halt in front of our new home on Prestwick Park. I was four years old, too young to understand what was going on, but I could tell by my parents' unusual warmth toward each other and their eager faces that something special was happening.

My mother and I got out of the taxi and stood on the sidewalk gazing at the house as my father paid the driver and unloaded the suitcases. The driver pulled away, leaving the three of us in the crisp silence of morning. I still recall the feeling of my mother's hand in mine as we stood there together admiring our new home. I had never seen either of them happier. It was a new beginning. My father was proud of himself, and for the first time in a long while, my mother was proud of him, too.

Although not grand by any stretch, the house did have a small garden at the front and another garden at the rear that was so big it constituted sixty percent of the property. All that green was truly glorious after so many years in a colorless flat. More importantly, it had electricity and indoor plumbing, facilities which were absent from many of the older homes in Belfast at the time. In those days, outside toilet facilities were the norm and gas lighting was still common. Except for those hearty souls who didn't mind midnight excursions in the midst of an Ulster winter to a rear yard toilet with ice on the seat, mere mortals were forced to use chamber pots, or "po's," as they were called, for nocturnal emergencies. There were two small bedrooms upstairs, one for my parents and one for me.

It was quite a pleasant house considering the times. Two stories, brick construction, and located in a new development on the outer northwest edge of the city. The first floor had a small living room with a fireplace, an entryway, a dining room, and a kitchen with a red-tiled floor. The kitchen shelving was open, which made the kitchen look like a mercantile store, with our food exposed for all to see. Arranged there side by side were the omnipresent cans of Bachelor's peas, HP sauce, assorted jam jars and Coleman's mustard. Beneath the cabinet, well within a child's reach, were Jeye's fluid (a cleaning solution), and a variety of toxic, germ-killing solutions, essentials required by my mother in her never-ending war against bacteria. The second floor had two bedrooms and a bathroom.

Our house (taken during a trip home in 1978)

The house was connected by a common wall to an identical home. When voices were raised, we could hear every word the neighbors were saying and vice versa. There were no secrets. I would later be happy about the paper thin wall between us and our neighbors because it was one of the few things that kept my parents from yelling at each other as loudly as they otherwise might have.

A privet hedge ran the full length of the front garden, and the entry path was secured by a wrought iron gate. A few years later, this gate and almost every other iron gate in Belfast would be removed by the government for use in the war effort.

The long garden at the rear of the house ended at a drainage ditch where holly bushes were planted, and where water flowed intermittently depending on the time of year. Over the years, my father would struggle to encourage the growth of a lawn, but swamp-like conditions generated by an underground spring would forever frustrate his efforts.

Our back yard

From the front upstairs bedroom window, we could glimpse the imposing Cave Hill*, which lent its name to our area of the city. Through the rear bedroom window, we had a fine view of the distant and ominous Black Mountain* overlooking west Belfast, where wholesale rioting would take place decades later.

Though class distinctions were beyond my comprehension then, I know now that our neighborhood was just a step or two above lower class. More than half of the people of Belfast at the time were working class, and life in general was very hard. Rent rates were controlled by the government so entire families usually lived and died in the same house, which was then passed on to the eldest child. People rarely moved voluntarily.

If only the years my parents spent together could have come close to the dreams dancing in their heads the morning we all stood together admiring our new home. The first three years of their marriage had been difficult, to say the least. They were hard times for anyone but especially a struggling young couple. Having no support from their families, they had no refuge from their woes and no one to turn to for advice. In a way, their marriage mirrored the history of the neighborhood and of Ireland herself - so full of new hope at the beginning, a too short honeymoon, and a steady decline into what was at best a state of mutual tolerance.

The house I grew up in seemed gigantic to me as a child, but it was actually very small. Over the years, I have thought about that little house and the typical street it stood on in the insignificant corner of Belfast, and how each house is its own universe, emotions swirling like constellations within it, in turmoil or harmony. The world outside its walls may as well not exist, for what happens within is all that matters, especially to a child.

My parents' first few years together, which should have been the happiest, were a time of dashed hopes and disenchantment. The home they entered with such anticipation would soon become a prison as the seeds of resentment and doubt planted by their families took root, slowly strangling their love for each other. They would live in that rented house for the rest of their lives. During the time I spent there with them, I never once saw them embrace or kiss. They never went on a vacation together and never won the approval of their in-laws. When I think of how hard it must have been for them, sometimes I still feel like crying.

Cavehill (Irish: *Binn Uamha*), historically known as **Ben Madigan** (Irish: *Binn Mhadagáin*), is a basaltic hill overlooking the city of Belfast in Northern Ireland. It forms part of the south-eastern border of the Antrim Plateau. It is distinguished by its famous 'Napoleon's Nose', a basaltic outcrop which resembles the profile of the famous emperor Napoleon and is said to have inspired the famous novel Gulliver's Travels. Cavehill is also the name of an electoral ward in Belfast. All of Belfast can be seen from its peak, as can the Isle of Man and Scotland on clear days. Like Arthur's Seat in Edinburgh, it lies just a few miles from the centre of a major city. The towering cliffs can be dangerous, with many people needing rescue after seeking a shortcut to the summit or the higher caves. Cavehill rises to almost 370 metres (1200 ft) above sea level. Most of its lower east side lies on the Belfast Castle estate, which has as its focal point the imposing 19th-century Scottish baronial castle. The castle was designed by Charles Lanyon and constructed by the Marquess of Donegal in 1872 in the Deer Park. The slopes of Cavehill were originally used as farmland but, from the 1880s, a major planting exercise was undertaken, producing the now familiar deciduous and coniferous woodland landscape. Belfast Castle estate was given to Belfast city by the 8th Earl of Shaftesbury in 1934. (Wikepedia)

Black Mountain (Irish: *an Sliabh Dubh / an Cnoc Dubh*) is a large hill which overlooks the city of Belfast. The mountain is one of the most prominent features of the city, towering above most of west Belfast. It reaches a height of 1,275 ft and is composed of limestone. There have been flint finds in the area, which also contains raths, deserted farms and overgrown paths joining the fields and homesteads scattered over the mountain. On a clear day there are views of Strangrod Lough, the Mournes, and the Sperrins, as well as Scotland and Donegal. (Wikipedia)

CHAPTER 4

WORLD WAR II COMES TO BELFAST

"Belfast was sorely tried, no other city in the United Kingdom, save London, had lost so many of her citizens in one night's raid. No other city, except possibly Liverpool, ever did. They wondered how the life of the city could ever be renewed".
~ The Belfast Telegraph, after a German bombing raid

"In the stink of human excrement, in the acrid smell of disinfectant these dead were heaped, body on body, flung arms, twisted feet, open mouth, staring eyes, old men on top of young women, a child lying on a policeman's back, a soldier's hand resting on a woman's thigh, a carter still wearing his coal-slacks, on top of a pile of arms and legs, his own arm outstretched, finger pointing, as though he warned of some unseen horror. Forbidding and clumsy, the dead cluttered the morgue room from floor to ceiling".
~ Ulster author Brian Moore

My parents were listening to the news on the radio in the kitchen one night when they became very quiet. My father turned the radio up and they both leaned in. They looked at each other with expressions I had never seen them make before. My father told me, "Go up to your room, son." I asked what was happening. All my father said was, "Another bloody war".

Conscription was taking place within the United Kingdom. However, even though Northern Ireland was part of the U.K., the draft was not extended to Ulster. I have never heard an official reason why but it was generally believed there was no draft in Northern Ireland because there were so many people living there who were disloyal to the Crown and because circumstances forced them to be there. To call these people up would invite too many problems. They would not be willing participants. It would take another army to watch them.

Northern Ireland, however, was deeply involved in the war effort and contributed through its ship and aircraft building capacity. This brought about an economic upturn in the north. A lot of unemployed people found gainful employment and more came up from the south to fill the demand.

After Britain's declaration of war against Germany, the commonwealth countries – Australia, Canada, and others – joined in. However, the Irish Republic to the south, which had gained its independence in 1919, decided to remain neutral. The president of the Irish Republic at that time was Eamon Devalera. His vision of Ireland was that it should retain its character as primarily agrarian, with particular emphasis on the retention of the ancient Irish language of Gaelic. In effect, he wanted to keep Ireland simple and rural, free from contamination by Britain and other industrial powers.

The decision of the Irish Republic to remain neutral during the war brought about the scorn and approbation of the people of Northern Ireland, who considered themselves loyal to the crown and the British war effort. Many southern Irish men also disagreed with their government's decision and went over to England to join the armed forces there. A similar number of people from Northern Ireland joined up as well.

My father attempted to enlist but was denied for some reason, perhaps because he had a wife and child. My strongest recollection of the war is listening to Prime Minister Winston Churchill on the radio. His frequent speeches encouraged the British people to continue with the war effort. In one of these speeches, he commented on a remark allegedly made by Adolf Hitler to the effect that Germany would "ring England's neck like a chicken". Churchill's response was, "Some neck. Some chicken!"

In April and May of 1941, the German air campaign against Britain extended to Northern Ireland. It was the ordinary working family which suffered most in these attacks. Almost 100,000 people were rendered homeless, nearly 1,000 killed, and 2,500 injured over three nights of blitzes.

Corner of York and Donegal after blitz, 1941

The powers that be at Westminster either did not anticipate or miscalculated the German's ability to reach as far as Belfast, in spite of the fact that Glasgow and Scotland had already been bombed by the Luftwaffe, the German Air Force headed by Hermann Goering and created surreptitiously by the Nazi's in the 1930's in defiance of the Treaty of Versailles. The Belfast Telegraph marked this monumental time in the provinces history with a brochure published in 1941. The foreword to that brochure records:

"In April and May, 1941, as the price of its loyalty to the British Empire, the Ulster capital endured the severest ordeal in its history. For several hours, without intermission, on the nights of the heaviest raids, relays of the Luftwaffe rained fire and bombs on a semi-defenseless city. There was a heavy death toll and material damaged involved works, stores, churches, halls, schools, shops, suburban villas, and humble homes. The many places of worship destroyed included the fine old sanctuary of Rosemary Street Presbyterian Congregation. But for the heroic exertions of the Civil Defense Services, the toll of human life would have been greater and the tale of smoking ruins more terrible."

On many nights, I was awakened by my mother to the banshee-like wail of the air raid sirens in the distance. She pulled me out of bed, dressed me hastily, and rushed me up the street to the glens north of where we lived, which we would follow up to Cave Hill and sit on the grass-covered cliffs overlooking Belfast. My father often worked at night so my mother and I would have to go alone or with neighbors. One night after a particularly hard bombing, the entire city looked like a sea of fire, an aerial view of hell. The Germans dropped incendiary bombs and land mines. The incendiaries were dropped in sticks, hundreds at a time. Once they had discarded their loads, the German planes strafed the city with machine gun fire. During the air raids, the light was cut to the city and surrounding areas to prevent the German pilots from finding targets. Nobody was even allowed to smoke a cigarette in case its glow was noticed from above.

Public air raid shelter

Even amid all this chaos, the war was like a game to me, unreal somehow. I can only recall feeling a vague sense of foreboding. This feeling grew as I looked at my mother and father, their worried faces illuminated by the distant flames. Then the all-clear would sound and we would return to our houses and take stock of the damage around the neighborhood.

My parents never knew what they would find when they returned home. Entire neighborhoods sometimes disappeared overnight. Rows of houses were completely erased. The machine gun strafing by the German's took huge chunks out of the sandstone buildings downtown. Some of those pock marks remained for years, a grim commemoration of the event.

After the air raids were over, my friends and I prowled around the surrounding fields and picked up burned out incendiary bombs, which had fizzled out harmlessly in the grass. We found that the fin assemblies at the end of the incendiary candles made good egg holders when stood on end. It was an application of the old philosophy, "If life gives you lemons, make lemonade." Or in this case, "If Germany gives you bombs, make egg holders."

There were a lot of false alarms so we wouldn't always head for the hills when the air raids sounded until we heard the distinctive dull thumps of bombs falling in the distance. During one raid, my mother decided that we should all huddle underneath the kitchen table. It was not a very sensible survival plan considering the fact that our flimsy kitchen table would surely not be much protection if a two-ton bomb landed on it. My father refused to suffer this indignity and stood defiantly at the rear kitchen door looking up at the skies, smoking his customary Woodbine cigarette.

"Ya know, Elsie," he once said to my mother, "I could hit those German bastards with a rock, they're so low tonight."

My mother said, "Fer God's sake, come inside! Or at least put out that bloody feg!" My father was due at work shortly and was waiting impatiently for the bombing to end so that he could leave. He wasn't about to let some pesky bombing raid ruin his perfect work attendance record. He never missed a day, no matter how badly he might have been feeling. He worked various shifts so he would often set off on his bicycle in the dark to travel the four miles to the station.

As if the bombs falling from the sky weren't enough, it began to rain torrentially. Despite my mother's protests, my father went outside, stood in the back yard, and yelled at the planes, "You bloody Krauts aren't goin' to keep me from my job!"

He jumped on his trusty Roadster bicycle, said, "See ya tamarra marnin" and headed down the street. My mother was livid. She chased after him yelling, "Come back here, ya bloody eejit!"

My father didn't even look back. His perfect work attendance record was at stake. Fighting German bombs and a thunderstorm - literally "hell and high water" - he pedaled feverishly in the direction of the train station. There was only starlight to steer by because the streetlights and electricity to all the houses had been cut and their windows painted black to prevent any light from escaping.

He was careening down the Oldpark Road at about midnight when the ground beneath him suddenly disappeared and he found himself flying ass over tit into a crater five feet deep. He landed flat on his back. After catching his breath, he climbed out of the hole, covered in mud from head to toe but uninjured, and pulled his bicycle out with him. After such an experience, most men would have felt quite justified in turning for home, but not him. He brushed himself off, mounted his trusty bike again, and continued dutifully on in the direction of the railway station, probably yelling up at the planes all the while, "You Nazi bastards won't make me late!"

On his way home from work that night, he found the area where he had fallen blocked off by police and bomb disposal squads. He thought he had only fallen into a hole created by street workers. Upon closer inspection, he realized that the hole had been created by an unexploded land mine, a brutal device which would have destroyed the entire block if it had functioned properly. Fortunately, this particular mine was a dud. Instead of exploding, it only tore up the street where it landed.

My father came home and said to us, "Jasus Christ, yar not gonna believe this! I was sittin' on top of a German bomb last night!" He told us the whole story, and we all laughed our heads off.

Our prize possession was our radio. It was a classic jukebox-shaped, wood radio with a fabric front that my father had picked up second-hand somewhere. It was so big, it actually put out heat and kept me warm as I sat in front of it listening to my favorite show, *Appointment with Fear*. I still think that's the greatest name ever given to any show, and it lived up to it. That show shaved years off my life. I once became so terrified, I ran into the kitchen and got three saucepans. I finished listening to the show with one pan on my head and the others in each hand, ready to go to war with whatever monstrosity might emerge from the mysterious crackling radio, my portal to other worlds immensely more interesting and dangerous than my actual one.

During the war, the city was humming with activity. Unemployment was at a minimum. The Belfast shipyard had a book full of orders, and the aircraft industry was also flourishing. Like the rest of the U.K., Ulster was gripped with a fervor to aid in the war effort, which arose from a sense of unity in facing the common threat. The downside was that many of those who joined up did not return. The Ulster regiments, the Royal Ulster Rifles, and the Enniskillen Fusiliers took their share of casualties. To the south, the Irish Free State remained neutral. This decision on the part of the Irish government in Dublin drove a further wedge between North and South. For Ulster's Protestants, this was just more proof that the Nationalists could not be trusted or depended upon.

In 1941, when the Americans entered the war after the Japanese attack on Pearl Harbor, Northern Ireland became the staging ground for the pending assault on Europe. The Americans brought their guns, tanks and other weaponry over and practiced war games on the fields of Northern Ireland, preparing for the assault on Europe led by Eisenhower and presaging D-Day in June of 1944. There were hordes of gum-chewing G.I.'s all over Belfast. Most people welcomed them but some didn't, particularly the local males, who found the intrusion of the G.I.'s to be a threat to their manhood. These G.I.'s brought with them American good manners, good looks, nice uniforms, higher pay, and charm that swept Irish girls completely off their feet. The sad fact of the matter is that Irish girls were not used to being treated so well. Discord and street fighting naturally resulted. The Americans gave Irish girls something to compare Irish men to, a perspective they had not previously enjoyed – basically, how they were used to being treated (not too well) versus how they should be treated. It had to be stopped. The Yanks were spoiling Irish girls and ruining everything! Many G.I.'s took some good batterings at first until they learned the local rules and began to give as good as they got. Roughly, these local rules were as follows:

The Duchess of Queensbury rules were for suckers.

Get the first "dig" in. (Punch, kick, knee, head butt, elbow, whatever.)

No area of the body is off limits.

Kicking a man when he's down is perfectly acceptable. After all, it's much easier than kicking a man when he's up.

The forehead is a weapon, too.

In Northern Ireland, that last one is known as an "Ulster Kiss". It is often used to punctuate the beginning or end of a disagreement. Being head-butted on one's nose or lips can be quite disconcerting, coming out of the blue as it invariably does. It takes a particularly hearty soul to retaliate after such an attack. In Scotland, which is largely inhabited by persons of Irish descent, the same technique is called a "Glasgow Kiss". The technique did not originate in either place, and has probably been used since prehistoric times. The Scottish and Irish just perfected it.

Another local phenomenon, and this is something I became aware of when I came to the states, is the position adopted by potential combatants prior to the actual outbreak of hostilities. While Americans tend to stand face-to-face, expanding their chests and carrying their air very high in the lungs, Irish hardcases always face to the side to avoid a kick to the groin. They are also hunched over somewhat, carrying little to no air in the lungs, the rationale being that they won't get the wind knocked out of them if there's no wind in there to begin with. Once the Yank's adapted to the rules, or lack thereof, a great many Belfast guys got good beatings. After all, the Yanks were generally better fed and stronger.

Like troops abroad anywhere else, the Yanks were anxious for a good time. Consequently, any girl seen with a Yank was immediately labeled a traitor or a "good thing", the Belfast euphemism for someone with low morality.

Around that time, the Belfast City Corporation operated trolley buses. Unlike their noisy counterparts, the new buses were incredibly silent, and people were getting knocked down all over the place until the danger was fully realized. Because of this situation, and with the arrival of the Yanks, the expression developed, "These Yanks are like the trolley buses. Before you realize it, they're on top of you!"

Belfast trolley

The Yanks had taken over downtown and along with it The Plaza, Belfast's largest dance hall. We kids were making a small fortune running messages for them. They either tipped liberally or made whopping mistakes, not knowing one coin from another.

One day, a big G.I. asked me to deliver a note to a girl and gave me an address up the lower Falls Road. I hopped on the bus and was there in no time. The girl opened the door, identified herself as the addressee and started to read the message. A large shipyard worker type came out from a back room, snatched the note out of the girl's hand and read it over. He then grabbed me by the lapels, yelling in my startled face, "You can tell that fuckin' Yank that the answer is no and if I get my hands on 'im, I'll kick the shite out of 'im!"

He then shook me like a rat to underscore his point, which was abundantly clear to me already, and I scurried off back to City Hall where my American friend was waiting for his answer. I told him what happened and he took the news surprisingly well. He then dropped a handful of change in my hand, said "Thanks, Kid!" and wandered off down Chichester Street in the direction of the Plaza to start all over again.

Belfast City Hall

One day, I was walking past the City Hall when a Yank came staggering along, bleeding profusely from a huge gash over one eye. I went over to him and asked, "What happened to you, mister? Did ya fall down?"

He looked at me kind of bemused and said with a southern accent, "I dunno what happened. Some sum-bitch just came up 'n popped me one right in the eye for no reason a' tall." That was typical of some of the hard cases in Belfast, but I'm happy to report it was a rarity. For the most part, the Yank's were welcomed and treated well, at least by those they weren't competing with for girls.

There was an army base near my grandmother's house near Dundonald, a rustic, country area. During the war, my mother shipped me off to my grandmother's to get away from Belfast and the air raids. I met a lot of G.I.'s as a result and was very impressed by them. They were exceptionally friendly and generous and would share their food and candy with us kids. One used to come to the house and have dinner with my grandmother and my aunt and uncle. Because all I knew about America was what I had seen at the movies, I asked him if there were cowboys or gangsters in the states and if he knew any of them. He humored me and said, "Yeah, kid. I know lots of cowboys and gangsters." I envied him, coming from such an exciting place, and silently vowed to myself that I would make it there someday.

That same army base was later replaced by a prisoner of war camp housing Germans and I met a lot of German prisoners, too. They would also give me and my friends little gifts. One of them was a very skilled carver who gave us little knives and soldiers that he made. We would give them food and felt no animosity toward them because we realized they were just young soldiers like the Yanks. Some of them were almost kids themselves, following orders they had no choice but to follow. Little or no effort was made to guard these prisoners. There were no fences or barbed wire enclosing them. They were on an island. Even if they ran off, it would have been nearly impossible to get back to Germany. I think they were happy just to be safe and out of the war.

Belfast had no effective anti-aircraft weaponry so there wasn't much we could do about shooting back at the German planes. The only effort I saw at resisting the air raids was the loosening of barrage balloons, which are similar to modern blimps - huge balloons suspended several hundred feet off the ground on wires and left up in the atmosphere in the hopes that a plane would run into them and crash. It was a pathetic defense. When the Yanks came to Belfast, they were appalled by the miserable weather and the endless rain. I was told that one of them remarked, referring to the balloons, "They should cut those damn cables and let this place sink back into the ocean."

During the heavier air raids when the whole city seemed to be going up in smoke, the Belfast Fire Brigade could not answer every alarm. The Lord Mayor of Belfast telephoned his counterpart in Dublin and asked for help from the Dublin Fire Brigade. The story goes that an official contacted Irish President Eamon DeValera and that he initially refused to send any help but relented within an hour or two saying, "After all, they're our people up there." We all presumed he was talking about the Catholics, who were also suffering from the bombing. The Dublin Fire Department then made the hundred-mile run north to Belfast to help put out the fires.

Another strange phenomenon from the war was the internment of British and American fliers whose aircrafts were crippled after sorties with the German fighters. Along with downed German pilots, American and British pilots, who had either crash landed or bailed out of their crippled planes, would parachute into Irish territory only to be immediately interned for the remainder of the war. The American Ambassador to Britain at the time took exception to this practice, pointing out that the south of Ireland was being supplied with oil and gas by Americans during the war and that this same oil and gas was being used in vehicles to track down and imprison American pilots! Not much is said about that ugly period in Irish history, and I doubt that many Irish Americans are aware of it.

Many unflattering and questionable stories used to come through about the South's activities during the war. One of them was that German submarines would refuel at Irish ports and then proceed on to sink ships bringing munitions from the States into Britain, which was allowed because their hatred of England and British rule was stronger than their hatred of Germany. Northern Ireland was particularly valuable in the war effort because of its strategic location. British submarines and warships would refuel in the city of Londonderry, which gave them direct access to the North Atlantic, thus allowing them to protect munitions ships coming from North America to restock the dwindling munitions on the British mainland.

The war finally came to an end in May of 1945 following D-Day, the collapse of Germany, and the introduction of Russia into the war. Hitler made a mistake by establishing two fronts. He was roaming all over Europe with his army, which at that time was the best army the world had ever seen. They just walked through France, the Lowlands, Holland, all of those countries, almost in a matter of days. But Britain proved to be a stiffer target. The British Air Force was particularly effective in fighting off the Germans, downing more German planes than they lost, and defeating the German Luftwaffe, which was led by Field Marshall Goering. Hitler then had to abandon his air war against Britain because of the loss of German planes. In the Battle of Britain, Young British, Canadian, Irish and even Polish pilots were sent up with hardly any experience to combat the German war planes. The Spitfire was developed by Britain, a plane which turned out to be superior to the German Messerschmitt. Churchill made a classic comment at that time, *"Never has so much been owed by so many to so few."*

Because of the attacks on shipping during the war, and as most boats were involved in the war effort in one way or another, food was in scarce supply and rationing had to be imposed on all of Britain. For instance, each person was only allowed two ounces of butter per week. All types of fruit were completely eliminated because they were all imported from Spain and other countries, mostly tropical. Eggs were also in short supply so throughout the war we ate dried eggs imported from America. Every so often, however, someone we knew or someone in the family would cross the border into the south and pick up some contraband butter or bacon, which became a special treat. I remember eating a banana for the first time in six years shortly after the war ended. How delicious it tasted! And the oranges! Oh, the glorious oranges!

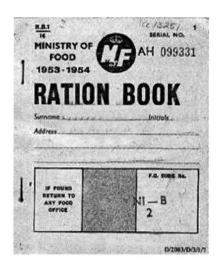

The day the end of the war was officially declared, the streets were alive with celebration, music and gaiety of every kind. Like most kids, I never felt the fear as acutely as the adults around me because death was an abstraction to me, not the reality it was to them. It was not until years later that I learned the horror and magnitude of what the Nazis had done, and realized how awfully different much of the world might have become if they had fully succeeded in their plans. Then again, just as the early Scots were overwhelmed by the Irish culture so much that their own cultural identity was gradually forgotten, I suspect that if the Germans had prevailed, there would be a lot of them in Ulster today speaking with thick Belfast accents.

CHAPTER 5

GERM WARFARE

"A sad soul can kill quicker than a germ."
~ John Steinbeck

Me at four.
Apparently, my parents had been hoping for a girl.

One morning, I heard a loud pounding at the door and walked downstairs to answer it. My mother grabbed me and pulled me behind the couch. It was the landlord looking for the rent again. Receiving no response, he yelled through the letterbox, "I know you're home! I'll be back tomorrow for the rent!" With pounding hearts, we remained quiet and stayed hidden until we were sure he had gone.

My mother's inability to save money was equaled only by her lack of housekeeping skills. Clothing and a vast array of odds and ends were strewn all over the floor in every room. When something was lost, my father would say, "Don't look up, look down" meaning that it could be found somewhere on the floor.

To her credit, though, she would go on the occasional cleaning frenzy when she got tired of hiking over the hills and valleys of bric-a-brac that blanketed the floors. She would plant me on the sofa while she hastily pushed the old Hoover around with a cigarette dangling from her lower lip. I would watch in fascination as the ash would get longer and longer until it eventually fell on the carpet. She would step back, vacuum up the ash and continue on, humming and puffing, puffing and humming.

Paradoxically, when it came to the elimination of germs, my mother's efforts bordered on the fanatical. If a fly landed on a loaf of bread, she immediately threw the entire loaf into the bin.

Because my father suffered from asthma in the earlier part of his life, he had a special cup for his use only. She threatened me not to drink from that cup so many times, I avoided it for fear of my life and imagined germs crawling all over it like miniature monsters. One day I drank from it by mistake and spent most of that day worrying about when I was going to start wheezing.

Somehow, her fear of spreading germs apparently wasn't severe enough to prevent her from spitting on napkins and using them to wipe dirt off my face. But there were times when her battle against germs went too far. When my friends from the neighborhood would come to the door asking if I could come out and play, she would examine them all for any sign of illness. If one of them had so much as a runny nose, she would pull me back into the house and slam the door without a word to any of them.

My ma

My mother and her brother Alfie were riding on the top deck of a double-decker Belfast bus one day when an ambulance drew up alongside it.

"My God, Elsie!" Alfie exclaimed. "There's the fever wagon!"

My mother gasped in horror and clamped her hand over her mouth and nose for fear of breathing in germs escaping through the cracks of the doors of the passing ambulance.

After the first year in the house, my parents began to argue more and more about money. Being a child, the words meant little to me. It was the angry tones that always drove me into my room until the dust had cleared.

My father either had the strongest work ethic of all time or he was just spending as much time at work as he could to avoid my mother. It was probably a little of both. His perfect attendance record was a major source of pride to him. When he came home in the evening, he would eat, read the paper, and listen to the radio for an hour or so before going to bed. This pattern never deviated in the slightest.

He rarely spoke to me unless I engaged him somehow, and then begrudgingly. As a result, my upbringing fell completely upon my mother, but I seemed to be a distraction to her as well. She was not one for overt demonstrations of affection, but she did show her love for me in less obvious ways, such as constantly stuffing me with various vitamins and elixirs. After putting the vitamins in my mouth, she would make me open my mouth and check under my tongue to make sure I swallowed it, which was no small feat since some of the tablets were as big as my thumb. She probably thought a vitamin was the opposite of a germ and imagined the two of them slugging it out in my system. Whatever her reasons, more tablets and potions were pumped into me than an Olympic weightlifter in training.

The dichotomy between her germ phobia and disinterest in housekeeping was a mystery to me even then. One would think the new home might have inspired her to change her ways, but her paranoia over microbes somehow didn't extend to the unwashed clothing strewn about the house, which was undoubtedly home to all manner of microscopic life forms.

My mother based her life and mine on old sayings passed down through the generations. One of her favorites was, "Don't cast a clout until May is out", which somehow meant one should not put away one's coat until spring was over. Thus she saw to it that I wore my overcoat straight through May even if the heat was splitting the trees outside. She dragged me all over town on her shopping rounds on warm spring days, sweating, red-faced and on the verge of fainting from heat exhaustion. I would plead with her to let me remove the coat but she would never relent. She was sure that deadly viruses and bacteria were following me around and waiting to pounce the moment any skin was exposed.

I tried to leave the house one afternoon without my jacket because it was the last day of May and I figured I had served my time. As I walked out to meet my friends, all of whom were reasonably dressed for the weather, I stiffened as my mother yelled after me, "Come you back here and put yar jacket on, Sidney!"

I walked back to the house to the chorus of my friends laughing and telling me what a mammy's boy I was. I felt ridiculous wearing a jacket when none of the other boys were and quickly shed it and hid it in some bushes the second my house was out of view.

Unfortunately for me, my mother's poorly thought out decisions concerning me did not end there. My hair was constantly falling over my forehead so one day she unwisely placed a girl's hair clip in it to hold it back. Too young to know any better, I went to school wearing it and was mocked mercilessly by the other kids.

She made another brilliant choice regarding my clothing the day she bought me a cap with the Belfast Royal Academy insignia on it. I didn't know it at the time, but the Academy was *the* school in Belfast where all the upper crust kids went. I realized later that she was trying to create the impression that I was a student there. Oblivious, I wore it to the public school I actually did attend. The other kids accused me of being a put-on and I was promptly beaten about the head, face and neck. When they finally relented, I threw the hat in a bin on the playground and walked home cursing my mother for setting me up for a beating. I decided that from that point forward, I would make my own fashion choices.

What I needed more than vitamins and clothes were for my father to take an interest in me, for my mother to put her arms around me and say she loved me, and to be tucked into my bed at night with a kiss on the forehead once in a while. I didn't think I was missing anything at the time because I had never known such treatment and had no other parents to compare my own to. I was also too young to know that only happy parents bestow such gifts upon their children.

I began to spend less and less time at home. My chums and I would climb the gentle slopes at the base of Cave Hill as high as we could, where we would rest and watch the ships entering and leaving Belfast Lough. On a clear day, we could see the southwest coast of Scotland in the distance. It was very close, but to me it was another world beyond my reach.

Cave Hill, County Antrim, 1890's

On summer days, hot and sweaty from the climb, we would lie on our backs in the heather and watch the white cumulus clouds drift like Spanish galleons across the pale blue sky.

There were caves on the north face of the mountain that everyone called "Smuggler's Caves" where it was said that pirates hid their booty many centuries before. We all wanted to climb them and we tried several times, but the terrain to the upper caves was too challenging and risky for us, young as we were, so we contented ourselves with exploring the lower caves. We never found a single doubloon in the lower caves, so I imagined the real riches were hidden in the caves that were out of our reach. My nights were filled with dreams of treasure-hunting. In those dreams, I was not the invisible child I was in my home. I was a hero, sword-fighting with skeleton sentinels, slaying dragons, exploring labyrinthine caves, and discovering secret chambers filled with treasure chests overflowing with glowing diamonds, emeralds and rubies, jewel-studded chalices and glittering gold coins. I would wake to a silent house, walk down the creaky stairs to the kitchen and find my parents sitting at the kitchen table like silent strangers. One morning, wanting to know if my parents had ever heard of the smuggler's caves, I broke the silence.

"Da?"

He looked at me over his newspaper.

"What?

"Have you ever heard of the Smuggler's caves?"

"What're ya talkin' about now?"

"Cave Hill. My friends say pirates hid their treasure up there."

"Ach, there's nuthin' in those caves. Don't be an eejit."

"How do you know?"

"I just know. Now stop botherin' me with silly questions."

"Aye," my ma said, "That's just an old wives' tale."

My father returned to his paper, indicating the conversation was over. I wondered why my mother didn't believe it if it was just an old wives tale. She was an old wife herself, and she had no trouble believing all the other old wives tales.

I went upstairs and looked out the back window at Cave Hill.

"How does he know there's no treasure?" I said to myself.

I decided he didn't know. He had never climbed that mountain. I swore to myself that I would make it to the highest caves someday and find the treasure, not to prove my father wrong, but to bring it back to them so they could finally stop arguing about money and be happy together.

CHAPTER 6

GRANNIES

"Grandmas don't just say "that's nice" -- they reel back and roll their eyes and throw up their hands and smile. You get your money's worth out of grandmas."
~ Anonymous

Both of my grandfathers died young, but I was fortunate enough to have two grandmothers as a boy. My maternal grandmother was English; the other Irish. Aside from being old and female, they had absolutely nothing in common.

My English grandmother was originally from London. She was a short-tempered, arrogant woman who succeeded in making everyone's life miserable around her. Her abrasive demeanor made loving or even liking her impossible. However, the main reason I didn't like her was because I knew she didn't care for my father. I never knew why but then she didn't usually need a reason. There were very few people she did like.

She spent most of her life in ill health, suffering from one disability after another. She was overweight and had bad feet and legs as a result, but her principal problem was her temperament, which I and everyone else found nearly impossible to deal with. There was no light conversation between her and me, only constant criticisms and frequent warnings to me to "hold your tongue." Another of her favorite expressions was the old classic, *"Children should be seen and not heard."* When I heard she was coming to visit, I would watch out the window until I saw her plodding up the street on her sore, swollen feet, then duck out the back and vanish for the next few hours hoping she would be gone by the time I got back home.

Because I avoided her so well, my mother forced me to pay her regular visits, which always involved my listening to her play the piano and being forced to sing songs made popular by the German tenor, Richard Tauber, such as "My Heart and I". This is a beautiful song but little appreciated by me at the age of nine, sitting beside her on the piano stool and wishing I could be outside in the sunshine playing with my friends. She had met Richard Tauber and greatly admired him. As a result, I was forced to spend hours with her singing his songs repeatedly until she felt satisfied with my performance. It wasn't the singing I disliked so much but enduring her humorless personality.

She started dying around sixty and stretched it out until she was eighty-seven. In her later years, she became afflicted with an unknown disease which would later be named Alzheimer's, and I saw less and less of her. I wish I could say something nice about her but for the life of me nothing comes to mind. In fact, the Alzheimer's symptoms were an improvement. At least she forgot who she hated and lost the ability to criticize somewhat, though I'm sure she squeezed a few insults out even through the fog of her condition.

Me with my English grandmother

My paternal grandmother, Tilly, was the exact opposite – a cheerful, petite woman from the country. She originated from the Dungannon area and worked hard all her life. She lived with my aunt Cissy and Uncle Tommy in a small cottage near Stormont on the south side of Belfast. Uncle Tommy was a small, quiet man from a country town called Guildford. Aunt Cissy was nervous and jittery. She never sat still for a minute. They never had children. In fact, I never even saw them kiss. Uncle Tommy never spoke much but he was very kind to me. Unaccustomed to such treatment, I grew very fond of him.

After one particularly hard bombing of Belfast by the Germans in 1941, my mother panicked and shipped me off for an extended stay with Grandma Tilly. I was ecstatic. I always loved visiting her because of her kind and calm personality, and because she lived in a pebbled-dashed cottage at the edge of a wild and sprawling forest. There were only a few neighbors nearby. I ended up staying with her for almost a year. After school, I roamed the woods with her dog, a border collie named Prince. Every day was a new adventure. I would ask Prince what character he wanted to play on our adventures, and he would lick my face excitedly. We were alternately Lewis and Clark, Robin Hood and Friar Tuck, Tarzan and Cheetah, the Lone Ranger and Kimosabe, etc. I especially enjoyed playing Tarzan, climbing trees and sprinting through the forest. Lost in fantasy, I didn't notice the cold wind as I sped along. I was in the muggy and humid Congo, surrounded by tigers, natives and evil, white hunters bent on killing my jungle friends, with only Prince and me to stop them.

Grandma Tilly was a devout Presbyterian. Every Sunday morning, she would dress me up and we would walk hand in hand two or three miles over hills and glens flanked by wildflowers to the small church in Dundonald village. Church bored me stiff but I had to go, and it probably did me some good. I enjoyed my walks with Grandma Tilly. She always pointed out anything beautiful. It was all she noticed.

After church, we invariably had Sunday roast for lunch. Prince and I would then be excused to play in the woods. In the evening, relatives visited for tea, which usually included cooked ham and other cold cuts, various cheeses and half a dozen varieties of bread my Grandma Tilly baked herself. There was almost always something delicious baking in the oven, and the whistle of the tea kettle could be heard a dozen or so times throughout the day. There was soda bread, potato bread, currant bread, brown and white loaves, and all manner of beautiful cakes. I always built up a powerful hunger playing and then stuffed myself with ten to fifteen slices of the fresh-baked bread soaked with sweet churned country butter. Grandma Tilly believed in abundance. Meals at her house were a celebration of life. Since I was used to dining in silence at home over a much more modest table, this was a big and welcome change for me.

The woods around the cottage abounded with badgers and the surrounding grasslands were home to an abundance of rabbits. Every now and then, Uncle Tommy would get out his .22 rifle and bag a rabbit or a fat pigeon for a change of menu. He never allowed me to handle the gun without his supervision but one day, he and Grandma Tilly had to go into town, and they left me alone for the entire day. I immediately headed for Uncle Tommy's rifle. I knew where he hid it so I took it and a pocketful of shells into the woods to play hunter. I had never fired a gun before so I was beside myself with excitement. I shot a tree first. The .22 slugs barely made a dent in the surface so I quickly grew bored and started looking for live game. I saw a few rabbits and shot at them but couldn't seem to hit anything. Searching for moving targets, I ended up at the local dump, which was located deep in the woods. It was completely deserted.

I was walking through the middle of the dump when a rat crossed my path. I shot at it but missed. It ran under a pile of rubbish. I could tell by the way the trash was sitting that the rat had nowhere to go and was stuck inside so I sat down about three feet away from the pile and fixed the sight of my rifle on the opening. After sitting quietly for about ten minutes, the rat finally poked his head out to see if I was still there. I fired reflexively. The rat scrambled around madly inside the box, ran out, jumped three feet in the air, and died at my feet. I was so scared and exhilarated by the thrill of the hunt and my first "kill" that I immediately keeked (pooped) in my pants, thus rendering examination of the game I had just bagged a lesser priority than finding a place to dispose of my underwear. Fortunately, I was already in a dump so this was not difficult. I walked home feeling quite proud of my marksmanship, but the more I thought about it, the more I began to feel sorry for the old rat who had done nothing to me and certainly didn't deserve to get his head blown off at close range. I decided that the hunting life wasn't for me and never shot anything else again in my life. The fact that I turned my underpants into a fudge factory was also an indication that I lacked the killer instinct necessary to be a successful trophy hunter.

I slept in bed with my granny that year, which was not uncommon in those days, the usual reason being a limited number of beds, but families also slept together because most cottages weren't heated by anything other than a small coal fire. During the coldest winter months, sharing bodily warmth was a matter of survival so it wasn't uncommon for entire families to share one bed. At my parents' home in Belfast, I had my own bedroom and had become accustomed to privacy so it was a little uncomfortable at first to sleep with Grandma Tilly, but after a week or so, I began to enjoy the feeling of having her next to me. She even smelled sweet, a mixture of her lavender perfume and the not unpleasant odor of sweat from a hard day's work. Besides, I loved her and felt very safe lying next to her.

It was ironic that my English, city grandmother struggled to be artistic while everything my simple, country Grandmother did was artistic and came to her naturally. Whether walking to church, working in the garden, preparing a meal or brushing her long, silver hair, she displayed beautiful grace and elegance with every movement, the kind of beauty artists spend lifetimes trying to capture.

Above her bed, there was a picture depicting the Pilgrim's Progress. No single image has had a more profound effect on me, probably because of my impressionable age at the time. On the left side of the picture, there was a wide highway filled with drunks, lechers, prostitutes, robbers, and other criminal types, their bodies crooked and their faces contorted with evil intentions. On the right side of the picture, there was the narrow "Christian path" along which strode the solitary Christian with back straight and head held high, avoiding the temptations the wicked world might place in his way. He ignored the broad path where all the sinners proliferated and wallowed in degradation. At the top of the picture, set in the clouds, was the all-seeing eye of God keeping track of what each of them was up to.

I studied that picture every day and it affected my behavior for years. In fact, along with Grandma Tilly's tutelage and example, that picture determined my character for the rest of my life. From then on, I always had the feeling that the all-seeing eye was watching me. I even tried to spot it in the sky a few times on cloudy days. If I was doing something I knew was wrong, I imagined myself among the sinners on the wide road and God watching me disapprovingly.

Though she must have been around sixty when I went to stay with her, I thought my Grandma Tilly was beautiful. I remember her strong, raw-boned, country face, her work-roughened hands and her perennial blue apron with multi-colored flowers stitched into it. She worked on the house constantly, vacuuming and scrubbing floors, cleaning and polishing furniture, and tending to the vegetables and flowers in her garden. She had steel gray hair, which she kept up in a bun during the daytime. At night, she would let her hair down, which stretched all the way to her waist, and comb it out in front of the dresser mirror by lamplight while I lay in bed. She wore no make-up, but the rosy glow on her cheeks gained from clean living and hard work made it unnecessary.

What made her most lovely to me, though, was her calm and peaceful nature. Unlike my mother, who was discontented with everything and everyone, Grandma Tilly was perfectly at peace with the world. This was not only a welcome relief to me but a demonstration that there was another way to live. While my mother complained incessantly about my father's income, Grandma Tilly, who had far less than my parents, always seemed perfectly content. She was living proof of the old adage that the person who is happy and needs little is richer than one who has much but constantly yearns for more.

It was two miles in each direction from her cottage to school. I wish I could say my year there was perfectly peaceful but, alas, that was not the case. I was plagued by a bully who lived in a house along the only path to and from school. I would try to avoid walking past his house as much as possible by walking through the woods to and from school, but he would hide behind trees or hedges then jump out, grab me, drag me off into an air raid shelter and threaten me. He never actually struck me, but he would hold his huge fist up and grind it into my cheek, threatening to knock my head off. He was about six inches taller than me, twenty pounds heavier and three or four years older so these assaults absolutely terrified me. He seemed to delight in terrorizing me and making my life miserable. I never told anyone about him as I considered myself fortunate that he did not make good on his threats. He probably tortured flies and stepped on baby chicks for laughs in his spare time. In later years, I wished I could run into him again and exact some revenge but shortly thereafter, I left Dundonald and never saw him again. I can only comfort myself with the thought that he probably ended up in a penitentiary.

That summer in Dundonald was incredibly warm with long, dry spells. The surrounding fields were baked by the sun and the grass turned to straw. One day, I found a box of wooden Swan matches at the side of the road. I went into a nearby field, struck a match and threw it on the dry grass. (I don't know what I was thinking, either.) I thought I could extinguish the fire anytime I wanted to, but it rapidly spread out of control. I took off my coat and swatted the fire with it but only succeeded in angering the flames and ruining my coat. Before I knew it, the entire field was ablaze. A man walking by looked over the hedge at me and yelled, "You'll never put that fire out, son!" I quickly ran home, told my granny what happened, then ran into the woods to hide.

A fleet of fire trucks came from Belfast and surrounding areas with sirens blaring to extinguish the fire, which had covered several acres by the time they arrived. For a while, the fire threatened some Nissen huts housing soldiers at a nearby Army base. The next day there was a write-up in the Belfast Telegraph about a "mystery fire" at Stormont. My uncle finally located me and brought me back, explaining that he had encountered the person who saw me set the fire. My heart was in my throat thinking that the man had turned me in, and my uncle was just there to bring me to jail quietly. I could have fainted with relief when my uncle told me that he had slipped the man ten bob in exchange for his agreement to forget the entire matter. Fortunately, no property had been burned, only empty grassland. It took me three or four days to get over my near brush with the law as a juvenile arsonist but in time the memory faded and I stopped worrying about a policeman knocking on my door to run me in.

After the year in Dundonald, my mother shipped me down to other relatives in Dungannon in the county of Tyrone, a farming area where we had distant cousins called Reid. There were two Reid families in the district of Iglish. One family ran a large and profitable farm. The second farm, owned by my Aunt Emily (She was not really an aunt, but that's what I called her), was much poorer, with a small cottage and no interior plumbing. There's an old Irish expression, *"He's a nice kid but he shites too close to home!"* Obviously, with no toilet facilities in the house, the further away one walked to do his or her business, the better.

Chickens would wander in and out of the house, and quite often we would find an egg in the bed. There were several pigs on the farm, and every day without fail one of the male pigs would break his way out of a ramshackle enclosure and run across the fields. My cousins and I would pursue the pig across several nearby fields, then it would turn around and chase us for several fields back. It was pure slapstick. Sooner or later, the pig ran out of energy or ambition and allowed us to lead him back to the sty.

Aunt Emily's farm in Dungannon

The farmer's helper was a big guy named Danny. Each night, he and I would round up the cows and corral them into the cow barns, or "byres" as we called them then. There were half a dozen cows, most of which knew the way home and followed the homeward path. However, one was a maverick by nature and at a particular crossroads, would always glance at us out of the corner of a brown eye and then trot off in the wrong direction. This occurred every night. Danny would run over and kick the cow up the ribs a few times with his

Wellington boots to divert him back in the right direction. The cow would belch and cough in response to these kicks, but she never seemed to learn the error of her ways. That cow was the stupidest animal I'd ever seen.

A few months after my arrival, my mother came down to visit. She was not impressed by Aunt Emily's house and summarily shifted me over to the other Reid family farmhouse down the road, which was large, spacious, and modern. Aunt Emily was grievously offended and cried. I wanted to stay with her, but my mother was deaf to my pleas.

Aunt Emily and Uncle Fred, circa 1960

For a short while, I also spent some time with other cousins in Lurgan, a small country town. One Saturday afternoon, we all went to a local picture house to see a western film starring Tom Mix. We paid our few pence and went in. The movie had already started, and we had to grope around in the dark to find a place sit. The theater was filled to bursting with other kids screaming and running around. It was absolute bedlam. I thought the kids in Belfast were tough, but these country kids were all half-mad. As I was searching for a seat and trying to keep track of where my cousins were, I suddenly received a stiff blow up the side of the head. At first, I thought someone had punched me. I didn't see it coming so I was almost knocked off my feet. Looking down, I found that someone had thrown a stale loaf of bread, scoring a direct hit. The only thing more bizarre than being hit in the head by a loaf of bread in a movie theatre was the fact that someone had actually gone to the trouble of bringing a loaf of bread to begin with, probably for the sole purpose of bouncing it off somebody's nut. Though my ear was ringing and filled with bread crumbs, I didn't take it personally. I was just a good target, silhouetted as I was in front of the movie screen. Even if I had taken it personally, there was no use trying to make sense of it. After all, this was Ireland where normal rules didn't, don't and never will apply.

Finally, the air raids eased up, my mother's fears subsided, and she came to bring me back to Belfast. Of all the relatives I was shuffled around to that year, I loved my Grandma Tilly the best, even as much my Uncle Alfie. This was quite strange considering that they were not at all alike. Alfie was a hell-raiser to whom nothing was sacred. Tilly was a devout Christian to whom everything was sacred. I attribute my hedonism in younger years and the often raunchy sense of humor I developed to Alfie. But I attribute any finer qualities I might have to my Grandma Tilly, who managed to instill Christian values in me during our short time together more deeply than anyone else did before or since. I have always maintained a belief in God and the idea that the good are rewarded and the wicked are punished somehow. Grandma Tilly's quiet nature and oneness with God was infectious, mainly because she never insisted that I believe accordingly. Though she did insist on my attending Sunday school, she never preached to me about religion or threatened me with eternal damnation if I did something wrong. She kept me safe but understood boyhood and did not overly control it. She taught in the best possible way, not by lecturing but by simply being who she was, the way a flower shares its beauty effortlessly with all who behold it.

She and Uncle Tommy went with my mother to the bus station in town and waited with me until the bus arrived. I wasn't looking forward to going back to Belfast. I thanked her for all she had done for me. She had taken me in without complaint and without expectation of reward. She said, "Thank you's are for strangers, not family and friends. It was a joy to have you here with us, Sidney. Come back again soon."

I told her I would, and I dearly wanted to, but she died before I was able to. Even her passing was completely opposite to that of my other granny. My English grandmother died slowly and painfully, trying to drag everyone she could down with her. My Grandma Tilly announced one afternoon, "I'm going to die soon." She continued to clean the house, work in the garden and cook her wonderful meals for another week or so before she stopped, walked to her bedroom, got into her bed, and died.

When I heard that she was gone, I cried for a week and intermittently for years. There was no way she could have known the depth of her influence on me, an influence which flourished because it was so unforced. Though I never attained her level of devotion, like the picture over her bed of the pilgrim's progress, I have tried to stay on "the straight and narrow" path ever since. When I've thought about my Grandma Tilly over the years, I would often see myself as the boy I was then, walking with her along the quiet country road we would take to church on Sunday mornings. And if I think hard enough, I can still feel her beautiful old hand holding my young, pudgy one and see her smiling down at me with her kind, soulful eyes.

CHAPTER 7

MY SISTER ARRIVES

"I was not only naïve, I was shamelessly misinformed. My parents told me I was bought with Green Shield Stamps."
~ Anonymous

Children don't understand much about adult relationships. It's enough of a challenge just trying to figure out their own lives and the world they've been dropped into. However, they do understand love. Even animals can feel the difference between a loving, peaceful household and a disharmonious one. It's wired into us from birth. My memories of my parents' relationship are bleak and sad for the most part, but they must have shared a few tender moments because when I was twelve years old, my mother gave birth to my sister.

American parents normally go to great lengths to psychologically prepare their children for the arrival of a new sibling. My parents, on the other hand, decided I shouldn't know about it or simply forgot to mention it to me. I was so naïve and uninformed, I didn't even know she was pregnant. As a result, when she went into labor, and they were hustling her into the car to take her to the hospital, I just thought they were late for an appointment of some kind. As I stood on the sidewalk waving goodbye to them, a boy who lived on our street, and who was much younger than me, said, "Yar mammy's gonna have a wee baby!"

Shocked, I shouted "She is not!"

"Of course she is, eejit. Whaddya think she's been carryin' around in her belly for the last year?"

He walked away laughing and shaking his head in disbelief. I couldn't think of anything to say. As I watched the taxi turn the corner, a tornado of emotions swirled in my head. A few agonizingly slow days later, she came home with a little bundle in her arms. They named her Olga. She spent the first few months of her life in an orange crate until my dad could afford a proper crib. My parents seemed happier in the weeks after Olga arrived.

I stared at her for hours every day for a week, not knowing what to feel, as she gurgled in her crate. I worried about my lack of emotion. I had heard my mother call my father an empty man so many times, I was afraid I was becoming an empty child. Now I know the emptiness inside me was a result of being kept in the dark by my parents. I wasn't told what to expect, so I didn't know what to feel.

My sister Olga at 12 in our back garden.

CHAPTER 8

NOT KEEPING UP WITH THE JONES'S

"Envy is the art of counting the other fellow's blessings instead of your own."
~ Harold Coffin

Even though my mother had a tendency to put on airs, in reality, she was very ill at ease around people whom she felt held a more advantaged station then she. Subsequently, her friends were the flotsam and jetsam of the neighborhood, the disenfranchised, and women she felt were inferior to her in some way. These downtrodden souls were constant visitors to our home, where my mother held sway. My father would often say, "Every misfit and nincompoop in the neighborhood has been in this house at one time or another." He tolerated it, though, because it kept my mother happy and, more importantly, off his back.

Resigned to misery, my father retreated more and more deeply into himself over the years, sitting in the kitchen listening grimly to his small radio crackling with the latest news, or buried in the Belfast Telegraph, his only connections to the outside world. The only time I ever saw him become animated was when he talked about his friends at work and their exploits. When he was in the mood, he was a very good storyteller. On these rare and happy occasions, we felt like a family for a change, and I relished every moment of it. The laughter was good medicine for all of us considering the usually somber mood of the house.

I always thought it odd that my father rarely spoke to my mother's friends or any of our neighbors. When passing them on his way to and from work, he would only nod or mumble a hello with a quick glance in their direction, which was actually more than I received. I would often come home after school and want to talk about the day's events, but he never asked. When I tried to talk to him, he would only grunt or give monosyllabic responses, rarely looking up from the newspaper as I spoke. Occasionally, he would look at me as if he was listening, but I could tell his mind was elsewhere. Eventually, I stopped trying to talk to him at all.

A nice couple named Freddy and Sherry Hull lived across the street from us. They were the exact opposite of my parents. Freddy was a professional man, an electrician. He was the first one on our street to own a car, an eight-horsepower Ford, which was the envy of all the neighbors. He was also the first one to have a television set. It was a small black and white set, probably an RCA, but it might as well have been the crown jewels the way we and the other neighbors who witnessed the grand spectacle were looking at it.

Unlike our house, the Hull house was always neat and well cared for with intricate doilies over polished wood furniture, sparkling glassware and silverware, exquisite paintings on the walls and beautiful carpeting. The front garden was always nicely trimmed, the hedgerows neat and uniform and the flowers perpetually blooming. My mother was in complete awe of the Hulls and was constantly falling over herself trying to impress them. Perhaps she was comparing their circumstances to our own, wanting to live that way but knowing it was impossible and probably always would be.

My mother wasn't the only one who was jealous of the Hull's, though. I would watch them laughing together, kissing goodbye as he left for work in the morning, holding hands on afternoon walks, and I wished that my parents got along as well as they did.

With my mother's tendency toward discontentment and my father's toward detachment, it's hard to imagine them being happy with anyone. Neither was receiving anything they needed from the other. Even if they could have divorced, they probably couldn't have imagined a better life for themselves. How would they begin again?

CHAPTER 9

NEIGHBORS

"Sometimes a neighbor whom we have disliked a lifetime for his arrogance and conceit lets fall a single commonplace remark that shows us another side, another man really; a man uncertain, puzzled and in the dark like ourselves."
~ Willa Sibert Cather

There was no terrorism in Belfast when I was young, only the seeds of the resentment that would spawn it. Comparatively, it was a blessed age and, despite the difficulties already mentioned, a happy time for Belfast.

Our neighborhood, while predominantly Protestant, had a few Catholic families scattered through it. The McCallister's lived several doors away from us. Mrs. McCallister, a staunch Catholic with a southern brogue, was from the south of Ireland. Her two children, however, were born in the north. Her son Thomas was an operatic tenor with a voice as good as any professional singer. One man's bathroom can be another's Albert Hall, and this was never proven by anyone better than it was by Thomas. When he was singing, his rich tenor voice could be heard for three blocks in every direction. Nobody ever complained. I used to lie in my bed listening to him sing late at night or in the early mornings as he was getting ready for school or work. Gazing through my window into the sky, it would seem as if his voice was coming from heaven. I would sing along with him sometimes and soon learned the words to many of the songs in his repertoire. I have had a love of singing all my life, and I credit much of it to Thomas and the sheer joy he took in belting out beautiful songs for the whole neighborhood. He had a gift. We were all just fortunate, accidental witnesses to it.

His mother had the reputation of being a bit of a mare who would eat the face off anyone with the slightest provocation. This propensity toward hostility, along with her Irish brogue and Catholic background, made her none too popular on our street.

The McCallister's had an Alsatian dog that seemed to hate my guts. Sometimes I would walk down the street so lost in thought that I would forget about the dog and walk too close to their garden fence. The dog would wait until the very last second then suddenly leap at the gate, barking and snarling, scaring me out of my shoes. As luck would have it, though, when I happened to be prepared for him, he would either be in the house or take no interest in me whatsoever. He only seemed to launch himself at the fence when he knew I was daydreaming. So in revenge for the years the dog had shaved off my life, I decided one day to stop at the fence and do an Irish jig while making faces at him. The dog struggled to squeeze its massive head through the iron bars, its jaws clamping at air like a bear trap, just hoping to catch a piece of my flesh in its teeth. The faces alone made the dog angry, but the dancing really worked him up into a feverish rage. It was such fun, I started doing it every time I walked by. I didn't think the dog could get more ferocious, but I was wrong. His mania seemed to increase with each performance. Eventually, though, I got bored with this routine and forgot about the dog again.

I was walking past the McAllister house one day a few weeks later, my mind a million miles away as usual, when the dog came tearing up to the gate right on cue. He succeeded in turning my hair instantly white yet again, so I broke into my usual Irish jig to torture him a little, but rather than snapping at me through the gate as expected, he ran off in the other direction. I looked over and saw, to my extreme horror, that someone had left the front gate open. Before I could move, he tore through the gate and ran toward me, clearly intending to tear me limb from limb. I knew if he got to me, I was dead. I looked around in desperation for something to protect myself with and saw a dislodged brick sitting on top of the wall. I grabbed it and threw it at him as hard as I could, hitting him squarely between the eyes. What a shot! He staggered for a moment, then ran yelping and whining back through the gate, disappearing into the deep recesses of the yard. There was a moment of elation as I realized I was not going to be eaten, but guilt quickly set in for hurting him so badly. This feeling also passed quickly, however. After all, it was him or me. Kill or be killed.

That night, Mrs. McCallister made inquiries and found out that I was the brick thrower. I heard someone banging on the door, and my heart froze when I saw it was her. I attempted to sneak up the stairs to hide in my room when my father yelled for me to open the door. I slowly opened it and peeked out. Mrs. McAllister stared at me through the crack like an angry ostrich. Her hair, sticking up in tufts in all directions, looked like an explosion in a mattress factory. She grabbed me by the collar and pulled me through the door.

"Who d'ya think y'arr throwin' bricks at my dog! I'll have ya in the boy's home 'fore the week's out, ya wee shite!"

I had never been yelled at by an adult like that. I was completely dumbstruck. My father came to the door, separated us and said, "Calm down for a wee second now, Missus McCallister. What happened?"

"That wee shite o'yours nearly kilt my wee dog with a brick, that's what happened! What kind of a wee sadist are ya raisin' here? That's wud I'd like t'know!"

She continued on for another minute or so before finally petering out. I was aghast at her language. I didn't think a lady could use words like that. I'd only heard the likes of it from ruffians and drunks when my mother took me into town. Throughout her tirade, the blasé look on my father's face never changed. She stood there for a moment, apparently embarrassed about being the only one participating in the argument, and said, "Well, wudder ya gonna do abite it?"

My father seemed to be considering his response carefully before he took a deep breath and calmly said, "Fuck off."
Her eyes went so wide, I thought they were going to burst.

"Ach, away and wash your dirty face!" she yelled.

To this day, I don't know what that meant. It was either an attempt at more colorful language or my dad actually did have a dirty face.

Storming away, she yelled over her shoulder, "Ya haven't heard the end o' this, ya fockin' bastard ya! I'll 'ave the peelers at your door!"

My father capped the conversation with what I thought was a brilliant retort, again delivered with perfect nonchalance.

"Missus McCallister, hell will never be full until you're in it."

As red as a rooster's headdress, she barreled off down the street, swearing up a storm. That was the last we ever heard of it. I expected Mrs. McAllister to sic the dog on me the next time I walked by. Since I couldn't depend on being so accurate with a brick again, I walked on the opposite side of the street from then on.

Several years later, while returning home one night after an air raid during the war years, my parents and I were shocked to see that Mrs. McCallister's home had received a direct hit from an incendiary bomb and was completely destroyed. My parents thought it was quite a coincidence that the only house on the street belonging to Catholics got smashed, and they immediately suspected foul play. However, it was confirmed later that the damage was caused by a bomb. My father's only comment was, "Couldn't a' happened to a nicer lady. There's some justice in the bloody universe after all."

I went up to take a look at the house the next morning and, while looking through her front window, saw the charred remains of the dog lying on the living room floor. The McCallister's were in the shelter at the time, so the dog was the only casualty of the blast. Once so fearsome, he was nothing more than a blackened skeleton. I felt sorry for him lying there despite his desire to kill me and the constant fear he caused me when passing his yard. However, the moment he died, I'm sure Satan immediately recruited him to guard the gates of hell. The McCallister's seized the opportunity to move out of the neighborhood, the house was rebuilt, and another family moved in.

Wee Dougie

I wasn't the only one in the neighborhood who came to blows with a murderous mongrel. Another kid named Dougie had a similar problem with a different dog on the street. Poor wee Dougie was about the same age as me but he was a bit challenged and had dropped out of school in the third grade. He spent his days wandering around the neighborhood while the rest of us were at school. When he was older, he had a paper route delivering the Belfast Telegraph to houses on our street.

One night, I was at my usual spot at the bathroom window when Dougie walked by delivering his newspapers. The lady across the street had a very large, bad-tempered dog of dubious heritage which, like the McCallister's dog, took great joy in scaring the daylights out of anyone who dared use the sidewalk in front of its house. The only difference was, in this case, there was no gate. Fortunately for Dougie, there seemed to be an invisible barrier surrounding the property in the dog's mind, and it would only chase a person to a certain point then proudly stride back into the yard having successfully defended its territory. Unfortunately, this barrier didn't end where a normal gate would be but at the curb, so anyone walking along the sidewalk was fair game. The only way to avoid dismemberment was to run into the street. Some of the men and older boys who refused to submit to the indignity of fleeing into the street would stand their ground and try to plant a boot somewhere on the dog as it approached. As a result, the dog received many vicious kicks but it never seemed to learn its lesson. Dougie tried the same thing on this fateful day but the great brute grabbed him by the ankle and shredded his leg pretty well before letting go. Dougie made sounds that reminded me of the tropical birds I'd heard in Tarzan movies. He dropped all his papers and took off like a shot as soon as the dog released its grip on him.

I was at the window again the following evening when I saw Dougie cautiously approaching the scene of the attack. The old dog came tearing out to finish the job, but Dougie ran into the street. The dog paced back and forth at the edge of the curb, snarling, growling and eyeing Dougie warily. Dougie then produced a chop bone from his pocket and meekly offered it to the dog, whispering, "Here ya go, boy. Nice doggie. Nice doggie."

Suspicious but desperate to get the bone, the dog stopped pacing and inched forward.

"There ya go, boy. A nice, big, juicy bone for ya," Dougie whispered.

The dog sniffed and showed its teeth simultaneously as it inched toward him, unable to resist the scent of the meat. It was then that I noticed Dougie was holding a splintered piece of wood in his other hand, hidden behind his back. The dog's desire for the bone overrode his normal instinct of inflicting pain, and as he opened his mouth to take it, Dougie struck it between the ears with all his might. The dog let out a chorus of yelps and staggered drunkenly back into the house. Its owner, Mrs. Walker, came running out, wondering what was wrong with her dog. Dougie took off down the street, jumping and cackling like a maniac. It was obvious he wasn't as stupid as he appeared, and the old mongrel gave Dougie a cautious berth from that day forward.

The Murphy's

Within Northern Ireland, Catholic families tend to be much larger than Protestant ones. Part of the reason for this, as everyone knows, is the condemnation by the Catholic Church of birth control of any kind and the general encouragement to "be fruitful and multiply". As a result, the Protestants have always suspected on some level that the Catholics are trying to outbreed them. In addition to Catholics having more children than Protestants, they also tend to emigrate in larger numbers. As a result, the balance of power has not yet shifted against the Protestants.

The Murphy family in our neighborhood had far too many children for a Protestant family - nine boys and one girl. The family income was barely sufficient to keep them all clothed and fed. At dinnertime, the children would squabble over why one had more potatoes or peas than the other, and Mrs. Murphy had a terrible time controlling them. Mr. and Mrs. Murphy were both very small in stature. They were like two geese with a gaggle that had grown too large for the nest.

Despite their impoverished state, the boys all grew up to be strong and healthy – except one, Henry, who developed rickets. As a result, he was always somewhat sickly. Despite his ailment, however, Henry's sense of humor made him the biggest character of the bunch.

Everyone tried to stay on good terms with the Murphy's because of their rough reputation and sheer numbers. The Murphy girl was the safest girl in town, and if someone hit one of the boys, he had the other eight to contend with.

When they reached their teens, most of the children moved away to Australia or Canada, and they all became quite successful. Several stayed behind and did not do so well, ending up in and out of jail for minor transgressions such as fighting and raiding gas meters. In those days, no credit was allowed so gas was delivered to the houses through meters which had to be fed with shillings. Theft from the meters was commonplace. Neighbors who found their meters broken into immediately suspected the Murphy boys and would often complain to Mrs. Murphy after Mr. Murphy had gone to work. Everyone liked Mrs. Murphy so the complaints were always delivered apologetically and, afterward, the complainants would usually be invited in for tea.

They weren't bad kids as much as adaptive. They were as tough as their surroundings. Mr. Murphy seemed angry most of the time, probably because of the constant mayhem in the house, and perhaps he had passed some of his rage on to the boys. Whatever the reason, someone on the street was always complaining about one of the Murphy boys.

Like most kids, they were made up of equal parts of their mother and father. They exhibited their mother's friendliness and graciousness when one spoke to any of them alone, but they were unapproachable and volatile like their father when they got into their groups and were trying to uphold their reputations. In fact, this was true of most of the tough guys around the city. A kind of auto-pilot would kick in, and it was immediately obvious that they weren't in their right minds and couldn't be approached safely.

On Friday nights, after getting his week's pay, Mr. Murphy would often stay too long at the bar and come home tanked up around nine o'clock. I was at the Murphy house one night playing with Danny, the youngest son, who was closest to me in age, when Mr. Murphy arrived home, three sheets to the wind. Mr. Murphy was barely in the door when he yelled to Mrs. Murphy, "Whar's me dinner? Is it still warm?"

He sat down at the table in a fierce temper, waiting to be fed. Mrs. Murphy answered, "It should be. It's been in the back o' the fire these past three hours!"

She then pulled a piece of meat out of the oven that looked like a lump of coal and slammed it down in front of him. Mr. Murphy looked at it as if he was trying to figure out what it was. His expression almost made me burst out laughing. Mrs. Murphy could always give back as good as she got.

She would usually recount the complaints made by the neighbors at some point in the evening after he had cooled down. Fortunately, she had the good sense to let him unwind a little first.

Several nights a week, Mr. Murphy would get plastered and stand in the center of the street, proclaiming to all the neighbors at the top of his lungs, "Are thar any more complaints about the Murphy's? If anyone has anythin' to say, let 'im come out and tell me now!"

Nobody wanted to mess with Mr. Murphy when he was in one of these moods so he was usually ignored. However, after listening to his ranting for about an hour one night, Mr. Parker, who lived across the street, came barreling out in his pajamas, grabbed Mr. Murphy by the throat and yelled, "Yeah, I 'ave a fockin' complaint, ya wee bastard! I'm sick t'death o' listenin' to yar bloody gulderin'!" For punctuation, he planted a sweeping right hook on poor wee Mr. Murphy's chin, stretching him out on the pavement, where he lay until his wife and kids came out and carried him back into the house.

Mr. Murphy's street performances temporarily ended for a while after that until the complaints started to mount up again, and he went back to his old tricks. I used to watch him from my bedroom window, laughing as the responses were called from around the neighborhood.

"Shaddup, ya eejit ya!"

"Give m'head some peace, far fok's sake!"

"Sleep it off, ya drunken git!"

To me, it was high comedy. I did notice, however, that Mr. Murphy now stood with his back to Mr. Parker's house and threw his voice in the other direction.

Danny and I became good friends in school, and he was generally considered to be the most fun-loving and friendly of all the Murphy boys. Unfortunately, he too ran into trouble growing up and ended up becoming the wildest of the bunch. He spent some time in jail for various offenses until one night when he was arrested for being drunk and disorderly. In the holding tank, he fell asleep on his back and choked to death on his own vomit. He was only nineteen. I was heartbroken by this news because I still remembered him as a fun-loving boy with an easy laugh.

The remaining children moved away and Mr. Murphy passed on a short while later, leaving Mrs. Murphy alone in the house that was once filled with the voices and laughter of her ten children. On the occasion of her seventieth birthday, the entire family got together and bought their mother a world cruise on a luxury liner. Despite her lack of education or social status, the other passengers on the liner voted her the most popular person on the ship.

Even while raising ten children through difficult times over all of those years, she had maintained a bright spirit and a strong ability to cope with the vicissitudes of life. However, she was as remarkable as she was common. A Cheyenne proverb states, "A nation is not conquered until the hearts of its women are on the ground. Then it is done, no matter how brave its warriors or how strong its weapons." Mrs. Murphy was a classic Irish woman. No amount of adversity could suppress her charm. She was extraordinary and unusual at the same time, for there were many Mrs. Murphy's" all over Belfast when I was a child, and they were a source of inspiration to those of us who lived through the leanest years of the 20th century.

CHAPTER 10

THE LITTLE BOY THAT SANTA CLAUS FORGOT

He's the little boy that Santa Claus forgot,
And goodness knows he didn't want a lot.

He sent a note to Santa
For some soldiers and a drum,
It broke his little heart
When he found Santa hadn't come.

In the street he envies all those lucky boys,
Then wanders home to last year's broken toys.
I'm so sorry for that laddie,
He hasn't got a daddy,
The little boy that Santa Claus forgot.

You know, Christmas comes but once a year
for every girl and boy,
The laughter and the joy they find
in each brand new toy.
I'll tell you of a little boy
that lives across the way...
This little fella's Christmas
is just another day.

The first time I heard Nat King Cole sing that song, I thought it had been written about me.

Some say a home is a reflection of the occupants. A tidy home indicates that the owner is organized, and a messy one that the owner is scatterbrained or worse. I'm afraid this was true in my ma's case. I never thought much about the disarray in my house growing up until I was able to see the homes of some of my friends and became aware of the difference. Increasingly embarrassed, I never invited friends to visit me at home. If anyone came over, I would meet him outside and suggest we go somewhere else. However, one afternoon, one of my friends ran up the front walk and started banging furiously at the door. I opened the door to see what the ruckus was all about. He rushed past me into the house claiming that a group of boys were threatening to beat him up. He jumped behind the couch and landed on top of some dirty clothes left there by my mother in the distant past. I looked through the window but could see no one on the street and realized that his claim of being chased was just a trick to see inside my house. I was mortified and certain the news that Sidney Rickerby lives in a hovel would be spread far and wide in short order.

Perhaps because of the disarray in the house and the discord I felt between my parents, I took an interest in reading very early in life and spent most of my time alone in my room escaping into the other worlds contained in books. When a birthday or Christmas was approaching, realizing my parents couldn't afford anything too extravagant like a bicycle or a sled, I would always ask for a book. My mother would usually answer, "We'll see." Usually, though, birthdays and Christmas mornings passed without any gifts. I assumed at the time that they couldn't afford to buy one for me and were too ashamed to admit it, but I realized in later years that books were not expensive at all and could be bought even more cheaply when used. Resentment or anger, however, did not seem to be part of my repertoire of emotions at that young age, and I just assumed they had their reasons for not celebrating holidays or birthdays. They never apologized for not buying me gifts. They didn't even try to lay the blame on Santa for forgetting our house. Being a naïve and gullible child, I would have readily believed it. With every gift-less Christmas, I grew more and more confused about why Santa Claus kept skipping me. I thought I was a good boy and had done nothing to make the naughty list. I held onto hope that he was just missing my house somehow.

One day, I looked up the chimney to see if it was wide enough for him to come down. It clearly wasn't, so on Christmas Eve I crept downstairs after my parents had gone to bed and unlocked the back door so Santa could get in. I lay in my bed listening all night for the sound of the knob turning until I finally fell asleep. I woke early the next morning and ran down the stairs praying that Santa hadn't skipped me again. I looked into the den by the fire. I looked in the kitchen. I even looked at the front step. Nothing. He had forgotten me again.

I often wondered if my parents were hoping I would just forget it was Christmas. Of course, this is impossible for a child so I usually spent Christmas morning looking out of my bedroom window at the street below where other kids played happily with their new toys. They would sometimes come to the front yard and call for me but I would duck down, too embarrassed to go outside and reveal that Santa hated me.

As I got older, and after enough barren Christmas days, I stopped believing in Santa and started blaming my parents. There were probably other parents in the neighborhood that couldn't afford to buy gifts for their children, but every Christmas morning, it seemed to me that every kid in the world except me was playing with a shiny, new toy. And it was Christmas mornings that I felt most acutely that my parents were poor in more ways than one.

Me at 12

CHAPTER 11

"T"

"The torment of human frustration, whatever its immediate cause, is the knowledge that the self is in prison, its vital force and mangled mind leaking away in lonely, wasteful self-conflict."
~ Elizabeth Drew

My poor ma was constantly on the verge of a nervous breakdown. The slightest annoyance could set her off. The most consistent outward manifestation of this perpetual exasperation was a "t" sound she emitted every five minutes or so during her entire waking life. It is the universal expression of exasperation, performed by clicking the tip of the tongue against the roof of the mouth. Sometimes I would know the reason for her t'ing, but most of the time it seemed without purpose as if her tongue was on some sort of a timer. The "t" would sometimes be followed by a complaint, but most of the time she did it for no reason at all that I could see, and it was usually followed by a shake of the head and a deep sigh of exasperation.

Despite her shortcomings, my mother had delusions of grandeur about herself and her appearance. I used to watch her putting on her make-up when she was getting ready to go out and was fascinated by the expressions she would make. She was quite pretty when she was young, with nice legs and an hourglass figure. Unfortunately, she had inherited the prominent McKee neb (nose), and no amount of powder or paint could detract from it. I once saw a picture of her with her mother and brother sitting on the rocks by the seaside at Pickie Pool, my mother in 1920's bathing suit attire, my grandma in her standard baggy, black dress, attempting to hide her overblown figure, and my Uncle Alfie in white sports pants and jacket with his equally prominent proboscis. Between the three of them, the noses could have made a fourth person. Despite this, however, they all had a bit of a wire about themselves, and none of them suffered from any lack of confidence.

Like my father, my mother's moods were completely unpredictable. One summer day when I was nine or ten, she and I were walking around Bangor together, a harbor town with a small beach. The streets were packed with summer revelers. My mother was holding my hand as we walked along the boardwalk. She had just bought an ice cream cone for me, and I was about to take the first lick when a street waif ran by and snatched it out of my hand, leaving my tongue lapping at thin air. He darted off into the crowd and was out of sight before I knew what happened. I looked up at my mother and started to cry. Instead of consoling me, the obvious and clear victim, she gave me a smack in the ear and yelled, "Ach, why'd ya let 'im take your ice cream?"

I was then crying not only for my stolen ice cream cone but for my sore ear and the general injustice of it all. I got a clout in the ear hole while the thief was greedily devouring my ice cream cone in some alleyway. This was yet another lesson to me that the world was neither a fair nor equitable place.

CHAPTER 12

PRODS AND TAIGS

"Ireland is a country in which political conflicts are at least genuine: they are about something. They are about patriotism, about religion, or about money: The three great realities."
~ G.K. Chesterton

No book about Northern Ireland would be complete without at least some mention of "the troubles" between the two tribes of "Nor'n Iron" – the "Prods", also known as the Protestants, and the "Taigs", also known as the Roman Catholics. The Prods are a majority in Northern Ireland, especially around the capital city of Belfast, and outnumber the Catholics two to one.

In conversation, Protestants will routinely refer to Roman Catholics as "Taigs". No one can seem to agree on the origin of this term, though the most popular theory is that it is derived from the common Irish male name of the same spelling, or the surname of Teague, as the term "Paddy" came from "Patrick". Another common Protestant slur of Catholics is the term "Fenian", undoubtedly a reference to the Irish-Catholic Fenian Brotherhood, a secret revolutionary organization in the United States and Ireland in the mid-19th century dedicated to the overthrow of British rule in Ireland. The appendage "bastards" is also common, as in "Taig Bastard" or "Fenian Bastard".

When I grew up in Northern Ireland, the term most used by Protestants in referring to Catholics was "Mickey's", probably because many Catholics are named Michael. The use of the term "left-footer" is also popular. For example, when inquiring about someone's background, the question is often asked, "Does he kick with the left foot or the right?" It is known that Prods kick with the right foot, Catholics with the left. When using the pejorative "Fenian" or "Taig", Prods often do so with a contemptuous curl of the lips or a scowl to accentuate their distaste for "those people."

Despite the colorful use of epithets in referring to Catholics, the response from Catholics has been either mild or comparatively unimaginative. The worst put-downs I've ever heard a Catholic use toward a Protestant are "Prod bastards" or "Orange bastards." Catholics just don't seem to have the desire to create as many colorful descriptions of Prods as the Prods have for them. I think the answer can be found in how each community views the other. The Prods, while a majority within Northern Ireland, are the true minority in the whole of Ireland with all of the attendant fears common to minorities who consider their community under siege.

Most Protestants have long believed that the Catholics are intent on the destruction of the Northern Ireland State and the Protestant way of life. This fear eats at the soul of the Protestant community in Northern Ireland and is the source of their hatred of Roman Catholics. The Catholics, on the other hand, know that time and history is on their side and that sooner or later they will prevail and Ireland will be "united and free". The prospect of this eventuality terrifies Orangemen.

Another example of the bitter hatred the Prods have for the Taigs can be found in the nature of Orange music or "party" songs. One of these songs goes as follows (with apologies to the author of "Galway Bay.")

If you ever go across the sea to Ireland,
Be it only on the Twelfth Day of July,
Just to see again the lily and sweet William
And to watch the Orangemen as they walk by,
And if there's gonna be a fight hereafter
And, somehow, I'm sure there's going to be,
We'll make the fenian's blood flow like water
Down the Belfast Lough into the Irish Sea.

Another song goes –
Do you think that we would let
A dirty fenian git
Destroy a leaf of the lily-o?

Alongside the political divide, which has to do with the future of Northern Ireland or lack thereof, there are other divisions. Catholic schoolchildren attend Catholic parochial schools. Protestant children attend state schools. Some efforts have been made to have Catholic and Protestant children attend non-denominational, mixed schools but with only limited success. There are also exclusive Catholic sports such as Irish football and hurling in which Protestants do not participate. One of the few common interests the two communities share, however, is soccer. In the past, certain teams had a Catholic following and others an exclusively Protestant fan base.

The division even extends to the national newspapers. Catholics will receive their version of events from the Irish news and Protestants from the Belfast Newsletter. Both tribes, however, will purchase the Belfast Telegraph, which attempts to remain somewhat neutral.

Where one lives is often an indicator of one's religion. Working class Catholics and Protestants tend to congregate within their own communities. These communities have unofficial but strict borders. A common practice during periods of communal violence was to raid the other's territory and toss Molotov cocktails through parlor windows, a particularly despicable practice given that the victims had little enough in worldly possessions. During the height of the troubles, the authorities erected tall fences between the two communities to deter cross community raiding.

The worst of the violence and the greatest degree of hatred is found within the working class neighborhoods in Belfast, Derry and other Northern Ireland cities. The middle and upper classes remain aloof from and experience less of the effects of the conflict. There is little difference to be found between a rabid, working class, Roman Catholic nationalist and a working class, Protestant fanatic. Neither can find any good with the opposite side. The provisional Irish Republican Army, the IRA, a mostly Catholic group vehemently against English presence and rule in Ireland, drew its recruits from the blue collar, nationalist neighborhoods and their counterparts in the Protestant community from the Protestant ghettoes. They are mirror images of one another.

A solution to Ulster's political and religious divide would bedevil even the most rational thinker. For the fanatics, it's impossible. Yet apart from a few psychopaths on each side, the working class people caught up in this conflict are basically good people confused and torn apart by history. As a community, Northern Ireland's Protestants and Catholics contribute more to national charities per head than any other group within the United Kingdom.

Of the two groups today, the Protestants exhibit the greatest degree of pessimism. They feel betrayed and let down by the British government whose perceived "concessions" to Ulster's Catholic minority has weakened the Protestant power base. The common sentiment now heard around Northern Ireland is, "The Catholics are being handed everything they want." The beloved Royal Ulster Constabulary has been restructured and is now the Northern Ireland Police Force. With the peace process, IRA gunmen guilty of murder are being prematurely let out of jail, although the same is true of Protestant militants. Former IRA militants are now political leaders in the prominent Catholic parties in Northern Ireland. They draw handsome salaries from White Hall while in the past they drew only guns. The hated Roman Catholic tri-color flag now flutters over former Protestant neighborhoods in Belfast. The British "sell-out" is well underway.

The sad fact is that Northern Ireland is an embarrassment to Britain. The claims of the Ulster Loyalists for inclusion in the U.K. as British subjects are unwelcome. The absorption of Northern Ireland by the Irish Republic would free the British of any financial obligation to Northern Ireland. Thus, for the most part, the Protestants are on their own.

However, for the sake of the health and sanity of the people of Northern Ireland, a settlement is mandatory. If they can only put their history and their divisions behind them, as appears to be the case with the recent agreements, they can turn Ulster into a decent place to live in and bring up children. It would be an even greater place than it already is if they could combine their talents for the good of all the people of Ulster, particularly the children, who are always the innocent sufferers of the ignorance of their parents. Whether the two communities have the will and the courage to change things for good and all remains to be seen.

As a Protestant, it pains me to say this, but one of the main hurdles to achieving a lasting peace in Northern Ireland is Protestant gloating about ancient battles through the constant parading of Protestant power by the Orange Order. The Twelfth of July Parade is a prime example of this. In any other country, such ancient victories would be nothing but a sidenote in the history books, only vaguely recalled by anyone but history buffs. For instance, the Fourth of July in the States is more of a national holiday for independence than it is a celebration of victory over the British. In fact, most Americans now love all things British. In the case of the Protestants, however, the defeat of the Catholics is the core of their sentiment, and the Orange parades are a demonstration of the supposed superiority that the Protestants hold in the north. Protestants even used to walk along the wall bordering the city of Derry and throw pennies down into the Catholic ghettoes where the poor Catholic's were living, obviously a very demeaning act. Until this kind of behavior stops, there will be hatred. And as long as there is hatred, there can never be complete or lasting peace.

The main reason for all the Protestant celebrations is the strong emotional attachment they have to the soil of Ulster; to the six counties. It's almost ethereal how they feel about it. There are many reasons for the problems between the two groups - the Celts and the Anglo-Saxons (the Celts being the Catholics and the Anglo-Saxons being the Protestants) - religious, ethnic, historical, political, even racial, but it all boils down to who controls the territories. In that sense, the conflict in Northern Ireland is a turf war. Getting the British out of Northern Ireland will not solve nor end the problem. There are still the Protestants to deal with. In fact, the English wouldn't even be there if it were not for the Protestants, who are still their subjects and who number approximately one million out of about one and a half million in Northern Ireland. The British would dearly love to cut the tie once and for all. There is no benefit for them in having Northern Ireland. It has ceased to be of strategic importance to them. Funding Northern Ireland to keep it up to the standards of the mainland is an economic drain financially. They would love it if the Protestants gave up but that's not going to happen in the foreseeable future. The British are also too proud to be chased out of Ireland by a bunch of ragtag revolutionaries like the IRA.

Growing up in such a divided environment, I absorbed some of these attitudes by osmosis. Nobody ever sat me down as a child and gave me a detailed history. In fact, we were not even taught Irish history in school as Protestants. The Catholics were taught Irish history and had a keener sense of their own background than we did. It is still that way today. So through the attitude of our parents and the people in the neighborhood we lived in, all we were taught was that we were Prods, that the Catholics were against us, and that they were no good and could not to be trusted. We were taught they were feckless and lazy and did not have the qualities of thrift, hard work and cleanliness that the Prods had. Ironically, these were and are the very same comments made about blacks by racists in the deep south of the United States. The mass generalization inherent to prejudice is always the same, no matter where it is or who it is directed toward.

CHAPTER 13

FENIANS AND MILK BOTTLES

"Tourists have nothing to worry about in Ireland. The Irish love everyone . . . except each other."

~ A comment made to my son, Mark, by a Belfast cab driver.

My father had good, close Catholic friends at his work at the railway, and he always made exceptions for them when he castigated the Catholics as a group. During a vacation back home one year when I was in my forties, he and I went to a soccer game at Windsor Park. We took a bus home and were walking the several blocks to our house when he said, "I can always spot a Catholic house."

"Oh yeah? How can you do that, da?" I asked.

"By the milk bottles," he replied.

"Milk bottles? What do you mean?"

"They're always dirty. Catholics are lazy bastards. They don't wash out their dirty milk bottles before settin' 'em out on the steps for the milkman t'pick up."

"Really, da?" I said. I thought this was an interesting anthropological observation on his part and I pondered it as we walked along.

"I was visitin' a Catholic friend'a mine one time," he continued, "and 'is wife put out a saucer'a milk fer the cat. The cat turned its nose up to it and do you know what she did then?"

"I don't know, da. What'd she do?"

"After the bloody cat got through sniffin' at the milk, the oul' doll picked up the saucer and poured it back into the bottle! I never saw anythin' so disgustin' in my whole life! There's Catholics for ya! Only a fenian would do somethin' like that – pour milk a bloody cat sniffed over back into a bottle fer human consumption."

Playing the devil's advocate, I argued, "Well, maybe the cat didn't actually drink any of the milk."

This threw my da into a fit of anger.

"Ach, it doesn't matter if the cat drank the milk or not! The milk was fouled just by the bloody cat sniffin' at it, ya eejit! Don't be daft!"

"Okay, da. I guess you're right."

To accentuate his point, he pointed out dirty milk bottles on various front porches and clean bottles on others, saying, "Catholic house, Protestant house, Protestant, Catholic, Protestant, Protestant, Catholic" and so on.

The more dirty milk bottles he saw, the more his disgust and contempt mounted, until he had finally worked himself into a seething rage. It was obvious he could not conceive of a Protestant family anywhere in the world leaving a dirty milk bottle on their porch.

When we arrived home, I noticed that there were three empty milk bottles on our own front doorstep with a film of congealing milk inside all of them.

I said, "Jesus, da! Look! Catholics must have taken over our house!"

He gritted his teeth, stormed into the house and didn't talk to me for two days.

CHAPTER 14

THE GOOD AND BAD OF IRISH FOLKLORE

"The Irish believe that fairies are extremely fond of good wine. The proof of the assertion is that in the olden days royalty would leave a keg of wine out for them at night. Sure enough, it was always gone in the morning."
~ Anonymous

Everyone knows the classic and positive images of Irish folklore – dancing leprechauns, pots o' gold shining under rainbows, screaming banshees, harps and four-leaf clovers. And just as there is cultural folklore, there is folklore created within families - tall tales told and retold through the ages, elaborated on with each retelling until no one remembers how much of the original event matches the myth. The evolution of Homer's epic poems was probably not much different. But as happy and whimsical as folklore can be, it can also be used to spread and perpetuate negative half-truths and outright lies. Thus the seeds of prejudice were planted in us early through stories passed down from generation to generation.

For instance, my paternal grandfather, whom I never knew, was reputed to be a bit of a character. He didn't mind Catholics but he hated Protestants who became Catholics. In the small town where he lived, there was a Protestant who had changed his religion so that he could marry a Catholic girl. My grandfather considered this unforgivable treason so there was deep resentment between the two of them.

One day, they met outside the town at a crossroads and words were exchanged. Punches flew and the turncoat, as my grandfather would have called him, was knocked head over heels into a duck pond at the side of the road. My grandfather walked off and left him there. The word spread back to the village. The poor guy's wife heard her husband had been beaten up so she tore out there. It was the Victorian era when ladies generally wore long, heavy skirts and underskirts. She saw her husband's hat floating on the top of the duck pond, assumed he had drowned, and dove in to get him out. The pond was only about four feet deep but she couldn't dive to the bottom because all her heavy clothes were forcing her to float on the surface. She screamed, "Oh, my husband's drowned! God help him!"

Seeing his hat floating on the surface of the pond, she had assumed the worst, but her husband had actually crawled out and was sitting at home waiting for her when she got there.

Though this story was told to me many times ostensibly for the humor in it, it also served to firmly embed in my psyche the idea that converting religions for love or any other reason was never to be considered. Through stories such as these, the social indoctrination took place. I'm sure the Catholics had similar stories designed to discourage intermingling with Protestants. Hatred can be bold-faced or hidden, but the effects are the same.

CHAPTER 15

THE PAPERBOY FROM HELL

"He's a mean kid, I tell ya. He tapes worms to the ground and watches the birds get hernias!"
~ Rodney Dangerfield

Our street, Prestwick Park Road, County Antrim

Since I was entering my teen years when my sister Olga was an infant, much of the responsibility of minding her fell to me. My mother forced me to walk her around the neighborhood every day in her pram. I would dread these walks because of the endless harassment I had to endure from the tough neighborhood kids. From perpetually dirty faces, they would yell comments like, "Awww, how sweet! Loogit tha wee mammy's boy!" and "Look at her, would ya!"

The meanest of the lot was a kid who delivered newspapers around our neighborhood. He had jet black hair dangling in greasy clumps over steel-blue eyes and a stubble of beard on his chin at only fourteen or fifteen years of age.

I was out walking my sister in her pram when he passed by on his bicycle and without warning, gave me a tremendous blow in the solar plexus, knocking every ounce of air out of me. I was completely unable to retaliate and dropped to my knees, gasping and wheezing. I could hear him laughing as he rode away. It took me about ten minutes to recover. Once I was able to breathe again and realized I would live, I made up my mind to seek revenge.

All I could find out about him from my chums in the neighborhood was that he lived in Old Park Village in a row of dilapidated, pre-century housing. The next day, I put on a pair of my father's leather gloves and waited behind a hedge for him to come around the corner on his afternoon rounds. After about an hour, I saw him coming up the street. I widened my stance, cocked back my fist, and as he came around the corner, belted him as hard as I could on the chin. There was a very brief moment of elation as he crashed to the ground and his bike rolled ahead without him. To my horror, he immediately jumped back up, shoved me to the ground, sat on my chest, pinned my arms to my side and proceeded to gouge my left eye with his thumb. The pain was excruciating. I screamed for help, but all I heard in response was someone yelling, "Shut up out there!" It was like a bad dream. I was certain that my eye would be popped out of the socket at any moment. Knowing the treachery of this wee bastard, I was sure he would grab my dislodged eyeball, put it in his pocket, and ride away on his bike laughing hysterically. I increased the decibel level of my screaming as Olga gurgled happily in her pram. Finally, someone came to the upstairs window of the nearest house and said, "What the bloody hell is goin' on down there?" Fearing discovery, he finally removed his thumb from my eye and stood up. Looming over me, he said, "If I ever see you again, I'll marder ya."

He then gave me a kick in the stomach to accentuate his parting remark, picked up his sack and rode off, leaving me sucking air and totally humiliated for a second time. I laid there for a while looking up at the sky, waiting for the air to return to my lungs, which was becoming a familiar sensation, and testing the mangled eye to see if it was still operational. I finally stood up and staggered home. My eye was getting redder and more swollen by the minute. When I got home, my mother saw it and actually screamed. I was glad to be safe at home and was looking forward to a little sympathy and tender loving care. Instead, when my mother saw my swollen eye and generally disheveled appearance, she yelled, "What happened?"

"I got beat up," I said.

"Can't ya even take your wee sister for a walk without gettin' into trouble?"

"But ma, it wasn't my fault!" I pleaded. "It was the paperboy! He beat me up for no reason."

"No reason, eh? Then what are you doing with your father's gloves? You went out looking for trouble."

"No, ma! I didn't! I swear!" (I lied.)

"Ach, ya must'a done somethin' to him. Nobody hits someone for no reason a'tall!"

My mother obviously had no clue about the harsh realities of boyhood, and certainly had never met this particular paperboy. I started to cry at the injustice of it all. Her face softened. She fell to her knees and hugged me.

"There, there now. It's all over. We'll just go wash your eye, and then you can have a wee lie down."

She walked me to the bathroom sink and splashed cold water on my face, dried me off with a dish towel and put me to bed.

This reaction is universal to parents. It seems when a child worries them or gets hurt, they have to get their anger out of their way before the compassion can come through.

I lay in bed for hours seething with anger, my eye throbbing in agony, and it took more than a week for it to recover. I entertained the most violent fantasies about how I would exact my revenge on the paperboy, perhaps using a board or an iron bar on him next time he rode around the corner, but the fear of another eye-gouging session squelched my resolve. He deserved a good beating, but I just wasn't big enough or strong enough to give it to him. Finally, I chalked it up to yet another of life's little inequities.

To this day, that eye still gives me trouble now and then. I comfort myself in imagining that the paperboy somehow met a ghastly death, or he's still the neighborhood paperboy to this day.

CHAPTER 16

STREET VENDORS

"No one can possibly have lived through the Great Depression without being scarred by it. No amount of experience since the Depression can convince someone who has lived through it that the world is safe economically."
~ Isaac Asimov

When I was a kid, a whole procession of street vendors would come up our street on weekdays hocking their wares. This routine gave a comforting predictability to life. I remember the bread man from the Ormeau Bakery with his horse-drawn cart selling bread and other bakery products to the housewives - the wonderful, intoxicating smell of fresh-baked bread flooding from the back of his cart. There were crusty loaves, or Ormeau bread as we called it. There was sliced Pan bread, which had a different texture and a sweeter taste. There were Barn Bracks, thick rolls with currants inside of them, which could be sliced in half and were delicious with fresh dairy butter. Those were always my favorites in the morning. There were currant squares, flaky pastries with raisins. There was soda bread, or "soda farls," as they are known in Belfast, which were triangular in shape and a staple of just about everyone's diet. Then there were scones, or potato bread. Without soda bread and potato bread, an "Ulster fry" would not have been complete. My mother and I would go out to the cart with the other mothers and children from the block. I would stand there and bask in the aroma until I was dizzy. It was also a good chance for neighbors to socialize, something else the supermarket has all but done away with.

Bread man, 1950

Then there were the coal men in horse-drawn carts who delivered bags of coal. There was no central heating in those days so coal fires were essential. These men would carry the bags of coal on their backs and dump it into the coal bin at the back of the house. They were always black and dirty from the coal dust sticking to their sweat. There was another coal man who sold bricks of coal made from coal dust compressed together. They were the next best thing to actual coal.

We could always depend on the stick man, who delivered bundles of kindling tied together with string. Before we could start a coal fire, we had to put paper in the fireplace, then short sticks. Once the sticks were burning well, we added the coal. The coal fire would blow in the hearth, spreading heat throughout the house and warming up the water heater.

The fish man would come around a few times a week in his truck selling Ardglass herrings, which were freshly caught by the fishermen in the village of the same name. He also used a horse-drawn cart and would announce his presence with the cry, "Ardglass! Ardglass! Ardglass herrings!" All the housewives would run out and make their purchases, chatting as they waited in line. The fish were in their original condition, not cleaned or filleted, plucked right out of the sea the day before. The housewives would gather around and ask him if the fish were fresh. And he'd always say, "'Course they are, Missus. Look, their eyes are still open!"

The Delft man also made regular rounds. His street cry was, "Any old rags for Delft?" For old rags, he would give somewhat cheap Delft cups, saucers and plates in return. That was their medium of exchange.

There was also the refuse man who collected scraps of food, potato peelings, and other throw-away items, which were then used for pig swill. As far as I can remember, he didn't pay out anything for whatever contributions were made by the housewives. That was just a way for them to get rid of some of the garbage.

All of these characters were very jolly and friendly. They kidded with the housewives and added to the feeling of community which existed then. The parade of horses left deposits on the streets, and people in the neighborhood who had flower gardens eagerly went out with pails and shovels to collect the steaming droppings, which were then liberally deposited around the roots of rose bushes and flower patches.

The Ormeau bakery man had a very tall cart with two doors at the back which opened outwards from the center. He sat up on a raised seat at the front of the cart with a whip which he cracked to move the horse along. As kids, we ran along behind his cart, jumped up and grabbed the handles and held on as the horse pulled the cart along the street. The bakery man always seemed to know when we were back there because he would flip the whip backwards with deadly accuracy and catch us around the ear or the back of the neck, which always left a welt. I thought this was quite cruel and couldn't understand how someone so nice just moments before when selling his bread to the ladies could suddenly become such a bastard. But we continued to ride on the cart, anyway. I guess we couldn't resist the challenge of jumping on, hiding from the driver, and avoiding the whip if he did see us. For months, we labored over the mystery of how he could see us when we couldn't see him. It finally dawned on us that he could see our reflections in the house windows as he passed.

When the bakery man stopped his cart to sell his bread, and the horses were resting, my mates and I would run between their legs on a dare. One day, one of my friends was halfway through when the horse released a strong jet of urine, drenching him from head to toe. My friend screamed and ran home to wash it off. We laughed all day about it.

I don't know why we didn't complain to our parents or the police about the bread man using a horsewhip on us. I suppose we felt that we were doing something we shouldn't be doing, so we must have deserved it. I did get my own back on him one day, though, years later and completely by accident.

I was about fourteen years old, flying down the street, late for work as usual, pumping my dad's old roadster bicycle, which was definitely no racer. The horse and cart were facing me as I approached. As I passed on the side, one of the heavy, wooden side doors flew open, completely blocking my path. I couldn't avoid the door so I stuck out my leg to keep it from hitting me. The door slammed hard and swung back open, hitting the bread man in the back of the head with a loud bang. I heard an anguished scream of pain followed by a loud thud as I rode away. I had a momentary feeling of guilt, but it dissipated as I recalled his former cruelty to me and my mates. He had it coming.

Two street sweepers employed by the Belfast City Corporation used to come around our neighborhood. They always reminded me of Laurel and Hardy; one very fat with an assertive nature and the other very thin with a passive nature. The smaller one always had a Woodbine cigarette stuck behind his ear while he puffed away on another. Cigarettes were unfiltered in those days. For the average person, it was an expensive hobby, so cigarettes were treasured and smoked to the nub. A few puffs would be drawn, the cigarette would be nicked, and the remains were then placed in a vest pocket or behind the ear for future pulls. Nothing was wasted. There were some people who would even use pins or needles, which they would insert into the remains of the cigarette so they could smoke the last few flakes of tobacco right down to the very end.

My wife, Rosaleen, knew a lady up her street in Belfast who would come out every day and give a slice of hard bread to one of the vendor's horses. The old horse got so used to this daily treat that it began to look forward to coming to her house. One day, she didn't come out for some reason and the horse, which had been left unattended, walked up the sidewalk and tried to enter the front door, pulling the cart behind it. Most houses back then had an exterior door right on the sidewalk, a small front entry, and an interior door on the inside which was kept locked to keep out the heat, flies and dust. The outside door was often left open. The wagon got wedged in the doorway and the horse started to panic. The cart was making a racket hitting the sides of the entrance. The old horse couldn't go in any further and couldn't back out. When the lady opened the interior door to investigate the commotion, she was greeted by the horse's face looming over her. She let out a scream and almost fainted. Her scream spooked the horse even more and it started rearing up, almost destroying the cart and doorway in the process. It took half an hour to calm the horse down and coax it to back out slowly.

The horses that the vendors used to pull their carts really had no business walking on the cobblestone streets around Belfast, and would often stumble and hurt themselves, especially during the winter months when the ground was wet and slippery. If they did fall, the horses would have a difficult job getting back on their feet again. The cobblestones were also an extreme hazard for bicycles. The stone and the iron tracks the trams ran along made bicycle-riding quite adventuresome, too. I would sometimes get stuck in the tracks and it was a hell of a job to get the bike tire out of it. Since the tracks criss-crossed madly, it was almost impossible to miss running into at least one of them. The tire would slip into the grooves of the track, making it impossible to turn or maintain balance. Eventually, I would either go arse over tit, grind to a stop, or dive off and watch the bike ride away without me in another direction along the track. I would then walk over to the bike, extricate it from the tracks and ride on red-faced as all who witnessed my Chaplin-esque antics laughed uproariously.

The vendors were a big part of everyday life in Belfast. One got used to this parade of characters coming around and everyone knew them on a first-name basis. The feeling of community it created is sorely lacking in the modern world. The only street vendors we have now are people hanging fliers on door knobs. The ice cream man is the closest modern equivalent to the horse-drawn carts. The street vendors were like characters from a Disney movie. They weren't bitter about having hard, low-paying jobs. They were happy to be employed when so many others weren't.

Appreciation for one's health, a job (any job), and food on the table, however humble, may have been the greatest side-effect of the Great Depression, and one many could learn from today. We have so much comparatively, yet depression is at such an all-time high, pharmaceutical companies are making a fortune selling us drugs to treat it. It seems that greed, discontent and a sense of entitlement constitute the Great Depression of our age.

CHAPTER 17

BUSKERS AND ASSORTED HEADCASES

"A man snuck behind a tent to see the inner workings of the circus. He saw a man picking up elephant droppings with a large shovel and engaged him in conversation. The odor was so overwhelming, he asked the man if he ever thought of quitting his obviously unpleasant job. The man answered, "What? And give up show biz?"
~ Dusty old joke

When I got a bit older and could go downtown by myself or with my mates, there was a whole new variety of street characters. A plethora of street singers, or buskers as they called them in England, would assail the city on weekends entertaining the queues at the picture houses. As a result, people usually had a better time outside waiting in line than they did inside the theater.

On Saturday mornings after a week's work, there was the usual "lie-in", a good Ulster breakfast of bacon and eggs, sausages, tomatoes, mushrooms, and black sausage, then we would all go to a soccer match or play in a game ourselves. After the game, the next stop was the pub for a few pints, then home to freshen up for the Plaza, Dossors, or The Gala around nine or ten to see how the girls were doing. With a bit of luck, a connection would be made. With extreme luck, we would land a "knee-trembler" at the end of the evening. This was a term we all used for the awkward but unavoidable necessity of necking with a girl against the wall of her doorway or entry, since they always lived at home, and we had nowhere private to go. After a while, due to the combination of cold weather and frustrated excitement, the knees would start to tremble.

If money was tight on a Saturday night, instead of going to the Plaza Dance Hall, we would go to the Park Picture House, Belfast's only movie theater at the time. Everyone in Belfast loved the movies, so a two-hour wait was standard to get into the second show at 8:30 on weekends. The picture queues stretched around the block starting after the first house was filled. The movie screen at the Park Picture House was nothing less than a window to other worlds, whisking us away from the perpetual rain of Ireland to a tropical beach or jungle paradise. These exotic locales might as well have been another planet to us. Our heads would swim as we watched them, dreaming about seeing them all for real one day. So we would wait the two hours without complaint, rain or shine, for the second house.

The variety show on the sidewalk in front of the Picture House was every bit as entertaining as anything Ed Sullivan ever put together. There were players of every kind of instrument imaginable, mainly fiddles and accordions, as well as acrobats, magicians, mimes, clowns, even whistlers, a true art form in Belfast. Accompanying the entertainers was an army of beggars. Hunchbacks and cripples of every variety all vied for loose change from the crowd. There was a man with no legs who pushed himself around on a board with wheels on it. He was very adept at maneuvering the contraption through the crowds. He always got into the movie for free. We used to joke with the owner of the theater that we shouldn't have to pay either since he had "bummed his way in". The man would sit in the aisle or by the door and people would often trip over him in the dark. He was not shy and would startle them by yelling, "Watch where yer goin', ya silly bugger!"

There was a man who apparently had no marketable talent, so he invented an act pretending to tie his face together with an invisible needle and thread. His facial expressions would distort as he sewed up the ends of the string. Once the "strings" were attached, he would then pull them wildly in every direction, his face contorting along with the movements of his hands. It was startling to witness and somewhat macabre.

Another man would dress as a cowboy and sing songs of the American west. The overall effect was diminished somewhat by his Belfast accent.

An old woman we called "Old Corky" was always good for an appearance. She was Belfast's premier hooker and mainly catered to the working class. Her nickname was given to her because of her most distinguishing characteristic – a wooden leg. Apparently, none of her customers seemed to mind it because she never seemed to be short on cash.

I remember the "Mountain Man", a tall, bearded, barrel-chested brute who always carried a small medical bag containing his toiletries. He was never without an apple. He would inspire a mixture of awe and fear in everyone he passed, but he seemed to exist in a world separate from ours. He looked neither right nor left and never spoke with anyone. He would simply walk through town every morning with his bag, his stride full of purpose as if on some important business, carefully wash his face and teeth in the drinking fountains in front of the City Hall, and disappear for parts unknown. We all wanted to learn more about him, but nobody had the guts to talk to him because of his imposing size and fearsome appearance. We were too young to know it then but he was probably homeless and his lack of contact with people was a defense to avoid social contact, perhaps out of shame for his situation. That or he was just crackers.

"The Colonel" was another favorite character around town. He got the nickname because of his manner of dress and the stiff way he carried himself. He was always exquisitely attired in a hounds tooth jacket, cavalry twill pants and, tucked under his arm, a military-style swizzle stick. His moustache was waxed and curled at the ends in the common style of a British military man. Every time a plane would pass overhead, he would snap to attention and briskly salute in military fashion. We all reached the conclusion that he was shell-shocked and a possible victim of World War I. Like the Mountain Man, he made no effort to talk to anyone and barreled around the city at a brisk pace, pausing only to salute planes. Like the others, however, he was harmless and accepted as part of the daily scene.

Then there was "Daddy" Rice (I was never sure how he acquired that nickname) who could almost always be found walking around the city, eyes rolling, tipping his hat and smiling at everyone he passed. He was obviously "touched" but in the nicest of ways. The most impressive thing about him was the sheer speed with which he walked. He was like a human locomotive. When people saw him coming, they just gave him plenty of room to sail on through, saying things like, "Look at him go!" and "Late again, Daddy?"
I'd often see Daddy Rice walking along the sidewalk while I was riding the bus along Royal Avenue. He was difficult to miss darting in and out of the crowds as fast as his long, boney legs would carry him. He actually kept up with the bus as it made its way through the traffic and my mates and I would cheer him on, imaging that he was racing with us. He would always just smile and tip his hat in response.

There was another man we called "Beautiful Dreamer", a sepulchral figure who entertained us with his stammering rendition of the song of the same name. He was often accompanied by a small, doleful accordion player who was half a bar ahead of him most of the time. They were not the most talented pairing I've ever witnessed, but they were committed (or should have been.)

There was a horrible, old woman who, God help her, had sleeping sickness or something akin to it. She used to haunt the queues like a ghost, dangling an old, woolen sock from filthy fingers. If someone failed to drop in a coin, she would fasten her talon-like hand on the offender's arm, digging her nails into the flesh, and nip and pinch until he anted up. She never spoke a word, but somebody said she had a big house up the Malone Road and went to church on Sundays dressed to kill.

When *The Jolson Story* starring Larry Parks came to Belfast, everyone was Al Jolson for about a year afterward. There were "Mammy" singers on one knee up and down the block, all doing their best to drown each other out. One enterprising lad cashed in on the boom by fitting himself out in a Jolson wig and black face. He looked exactly like him and had all of Jolson's movements down pat. He would drop to one knee and belt out "Mammy" whether it was dry or wet. He must have made a fortune because everyone threw change into his hat in appreciation. All the other Jolson's were sick with envy.

We were all very familiar with all of these characters and they were affectionately regarded by everyone. They added a great deal of vivacity to the city, and we would have missed them had they not been there. The mentally or physically handicapped were not just tolerated, they were taken care of. We all felt responsible for their well-being, and they never lacked for a warm blanket or other necessities. In small villages or towns like Belfast, we all kept tabs on the "village idiots", as they were called then, and made sure they were okay.

Most of the street performers in Belfast weren't insane. They were just wild characters with an excess of personality and probably a hope somewhere in their minds to escape the rough and tumble world of Belfast and somehow enter the one they saw in the movies at the Park Picture House. They could always be found in or around the central area of Belfast, which was where I usually ran into many of my friends, also. Life was never lonely. That's what I miss most about Belfast. It was a big city to me but I ran into people I knew everywhere. My circle of friends encompassed the entire city. I've lived in Los Angeles for over forty years now and still don't know most of the people on my street. It takes an earthquake to get everyone out of their houses at the same time.

Something else Belfast had that modern cities lack is accountability. A criminal can disappear into a crowd and be fairly certain they will never see their victim again. In the Belfast of my youth, and probably still today, if someone insulted someone else one day, they would answer for it the next or not long afterward. There was nowhere to hide. A walk downtown in Belfast was always a reunion, for better or worse.

Whistling Competitions

One thing the Irish are famous for is whistling. Most people will whistle parts of tunes or no tune at all just to pass the day, but there were guys in Ireland who would whistle entire songs from start to finish. They even had whistling contests. My friend Bill Cunningham told me a great story of one such contest he went to in Belfast. The reigning champion was a guy named Ronnie Ronald. Why his parents named him Ronald when his last name was already Ronald is another story. Ronnie could whistle with amazing, fluttering tones. He was whistling away in this contest when a guy in the audience started to whistle back at him, cupping his hands over his mouth like he was playing the harmonica. Ronnie was starting to get annoyed that this guy was hitting higher notes so he kept going up to higher octaves. The man in the crowd would do the same, and Ronnie would go up still higher. This continued until both of them looked like they were about to bust a corpuscle. It was like *High Noon* with lips instead of guns.

The most powerful whistler I ever knew was Ted Wallace. He was a big, good-looking guy and sane enough, but he whistled incessantly to the point where people began to think he was a bit touched in the head. He could hit piercing notes that seemed to travel to infinity. We used to say, "Oh, there's Ted coming" because we always heard him a full minute before he arrived.

The Musical M's

Two or three times a year, the Park Picture House would have a midnight matinee, usually on a big event like St. Patrick's Day. That was a much-anticipated day because we got to stay up until midnight watching movies and, sometimes, a live variety show. We wouldn't get home until one or two o'clock in the morning. It was a complete departure from what the rest of the year was like.

One year, the show was held at a theater on the Shankill Road, the heartland of Protestant Belfast. There was a group in the variety show who called themselves "The Musical M's." They were three guys with a guitar, an accordion, and a banjo, and they weren't too good. Truth be told, they were bloody awful. I suppose they chose their name because they all had names beginning with M.

Belfast audiences at the time and probably still today were much like the audience of Harlem's Apollo Theatre. If someone didn't cut it, they would boo them right off the stage, but if they were good, they'd give them their undivided attention and a rousing round of applause at the end of the act. They really had to earn respect from a brutally honest audience. It was a great proving ground for talent, and hell for anyone who had delusions about their own abilities. Sinatra's famous *"New York, New York"* could just as easily have been "Belfast Belfast" because if someone could make it there, they really could make it anywhere. It was like bringing culture to the savages, much like the theatre groups which toured around the old American west entertaining the cowboys and outlaws.

The Musical M's were ambitious because, rather than just singing established hits like almost everyone else did, they insisted on writing their own songs. But despite this extra effort, they were as bad as bad gets. I don't remember the lyrics. I only remember the chorus, which they repeated over and over while dancing with canes and hats –

We're the musical M's!
We're the musical gems!

Everyone was yelling very insulting remarks like "Get the fock outta here!" and "Get off the stage! You stink!" - the usual comments any performer doesn't want to hear. Finally, the audience got so loud, the Musical M's couldn't sing loud enough to be heard. The M.C. came out about three times and said, "Come one now, guys. Give 'em a chance. These boys'r tryin' tuh antertain ya. Let's be nice now. Give 'em a chance, boys. Awright, away ya go, lads."

They'd come back out again tap dancing and tipping their hats.

"We're the musical M's! We're the musical gems . . .*"* and all the catcalling would start up all over again.

"Get off!"

"You're awful!"

"Piss off!"

The leader of the group was getting madder and madder by the minute. Finally, he took off his accordion, threw it on the stage, singled someone out in the audience and yelled, "There's the bastard down there that's starting it all!" He hopped off the stage and chinned a guy in the front row and started a melee with half the audience that lasted ten minutes.

After the fight, this old boy came in from the street. He was an old drunk in the neighborhood, and everybody knew him. The crowd got him up on the stage and started chanting, "We want Jimmy! We want Jimmy!" We want Jimmy!" So they got old Jimmy up on the stage, and he started singing. He was drunk as usual and sounded like someone twisting a dog's hind leg. He probably couldn't sing at all, drunk or not, but the crowd gave him wild applause anyway.

This was typical of a Belfast crowd - applauding the drunk who couldn't sing and booing the professional entertainers off the stage, or the people who fancied themselves as professionals. The M.C. came out and tried to get old Jimmy off the stage a couple of times but Jimmy was enjoying the limelight too much and wouldn't leave. He just kept repeating the few songs he knew. The M.C. kept trying to politely pull him off the stage until a hardcase from the audience finally got on the stage, grabbed the M.C. by the lapel, held up his fist and said, "He stays on or you get this."

The M.C. thought it over for a few seconds then announced, *"Er-uh . . . ladies and gentlemen . . . Jimmy!"* With that, he put the microphone down and walked off the stage, apparently abandoning the entire effort, maybe even retiring from show biz altogether. Old Jimmy then ran through his entire, three-song repertoire again several times while all the other acts waited in the wings. When Warhol said everyone is famous for fifteen minutes, he might have been referring to Jimmy, except for the fact that Jimmy got forty-five. When he finished, though he was the worst performer there, he received the only standing ovation of the night.

One year, a Shakespearean troupe came through Belfast and put on a production of *Romeo and Juliet*. The tickets were cheap so every hooligan in town showed up. The performers were up there in full regalia performing their hearts out. As usual, though, the crowd was ridiculing them and writing their own dialogue as if they were part of the show. At the end, when Romeo found Juliet's body and was in a quandary about what to do, someone yelled, "Buck 'er while she's still warm!" The actor was so appalled he could barely finish the play.

CHAPTER 18

MY MA THE CHANCER

"To get the fruit, sometimes you must go out on a limb."
~ Anonymous

Ma striking a pose.

My mother had spent some time in England as a child and could affect a passable London dialect. Thus, whenever she felt the need to impress someone, the Belfast accent would be ditched, and the English accent would kick in. One of the times she employed her English accent most successfully was when one of the most popular British entertainers of that time visited Belfast. His name was Donald Peers. He sang on a radio show called *Housewife's Choice* every morning on BBC. My mother fell madly in love with him. One of her favorite songs was "I Remember the Cornfields" -

I remember the cornfields
In the wind softly sighing
And the swing beneath the chestnut tree

I remember my school friend
Happy days swiftly flying
And my room still waiting for me

The old harvest moon
Shining over the city
Discovers me there
And regards me with pity
While sad of heart I roam

I remember my first love
And the last time she kissed me
By the golden cornfields of home.

The old harvest moon
Shining over the city
Discovers me there
And regards me with pity
While sad of heart I roam

I remember my first love
And the last time she kissed me
By the golden cornfields
Those lovely cornfields of home.
Sweet home.

Donald Peers signing autographs in England, 1953

My mother learned that Donald Peers was appearing in a variety show at the opera house in Belfast and that he would be staying at the Grand Central Hotel on Royal Avenue in the center of town. She immediately made up her mind to meet him in person. She went to the Grand Central Hotel posing as a writer with *Women's Own* magazine, a popular women's magazine of the day. She laid the London accent on with a trowel.

The hotel personnel notified Mr. Peers that there was someone in the lobby who wanted to interview him. Mr. Peers had them send her to his suite. She carried on this subterfuge for about twenty minutes until she finally broke down and confessed she was not what she claimed to be and was merely one of his local fans. Mr. Peers took it all in stride and was quite kind to my mother. He ordered tea and cakes, and they sat down and chatted for about half an hour. My mother came home floating three feet off the ground, absolutely enchanted by the encounter. She would drift off in reveries for weeks afterward. My father would nudge me and whisper, *"Look at her, would ya? She's off skippin' through the cornfields with Donald Peers again."*

Grand Central Hotel, Royal Avenue

CHAPTER 19

SEASONS

"Blessed is he who, in growing old, retains his child's heart. "
~ Chinese proverb

There was a season for everything when I was a kid, and one would usually overlap the other so there was always some way to entertain ourselves. Since most of our parents couldn't afford to buy us actual toys, we created toys out of scraps we found in the street.

Hoop and Cleak

A favorite homemade toy was the *hoop and cleak*, which was the rim of a discarded bicycle tire and a metal rod with the end curved to fit within the edge of the rim. Once the rod had been shaped to match the rim, the hoop could be guided in any direction, even in circles or around tight corners. There's a corny old joke about a boy who pushed his hoop the twelve miles from Belfast to Bangor. His hoop and cleak were stolen, and he was very upset that he had to walk all the way home.

Marlies

Marlie (marble) season was most popular in the summertime but extended all year long. We bought as many glass marbles as we could afford and played with them in the gutters, stopping occasionally to dodge cars or horse-drawn carts. With a marlie wedged firmly between the thumb and forefinger, one eye closed, chin as close to the ground as possible for better accuracy, and the all-important tip of the tongue resting at the corner of the upper lip, the goal was to hit the marlies owned by one's opponent and take ownership of them. We played so much that our thumbs turned black with bruises. Sometimes, the thumb nail even fell off from the damage that was caused to it. An exalted few of us became highly skillful and could not only hit a marlie from any conceivable angle but could even hit it with a ricochet off the curb or another marlie, or both, using complex geometric calculations, like billiards.

A recurrent problem was losing marlies which rolled down the gutter and into a drain (which we called a gratin.) To retrieve the marlie, we had to remove the gratin lid, which extended into the ground several inches and seemed to weigh about a hundred pounds. It had to be lifted up by the grates in the lid. A couple of us would grab the grate and lift it up out of the ground, roll up our sleeves, put our arms into the sewer water and retrieve the marlies that had fallen in. This job was not for the squeamish, as none of us were quite sure what kinds of creatures the foul, soupy mess might be home to. The urban legend of alligators in the sewer system was alive and well even then and everyone knew someone who knew someone who had lost a finger or an entire arm searching for a lost marlie.

Cheesers

In autumn, chestnuts formed in the trees and fell to the ground, signifying the beginning of the "cheeser" season. We would all collect the largest and hardest cheesers we could find. Cheesers were amazingly dense in their natural state, but we would bake them on a fire until they became even harder. We would then drill a hole through the middle and run a string through it. The string was knotted at one end so the cheeser could hang from it without falling off. The game was to try and crack each other's cheesers by swinging them and slamming them together. The quality of one's cheeser was measured by the number of other cheesers it could crack. This game resulted in numerous injuries, mainly to the knuckles and elbows, but sometimes to the face as cheesers careened wildly off each other or shattered, spraying sharp cheeser shrapnel into the air. It's a wonder one of us didn't put out an eye.

Peeries

Eventually, the "peerie" season would roll around. (Pun intended.) Peeries were spinning tops. Everyone had a peerie and the streets were filled with kids gleefully whipping them faster and faster until some over-enthusiastic boy whipped his peerie right through someone's window, causing us all to momentarily freeze in horror, then scatter to the bellows of the irate owner. Our peeries were nothing less then Roman gladiators, and the circle we kids made while watching two champion peerie's battle it out, a miniature Coliseum.

Guiders

Guider season also came along every autumn. They were makeshift go-carts made of wooden boxes with metal, ball-bearing wheels. We zipped down the hills at breakneck speeds and zigzagged in and out from under the vendors' carts, startling the horses, angering the drivers, and frightening our mothers half to death. Most of the guiders were flimsy contraptions which had to be repaired after almost every run. With infinite patience, we carefully replaced the nails that acted as cotter pins in the axles and held the wheels in place. Now and then, some lucky soul found an old, discarded pram (baby carriage) and removed the larger, rubber wheels, then sailed cheerfully past us in our more meager vehicles of the ball bearing variety, drawing our resentful and envious glares.

I guess it's just built into human beings to compare our possessions. I'm sure there is someone living in the most squalid conditions right now envying a neighbor whose mud hut is constructed of a higher quality mud than his own.

Sledding

In the wintertime, the sledding season began. If it snowed or became icy, boys with homemade sleds came out en masse and raced each other down every hillside or street with even the slightest grade. The sleds were made of anything flat - trash can lids, pieces of cardboard, wood planks - whatever we could find. More enterprising kids built their sleds with metal runners which glided along at great speeds. With the total obliviousness to danger known only to childhood, we flew down the street with reckless abandon. There were occasional crashes and mouthfuls of ice after being catapulted face-first into a snow bank, but what I remember best is the glorious rush of speed, the cold, fresh air in my face, and the laughter and cheers of my friends hurdling along beside me.

One year during the war, the government had blocked a road with a concrete stanchion to slow down or stop German tanks in the event of an invasion by land. One of the lads laying face down on a sled ran head first into the concrete barrier and killed himself. We were all horrified and very few sleds were seen for weeks afterward, as if every child in town was in mourning. But death was still an abstraction to us. We still wanted to play in the snow, but our mothers had confiscated our sleds in greater fear themselves. After enough moping around and looking out the window during new snowfalls, our mothers finally relented and gave us back our sleds, but my mates and I were more careful and less joyous. The next year the loss in our ranks was forgotten, and sledding was pure joy again.

Soccer

Soccer, or football as it's called outside of America, was played year round, but most of the league games were in the winter months. In the summer, we played the odd game of cricket, but this was considered to be a "sissy game" by many of the boys. Rugby on the other hand was for the advantaged classes and out of our reach. In fact, an adequate soccer ball was usually out of our reach as well so we made due with a ball of any kind or just a rolled up bundle of cloth, as long as there was something to kick.

To a healthy child, boredom is impossible. Every day for me was filled with new challenges to overcome, cheesers to break, peeries to capture, and races to win. It took growing up for me to discover what boredom was. I suppose this is one of the reasons poets often reflect fondly on their early years. It is a balancing act we all must perfect if we are to be happy – to observe our adult responsibilities while holding on to the wonder and natural joy of childhood. As Jesus Christ said, to enter the kingdom of heaven, we must become like little children again. I think that's true of earth as well.

CHAPTER 20

THE DREADED "HOME"

"Parents need to fill a child's bucket of self-esteem so high that the rest of the world can't poke enough holes to drain it dry."
~ Alvin Price

When the McCallister's house was destroyed by a German bomb, several carpenters and others were engaged for months in rebuilding it. One of them was a big, strapping fellow named Joe Cairns. The workmen needed hot water for their tea breaks and Joe would come to our house with his tea can. My mother would boil the water for him on the stove. It seemed to me he was making more trips than necessary and was taking a hell of a lot of tea breaks. He looked a bit like the actor James Mason and I sensed my mother fancied him. He took a liking to me and brought me books on my birthday and on Christmas. During these times, my father would be off at work, sometimes for a day or two at a time, working double and triple shifts in an effort to make more money for my mother to waste. I wasn't so naïve as to miss that there was something going on between Joe and my mother and thought it rather scandalous at the time. In retrospect, however, I can't blame her. The poor woman had no romance at all in her life.

I remember coming home from school quite often, expecting to see my mother and get some afternoon lunch, and she would be gone God knows where. One rainy day, I stood outside in the rain letting myself get drenched to the skin in an attempt to make her feel guilty when she came home. When she arrived, rather than bursting into tears for neglecting me, she gave me a crack in the ear and dragged me into the house by my collar screaming, "Even a bloody cat has enough sense to get out of the rain!" It may have been displaced anger with herself for not being home when I needed her.

One of her favorite tactics when she got upset with me was threatening to put me "in a home." I never knew exactly what she meant by that. All she told me was that it was where all bad children were sent, and that it was bloody awful. The more she threatened me with banishment to the dreaded "home", the more fearful I became of the idea. And the more fearful I became of this threat, the more she employed it. Any infraction on my part was met with, "I'm gonna put ya in a home!" I would cry and wail, "No, ma! Don't put me in a home!" and she would repeat it over and over again, sometimes even taking me by the arm and walking me toward the door, only relenting when I was sufficiently terrified.

Her second favorite method of psychological torment was to use the classic line, "You just wait 'til yar father gets home. He'll know how to take care of you!" This veiled threat was always delivered in an ominous and foreboding tone, and would leave me trembling with fear of being beaten to a pulp by my father after arriving home from work exhausted only to have to listen to a complaint. However, my mother rarely reported me to my father except under the most extreme circumstances. His reactions were unpredictable when she did tell him, leaving me in doubt as to what to expect. He would sometimes punish me for a minor infraction but let me off the hook for something major.

For instance, one morning I was polishing a pair of shoes with Cherry Blossom boot polish. I was so determined to impress him, I polished the soles of the shoes as well. He saw what I was doing and gave me a smack, yelling, "What are you wasting the good boot polish for?"

"I – I thought I was supposed to!" I stammered.

"Ach, ya don't polish the soles, ya stupid bugger!"

I ran to my room and cried. When I was cried out, I sat in the window and watched my neighbors walking by. I saw a father kicking a ball in the street with a boy younger than me, something my father had never done with me, and I wondered what was wrong with me and what I had done to make him the way he was.

A few days later, I was attempting to light some sticks in the fireplace. The sticks were damp and wouldn't light so I decided to help it along with lighter fluid. The can ignited in my hand and fell to the floor. Fluid squirted all over the floor and before I knew it, a fire erupted. In a panic, I threw a rug on top of it, but the living room carpet and the floorboards beneath were charred before I could extinguish it. Since I had been smacked a few days earlier for using too much shoe polish, I was sure my father would just kill me outright for setting the house on fire. When he came home from work and saw the charred floor, I spluttered out an explanation, closed my eyes tight, and waited for the worst. To my surprise, there was no customary clout in the ear hole. I opened my eyes again and looked at him. Seeing my distress, he merely said, "Ach, it wasn't your fault. Don't worry about it." He tousled my hair and walked away. Gradually, I realized that my fate was determined not by anything I said or did but by the whims of his mood.

CHAPTER 21

SCHOOL DAYS

"A teacher affects eternity; he can never tell where his influence stops."
~ Henry Adams

My first day at school was in the fall of 1939. War was just around the corner and Great Britain was preparing for its role in the conflict. My mother strapped my leather schoolbag on my back, took my hand and led me down the Ballysillan Road past Carr's Glen, down a steep brae, over a trout stream, past Maggie Moore's Confectioners, and on to the small schoolhouse at the Cave Hill Road crossing. This school was to be temporary pending completion of Carr's Glen Public Elementary School which was under construction at the top of Oldpark Road.

The school had a fence made of tubular steel running along its front. We found out early that we could talk to each other from opposite ends of the fence through the hollow metal. This was our first exposure to a telephone.

One day, there were about twenty of us all seated on the fence when an army lorry loaded with soldiers passed by. We cheered them on because, young as we were, we somehow knew what lay ahead for them. The schoolmaster became extremely angry and berated us. He then led us inside and caned us one at a time. None of us had any idea what was wrong with cheering the soldiers.

That night at the dinner table with my parents, my father grabbed my hand and turned it to look at my palm, which was red and swollen from the cane. He asked me what happened. I told him the schoolmaster had caned me and the other boys. When he found out why, he almost hit the ceiling and said he was going to go to the school in the morning to "knock his pan in." My mother prevailed upon his good sense, and he eventually calmed down. Convinced that attacking the schoolteacher would be unwise, my father contented himself by mumbling, "He's probably a fenian."

As previously noted, the fenians, or Roman Catholics, did not appear to be as concerned as we were about the war between Britain and Germany. In fact, it was rumored that some of them were backing Germany because they hoped that if Germany won it would free Ireland from the English. My friends and I were too busy trying to survive childhood and enjoy it once in a while to have any thoughts about the war one way or the other. It was just some problem adults created for themselves because they got bored.

I remained at this small schoolhouse for a few months and then transferred to Carr's Glen Public Elementary School. It was a beautiful, new brick building with large windows and airy classrooms for grades one through eight.

Miss Semple

My first grade teacher was Miss Semple, an elderly spinster with a kind face and an even kinder heart. I was a very shy and retiring child. I felt that I was incredibly stupid and couldn't be taught anything. As a result, I tried to be inconspicuous in class and sat as close to the back of the room as I could. I would have sat behind the building if I could have. There were several students in the class I looked up to and whom I felt were my superiors because they seemed so confident.

One of these students was Tudor Edwards. He was one of the leading lights in the class that year, well thought of by the teacher, good looking, and always the first one to answer the teacher's questions. He sat in the front row. I even admired Tudor's name. It seemed so dignified compared to my own, Sidney Rickerby. For some reason, my parents called me by my middle name instead of my first name, John, and it was singularly inglorious to me. A Sidney is an easy target in a sea of Tommy's, Willy's, Jimmy's, and other ordinary names.

I developed a crush on a pretty, blue-eyed, blonde girl named Joan Barkley. I had made my feelings known to some of my friends but did not know at the time that Tudor Edwards also fancied Joan. I was seated in the classroom when he approached me with two of his friends.

"I hear you fancy Joan Barkley", he said.

I looked up at him. "Well, yes, I - I do," I stuttered.

"Well, I want you to know she's my girlfriend, and you can stay away from her, or else."

I didn't know what to say. I decided to avoid Joan Barkley for the rest of the year, though she would occasionally smile coyly at me having probably heard I was smitten by her. I never overcame my fear of Tudor enough to talk to her, though, so he never had reason to make good on his threat.

Throughout the school year, Tudor and his friends sat in the front row of the classroom raising their hands eagerly when questions were asked, while I sat at the back trying to stay out of sight. One day, Miss Semple asked the class how prehistoric cavemen combed their hair. The answer was obvious to me so I gathered up my courage and raised my hand, along with the elite few, for the first time. Fortunately, Miss Semple didn't pick me because my answer was going to be "a comb made of rock." Once I heard the actual answer - that cavemen combed their hair with their hands, I consider my idea to be so idiotic, I thanked God that I wasn't chosen to answer the question. I would have been laughed out of the room. The better question is why Miss Semple thought this piece of information would be useful to a small boy in 1940's Belfast. In any case, that event was enough to do me in with volunteering for anything. I kept a low profile for the rest of the year until the following June when the class broke up for summer recess.

On our last day of school, Miss Semple announced that she was retiring, and that it was her last day as well. We all liked her and were saddened by this news. She thanked all of us for our attendance and interest that year then dismissed the class. The class gave her a rousing send-off. As we were walking toward the door, she stopped me and said, "I want to talk to you, Sidney. Please stay behind."

I was completely bewildered. I had not spoken directly to Miss Semple for the entire school year. I didn't even think she knew I existed and wondered what on earth she wanted to talk to me about. After all the other children had left, to my complete and utter astonishment, she said, "Sidney, you are my favorite pupil. I always knew you didn't want me to call on you for answers, so I didn't. I felt you were a wee bit shy so I left you alone, but I will remember you before all of the others. There is something very good and special in you. I wanted you to know that."

I was dumbfounded. I wasn't accustomed to receiving such praise.

She then said, "I would like to give you this small gift as a token of our friendship this year."

She handed me a book with color illustrations of the Lake District in Northern England. She signed it, "To my favorite student, Sidney Rickerby" with her name and the date beneath.

She said, "I know you enjoy reading, Sidney, and I thought this would be a nice gift." She smiled gently, and I mumbled my thanks, still somewhat stupefied by all the attention, and left the classroom. I never saw Miss Semple again.

The knowledge that she had singled me out of a classroom of people for this special treatment touched me so greatly I have never forgotten it. Maybe she knew that I needed a confidence booster. It worked, too. There were many times later on when I was feeling doubt in my abilities but felt a little better when I reminded myself that I was Miss Semple's "favorite." I treasured the book she gave me for many years and on my bookshelf, among the classics of literature I was able to acquire, Miss Semple's book held an honored place. I would probably still own it today, but my mother hocked my entire book collection at a used bookstore in Smithfield in Central Belfast when she ran short of money. I was in my twenties and living in England at the time. I was enraged and confronted her about it, but she denied it and refused to discuss it.

Mr. Hamill

For the remainder of my years up to age fourteen at Carr's Glen Public Elementary School, I encountered several more teachers and only one made an impression on me as strongly as Miss Semple had. His name was Mr. Hamill, my sixth grade teacher. By that time I had become more assertive and sure of myself. Mr. Hamill was a kind-hearted man and infinitely patient. I know this to be true because I tested the outer reaches of that patience on many occasions.

I was in class one day during cheeser season. I had my cheeser on a string. It was chipped a little from numerous battles but still unbroken. It was the hardest cheeser I had ever owned. I had competed with it for weeks, climbing up the ranks of cheeserdom to elite status. My friend, Teddy Weatherhead, was sitting next to me. Teddy was attacking me with his ruler every time Mr. Hamill turned his back to the class, and I was keeping him at bay by swinging my cheeser at him. Mr. Hamill was studiously engaged in drawing a bridge on the blackboard, his back to the class. Suddenly, my knot came undone and my cheeser flew off the string, shot across the classroom like a bullet, and hit the blackboard with a deafening crack right beside Mr. Hamill's head. He jumped about three feet in the air then whipped around and yelled, "Who did that?" Nobody answered, of course, so he proceeded to walk up and down the aisles, pointing and yelling at each child individually, "Was it you? Was it you? Was it you?" He finally came to me and could tell by my flushed cheeks and nervous expression that I was the culprit.

"So it was you, Rickerby," he said.

I closed my eyes hard and prepared for the worst but all he said was, "I thought the bridge I was drawing had collapsed!" Then he laughed and went back to the head of the class. I almost fainted with relief.

I always had a soft spot for Mr. Hamill after that, especially since corporal punishment was allowed and often encouraged in those days, and he could have laid a stick across my palms or rear end.

Another time, Mr. Hamill took us out to the schoolyard to play a little soccer. Other teachers wouldn't bother to let us out but would punish us when we got out of line in class. But he seemed to understand that boys need to let off some steam once in a while or they get restless and disobedient. He couldn't play soccer himself so he brought out a little tennis ball for all thirty or so of us to kick around. This minor technicality didn't bother us. We usually didn't have a soccer ball anyway so anything round would do. When the ball bounced in Mr. Hamill's direction, rather than dribble it or try to get fancy, he would just take a wild, completely unscientific kick at it as hard as he could in any direction.

On one such occasion, the ball landed between him and me. Trying to impress him, I decided I would do the same thing. I ran at the ball full speed and kicked it as hard as I could. The ball shot up and hit him directly between the eyes, shattering his glasses. I was mortified once again. This made a grand total of three times that I had almost caused him a severe head injury. I thought he was going to lose his patience this time for sure, but sweet, old Mr. Hamill just picked up the shards of his broken glasses and said, "It was just an accident, Sidney. It wasn't your fault."

We had an unusually heavy snowfall that year. We were all out on the playground one morning throwing big, slushy snowballs at each other when I saw Mr. Hamill walking by on his way into the school. I picked up a ball of slush, compressed it in my mittened hands, and threw it at him. He was a good thirty or forty yards away so I really just expected it to land at his feet or somewhere nearby but I scored a direct hit right in the back of the head. I recoiled in horror, quickly turned my back to him, and pretended to be innocently playing with the other kids. Luckily, the playground was full of people so he didn't know who had thrown it.

I couldn't believe my bad luck. He was my favorite teacher and I couldn't seem to stop accidentally assaulting his person. Another unfortunate coincidence was that all of these events took place within the space of about a month. I wondered if the incidents with the cheeser and the tennis ball made him realize that I was responsible for the snowball attack, too. I suspected that he knew somehow. While recuperating in the teacher's lounge, he probably told his colleagues, "Sidney seems like such a nice wee lad but I swear to God he's trying to kill me."

Mr. Hamill's repeated forgiveness of me for my mistakes only served to make me even more fond of him, and we got along wonderfully for the rest of the year. To avoid causing him serious bodily injury, I got into the habit of standing still and avoiding any rambunctious activity when he was nearby.

Miss Meyers

Miss Meyers was a looker with impossibly long legs and platinum blonde hair always arranged perfectly. I passed into her class for a year and, like most of the other boys, developed a massive crush on her. She had a disquieting way of tickling the back of our necks while leaning over us to discuss problems. I would get dizzy from the scent of her perfume. It was completely unnerving for us, being on the brink of puberty as we were. She had to have known the effect she was having on us but persisted nevertheless. For most of that year, I had erotic dreams about Miss Meyers, although my complete lack of knowledge in the field of sexuality was such that these dreams would be considered quite tame by today's standards. They would always start and end with kissing because I had no idea what was supposed to happen next.

After one of the first dreams starring Miss Meyers, I woke in a cold sweat to find my sister Olga staring directly at me. She had apparently been fascinated by whatever noises I was making, which must have been very unusual to hear coming from me. I felt as if she had witnessed the whole sordid event somehow. I rolled over and pretended I was still sleeping. She yelled, "Ma, Sidney's sick!" My ma came up to check on me. I was too embarrassed to show my face and kept pretending to be asleep. I was sick alright. Sick with primal desire.

Da Bunting

Da Bunting was the custodian of the school, a somewhat disgruntled man, and very obviously unhappy in his job. The best perk his job had was a house on the school premises. During my last year, I would sometimes help Da

Bunting stoke the school boilers or deliver the free milk the government gave us kids each day. He was usually somber and silent during these outings except for the occasional grunted command.

One winter, he and I were delivering milk to the classrooms when we found a cat perched on a second floor window ledge overlooking a steep hallway. The cat must have strayed into the building the night before. Da Bunting became enraged, picked up a long pole, and shoved the cat right out the window, causing it to fall two stories to the ground. Miraculously, it didn't seem to be hurt and scampered off after landing on its four paws. I was outraged at his cruelty and yelled, "That was a terrible thing to do, ya miserable ol' bastard! Ya can deliver your own bloody milk!" I left him standing there with his mouth open. I was usually very mild-mannered so he was too shocked to respond.

A few weeks later, a group of us were playing in the gymnasium, which had a hardwood floor. We were not supposed to be in the gym at that particular time. Da Bunting came in and chased us out, but he singled me out for special attention to exact revenge for yelling at him before about the cat. As I ran for the door, he swung his boot at my backside. Attempting to avoid the kick, I slipped on the hardwood and landed hard on my tailbone. The pain was intense and lasted for weeks. I should have reported the old bastard for child cruelty but in those days such events were not taken very seriously. For fifteen years afterward, I had recurring swelling of the coccyx, which I am sure was a result of that fall. I contented myself with the knowledge that Da Bunting must have been a miserable man to display such cruelty toward stray cats and small boys, especially since he was in a position of trust. He's dead and gone by now, and perhaps receiving similar treatment himself in the netherworld.

Geordie Powers

Geordie Powers was a teacher who had formerly been a physical education instructor and was quite athletic. One day, he came back to the classroom after a short departure and found Teddy Weatherhead and Ronny Stevenson fighting with each other. He separated them, said "Hang on a minute" and left the room. He came back a few minutes later with two sets of boxing gloves and, in Father Flannigan-like fashion, told Teddy and Ronny to put them on.

"Okay," he said, "Now you two can go at it."

Teddy and Ronny blattered away at each other for about fifteen minutes until both were totally exhausted and had to stop, but the gloves were like big pillows so neither of them was hurt. They both sat on the ground panting.

Mr. Powers said, "Now you can go back and sit in your seats." With all the anger out of their systems and thoroughly exhausted, they returned to their studies. It was a quick and effective way of ending a dispute, which probably would have continued outside the classroom following school if they had any strength left.

Sammy Smiley

One of my schoolmates at Carrs Glen Public Elementary School was Sammy Smiley. Sammy didn't come from our neighborhood but lived in the adjoining Ardoyne. Even back then, the Ardoyne was considered to be a tough neighborhood and would later become almost exclusively Roman Catholic and a breeding ground for IRA gunmen. Sammy, however, was a Protestant. He was a great soccer player. He had the physical advantage of being somewhat pigeon-toed, a necessity for a good ball dribbler.

Sammy got picked for the Northern Ireland youth soccer team and traveled to England to play an English youth team. As Sammy told the story, he took the legs out from beneath the opposing English center-half, to which the Englishman said, "I say! Steady on there, paddy! You're in England now!" Sammy smiled and replied, "Fuck England and fuck you, too!" He told the story with great relish. We all enjoyed his account and the fact that the Irish team had won.

Our teacher was "Da Morgan" (we called everyone over 30 "Da") whom we all agreed was a vicious and unpredictable brute. If he caught us not paying attention to him while he was speaking, he was apt to fling a blackboard eraser at the offenders' head. This does not sound particularly cruel until one considers that erasers in those days were soft on one side but wood on the other. I had received a few nasty knocks on the noggin from this in the past. Complaining to parents was useless. In those days, teachers were on the same level as other professionals and were meant to be obeyed. Corporal punishment was commonly administered by a bamboo cane over outstretched, grubby palms, as I had learned already many times. Someone told me if I put a hair on my palm, it would cause the cane to split. Though obviously a silly wives' tale that would not hold up to scientific investigation, I tried it a number of times, but the hair was never any match for the cane and the relish with which the nastier teachers employed it.

One day, Sammy was summoned to the front of the class for some obscure offense. Apparently, he didn't move quickly enough because as he approached Da Morgan, with his hands in his trouser pockets as usual, he was treated to a ringing slap across the side of the head. Almost instantaneously, Sammy delivered a right hook to Morgan's chin that would have made Rocky Marciano proud. Morgan went down like a sack of potatoes, bringing the blackboard and easel crashing down with him. We all gasped with a mixture of horror and elation. No one had ever punched a teacher before, let alone Morgan. He sat on his haunches with an incredulous look on his face. He couldn't believe what had just happened any more than we could.

Scrambling to his feet with his eyes bulging, Morgan exclaimed, "Well, now you've really done it, you wee shite! It's the Principal for you, my lad! You'll be expelled for this!"

Sammy looked him up and down.

"Ach, away 'n fock yarself!" he retorted, turning on his heels and strolling proudly out of the classroom.

Sammy's reputation took an immediate upturn and gave us all something to talk about for the next few weeks. Eventually, he returned to class, and no comment was made by Morgan upon his return. We later learned there had been a meeting between Mr. Morgan, the school Principal, and Sammy's parents, and it was generally agreed to let the matter die without further action. For the remainder of the school year, Da Morgan seemed a lot quieter, and no more blackboard erasers were thrown.

Eighth grade was our last year at school. By that time, the school had educated us about as much as possible, and many of the boys were getting ready to go on to work or to secondary school. I decided that I'd had enough of school. At fourteen years of age, I advised my parents that I intended to start working. They raised no objection.

Most if not all of the teachers mentioned in this narrative are dead and gone. On each visit to Ireland, I pass by Carr's Glen Public Elementary School, which is now somewhat faded and worn, and warm memories flood back of the days I spent there from seven to fourteen years of age. I wouldn't say the education it gave me was stellar, but the old place did provide me with the basics of reading, writing, and arithmetic, which gave me some preparation for the working world.

Dear, old Miss Semple has always had a place in my heart, and always will. I wonder if she ever realized that I would remember forever the kind words she spoke to me on that day in 1940, words made even more meaningful to me because I was not receiving any of the spiritual nourishment I needed at home. Perhaps in her great wisdom she sensed it. I don't know. The right words at the right moment in a child's life can work miracles. Starved as I was for praise, that little compliment went a long, long way. It took her only a minute for her to say it, but I remembered it forever.

CHAPTER 22

SAMMY

"When Jesus Christ asked little children to come to him, he didn't say only rich children, or white children, or children with two-parent families, or children who didn't have a mental or physical handicap. He said, "Let all children come unto me."
~ Marian Wright Edelman

One of the people I remember best from the old neighborhood and have had a lingering fondness for in my memory over the years was a kid called Sammy who lived at the other end of my street. Sammy was mildly challenged mentally and would hang around with us wee kids, though he was about fourteen years of age himself. At only eight years old, we were more mentally advanced than he was. But there was one thing about Sammy which made him immensely popular with the neighborhood kids aside from his gentle demeanor - he had a storehouse of pre-World War II comics. That is, prior to 1939 when comics began to be rationed for the war effort.

I loved reading comics. My favorites were *The Dandy, Film Fun, The Beano, The Champion, Radio Fun, The Wizard,* and *The Adventure.* Some were just comic strips, but some were stories serialized from week to week. Because paper was rationed along with everything else during the war, the stores would only order magazines and comics for customers who had placed an order with them. This meant that one had to make a commitment to a shilling or two each week to pick up three or four comics. My family couldn't afford that, but on Tuesday when the comics came into the store the delivery people would always leave a few extras on top of the ordered count. All of us kids knew when it was delivery day so at lunchtime several of us - myself, Teddy Weatherhead, Ronny Stephenson, and a few others - would dash round to the news agent's store. The store was called The Endeavor and was next to the school. When we got there, we would try to grab up the comics, which were left on the shelves for anyone who wanted to buy them.

The competition was so fierce to arrive first and have first pick of the best comics that we tripped each other up as we ran at great risk of bodily injury. The preferred technique was to click the heels of the person in front with the tip of the toes causing one of his feet to get caught behind the other. It was kind of a mean version of leap frog. In our mad dash for the comic shop, we would take turns sprockling on our mouths and noses on the pavement. Then the tripper would go running past, perhaps stepping on the trippee in the process, as the former leader writhed on the ground whining about his injuries. He would get back up as quickly as he could and try to return the favor.

The serials kept us all on pins and needles from week to week, wondering what was going to happen next to our favorite characters. There was a serial story about a guy called Wilson, a real loner who lived in some moor in the south of England and dressed all in black. He just ran all day and ate natural food at nighttime. He didn't like being around people so he turned himself into a championship runner, which contradicted his loner lifestyle because one would assume he was preparing to actually compete with other people at some point. One day he was out running in the wild, desolate moors when, way off in the distance, he saw a young couple, just two tiny specks. "This place is getting too crowded," he said to himself, and immediately moved somewhere else.

Among the comic strip characters, there was Desperate Dan, a big cowboy type with a gigantic chin covered with stubble. He was always getting into all kinds of crazy predicaments. He was the world's strongest man, able to lift a cow with one hand. His beard was so tough he had to shave with a blowtorch.

Desperate Dan

Then there was Keyhole Kate, a tall skinny girl a bit like Popeye's Olive Oyl with glasses and a long, pointy nose, so named because she was always looking through keyholes and spying on people.

Keyhole Kate

Another favorite was Lord Snooty. He was a rich kid with a top hat who had a bunch of scruffy-looking friends. Korky the Cat was another character in *Dandy*. Originally a mute character, Korky was given a voice in 1940. Speaking or not, Korky's antics were always hilarious. We younger kids like *Dandy* and *Beano*. The older kids liked the *Wizard, Hotspur* and the *Champion*. The Dandy pulled no punches parodying our WWII enemies, either. Hitler was regularly lampooned and humiliated in a variety of ways.

Because of the brutal competition for comics every month, we all lusted after Sammy's collection and spent hours brainstorming about how we could get him to part with them. It was a seemingly impossible mission because Sammy never let them out of his sight. He treasured his comic book collection and would have fought to the death to protect it. One day, however, we hit upon a plan.

Even though Sammy was much larger than us, he joined us in our hockey and soccer games in the street. Sammy's mother always told him not to play too roughly with us because of his size. She yelled to Sammy from the window, "Now don't you be hurtin' those wee boys, Sammy, or it'll be too bad for you!"

Since none of us could afford hockey sticks, we used tree branches roughly cut into an L-shape instead. Knowing that Sammy was mortally afraid of what his mother would do to him if he hurt us, we pretended that he had injured us somehow and fell to the ground, screaming and yelling. Afraid that his mother might hear, Sammy stroked and shushed us, but we would just keep crying until he ran inside and got a comic book to shut us up. (Cruel, yes, but effective.) When he brought out the comic, we shut up immediately. He reluctantly handed over the comics but warned us to take good care of them. The comics were maintained by Sammy in mint condition, and he insisted that they be returned to him in the same condition after we had read them. When we brought them back, he carefully inspected them page by page for any sign of damage. If the comics were in less than perfect condition, he would chase the offending party, smacking him up the ears and neck until he got away. I had even gotten into the habit of lightly ironing the comics to avoid Sammy's wrath.

One day, distracted by a friend calling outside, I had carelessly left one of Sammy's comics on a chair in the kitchen. Forgetting about the comic, he and I ran off on some adventure. When I returned, I discovered to my immense horror that my mother had been sitting on it for quite some time. I found the forlorn-looking thing sitting on the chair (the comic, not my ma) wet with perspiration and collapsed in the middle with wrinkles extending outward toward all four edges. I shuddered at the thought of what Sammy would do to me when I handed it to him in that condition. Panicked, I got the iron out and attempted to give it the usual treatment. Usually, comics which were slightly crinkled from normal use needed only one light going-over with the iron, but this one was in such terrible shape, I had to keep going over it again and again while dabbing it with a moist towel. I was relieved when it finally looked straight. However, when I went to pick up the comic from the ironing board, it was as stiff and dry as a roof shingle. I had ironed all the moisture out of it. I attempted to open it, but the pages just crumbled in my hand like dry leaves.

I was a nervous wreck returning it to Sammy in this condition and attempted to avoid guilt by inserting the comic into a stack of others he had loaned me. He took them and went inside to put them back while I joined the other boys playing in front of his house. As I played, I kept an eye on the house, knowing that Sammy was in there scrutinizing his comics one by one for any sign of abuse. As expected, a few moments later, I heard a guttural moan come from the house and knew Sammy had discovered the petrified comic. He came barreling out of the house yelling, "What have ya done to muh comic, ya wee shite?"

I took flight and yelled, "I'm sorry, Sammy! It wasn't my fault! My ma . . ." trying to explain as I ran. But it was no use. Sammy was on the warpath. He chased me around the street for ten minutes, smacking me around the head and ears as I ducked and dodged, futilely screaming my excuses into the uncaring wind. This provided great amusement for my friends. I finally decided to run home and return at some later time when Sammy's rage had dissipated. Maybe it was because of his ailment but Sammy never held a grudge for too long. In fact, he and I became quite good friends despite my torture and execution of one of his comic books.

One day when Sammy was about sixteen and I was ten, we decided to take a bike trip to Bangor, which is about twelve miles down the coast. It was quite a feat talking his mother into letting him go away for the day. She made me promise I would watch out for him. To anyone looking on, this would have sounded like a strange request, considering Sammy was older and a good foot taller than I. After winning her trust, I got my da's old bike out for the journey, Sammy got his bike, which was much nicer than mine, and the two of us took off along the Bangor Road with the wind in our faces. The trip to Bangor was quite an adventure for two kids. We had to go through the city then beyond it to the south, down the coast past Millisle and Helen's Bay before we arrived at, glory of glories, Bangor.

We rode our bikes right down to the sand. I saw the sand approaching so, naturally, I slowed down and got off my bike. I was expecting Sammy to do the same but he just sailed right past me at about thirty miles per hour, apparently trying to ride right to the ocean's edge. When the tires made contact with the sand, the bike came to a complete halt and Sammy flew over the handle bars landing flat on his back in the sand about ten feet ahead. Once the crowd knew he was unhurt, everyone had a good laugh, including Sammy.

Bangor, 1940

The smell of salt water was always the first thing I noticed when I went to Bangor because it was such a refreshing change from the coal-laced air of Belfast. The promenade was always packed with people walking back and forth. Ice cream cones and soft drinks were sold from dozens of shop windows. The soft drink manufacturer then was Cantrell and Cochrane, and they made delicious lemonade. The bottle fizzed over after I pulled the cork (No twist-off's in those days!) and I held the cold bottle to my head for relief from the sun. And, oh, the taste! On a warm summer day, it was nectar of the gods.

After our lemonades, Sammy and I headed for Pickie Pool where all the bathing belles gathered. After we had given them all a good ogling, we walked over to the amusement park, which had swings, musical chairs, and all kinds of rides. The chairs flew around at the end of a chain. It was a lot of fun if one hadn't eaten too much beforehand, but every now and then, a kid would lose his lunch halfway through the ride. Vomit would spray outward in a giant circle, sprinkling any pedestrians who were unlucky enough to be walking below. I never saw Sammy happier than that day. I guess it was a relief to get away from his parents and feel like a normal kid for a change.

Sammy got steadily worse as time went by. About a year later, his parents must have decided that they needed some help, and they sent for the sanitarium wagon to come and pick him up. The wagon pulled up to take Sammy away. Three burly men dragged him out of the house. He fought like the devil, total confusion and panic on his face. The men were wearing white but they didn't have a net like they did in the comics. There was nothing funny about this, either. My heart was breaking for Sammy. I wanted to run and pull him away, get on our bikes, and ride back down to Bangor where he would be safe and happy again. Sammy was strong, but they overpowered him, forced him into the wagon, and slammed the door. Sammy looked at me through the back window, tears streaming down his face. I waved goodbye, but he didn't wave back. He looked toward the house, yelling for his mother, who was crying into his father's chest.

I don't know where they took Sammy, but we didn't see him again for about two years. When he came back, he was very quiet. The other kids and I wondered what had happened to him, but he was too unapproachable to ask. There were rumors about shock treatment and drugs. Whatever they did, it didn't improve him. Sammy had become very morose, a word no one would have used to describe him before. He wouldn't talk or play with any of us anymore. We'd see Sammy sitting in the front window of his house and yell over, "Hi, Sammy!" as we walked past, but he would just glance over, sullen and silent, and look away again. We all felt sorry for him but we were scared of him now, thinking he'd finally gone completely mad and might suddenly turn violent on us. Sammy just moped around the neighborhood, eyes on the ground, and would only mumble if we said hello to him. He didn't even seem to remember us.

I always wondered what went on at that hospital to reduce him to such a state, whether something sinister had happened or if Sammy was just devastated by the fact that his parents had sent him away. I suppose no matter how mentally challenged someone is, they know who loves them and who doesn't, and that makes all the difference. Either way, I was glad that Sammy was back home.

About fifteen years later, I came back to Ireland after living in Canada and the States. I was thirty-five years old or so and I hadn't seen Sammy in all that time. In fact, for five years before I left Belfast, he had disappeared from view entirely so it was more like twenty years since I'd last seen him. I was walking down the street one day, and his mother was out at the front door talking to one of the neighbors.

"Hi, Misses Todd!" I said.

"Sidney! Are you back from the states?" she said.

"Yeah, I'm over for a trip. How's Sammy doin'?"

She yelled toward the house, "Sammy, come on out and talk to one of your friends!"

Sammy came out of the house and stood next to his mother, looking at his feet.

His mother said, "Do you know who that is?"

Sammy raised his eyes, looked at me for a second and said, "That's Sidney Rickerby."

I was amazed. Deep down, his mind was still working. He was completely incapable of taking care of himself, but he still remembered me after twenty years. My heart swelled with fondness for him, remembering the boy who loaned me his prize comics and took a ride to Bangor with me one sunny day twenty-five summers earlier.

Sammy had a brother, Harry, who was also a friend of mine, and a sister, Agnes. Harry and Agnes had both married and moved away. Finally, Misses Todd died and Sammy's father then had to take care of him all on his own. They sold their house and moved up the Ballysillan Road.

About ten years ago, I went home again and stopped in to visit Mister Todd, who was then in his nineties. He was still taking care of Sammy. Here was this poor, old man, almost a hundred years old, taking care of a son in his seventies and still loving him. I asked him how he did it. While some might have taken this opportunity to deliver a speech on how selfless and noble they were, Mr. Todd only said, "Well, I can't leave 'im alone, can I? He'd set the house on fire." And that was that. He brought Sammy into the world, and it was his job to take care of him, no matter what.

Many Americans think the people of Belfast are all half nuts because of the political violence there over the years, but many of them are absolute saints. There's a warmth and kindliness and devotedness that isn't mentioned on the telly. These people are much more common than the other kind; people like Mr. and Mrs. Todd, who accepted their lot and did what the Lord and the dictates of their own hearts commanded them to, without self-celebration and without complaint.

CHAPTER 23

THE ORCHARD WHERE I MET GOD

There was a place in childhood
That I remember well,
And there a voice of sweetest tone
Bright fairy tales did tell.
~ Samuel Lover

There was an orchard at the top of our street that my friends and I explored every inch of. It was actually an old, abandoned estate overgrown with apple, lemon, and lime trees, gooseberry and raspberry bushes and a variety of others. The orchard was in the middle of our neighborhood, and a decrepit old mansion stood at the center in a state of ruin. It was a Garden of Eden during the day and spooky as hell at night. We all believed the old mansion was haunted. We would often meet in the orchard at night and if we looked at the old house long enough, its old face illuminated by the moon, we always saw or imagined seeing figures gliding back and forth in the dark rooms behind the dirty windows and tattered curtains. It was rumored that these ghosts were two old ladies who had occupied the house for many years.

The grounds were overrun with rabbits, rats, cats, field mice, and every other kind of critter indigenous to the area. Sitting in the dark with friends, we were surrounded by the calls, cries and footfalls of these creatures, sounds which were assumed to be of supernatural origin. We gathered regularly under a giant oak tree to roast potatoes over crude fires, catch up on the latest gossip about our schoolmates, and tell stories of banshees and leprechauns allegedly spotted by some of us in the orchard. At night, the orchard was made even more ominous by its distance from the streetlights on the adjoining Ballysillan Road, the main road leading to the bus station. I often used the orchard as a shortcut during the day and did so intentionally when I was hungry so I could pick up a fallen apple or a handful of raspberries.

Because the main pathway through the orchard started at my street and ended at the Ballysillan Road, the orchard became a short cut for the entire neighborhood to the bus stop, even for adults. Strictly speaking, the orchard was private property and the police would come around and chase us out occasionally, but it was a playground to us kids night and day.

We got our potatoes from a store called The Hillcrest on the Ballysillan Road across the street from the orchard. This store sat at the top of a steep driveway so as the storekeeper weighed potatoes on the scales for the customers, one or two sometimes fell out and rolled down the pathway to the curb. We would then casually walk by, stop next to the fallen potato, lean over and pretend to tie our shoe, then furtively pick up the potato and dart off into the orchard. If there were no spuds lying on the ground, we snuck into the store and pinched a few. Because we cooked them over an open flame, they were often a bit overdone on the outside or burned and hard on the inside but with a little bit of salt, they were delicious, and even better since we had baked them ourselves. Stealing spuds and cooking them unassisted made us all feel quite self-sufficient, like Robin Hood stealing food and delivering it to the poor, with the small exception that we were the poor. We all imagined the orchard to be Nottingham Forest.

There was a big yew tree in the orchard. Yew trees were used in medieval times to fashion bows because the branches are very flexible and since they have a natural bend to them, can be bent into a complete circle. We climbed that big yew tree all the time because it had low branches which were easy for us to reach. One night around eight o'clock, we were sitting around the fire cooking our spuds when a big cop suddenly appeared and yelled, "Hey! What are you kids up to?"

We panicked and ran like hell in different directions. Everyone else made a clean getaway but I made the brilliant decision to run up the yew tree, ample evidence that I was not cut out for a life of crime. The cop, who was badly overweight, stood on the ground and ordered me to come down. I refused. He tried to climb the tree but couldn't because of his deplorable physical condition. After a few minutes of pathetic attempts to get onto the first branch, he just sat down exhausted and said, "Well, my boy, I'm gonna stay right here 'til ya come down. I've got all the time in the world."

He was a man of his word, too, because he kept me up in that tree for about three hours. I couldn't understand how anybody could be so dedicated to arresting a ten-year old boy. Eventually, he went off into the bushes for a pee. Since we used to pretend to be Tarzan and swing from the upper branches of the tree, I was well practiced at it and seized upon this opportunity to escape. I grabbed a branch of the yew tree, swung down like Tarzan, landed on the ground, and ran out of the orchard and down the street before the cop could even zip up his pants.

I won that time, but that same cop caught me eventually. A few weeks later, we were sitting in the orchard again, gathered around our little fire as usual when somebody shouted, "Here come the peelers!"

We all split up in different directions, as usual, and I dove for a hole in a hedge surrounding the orchard. But as I came out the other side, I ran face first into a pair of black boots. I looked up and saw the same fat cop staring down at me with a look of pure satisfaction. Looking down at him from the tree, he didn't seem so tough, but from this angle he appeared to be fifty feet tall. Having no defense, I smiled, hoping he would be merciful. No such luck. He grabbed me by the scruff of the neck and dragged me over to the squad car, my feet barely touching the ground. Some other cop had picked up another friend of mine in the same raid, and together we were driven down to the Antrim Road barracks for an interrogation.

I thought we had been rounded up because we were trespassing and lighting fires in the orchard, but it turned out they were investigating a more serious crime in the neighborhood. Within the old, abandoned mansion, the City Corporation had stored a bunch of wheelbarrows and other tools for some project nearby. Someone had broken into it and stolen everything. They either suspected us or thought we might know who the thieves were. I had a pretty good idea who had done it, a rough kid from the neighborhood called Jimmy. He was about seventeen, and I knew that he had suddenly come into a lot of money.

Since squealing was and is one of the cardinal sins of childhood, we all feigned ignorance and stupidity. After grilling us for about an hour, the cops were satisfied that we knew nothing and took us back home. As we rode in the police car, they joked around with us and let us ring the alarm bell. They dropped each of us off right at the front door of our houses. Cops weren't so serious in those days, at least not with kids. But then, they had much less to contend with.

Another night, I was walking through the orchard alone on my way home from the picture house. It was so dark I couldn't see where I was stepping. About halfway through, a severe case of heebie-jeebies set in, so I picked up a stick for protection from things of or not of this world. I was passing a large clump of bushes when there was a sudden rustling in the dry leaves at my side. My heart leapt into my mouth, and I instinctively started slashing wildly at the source of the sound. I made contact with something solid and heard an anguished yell and saw what appeared to be a white face rising up from the ground toward me. I froze in horror thinking it was a ghost. With a thundering heart, I took to my heels and didn't stop running until I reached my house, nearly knocking down the door in my haste to get inside. I stammered out an explanation to my mother about seeing a white ghost in the orchard. She laughed and said, "Ach, ya prob'ly just surprised some oul' tramp or caught a couple havin' a curt!" After thinking about it, I concluded that the "ghost" was probably just somebody's white arse.

Despite our encounters with the mean or scary denizens of the orchard, there were times when I would go there alone when I needed to think. I would lay in the tall grass and watch the clouds roll by during the day and the stars come out one by one at night. A pleasant, tingling calm would often fill me. I could feel the "thoughts" of all the living things there, dozens of different kinds of consciousnesses all relating to each other. I watched birds collecting twigs and branches, flying into the treetops and building their nests and wondered at how smart they were. I noticed that the flowers turned toward the sun on bright days and wondered how they knew to do that. I marveled at the variety of colors and designs they came in, as if God had commissioned his most talented angel artist to create them. They just seemed too varied and beautiful to have been an accident.

I heard the adults talking about God all the time, but they usually only brought him up to make a point or support an argument. When I said something adults disapproved of, I would hear "God forgive you!" When someone was sick, I would be told to pray for them, and I would, not really knowing who or what I was praying to. I could never feel God when adults would say these things to me. The first place I felt God was in the orchard. No matter what my problems were, if I just sat in the orchard long enough, the crash of scents engulfing me, a natural potpourri, a feeling of peace always washed over me eventually, as if God knew all my worries and was whispering in my ear, "Don't worry, son. Everything will be alright."

The orchard was the closest thing to a natural park in our area and the stories we kids told as we huddled around fires about leprechauns, banshees, wood nymphs, fairies, ghosts, and other creatures of the netherworld did wonders to develop our imaginations. I have always felt sorry for children in the inner cities who have no parks or wild areas in which to find such solitude and wonder. It should be law that city planning always includes an area of woods or an orchard in every neighborhood for children to explore. No attempt should be made to tend it. There should be some places even in cities which are left alone to grow wild, where a child can sit quietly or lie in tall grass and feel that he is part of something greater than himself, like I did. There should also be at least one run-down old mansion in every neighborhood that looks like it might be haunted, for no other reason than to scare the wits out of children. If the neighborhood is a new subdivision, this house should be built to look old. It is good and healthy for children to believe in extraordinary mysteries, and this illusion should be maintained as long as possible. The world will become ordinary soon enough.

CHAPTER 24

THE GLORIOUS 12TH

"In Japan for an international conference on religion, (Joseph) Campbell overheard another American delegate, a social philosopher from New York, say to a Shinto priest, "We've been now to a good many ceremonies and have seen quite a few of your shrines. But I don't get your ideology. I don't get your theology." The Japanese paused as though in deep thought and then slowly shook his head. "I think we don't have ideology," he said. "We don't have theology. We dance."
~ Joseph Campbell and Bill Moyers – *The Power of Myth.*

July 12th bonfire awaiting a torch

The highlight of the summer months was "The Twelfth." Every twelfth day of July, the Orangemen celebrated the victory of the Protestant King William the Third (King Billy) over the Catholic King James at the Battle of the Boyne in 1689, which saved the English throne from Roman Catholicism and Ulster for the Protestants. We celebrated with large bonfires, which were burned in the streets on the evening of July eleventh.

For Ulster's Catholics, this was a day to lay low, to stay home behind closed curtains or, better yet, to go on vacation. However, they would have their own celebration the following month, so most just waited their turn with bated breath. The fact that the two celebrations are only a month apart probably prevented a lot of trouble. Angered by the strutting Protestants, many Catholics undoubtedly thought, "Wait until August. We'll get our own back!" For some Protestants, the twelfth of July was an opportunity to drive home to the Catholics who was in charge of Ulster. For others, it was merely a celebration and an affirmation of culture and identity with no ill feelings toward the Catholics at all.

For weeks prior to the big night, we scoured the surrounding hills and glens for fallen trees, which we cut up and carried to the bonfire area. Mostly, our offerings ended up being old mattresses, tires and anything else that would burn. We hid all this junk in secure storage points, which were guarded night and day from other groups of marauders. Some was also stacked at street corners all over town for smaller fires.

One year, we set about our usual task of gathering up materials for the bonfire to be lit on the eleventh night. For weeks, we had been searching the neighborhood and surrounding areas for materials for the fire. We had scoured every alley and emptied every trash bin looking for discarded items, but the pickings had been slim. As we examined the pitiful results of our efforts, we tried to come up with ideas to improve our supply. Our friend Lionel, who you will be properly introduced to later, came up with the first workable suggestion.

"Why don't we chop down a tree?" he said.

After some discussion, everyone agreed this was a great solution. The question was where we could find a tree to chop down. After laboring over this for a while, one of us suggested the orchard. We found a couple of rusty hatchets in our parents' tool shacks and walked up to the orchard to select a suitable candidate for the bonfire. The tree we chose bordered the Ballysillan Road. Big Lionel, a consummate bluffer, claimed to have inside knowledge of how to cut a tree so that it fell in the preferred direction - in this case, backward toward the orchard. He must have read that page of the lumberjack manual backward because when we finally managed to hack through the trunk of the tree, it fell directly across the main road with a deafening crash, sent several pedestrians scrambling for their lives, and nearly flattened several cars.

At this moment, old Joe Heslip who ran the grocery store across the street came tearing out of his store screaming at the top of his lungs, "What the hell d'ya think yar doin'? Why'd ya cut down that tree?"

"It's for the twelfth. We need it for the bonfire!"

Old Joe screamed, "Do you mean ta tell me ya cut down a parfectly good tree for a bloody bonfire? Well, I'm calling the police!"

He scurried back across the road to make the call. Big Lionel immediately bolted and was long gone before the rest of us realized the gravity of the situation. Fortunately, several of the men from the surrounding houses came out and, seeing our predicament, joined together and helped us pull the tree off the road and back into the orchard. Afterward, we decided it would probably be a good idea to make ourselves scarce before the police arrived, as Lionel was wise enough to do immediately.

After a suitable period of hiding and waiting, we returned, chopped up the remains of the tree, and stashed it in the local air raid shelter. Whether the police came or not, we never knew. In retrospect, it was vandalism and a shame that we had killed a perfectly good tree, but the demands of the moment were more important.

Before going to bed on the 11th, the Orangemen of Ulster set out their best dark blue and black Sunday suits and shoes, white gloves and orange sashes for wearing the next morning. In the Orange Halls, huge banners were unfurled and prepared. These banners, which required two men to carry, depicted the glorious moments in Irish Protestant history, mainly the exploits of King William of Orange from whom the Orangemen drew their name. As well as the Battle of the Boyne, a banner is also dedicated to the relief of Derry when the starving Protestant Apprentice Boys held the Catholic armies at bay for months until they were finally rescued by the arrival of the relief ship *The Mountjoy.*

Orange Hall, Belfast, 1941

In the days leading up to the event, the deep thundering of the giant Lambeg drums sounded throughout the hills and valleys of Ulster as wiry men with the massive drums strapped to their chests beat them until their wrists were swollen and bloody.

Finally, the magic moment came when the fires were lighted. Petrol was splashed on the debris, and men with torches would set it ablaze. An effigy of the Pope made of straw and rags was produced by the crowd at each bonfire, which was then torched to the cheers of the onlookers. Everyone was out on the street, and the adults danced into the wee hours to music broadcast from a hastily constructed PA system. Children leapt and skipped around the edges of the flames and through the smoke, whooping with delight while their elders looked on approvingly. The massive, bright orange bonfires burning around Belfast with all the revelers dancing around them must have been quite a sight from heaven, though I'm not sure God entirely approved. And our bonfire burned much brighter after a brigade of dirty kids carried dozens of pieces of a tree by hand and wagon to feed the flames.

On the morning of July twelfth, while the bonfires from the night before were still smoldering, the Orangemen gathered in the city center and marched to the field at Finaghy several miles away, along with massive accordion, pipe and brass bands. Exuberant crowds lined the route and cheered the parades on their way as the bands struck up the old familiar tunes, "Dolly's Bray", "The Sash My Father Wore", "The Green, Grassy Slopes of the Boyne", and best of all, "No Surrender!"

The excitement and emotion that accompanied the July Twelfth celebrations was palpable. It was an annual pilgrimage to our roots and a warning to the Catholic hordes in our midst that we were not to be taken lightly. However, in those days, it was not a call to arms, nor even slightly aggressive. In fact, many of the Catholics who didn't leave town or stay indoors joined in the celebrations and were accepted enthusiastically.

Then and still today, the Twelfth day procession ranks as one of the largest in the western world, rivaled only by the Mardi Gras in New Orleans, with over 250 bands amassed from all corners of Ulster and from as far away as Scotland, Canada and Australia. One year, we even had representation from the Orange Order Branch of a country in Africa! A solitary black man, grinning broadly with magnificently white teeth, sash proudly in place, got the biggest cheer of all who passed that day.

When the bands reached Finaghy field, the celebrations continued. Great quantities of Guinness and whiskey were consumed, songs were sung, and the bands played on and on. After much revelry, the parade resumed and returned to the city. Once there, the men returned to the lodges, and the drums and the banners were put away until the following year.

This annual event was benignly tolerated by the police. I suppose they felt that the parade was a relatively safe way for the Protestants to express themselves and flex their muscles once a year. It was also a less troublesome way for them to get it out of their system. The bonfires glowed orange for days afterward until the Belfast City Corporation came around to sweep up the ashes. Homeowners closest to the fires touched up the scorched paint on their walls and replaced the heat-cracked glass, if they had the money to do so.

Though the Orange Order had been responsible for a lot of the trouble in Northern Ireland, not everyone in the Order had bad intentions. In fact, most were very peace-loving. They weren't against the Catholics as much as they were for themselves and proud of their heritage. I'm sure there are many Catholics who felt the same way. The English thought we were all mad. To them, the spectacle of grown men dancing around bonfires and parading around while beating drums which were sometime bigger than the men carrying them was something better fitted for deepest, darkest Africa. It was all very unseemly and embarrassing to them. However, an Irishman might respond to this with an expression African-Americans are fond of (slightly altered) – "It's an Irish thing. You wouldn't understand."

The fact is, with few exceptions, the English have little of the vitality or exuberance of the Irish, or the Scottish either for that matter, and their love of country and heritage vanished around the 1950's when their commitment turned to the trade unions. Only the history buffs realized the events in Ulster represented the last gasp of the former British Empire and that history was being played out before their eyes.

The Twelfth Day celebrations meant little to me as a young child except a lot of noise and excitement. However, the day would come when I would realize the nature of the society into which I had been born and how that society would forever shape my character. Some of what I would learn I would have to put aside - the narrow-mindedness and parochialism, for instance – but the remainder I would retain - the blunt honesty and the rugged individualism that forever marked the Ulster Scots, whether in Northern Ireland or in the New World. Those characteristics would remain with me for the rest of my life.

Would that this steadfastness and loyalty were to be reciprocated by my fellow British subjects on the mainland. Instead I would find years later that Loyalist allegiance was unwelcome there. Indeed, it was a source of embarrassment to many. Like bastard children, the Ulster Loyalists were unpleasant reminders of past English dalliances with Ireland, best forgotten. To my co-habitants in Ireland, the Irish Catholics, my kind was equally unwelcome. To them, the Ulster Loyalists were usurpers, Anglo-Saxon invaders and unlawful occupants of Irish soil.

While the rest of the world knew little of these passions, conflicts, and historical grudges, it *would* learn the depth of the passion and rage that exploded on the streets of Belfast and other cities in Northern Ireland in the late 1960's. But that is a story that has been told many times by others and one I am determined to avoid adding further volumes to. It is my intention to reveal the character of the people of Belfast beneath all the anger and mutual distrust. Frankly, enough has been said about it already and I'm bored with the entire subject. Exposing negative qualities does not promote healing. Hopefully, revealing positive ones will.

CHAPTER 25

MY MA AND THE BIG CHURCH HEIST

It's the lure of easy money.
It's got a very strong appeal.
    ~ Glenn Frey

One of my mother's finer qualities was that she didn't seem to care at all about whether people were Protestants or Catholics, which was very unusual then and even now. Traditionally, a Protestant would never set foot inside a Catholic church and the same was probably true for Catholics. However, if my mother felt that she needed some divine guidance, she would be just as likely to walk into a Catholic chapel, a Jewish synagogue, or whatever was handy. I thought it was very open-minded of her.

The churches always seemed to be holding some kind of fundraiser. My mother entered me in one collecting for an organization called *The Orphaned Protestant Children's Fund*. The minister, a tall man with white hair and red cheeks handed me my materials and said, "I'm proud of you, son. Doing the Lord's work at such a young age. You're wise beyond your years!"

I was anxious to make the minister proud and live up to his high opinion of me. He gave me and the other boys a board with punch-out holes. The price for each hole was sixpence. The purchaser would punch out the hole and a piece of paper would come out with or without a money prize. The prize amount could be as much as two shillings. I went door to door in my neighborhood. I was shy at first but became more bold as the change began to accumulate in my pocket.

The Protestant people of Belfast are very altruistic and almost always say yes to reasonable requests for charity. Before I knew it, I had sold off the entire board. Walking home, I counted the money I made, about thirty shillings. Proud of my accomplishment, I couldn't wait to tell my mother about it when I arrived at home.

"Thirty shillings!" she said. "Good lad! Let me see it!"

I handed it to her and she counted it out on the table.

When she was done counting, she paused and said, "Sidney, we're a wee bit short this week so I'm goin' ta barrah this from ya. I'll pay ya back next week when yar da gits paid."

I was shocked. I was looking forward to giving the money to the minister and being praised as one of the Lord's best foot soldiers.

"But ma," I protested, "I need to give that money to the church like ya told me to."

"Ach, we'll give it to them next week. They can wait a week surely!"

The next week came and went with no mention of the money. As time passed, I realized I would never see it again. The pride I felt in serving the Good Lord and making money for the church slowly turned to guilt. I imagined the minister who had put so much faith and trust in me looking out of the window of the church and wondering why I never returned with his board. The guilt about that unresolved thirty shilling debt lasted for decades. I even tried to locate the organization one year during a trip home to repay the debt but, alas, they were no more. I comfort myself with the knowledge that I have supported other charities of a similar nature since that time and hopefully have redeemed myself to some degree in the eyes of the Almighty.

CHAPTER 26

UNCLE ALFIE TO THE RESCUE

"If a child is to keep alive his inborn sense of wonder, he needs the companionship of at least one adult who can share it, rediscovering with him the joy, excitement, and mystery of the world we live in.
~ Rachel Carson

Uncle Alfie

I became interested in soccer at an early age and, on one occasion, asked my father to come watch us play at the nearby Ballysillan playing fields. He had never come to any of my games before so I was elated to see him standing on the sidelines about fifteen minutes after the game started. I played my heart out trying to impress him and felt I did fairly well. At halftime, however, I looked around and discovered that he had left. My disappointment was so great, I could barely muster the energy to play the second half of the game. I dragged myself home afterward and asked him why he left. Without looking up from his paper, he said, "You guys don't know how to play soccer."

Later, I took up boxing and would often come home with a split lip or a black eye. My father would make no comment at first but eventually would put down his paper and ask, as if out of obligation more than concern, "Alright, what happened?" He would listen briefly then return his attention to the newspaper.

I never understood why my father seemed so distant and, as children tend to do, I took it personally. I now understand that it was simply a character flaw and probably a result of his relationship with his own father. Unhappy people don't go around making others happy, not even their children. That's just not the way it works. We can only give what we have inside. But I didn't have the benefit of philosophy back then. All I knew was I needed a pat on the back from him, or a word of praise, and never received either.

The best thing I can say for my mother's maternal instincts is that she saw to it that I was fed properly. Aside from that, she was scatterbrained, impulsive and, like her own mother, overly opinionated. Most of her criticisms and opinions, however, seemed to be inherited directly from her mother. I don't think she had an original thought in her entire life. My mother couldn't have an intelligent conversation with me and my father wouldn't. I suppose my da was too wrapped up in his own problems to be very concerned about mine or to even know that I had any. And compared to his, I suppose I didn't.

The home is the last place one should feel lonely, but it often is that way. As I grew up and my thoughts became more complex, I longed for a wise adult to ask questions of. It was at this point that my parents started sending me for days at a time to stay with my Uncle Alfie in Coleraine. Alfie was a godsend if ever there was one.

Of all my extended family, I loved my Uncle Alfie the most. He was my mother's brother and, though he was born in Belfast, lived his entire married life in a little town called Coleraine on the northern coast of County Antrim. I always looked forward to visiting him and his wife, my Aunt Flo. He was rough around the edges, but he was good to me and lavished upon me the warmth and affection I longed in vain to receive from my father. He was a bit of a wild man but sincere and good-natured.

Alfie met Flo at a country dance. She was the local beauty with wild, dark-hair and clear, pale skin. Unlike Alfie, she was quiet and shy, and spoke sparingly and softly. Alfie was the exact opposite, gregarious and brash, always the life of the party. They made a great pair, and it was inevitable that they would marry and settle down together. I suspect that Alfie may have wanted to wander the world a bit but he chose to live in Coleraine because it was Flo's hometown and despite his wild character, he loved her completely and desperately.

My beautiful Aunt Flo, Uncle Alfie's better half

Alfie worked for the Automobile Association helping stranded motorists. It was similar to America's AAA. Alfie became a fixture around town astride his BMW German WWII motorcycle with sidecar, wearing a leather jacket, boots and matching leather skullcap with fur lining and built-in goggles. The sidecar came in handy for taking stranded motorists home when their cars could not be fixed with the tools he carried with him. I used to think Uncle Alfie looked like a dispatch rider delivering important messages.

Alfie's house was next to the railroad crossing at the north end of the city. There was a pub three doors away, and beyond that, the railway station. As is typical throughout Ireland, the pub was a gathering place for the locals. Alfie could almost always be found there, regaling all who would listen with his exploits; some true, some exaggerated for dramatic effect, and some outright lies. They were happy times. There must be some truth to the old idea that opposites attract because Flo was the antithesis of Alfie. She probably never swore once in her life and was the picture of class and refinement.

Alfie's house was very cozy, but it had one problem. Its only bathroom was right next to the kitchen, with a door that had the unsettling habit of suddenly swinging open at the most inappropriate times. Alfie tried to fix it, but the old house must have developed a lean over the years, which left the door irreparably out of kilter. At my tender age at the time, bathroom ablutions were a sacrosanct affair, and I had great difficulty performing even the simplest bodily functions while simultaneously holding one foot against the unpredictable door. After several unsatisfactory forays, I deemed it more practical to spend a penny at the public toilet in the railway station where privacy was more dependable than continuing to risk exposure in the middle of a keek.

Alfie and Flo had two children - Sylvia, who was the eldest, and Wee Alfie. They all lived in a three-story brick row house built in the latter half of the 19th century. The house was full of nooks and crannies and secret rooms, which made for great exploring and hiding as a boy.

Alfie was known and loved for miles around so people were always dropping into his house. He swore like a trooper no matter who was present, whether at the pub or at home, and whether drunk or sober. But somehow it never seemed vulgar coming from him. No one ever took offense. They were usually too busy laughing to care. My Aunt Flo just sighed in resignation. She knew there was no fighting it.

During the war, Uncle Alfie joined the Ulster Home Guard, a volunteer force to help thwart the German invasion. In training practice one morning, the instructor lobbed a hand grenade in Alfie's direction and told everyone to duck. Not being one to take orders seriously, Alfie casually looked over and got one of his eyes blown out by shrapnel. He later told me that the pain was so intense, he begged them to shoot him. He was fitted with a glass eye. Either the quality of glass eyes was not very high in those days, or Alfie had purchased the cheapest one, but he was more comfortable with it out than in and would only wear it when going to the village. As a result, the eye was constantly on display for all to see on the mantelpiece or kitchen table. When I first saw it, I thought it was a marlie and took it outside to play with it. I showed it to a few of my friends. It was the most unusual marlie any of them had ever seen because, of course, it wasn't a marlie at all and it wasn't quite round. We ended up in a competitive game. Fortunately, I managed to avoid losing Alfie's eye to another player, or worse, down a sewer.

Halfway through the game, Uncle Alfie went to the table, saw the eye missing, then looked out the window and saw me on my hands and knees, ready to let it fly. He was not pleased. The eye looked false enough already without being scratched up and dirty. I had been skiting it across the cement for fifteen minutes when he came running out of the front door and grabbed it.

"That's not a toy, ya wee skitter! It's my eye!" he said.

"Oh! Sorry, Uncle Alfie! I didn't know."

"Oh, really now?" he said with mock anger, "The pupil on it wasn't a good enough hint, I suppose!"

"I'm sorry," I replied with my head down.

"Ach, there was no harm done, lad."

With that, he fogged up the eye with his breath, polished it on his lapel, popped it back in his head, winked at us all, and dandered off down the street. My playmates were frozen in wide-eyed amazement. Alfie had a special talent for shocking people. The eye just gave him another prop with which to ply his trade. After he left, I spent a half hour telling my friends heroic tales about his days in the military. The story of how he lost his eye was altered a bit for dramatic effect. I felt compelled to make up something more interesting than he had simply forgotten to duck.

One morning, Alfie was gutting a chicken. Back then, chickens bought from the store still had the guts in them. There was no way of getting rid of unwanted food because disposal units hadn't been invented. He didn't want to leave it outside to stink up the whole yard, so he got a shoebox out of the closet, dumped the guts in it, wrapped the box in Christmas paper, and stuck a bow on it. He then walked across the street and left it on a bus stop bench. We sat in the window watching and waiting to see who would take the bait. Eventually, a young ruffian sat down, gradually scooted over next to the apparently forgotten gift, looked around to make sure nobody was watching, then tore the box open hoping to find some valuable present. The expression on his face when he saw the chicken innards was priceless.

Alfie's grandson Darren told me that the gift of giblets was a Christmas tradition at Alfie's house, and the whole family would gather at the window to watch unsuspecting would-be gift-nappers open box after box of turkey or chicken guts. It never stopped being funny.

Before you judge too harshly, dear reader, please keep in mind that these were the days before television when people had to invent their own entertainment!

The constant flow of visitors to Alfie's house was a blessing and a curse. Though he welcomed everyone equally, Flo felt a bit put upon at times, having to prepare tea and snacks repeatedly throughout the day.

Alfie became friends with a fellow named Jimmy Malone who was a little backwards and shy. Though over forty years of age, he still lived with his mother and had never had a girlfriend. Alfie said he felt sorry for Jimmy because, as he poetically put it, he had "never had his hole."

Because of Alfie's kindness, Jimmy got himself into the habit of dropping by every Saturday at about five o'clock just before dinner time. This meant that my Aunt Flo had to arrange another setting at the table and divide up the dinner for the extra mouth. At times, this was difficult for her because these were lean years after the war when food was scarce. After about six Saturday's in a row of this routine, Aunt Flo said to Alfie, "I wish you would tell that Jimmy Malone to stop coming here on Saturday nights." Alfie agreed that he was becoming a burden and said, "Don't worry, Love, I'll take care of it."

The next Saturday, Jimmy showed up as usual and positioned himself near the kitchen table, waiting for the grub to come out.

"Would you like a drop of tea?" Alfie asked.

"B'Jesus, I'd love a cup'a tea," Jimmy said, "and maybe a wee biscuit if you have one."

"No problem," Alfie cheerfully replied, preparing the tea. He handed a mug to Jimmy and set a few biscuits beside him, at which point the two of them set to talking about the soccer game that afternoon. As Jimmy finished his tea, he saw Alfie's glass eye staring up at him from the bottom of the cup.

"In the name'a Jasus!" he yelled, "What's that?"

"Ahh, fer fock's sake, there's me eye!" Alfie answered. "I've been lookin' for it all day!"

"You did that on purpose, ya rotten git!" Jimmy said. "Yar trying ta sicken me!"

Jimmy bolted for the door and took off down the street, swearing and spitting in disgust all the way. That ended the Saturday night visits for a while. In his own unique fashion, Alfie had solved the problem.

As a young man growing up, I didn't have a clue about women and their motivations. The bizarre nature of my parents' relationship had left me almost completely ignorant about love and sex. Uncle Alfie was ready to help me through this important stage. One valuable piece of information he gave me about the opposite sex was, "They give you their pussies, but they want your soul." Another piece of sage advice he gave me was, "Just remember this . . . no matter what a woman says, what she really wants is a man who will yank off her knickers with no apologies."

This information was startling to me but I assumed he knew what he was talking about because he reputedly had yanked off quite a few pairs of knickers around Coleraine in his time and had become quite popular in the process.

Alfie had a German Shepherd named Lassie that was very well-trained. Behind Alfie's house was a back lane and backing onto this lane was a distribution centre for a bakery. Lorries would come down from Belfast in the morning to deliver fresh bread products, which would then be moved on to local bakeries. Alfie somehow trained Lassie to steal bread and cakes when the delivery men turned their backs. This booty was then returned to Alfie, who would cut off the slice the dog had in its mouth for it to finish and keep the remainder for the family. With a trained dog like this, its skills were also applied to the local butcher shop.

Alfie had somehow come into the possession of some high-end radios of dubious origin that were smuggled over the border. On hearing a rumor that the police were on their way, a friend woke Alfie and his daughter Sylvia. , Bleary eyed, they dumped the radios in the River Bann, still in their pajamas.

Two young male friends that had caught an STD asked Alfie for advice. He recommended rubbing their genitals in petrol (gasoline). I never heard the outcome. I only heard that it involved considerable pain.

Alfie took the family to an airfield one Sunday afternoon to give the kids a go at riding his motorbike. Flo decided she wanted to try riding it, too. After many laps of the airfield and many whoops of joy, everyone was under the impression that Flo was thoroughly enjoying the experience. Eventually, Alfie realized they weren't whoops of joy but shouts of panic. Flo had no idea how to stop the bike! Alfie had to ride alongside her on another bike and climb from one to the other to stop it for her, a modern reenactment of the runaway horse scenes in old westerns.

When Alfie's daughter Sylvia was young she was hanging off the railway bridge spitting down the funnels of the steam trains. When reprimanded by a concerned lady, she said "Ach, go on away, you auld bitch." She was taken home to be punished. Flo left it to Alfie to spank her. He took her upstairs, took off his belt and told her to scream in pain as he whacked the back of the chair with his belt. He was too kind to punish his child even when she deserved it.

Even as a child, Alfie was just too alive for his own good. He and his friends Jordy and Albert, used to break into a jam factory through the skylight to steal jam.

One of Alfie's uncles passed away and the wake was held in the departed's parlor. Everyone was sitting around talking about what a great man he was. The corpse was upstairs in his bed. He had been stripped and dressed in proper funeral attire. Suddenly, from the top of the stairs, everyone heard the dead man shout, "Where are me clothes?" Several mouthfuls of tea were spit across the room and every woman in the place screamed in terror. His uncle had been in a coma, not dead.

Alfie was also trained as a medium. At his first seance, a family was trying to locate the will of a recently departed father. Alfie was convinced that the will was on top of a wardrobe. After much searching, no will was found, but Alfie remained adamant. "Check again," he said. "You'll find it on top of a wardrobe." The family stood in front of the wardrobe again. One of them noticed a loose corner and lifted the wood veneer on top of it. Hidden beneath it was the father's will.

Irreverent about his own psychic powers like he was about everything else, Alfie capitalized on his growing reputation as a mystic to play tricks on his houseguests. When he had company staying the night, he would begin the evening by winding everybody up that the house was haunted. He hid bells and chains in their rooms and in the attic ahead of time. Using various pulleys, he would give them all a very uncomfortable night. With Alfie, there truly was never a dull moment.

Alfie helping a stranded motorist, circa 1940

CHAPTER 27

"JACK RICKERBY, PLEASE"

"The man wants to be admired and the woman wants to be cherished. If that's not happening, the relationship is doomed."
~ Anonymous

I think my parents knew that my Uncle Alfie was probably not the best influence on me, but they sent me to stay with him and his wife Flo more and more frequently as I got older because they enjoyed the break from taking care of me. My sister apparently wasn't as much trouble as me because they usually kept her home.

Except for the occasional day trip to visit relatives, we never went on a vacation together as a family. Even during short visits to visit in-laws, arguments usually broke out because of some unsettled family issue, and everyone parted with their negative feelings toward one another reaffirmed. This mutual condemnation contributed more to the collective loneliness in my family than anything else. Rather than bringing my parents closer together, the persistent disapproval of their in-laws drove them further apart.

Perhaps because of the combined stress of work, family and marriage, my da's asthma grew worse and worse over the years, and he had frequent and violent bouts with it. The fact that he never took time off from work because of his asthma and, in fact, seemed eager to get to work, further demonstrated that most of his stress – namely, my ma - was in the home. Arguments with my mother seemed to trigger his attacks. He had a little tin can full of a mustard-colored, powdery substance to help him overcome these episodes. He would begin to wheeze and then yell to me, "Sidney, get my powder! Hurry!" I would run to his room to find it, and run back to him. When I returned, his breathing would be short and pained. He'd take some of the powder out and ignite it with a match, breathe in the fumes, and his breathing would gradually come easier. I was so frightened by the severity of his attacks that I would become short of breath myself just watching him and would only breathe normally again when he could.

Because my father was paid on Thursdays and my mother had it all spent by Tuesday, she would often ask me to go down to the railway station on Thursday afternoon to pick up my father's pay packet before he could do it himself, which meant I had to wait in line with my father's workmates towering over me. I never saw any other children in the line, so I was apparently the only one who did this. Whether or not my father was embarrassed by it was beyond me at the time.

I had to struggle to see over the edge of the counter as I said, "Jack Rickerby, please." The clerk got to know me after a while and would toss the little brown envelope across the counter to me. I would run home with it and give it to my mother. Presumably, she would then dole out some to him when he got home. This was one of the things I saw no wrong in as a child and only realized many years later how humiliating it must have been for my father to have his son collecting his pay for him before he could get to it himself, only to be rationed to him later by his wife.

For this reason more than any other, I came to understand my father's bitterness, even the way he behaved toward me. As strong-willed as he could be on occasion, it's a mystery to me why and how he put up with this treatment.

CHAPTER 28

MAGIC MOMENTS

"People are beginning to realize that there is a kind of mystical bliss that comes when the body is overtaxed. I experienced this when I was running in college and a couple of years after college. As I look back now there were a couple of moments in the last eighty yards of the half mile when I was running in championship time . . . you know, you're spaced out then. If anyone would ask me what the peaks were, the high moments of my life experience – really, zing! – the whole thing in a nutshell – those races would be it. More than anything else in my whole life."
~ Joseph Campbell

The soccer season (or football season, as we called it) was in the wintertime. We had a game every Saturday afternoon at about two o'clock. I looked forward to playing soccer every Saturday so much that the rest of the weekdays were only minor annoyances to get through as quickly as possible.

The first thing I always did on Saturday mornings was to look out the window to see if it was raining. A light mist wouldn't disrupt our plans but a downpour would. My heart soared if it was dry and sank if I woke up and heard the rain tapping on the roof.

On sunny Saturdays, I usually woke to the sound of my mates yelling outside. I couldn't get dressed fast enough with the combination of the sunshine streaming through my window and my friends voices beckoning. Ralph Waldo Emerson wrote, *"Give me health and a day, and I will make the pomp of emperors ridiculous."* That's how it was. Soccer was the greatest joy in my life.

Soccer cleats in those days were real leather with leather studs. We put on the new cleats, tied them tightly, and submerged our feet in buckets of hot water to mold them to our feet. With boots, jerseys, shorts, socks and shin pads packed in brown paper bags, we embarked on the journey to the Newforge playing fields on the far side of town. Newforge had several beautiful playing fields on the south side of the city. It was a long trip and took several buses to get there, but we didn't mind.

When we arrived, our trainer was already there talking to the groundsmen and inspecting the pitch to see whether the rain had been severe enough to warrant calling off the game, or if the game could go forward. We solemnly waited for their decision, praying that we would be allowed to play. If they let us play, we rushed ecstatically onto the field. If they said we couldn't play, we returned home deflated and miserable, life completely ruined for another week.

I lived from Saturday to Saturday and thought about soccer incessantly. I was never a great player, but I enjoyed the game immensely. I usually played center-half, a defensive position, because I was not very fast on my feet. However, I developed a chant which I would repeat to myself during games. This chant heightened in intensity as the players of the opposing team rushed toward me. It was "They shall not pass." A bit dramatic perhaps, but it gave me a strong sense of purpose. As a result, I zealously threw my body in front of the player or the ball to stop either from passing. Nobody wore cups in those days so a heavy thump in the jewels by a muddy leather ball was not a lot of fun. Receiving a direct blast up the pie hole was no day at the beach, either.

Sometimes it began to rain when the game was almost done. By this time, I had usually been pummeled from head to toe. The combination of physical exhaustion, being covered with muck and freshly cut grass, and bleeding from the nose and lips, made me feel like a medieval warrior defending king and country on some field of battle.

When we had no Saturday game, we would visit our local football stadium and cheer for the home team, in our case Cliftonville, an amateur team in a professional league. My favorite player was a left back named Herbie Hegarty. At least once in every game, Herbie would succeed in kicking the ball over the stadium roof to the street outside, which always drew a big cheer from the home crowd. It was his trademark.

Cliftonville Football Club, 1952
Back row, left to right -
Swann, Weir, Calow, Hegarty, McCleary
Front row –
Sheills, Beggs, Wilson, Gilmore, Reid, Boyde

If there weren't many fans in the stadium because of rain, they sometimes opened the gates at halftime and let everyone come in free of charge. My mates and I always took advantage of this opportunity.

One day, I was standing with the crowd at the sidelines. A light drizzle was falling. I was watching the game when a wiry, wee man walked up and stood next to me. He looked like a civil servant of some kind. He was wearing a black jacket, pin-stripe pants, and raincoat. He had a briefcase in one hand and a rolled up newspaper under the other arm. A neat derby hat and a fancy mustache completed his prim appearance. He stood out like a sore thumb from the rest of the crowd; most of whom were working class types.

The action of the game was heating up when one of the players sliced the ball and it spun into the crowd, landing right at the wee man's feet. He set down his briefcase and picked up the ball. The player was standing on the other side of the fence between the stands and the field waiting for the man to throw the ball back. Instead, he decided to demonstrate his own soccer skills. He tossed the ball in the air and dribbled it on his knees a few times. The player yelled, "Fock sakes, come on!" The crowd was also getting annoyed and yelling at him, but the wee man seemed oblivious to them. This was his chance to shine; to show all the world that he had the talent to be a professional, too. He ended his dazzling display by giving the ball one last dribble and taking a mighty whack at it. Unfortunately, because the ball was all wet and mucky, he sliced it, causing the ball to skite off his foot sideways and strike a very large, mean-looking man right up the side of his face. The bigger man wore gigantic construction boots, a duncher cap and a red scarf; a bit like Bluto from the Popeye comics. One of those characters one does his best to avoid at all costs. His hair flew to one side and a round, red mark began to form on his face, which was now covered with mud and bits of turf.

The crowd let out a collective horrified gasp followed by a deep and ominous silence as everyone waited for the wee man to be torn limb from limb. The wee man went as white as a ghost and actually appeared to shrink in size as he looked up at the giant and awaited his fate. The big man gritted his teeth and shook with rage for a second as the pain gradually set in to the side of his face. He slowly took his handkerchief out of his pocket, cleaned off his face, glared at the little man and hissed, "You stupid, silly, wee bastard." Mortified, the wee man snatched up his briefcase, ducked into the crowd, and speed-walked out of the stadium to the derisive laughter of the crowd.

On school days, we all usually went up to the big field and picked up games until sunset. In the summertime, the sun sometimes set around 10:00 P.M. My mother couldn't keep shoes on my feet. Even walking to and from school, I was always kicking something. If no ball could be found, a can or rock would do. In impromptu games in the street, two trash cans or piled up jackets substituted for goalposts.

The soccer stars of the day were Stanley Matthews, Wilf Mannion, Stanley Mortenson, Tom Finney and the rest of the international players. My personal favorite was Jack Vernon. He played center-half and captained the Northern Ireland team. All of us aspired to be soccer stars and play one day for Northern Ireland. A few of us even made the grade.

Tom Finney (Right)

Jack Vernon

The football crowd in Belfast was mostly working class. Their support was generally divided between Linfield, the Protestant team, or Belfast Celtic, the Catholic team. The town went nuts during the annual game between the Catholic team and the Protestant team. Strangely, not all of the Celtic players were Catholics, though all of the Linfield players were Protestant because the Protestants were more stern about not admitting Catholics.

Skirmishes often broke out in the crowd during and after the games. The Celtic center-forward at the time was a guy named Jimmy Jones. He was a Protestant and a rough and aggressive player. He bulldozed his way right through the defense and could put the ball into the goal from any angle. One day, he was flying down the field at his usual breakneck speed when he ran into Bob

Bryson, the Linfield right-fullback and captain. Bryson's leg snapped with a sickening crack that could be heard all the way to the back row. After the game, the crowd went berserk and stormed the field. They set upon Jimmy Jones and gave him a severe beating, making sure they broke the same leg. The fact that he was an Orangeman playing for a Catholic team may have doubled the wrath of the crowd, who considered him a turncoat. Jimmy Jones later sued the Belfast Corporation for lack of proper police enforcement at the game and collected a huge sum of money. It was reported that once he had cashed the check, he promptly threw away his walking stick and resumed playing soccer as aggressively as ever. Celtic dropped out of the league not long afterward, and they were greatly missed by us all.

I still watch soccer regularly on BBC America and love the game every bit as much as I did as a kid. Everyone who is born with their full faculties physically has a time when their body can do magic on a playing field or racetrack or wherever their chosen sport is performed. This was my time. I could run all day and never get out of breath. Every now and then, I would do something magical with a soccer ball, and my heart would sing.

I coached my son's soccer team in AYSO (American Youth Soccer Organization) for several years when he was a teenager. He was a good player, but I always felt that he could have been much better. He had a very laid back attitude on the field (a California thing), but he still managed to make the all-star team almost every year. I found it frustrating that I could not seem to arouse in him the same mania for soccer that he had for skateboarding, surfing or martial arts. Then again, if I wanted him to be exactly like me, I wouldn't have raised him in California. I pushed him a little harder than the other boys because he was my son but also because I saw myself in him and wanted him to feel his heart sing, too.

But there were a few moments when he did. Moments when he seemed to leave the ground while dribbling the ball down the field, when the ball went exactly where he wanted it to go, or when the crowd roared after he scored a goal. It was in these golden flashes that I knew he had discovered the magic, too. I could see it in his eyes. That's all there ever really is when anything ends, after all. A game, a love affair, a good day, or life itself. A few magic moments.

Me at 16 with the soccer team for my first employer,
Richardson Sons and Owden Irish Linen.
(First row, center)

CHAPTER 29

UNCLE OSSIE AND THE GUTTER SNIPE

"A sibling may be the keeper of one's identity, the only person with the keys to one's unfettered, more fundamental self."
~ Marian Sandmaier

My father had two brothers. One died at sixteen years old. The surviving brother, Ossie, and my father rarely spoke to one another. Decades passed without any contact between them. Something unforgivable had occurred, but I was never told the reason.

One summer when I was about eleven, I was living with my Grandma Reid, Aunt Cissy and Uncle Tommy in the Dundonald countryside when Uncle Ossie came to visit with his wife Jean and his son, Will. He was their only child. Uncle Ossie was afflicted with a pronounced stammer that had also afflicted his son. As a result, his parents were very protective of him, and I suspect he was kept apart from the normal rough and tumble most of us boys enjoyed growing up.

Sensing that Will didn't have much fun in his life, I thought he might enjoy exploring the forest near my Grandma's cottage. Unfortunately, time got away from us and we did not return until several hours later to find my Uncle Ossie pacing up and down in front of my Grandma's cottage, obviously agitated. He grabbed me by the shirt, lifted me to my toes and yelled, "Where the h-h-hell did you g-g-get to, you horrible, little g-g-guttersnipe!" spraying me with spittle all the while.

I didn't much appreciate being called a guttersnipe, though I had no idea what a snipe was and couldn't recall ever seeing one in a gutter.

Shortly after returning to Belfast, I asked my father, "Hey, Da. What's a guttersnipe?"

"What? Why do ya want to know that?" he asked.

"Because Uncle Ossie says I'm one."

"What? He called you that? What for?"

He was getting angrier by the second, and I stammered out the entire story. When I finished, he stood up, threw his handkerchief on the table and yelled, "I'll ring his fockin' neck for 'im!"

He was out the door and halfway down the street toward Ossie's house before my mother could say a word. She ran after him, and they stood arguing in the sidewalk for five minutes or so. Eventually, my mother talked him out of it and he returned home. He didn't say another word for the rest of the day. I was fairly certain at this point that "guttersnipe" was not a complimentary term.

My Uncle Ossie died suddenly of a heart attack a year or so later. We all went to the funeral but my father's complaints about the length of the drive and having to take time off work made me feel like we were going only out of obligation. Wee Will huddled close to his mother, thin and pale, as we stood at the graveside listening to the minister speak. I looked up at my father and was surprised to see a tear in his eye. I thought, "What the hell is he crying about? He didn't even want to come. It's been twenty years since they even talked to each other."

Since he loved his brother enough to cry at his funeral, I wondered why he didn't love him enough to call him and make up with him when he was alive. That kind of stubbornness is typical with the Irish but it's also as common to humanity as the rain that fell on that dismal day.

My father and his brother were not very far apart in age, so I started to wonder if my dad would die young, too. He was barely alive to me emotionally already, but the thought of losing him filled me with horror anyway. The death of his brother also amplified my panic when he would have one of his asthma attacks. This sense of impending doom added to my desperation to impress him somehow. I was not too young to know that death erased any possibility of improvement, but I *was* too young to know that I was not the problem. Thus, I spent my entire childhood holding about as much status with my father as a piece of furniture would, futilely hoping to get a pat on the head or a kind tone and receiving instead only the odd figurative or literal kick up the arse. Ultimately, this was all God's fault for not making foresight anywhere near as clear as hindsight. What we're confused by as children, we pity as adults as time and experience bestow the gifts of understanding, and forgiveness.

CHAPTER 30

UNCLE ALFIE AND THE MAGIC COIN

"When anyone asks me about the Irish character, I say look at the trees. Maimed, stark and misshapen, but ferociously tenacious."
~ Edna O'Brien

One Sunday afternoon I was sitting in my room with nothing to do when I heard a familiar engine rumbling outside. I looked out my window and was overjoyed to see my Uncle Alfie stepping off his motorcycle. Neighborhood kids had abandoned their games and were running over to admire the strange craft and its sidecar. Alfie removed his goggles, looked up at me and said, "Ah, there's my wee Sidney! How are ya, son?"

"Great!" I replied, which was true now that Alfie was there. I flew down the stairs two at a time to see him. Alfie had never come to the house before because of the distance between Coleraine and Belfast but also because of the discord in the family. He opened the gate and headed for the door. I rushed down the stairs to greet him. In my excitement, I forgot about the mess in the house. As usual, I was filled with embarrassment at the thought of anyone seeing inside, particularly him. In my rush to the door, I ran headlong into my mother, who was coming out of the kitchen to investigate all the yelling.

"Where are you rushin' to?" she asked.

"Uncle Alfie's here!" I yelled.

"Ach, the bloody eejit! Why didn't he let us know he was coming? This place is a pig sty!"

"What else is new?" I said.

Before she could respond, I threw open the door, and there was Uncle Alfie in the doorway looking every bit like a World War II flying ace. The neighborhood kids were standing on the sidewalk watching him. Having such an exotic and adventurous-looking relative was definitely making them reevaluate my importance.

He scooped me up and said, "How ya doin', lad? Ach, I've missed ya!"

"I missed you too, Uncle Alfie!" I said.

He set me down and hugged my ma. He looked around and, never one to mince words said, "For God's sake, Elsie! What the hell happened to this house? It looks like a bloody bomb went off in here!"

"Ach, shut yar gub and sit down!" my ma blasted back.

"I would, but I can't find the bloody couch!" he said.

The sibling rivalry was in full swing. It doesn't apply only to children. I laughed, and Alfie winked at me.

"Is that lump over there the couch, or is it that lump over there?" Alfie said.

"I'm gonna give *you* a lump in a minute," my ma replied.

"Ach, away and fix me a cup'o tea, woman. I've got a throat full'o dust from travelin' across hell's half-acre to see ya, and all I get for my troubles is a ration o' shite!"

My ma began to talk back as usual, but Alfie cut her short, "I'm going to sit and have a wee chat with Sidney now, if ya don't mind. I've already heard your gub enough for one day."

She rolled her eyes and went into the kitchen.

As always, Alfie had put me at ease immediately. I was too busy laughing to be embarrassed about the condition of the house.

"Come sit with me on this lump over here, Sidney. I want to hear what you've been up to, and don't leave anything out. Everything from A to Z!"

This was perhaps the main reason I loved my Uncle Alfie so much. He really cared about what was going on in my life, and he listened with rapt interest when I talked to him. This was completely unique in my experience with adults. He made me feel like my life was actually important, eagerly asking about my friends and school and girls and soccer and all the things I wished my da would ask me about. It was Alfie's nature to take an interest in others, but he probably also knew that I wasn't getting much attention from either of my parents. He didn't think much of my father, but he had no delusions about his sister, either, and knew her mothering skills were largely absent.

We talked for a little bit when my ma came in with a tray of tea and biscuits. Before long, they fell into the old rhythm. Alfie spun one tall tale after another as I sat enraptured. My mother would roll her eyes in disbelief and disdain now and then, but it didn't slow Alfie down a bit.

Word must have traveled around the neighborhood of the strange, new visitor to my house because I heard a rap on the door and opened it to find Big Lionel there with a group of kids behind him. He was as poised as ever, but they were all craning and peering around him to get another look at Alfie.

"Hi, Lionel! How are ya?" I said.

"Just fine, thank you! I thought I would stop in for a visit."

I knew this wasn't true because he never came to the door. He always yelled up to my bedroom window. He was dressed in his Sunday best. He had obviously heard about the visitor to the house and had dressed to impress.

"Well, are ya gonna invite me in, eejit?" he asked.

I didn't want him to see the mess inside but couldn't think of an excuse to keep him out, especially with Alfie listening, so I said, "Oh. Sure. Come on in."

Lionel came in and looked into the living room where Alfie was sitting by the fireplace. Before I could introduce them, Lionel strode boldly across the room, hand extended, and tripped over the dirty laundry on the ground. He almost fell but Alfie jumped up and caught him.

"Watch yarself, lad. Walkin' across this room is a journey only for the most adventurous."

My ma yelled "Shut yer gub!" again from the kitchen.

"Uncle Alfie, this is my mate Lionel," I said.

"How ya doin', son?" Alfie said.

Lionel extended his hand and said, "Good afternoon, sir. Lionel's my name!"

"Yes, I heard," Alfie said. "Those are beautiful threads you're wearin'. What's the occasion? Are you gettin' married today, Sidney?"

I started laughing and Lionel, never one to be outdone, calmly said, "I have a function to attend shortly. I was just passing by and thought I'd drop in."

Alfie wasn't one to harangue. He probably knew a 12-year old kid didn't have any "functions" to attend, but he allowed him the victory.

"Well, you're sure to make a splash in that outfit! 'Tis a fine suit, so it is!"

"Thank you very much," Lionel said. "Is that your motorbike out there?"

"Aye, that it is," Alfie said.

"Can I have a ride in your sidecar?"

"Of course you can! No problem a'tall. I'll be leavin' in a few hours, and we can do that."

Lionel's eyes lit up. This was clearly the main reason for his visit. Lionel did his best to attract Alfie's attention, but Alfie looked and spoke mainly to me.

"Did I ever tell you about the time I almost ran over a leprechaun on my motorbike, Sidney?"

"No!" I replied. I couldn't believe he had forgotten to tell a story like that.

"Aye, son, as sure as I'm sittin' here. It was the dead o' winter. I was ridin' through a terrible storm at night and was comin' around a corner when I saw the wee fella standing in the road."

Lionel and I were hypnotized.

"He was dressed all in green just like the storybook pictures and was no more than a foot tall. My headlight blinded him, and he put his hands up. I skidded off the road and crashed my bike into a bramble bush. I don't know how long I was lying there, but when I woke up, there was a gold coin in my pocket. Do you want to see it?"

"Yes!" we both yelled excitedly.

He reached into his pocket and held up a coin between his thumb and forefinger. It shone a brilliant gold, reflecting the fire's glow. He handed it to me. It had strange markings on it and words in a language I had never seen before. I couldn't believe I was holding a coin that had once belonged to a leprechaun; a coin that had been forged in a faerie land.

"Can I see it?" Lionel asked. I handed it to him, and he rolled it over and over in his hands.

"I think the leprechaun gave me the coin for luck," Alfie continued. "I only wish he would have magically removed all the thorns from me arse. I was plucking 'em out for a week!"

We both laughed. Lionel passed the coin back to me. Alfie could see how much I admired it. I was about to give it back to Uncle Alfie when he leaned in and said to me in a low voice, "Would you like to keep it, lad?"

I told him I couldn't take the coin that a leprechaun had given him because it was just too valuable, but he wouldn't take no for an answer.

I still have that coin to this day. I figured out somewhere along the way that it was a coin from ancient Rome, but by then it didn't matter. For my entire childhood, I carried a piece of magic in my pocket, and it was exactly what my Uncle Alfie told me it was.

CHAPTER 31

WEE HYNDSIE

"A friend is someone who knows the song in your heart and can sing it back to you when you have forgotten the words."
~ Anonymous

**John Hyndse with our friend, Harry Hutchison,
who you will meet shortly, circa 1962.**

Of all the friends I made growing up in Belfast, the one I spent the most time with was John Hynds, who we all called Wee Hyndsie. He was given the prefix "wee" because he was a few inches shorter than the rest of us. However, he was very powerfully constructed around the chest and shoulders from a combination of good genes, weightlifting and working on construction sites around the city. He had almost white blonde hair, very blue eyes and a pink complexion. In his youth, he had a somewhat cherubic look about him. For this reason, he may have appeared to be a soft touch to some of the hardcases who ran around Belfast. To their chagrin, however, many of them learned that Hyndsie could pack a wallop and wasn't slow about getting the first dig in. In fact, he was one of the most fearless fighters I've ever seen.

He and I roamed around the city visiting the bars and dance halls in Belfast and later on in England as well. After the dances were over, if we failed to "click" (meet a girl), we would often ride home on the upper deck of the red double-decker buses that were used in Belfast at the time. One of his favorite things to do to pass the time and alarm pedestrians on the sidewalk below was to sit near the window on the upper level of the bus, wrap a handkerchief around his head to give the appearance of a female headscarf, roll up his trousers, and then kick his legs in the air while yelling, "Yes! Yes!" To anyone on the ground, it looked like a woman having it off with someone. The expressions on their faces were priceless. The other bus riders would usually start out being shocked or scared by his antics, but by the end of the ride, they would always be laughing, too.

Another favorite prank of ours while walking around the city was to jabber away to each other in a language completely of our own creation to confound everyone who passed us. Foreigners were a strange sight in Belfast then so we drew a lot of stares and whispered comments. At times, to excite the locals even further, we would pretend to have ferocious arguments and shove each other to accentuate our gibberish. Everyone gave us a wide berth, thinking we were madmen from some exotic, far-flung land.

One Saturday night, we were headed for the Plaza Dance Hall as usual and stopped along the way to have a few pints. Once inside the Plaza, Hyndsie met a girl and disappeared. We had previously agreed not to get in each other's way once one of us connected with a girl. A few minutes later, I saw a large man propelling Hyndsie across the floor by his throat. Hyndsie yelled, "Who the fuck are you?" obviously surprised and none too pleased with the rough handling. I jumped in, grabbed the big guy, and took a swing at him. He snapped at me, "I'm a cop!" I stopped the next punch in mid-swing. At this point "Baldy" appeared; he was the Plaza's primary bouncer and had a reputation for extremely harsh treatment of troublemakers. The cop and Baldy escorted Hyndsie off to the romper room upstairs. We heard anyone taken there received a severe beating. Not wishing to leave Hyndsie to this fate, I told Baldy, "If he comes out bleeding, you're next!" Baldy merely gave me a dirty look and left.

About a half hour later, Hyndsie emerged with a sheepish look on his face. I asked him what had happened in the romper room. He said, "I've been barred for a month!" Being barred meant he could not come to the Plaza, our favorite haunt, and this punishment was considered extreme. I later found out that Hyndsie had ignited a firecracker and thrown it onto the dance floor, potentially causing injury to some of the dancers. His only excuse was he had a few pints in him and was not thinking clearly, a typical rejoinder that did nothing to calm the cop and bouncer.

Our second choice was one of the other dance halls around the city center near the Belfast Cooperative Society, a large grocery market on York Street. Again, Hyndsie found a girl immediately and disappeared. A few minutes later, he came over with a shocked look on his face and said, "I might need your help. Some big twat wants to beat me up."

"Ah, Jasus," I said, "Not again!"

He pointed toward the potential assailant, who was a bona-fide giant with a country boy look, red-face, open-necked shirt and sunburned chest.

Plaza Dance Hall then . . .

and in 1975.

He glared at us with clearly hostile intentions. Always operating under the philosophy that the best defense is a good offense, I sailed across the room at full speed and asked, "Okay, Desperate Dan, what the fuck is your problem?"

His eyes widened and he snapped, "Let's go outside."

Disappointed my show of force had little to no effect, I pressed on.

"Fine, ya big girl," I answered, "I'm gonna boot yer arse right off the fuckin' planet."

I walked toward the exit, hoping he wouldn't follow, breaking the first rule of survival – never turn your back on your opponent. He seized the opportunity to sucker punch me in the back of the head. I stumbled forward and turned around reflexively to return the compliment, but he was nowhere to be found. Hyndsie had seen it and beat me to him with a flying head butt, which was no small feat considering the big country boy was a foot taller than him. I never saw punches flying so fast in my life. He lit the big guy up like a Christmas tree, but before he could do any serious damage, the bouncers appeared from nowhere and grabbed all three of us.

While my arms were pinned behind my back by a bouncer, the country boy took another free shot at my chin. I was able to get out of the way of the sweet spot, but it still nearly knocked me out. Now I was actually mad, not just faking it. However, since no one was really hurt and since the fight was quelled quickly by the bouncers, they decided to let us stay on the promise that we would all behave ourselves. I gave them my word but was still smarting from the two sucker punches and knew that honor had to be restored and vengeance exacted. I wasn't sure I could handle the big country boy. He had fists like anvils and a chin that would make Jay Leno's look petite. But my youthful pride was at stake. I decided a good rap across the temple with a bottle would probably do the trick, but Hyndsie confiscated it and told me to calm down. We all gradually relaxed and had a good time, stopping occasionally to glare at each other warily through swollen eyes.

There are many reasons I would love to return to my youth. My pride and temper are not among them.

CHAPTER 32

LIONEL

"I am not eccentric. It's just that I am more alive than most people. I am an unpopular electric eel set in a pond of goldfish."
~ Dame Edith Sitwell

I've mentioned him a few times, but I would like to introduce you now to my best friend growing up - Lionel Frost, who we all affectionately called Frosty because of his last name. Ours was a competitive friendship, but a happy one. If anyone deserves a chapter of his own, it's Lionel.

Lionel had moved into a house four doors away from mine while I was away at my granny's house in Dundonald, where my parents sent me after the war started. We were about ten or eleven years old at the time. I knew right away that there was something special about him. He just had a way about him; an attitude which set him apart.

Though I was quieter than he was, we were very much alike physically. We were both about the same height, fairly tall for kids by Belfast's standards at that time, with light hair and the same general appearance. We were even put together the same way. People used to think we were brothers. However, when it came to our internal selves, he and I were total opposites.

We spent many fun-filled days rambling over Cave Hill and Black Mountain. One of our favorite games was "Cowboys and Indians." We always argued about who got to be the Indian. We decided that if we had not been Irish, our second choice of nationality would have been Native American, or "Red Indian" as we called them then, a race we admired a great deal for their strength and courage.

I was awed by his ability to talk endlessly about very little. He had the gift of the gab in abundance and used it unsparingly. In fact, he probably had too much energy for his own good. He was always jumping from phase to phase. He would be interested in something for two or three months, then he would become distracted by something else and turn all his attention to that. His hobbies were constantly changing. He decided once to become a demon bowler on our cricket team. That lasted about a month. (The term "demon" was used to describe a cricketer who bowled so fast, he terrified the batsmen.) Then he decided he wanted to be a soccer player. That one lasted about three weeks. Then he got involved in weightlifting. He stuck with that for a year or two and built himself up quite well but eventually moved on to some other activity.

We were all pretty good about going to school but Lionel constantly mitched. ("Ditched" in America.) We might have ducked out half a day early once in a while, but he took off for days at a time, climbing high into the mountains to lie in the grass and commune with nature. He would hide his schoolbag in the woods somewhere and frolic around for hours. While walking through the orchard at the top of the street, I would often see his bag, jacket and books under bushes and think, "Oh, there's Lionel's stuff. He must be mitching again."

His mother had remarried a tired, little man who worked as a drover, someone who drives a horse and cart and brings goods to the docks. Lionel used to say his real father was a captain in the regiment of the North Irish Horse* and that he himself was a bastard. Most people would be hesitant to label themselves in such a way but he said it with great pride.

"By the way," he said to me, "Did you know that I am a bastard?"

He added, however, that he was a blue-blood *because* he was a bastard. He told this story repeatedly with great aplomb and without the slightest sense of shame. After a while, he had me wishing I could be a bastard, too.

His mother was a woman of mystery. She looked a bit like Lauren Bacall, not very pretty in the classical sense but with the same sultry air and a kind of faded beauty. She was long and lean like Lionel, and she smoked incessantly. I fancied her a wee bit even though she was Lionel's mother. Actually, it was this forbidden aspect that made her even more enticing to my feverish adolescent mind.

Lionel's grandfather also lived with him. He was a somewhat uncouth man who had the revolting habit of removing his dentures after a meal and licking them clean, no matter who was present. This resulted in my studiously avoiding Lionel's house at meal time. To add to his charm, the grandfather would also break wind frequently. And great, foul gusts they were. Their dog, a mongrel of dubious heritage, would always be blamed. After each blast, Lionel's grandfather would always kick the poor creature up the arse and yell, "Go on, ya dirty brute ye!" In true Pavlovian fashion, the dog eventually got wise and immediately darted out of the room the instant he heard the old man break wind, leaving him to kick at thin air. Though this ritual made the dog a nervous wreck, the old man laughed uproariously every time and never seemed to tire of the joke.

Lionel and I had kind of a love-hate relationship. We wrestled and sparred constantly. We even had a few good punch-ups. We never intended to do any serious harm to each other, though. It was just the everyday roughhousing that all boys do.

One day, he said to me, "You can give it and take it. I can give it, but I can't take it."

I admired this candor. In Belfast, it was uncommon for a man of any age to admit to weakness, but Frosty made admissions like this without shame. At first, I thought he was just being modest, but I gradually found out it was true. He had no tolerance when it came to pain. One tap on the nose and he was finished.

Lionel and I were on the way home from the Park Picture House having just seen *The Sea Hawk* starring Errol Flynn, when Lionel asked me, "Did you ever hear tell of Captain Black?"

Given the context, I naturally assumed he was referring to some famous sea captain.

"Was he a buccaneer?" I asked.

"No, eejit!" Lionel said. Never one to pass up a play on words, he continued, "He's a buckin' IRA man and he's gathering up an army in the Irish Free State. He says he's going to march up to Ulster and drive all of us Protestants into the Irish Sea!"

Then, having delivered this somewhat shattering news, Lionel paused to see my reaction. Given his reputation for gilding the lily, I decided not to become immediately alarmed. After all, just a short time earlier, he had told all of us that he had seen a gnome with his own two eyes sitting on the fireplace hearth in his living room, and that his grandfather had seen it as well! We all agreed that he probably had been dipping into his stepfather's Guinness supply. His grandfather was hardly a better witness than Lionel. Anyone who would lick the left-overs from his dentures after a meal was disqualified as a credible source of information.

The whole neighborhood was always wondering what Lionel would be up to next. There was always something new and exciting happening to him. Half the city either knew him or had heard of him, and his outlandish adventures were the talk of the town.

One day, he was mitching from school as usual and his mother got wind of it. Neither his mother nor his stepfather could control him. In desperation, she telephoned her brother to intercede. He found Lionel goofing off somewhere, grabbed him by the ear, and walked him about a half a mile to school, tugging his ear every step of the way. Lionel's ear was the size of a bap (a loaf of bread) by the time he got there. His attendance record improved slightly following that incident, but in time he returned to his usual ways.

We were sort of an Irish version of Tom Sawyer and Huck Finn. Like Huck, Lionel was committed to a life of constant exploration and was completely beyond the control of the adults in his life. Like Tom, I had the same wile instincts but struggled to be a good boy, which wasn't easy with Lionel calling at my window at all hours of the day and night, urging me to come out and join him in some new adventure.

In those days, bodybuilding was not a recognized sport, but there were a lot of health gurus who touted chest expansion exercises and deep-breathing as a means of increasing one's musculature. Lionel must have bought into one of these courses because at about fifteen, he became a fresh-air fiend and a good posture fanatic. His enthusiasm for fresh air may also have been a result of watching his stepfather suffer from consumption for years. Though he wasn't close to him, I'm sure the idea of acquiring the same affliction didn't appeal to him. Lionel would walk up the street throwing his shoulders back to the point of contortion, sucking in air and holding it for incredibly long periods of time. He looked like a lovesick bullfrog. I think he felt it made him look impressive, but it was actually quite a bizarre spectacle to witness. He told me he had read that some British soldier could hold a sixpence, which is about the size of a dime, between his shoulder blades, so he persisted with that until he could do the same thing. I would often see him walking up the street with his back not only straight but arched backward, his nostrils flaring, sucking in air and holding his breath. Anyone who didn't know him would have thought he was a lunatic.

I didn't mind the chest expansion exercises when we were hiking or walking alone, but it was very embarrassing in public, particularly when we were trying to score points with girls. We were chatting up a couple of girls one day and just starting to make some headway when he suddenly started inhaling deeply and holding his breath for extraordinary periods of time. I continued to talk to the girls, hoping to keep them from looking at him. His face turned brick red. Finally he became impossible to ignore and everyone stopped talking, wondering if he was going to explode. This display scared the prospects away, who probably feared for their physical safety. He did this in the presence of girls several more times, and I chastised him every time, but it never had any effect. To his credit, he did manage to develop an enormous chest after a year or so of his chest expansion exercises, which started me doing them. However, I had the sanity to do them in the privacy of my bedroom.

One day, I went to Lionel's house and was told by his mother that he was out somewhere. I figured he was up at the orchard replenishing his fresh air supply. Sure enough, I found him there but with a pencil and notebook in hand, gazing into the heavens. Every so often, he would stop and make notes. After watching him for a while, I asked him what he was doing.

"Why, bird-watching, of course," he said.

He then spotted some rare species and darted off into the gooseberry bushes to continue his research. He kept this up for about two weeks, spending all his free time after school in the orchard until he had filled several notebooks with drawings and notes documenting his discoveries. After his sojourn into the world of bird-watching, he launched himself into long-distance running.

Finally, Lionel reached the age, as I did, when girls became his obsession. Class distinction in the world of dating was very prevalent in Belfast at this time. There was little or no mixing of the classes; everyone knew their place in society. Working class boys went out with working class girls. White collar workers went out with white collar girls in their professions. Even the way they spoke differed. Working class Belfast people spoke with a distinct "low class" dialect. The upper crust sought a more anglicized speech. The middle and upper classes found love at rugby club dances. The working class confined themselves to the Plaza Dance Hall in central Belfast.

All of us considered the best pickings among the girls to be the upper-class secretaries and other office workers. The wee girls who worked in the mills were good in a pinch, but everyone aspired to attain one of the more cultured types who worked in the downtown offices. However, we all felt like there was a world between us and them, that they were untouchable and would never lower themselves to talk to us much less date us. Lionel, however, set no such limits upon himself with respect to female conquests. Although just a laborer in the Belfast shipyard, he dressed like a college student when he went out on the hunt. While we squandered our meager pay on fleeting pleasures, Lionel bought nice clothes so he could dress like a professional person in his free time. The problem was he had to take the bus home at nighttime with the rest of us while he was still wearing his coveralls, and his face and hands were black with soot. Once home, Lionel cleaned himself up, put on his best suit, and went to the upper crust clubs where he introduced himself to girls as a student of law or a medical doctor in training. He was smart enough and looked good enough to pull it off.

There were even social divisions at the lowest levels. People who worked in offices or semi-professional jobs like secretaries or even just office filing clerks were at a higher level than the guys who worked with their hands and got dirty. So when Lionel went out dancing, he played the part of the professional rather than admitting to being part of the working class. The problem was, in a small town, one can't expect to perpetuate such deception indefinitely without being discovered by someone. Never one to do anything by halves, Lionel became an insatiable womanizer and maintained a bevy of admirers from one side of the city to the other, even as far away as Bangor.

He was coming home from work in his coveralls one day when he saw a girl he was going around with standing with a bunch of her friends at the bus stop in front of the City Hall. He had led this girl to believe he was a wealthy medical student. She looked over and saw Lionel with his dirty overalls, his face and hands black and sooty. She was absolutely astonished because she had seen him just the night before in his hacking jacket, twill pants, ox blood shoes, crisp white dress shirt and yellow tie with horse's heads on it.
The girl yelled over. Lionel turned away, hoping she would assume it wasn't him but she persisted.
"Lionel! Lionel Frost!"
He rolled his eyes and turned around.
"Your face is all dirty!" she said, as if he didn't know.
Most men would have been mortified at being found out, but Lionel didn't bat an eyelash. Knowing all was lost, he casually replied, "Just like your reputation, my love."0
The girl and all her friends were rendered speechless, and the crowd laughed uproariously. The poor girl had no idea she was dealing with a budding con artist.

Lionel's next job was as a driver's assistant moving furniture for a department store. I often saw the truck speeding around the city with Lionel sticking his head out of the window as far as he could, nostrils flaring, sucking in fresh air. It was quite a sight and gave me a laugh every time.

The driver of the truck was a real tough guy. He and Lionel were getting on the bus one day together. The driver was running up the stairs of the bus with Lionel behind him, yapping away about something. The driver got tired of listening to him and said, "Ah, shut the fuck up!" For added emphasis, he took a wad of chewing gum out of his mouth and stuck it in Lionel's hair. Poor Lionel had to go home that night and cut half his hair off to get it out. However, he didn't bother cutting the other side of his head to match, so he ran around for a month looking like a nutter.

The first thing my mates and I always asked when we ran into each other was, "What's Lionel been up to lately?" and we were never disappointed. Every day, there was a new story about him circulating around town. Even the grown-ups would ask us about him.

I was always amazed at the quickness of his wit. He never really thought about what he was doing or saying. He operated completely out of blind instinct. Whatever he thought about, he did it. Whatever he wanted to say, he said it. While I felt clumsy and awkward around girls, Lionel had a great line of chat with them.

We were all trying desperately to get laid, or "break the duck" as we called it then, but it was a nearly impossible task because Belfast girls at that time held on to their chastity as long as possible. In those days, both the boys and girls usually lived at home with their parents until they married. We were all about sixteen and seventeen, and none of us had unraveled the mystery yet. To make matters worse, even if one of us did find a willing female by some miracle, our living situations barred any thought of a comfortable rendezvous.

Naturally, Lionel was the first one to shed his cumbersome virginity. There was a wee girl who lived in our neighborhood called Sonia. She was quite attractive, but she seemed to have a screw loose. Her mother did, too. They weren't clinically insane; just lacking a little upstairs. In contrast, the father was perfectly normal. I often wondered what went on in their house and how he dealt with these two demented women. Lionel got pissed drunk one night and went to Sonia's house. When he woke up the next morning, he was lying in bed with Sonia and her ma! When he told us all this story later, he said, "I was screwing somebody during the night, but I couldn't figure out which one it was."

A sordid experience like that was so far removed from our day to day experience that we were all completely flabbergasted. Lionel ended his tale with, "I'm not only the first to break the duck; I'm also the first to do the daily double." Conceding defeat, I said, "You're the first one to do everything."

One day, Lionel, Hyndsie and I were chatting up three girls we met on the Antrim Road where all the young people walked on Sunday nights. There was always the chance of meeting some girl and having a wee court (make-out session) in a doorway. It was a good, cheap night out. One of the girls was very tall and kind of eerie-looking. To make matters worse, she was very quiet and glared at us while we were talking. Lionel was in the middle of one of his tall tales, lying his head off as usual, when I noticed her staring at him hypnotically. She was captivated by him, totally engrossed.

I said, "Hey, Lionel, you better watch out. Dracula's daughter has her eye on you." The next thing I knew, she turned and hit me a big crack up the mouth with her handbag. She busted both of my lips wide open. I was bleeding all over myself. I tried to pass it off like it was nothing, but I was in searing pain. No one had ever busted my upper and lower lips simultaneously before, not even in a fistfight.

I asked, "What have you got in your purse, a bloody brick or something?"

As if the blow up the lips wasn't enough, she then proceeded to call me every name in the book until I was finally forced to flee and seek safer environs. Hyndsie and Lionel came with me, probably fearing that they might be next.

One afternoon, Lionel and I were walking down the Antrim Road, flirting with some girls on the other side of the street. All along the sidewalk in those days, there were little phone booths with metal posts about five feet high. I think they were used by police to make emergency calls because they didn't have walkie-talkies then. The phones were housed in a square, metal box with very sharp edges right at face level. It was incredibly stupid to plant them right in the middle of a sidewalk. People who weren't being observant enough often walked right into them. But nobody sued anyone for anything back then, let alone the city itself. Lionel and I were walking along, yelling a conversation back and forth with a few girls across the street when I walked face first into the metal post. It made a very loud "doiiiiiiiiiinnnnnnnng" sound and a big knot shot up on my forehead almost instantly. I almost knocked myself out. The pain was incredible. Thankfully, the girls didn't notice or were too polite to let on if they had. Big Lionel, on the other hand, laughed himself sick.

Another time, we were standing at the bus stop waiting for the bus to go home when Big Lionel spotted a very attractive girl. When the bus came, she headed for the downstairs deck of the bus. We normally sat upstairs where we could see around us. Big Lionel whispered to me, "I'm gonna go chat her up." With his usual complete lack of hesitation, he shot down to the lower deck, sat beside her, and started talking away to her. About two stops later, he came back up the stairs again.

"What happened?" I asked. "Did she tell you to shove off?"

He said, "Well, she wasn't very receptive."

We got to Cliftonville Circus, an intersection close to where Lionel and I lived, and the girl got off. Knowing that Lionel wasn't easily put off, I pressed him to tell me what the girl had said to him, or what he had said to her. He said he had asked her where she lived and she told him, "I live in that house over there with the monkey puzzle tree."

There were quite a few monkey puzzle trees around Belfast. The common name for it is a Chilean Pine. It's called a monkey puzzle tree because the trunk and branches are covered with thorns that make it impossible for a monkey to climb it.

Lionel had to struggle to get the words out of her and she rarely looked at him, obviously not interested, so before he left her alone, he asked, "Well, have you figured out how to climb that tree, or are you still puzzled by it?" He said she was so mad, red traveled up her face like mercury in a thermometer and he thought steam was going to come out of her ears.

Lionel always had something colorful to say, and he never seemed to have to think about it. It just flowed. When I first introduced Rosaleen (my future wife) to him at the Belfast Plaza dance hall, I said, "This is Rosaleen, the girl I told you about." He knew that I had met her at work, at the linen manufacturing company. The first words out of his mouth were, "Ah, love amongst the linen threads!"

Lionel had a very special ability. A talent, if you will. There's no delicate way to say it. Lionel could fart. Perhaps it was all that air-swallowing he did to expand his chest. Whatever the reason, he applied the same passion and enthusiasm to farting as he did to his other interests. This was different, however, because it was the one interest which outlasted all the others; an abiding gift which he never tired of sharing with others. It was truly the gift that kept on giving. If farting was an art, Lionel would have been Michelangelo.

Bodily functions have long been a cornerstone of British humor. Most Americans are ashamed of and embarrassed by noises the body emits, but the British rejoice in them. They regale themselves in them and celebrate them. My mates and I were no different, but Lionel was the champ. He used to drop horrible, ghastly bombs. Often, to add a little more drama, he would crank his leg like he was winding it up, then let it go a little with each crank, and they were always rancid. It wasn't so much the smell but the burning of our eyes.

Our friend Hutchy would always say, "Ah, for God's sake, Frosty, that's disgustin'. Something must have crawled up your hole and died. That's bloody awful."

Lionel's usual answer was, "Jealousy will get you nowhere, my good man."

If he persisted in his criticisms, Lionel would shame him further by saying, "That's just envy talking. You see, that's not one of your pale, imitation farts; your bread and HP sauce farts like the kind you let. God knows what your ma's feeding ya. That's a good, old-fashioned meat and potatoes fart with a little dash of turnip thrown in."

Sometimes he would talk to his arse before a fart, saying, "Speak, oh toothless one!" or "Speak, oh chocolate lips that never told a lie." He would also sometimes talk to his arse after a fart with comments like, "Ahh, good ol' arse, I thought you were dead!"

When we got old enough to drink, a typical Saturday night was spent downing a few pints at Mooney's Pub at Corn Market. Mooney's was always full of life and bustling with characters. Professional fighters and hard cases, upper and lower class, straights, gays, old, young - everybody went to Mooney's. Mooney's served big meat pies, onions, and delicious pickles. We'd all have a pie and an onion and a few pints of Guinness then go round to the Plaza to meet a few girls, hoping to get lucky. Our usual pub-crawling group was Lionel, Harry Hutchison (nicknamed "Hutchy"), John Hynds (Hyndsie) and me. Lionel was the complete opposite of Hutchy, who was quiet and somewhat shy. This difference between them eventually erupted into arguments.

Me and Harry "Hutchy" Hutchison (right and far right)

There was nothing to do on Sundays because all the Protestant-owned or operated businesses in Belfast were closed. A few Catholic-owned businesses stayed open, but since the Protestants ran almost everything, the town came to a standstill. The city fathers took great pains to ensure that none of us had anything resembling a good time. All the picture houses, dance halls, markets, and especially the pubs were black. The Protestant church actually tied up the swings in the public parks in case some rebel tried to slip in a little fun when nobody was looking. There was even a story about a Protestant lady up the Shankill Road who took her faith so seriously, she tied up the little swing in the canary's cage so it couldn't entertain itself. Of course, it was a Protestant canary. With Belfast being rendered a ghost town every Sunday, we were forced to sneak into Catholic neighborhoods to find some fun. There was a subconscious taboo pleasure in our adventures into forbidden territory because we felt like we were sinning and that all the Catholics were sinning, too.

On Sunday nights, we usually ended up looking for girls at the Methodist church. Lionel was Presbyterian and I was Church of Ireland, but we both preferred to attend the local Methodist church because of the minister there, Reverend Redman. He was our Father Flanigan, a man who was good through and through and really knew how to talk to young people without sounding pushy or condescending. He also had a great sense of humor and never seemed to mind too much when we all sat in the front row and tried to drown out the choir. I suppose he figured it was better than us not coming to church at all.

Lionel would always arrive late. Reverend Redman would be delivering his opening comments when the back door would open and Lionel would come ambling into the church smiling at all the ladies. Mister Cool.

Reverend Redman would pause and say, "Oh, welcome, Lionel. Thanks for showing up. Is it okay if I resume now?"

With a dismissive wave of his hand, Lionel would glibly reply, "Carry on, Reverend. Carry on."

One day, in the middle of Reverend Redman's sermon, an unholy stench permeated half the church. We all knew damn well it was Lionel because the odor he could produce was legendary and unmistakably unique, kind of his own brand, and because we saw him leaning over onto one hip cranking it out just moments before. Everyone turned around and looked at each other, but Lionel never lost composure. He sat with an enraptured expression, intently listening to the Minister's sermon. No one said anything. They all just looked at each other with the same mortified looks on their faces. Apparently forgetting she was in a church, a woman whispered, "In the name 'a Jasus, what's that?" Everyone in the church looked at us, trying to discern who the culprit was. Hutchy's face reddened, inadvertently making himself the prime suspect. Though he was completely innocent, everyone was absolutely sure he must have done it and they all gave him glares of disgust and disapproval. His face turned so red, I thought a vain was going to pop out and spray blood all over us.

Hutchy had tolerated Lionel until this point, but that day, having been ostracized by an entire congregation, he'd finally had enough. Bad blood had been brewing for some time. After we left the church, they got into an argument. Full of false bravado, Hutchy challenged him.

"Suit yourself," Lionel said. "Just name the time and place and I'll be there." As usual, Lionel was all show.

"Next Sunday morning then!" Hutchy said. "Ten o'clock. The big field. See ya there!"

It was very dramatic, like the showdown at the O.K. Corral. Part of us wanted to stop them because we didn't want to see either of them get beat up, and part of us was happy that we had a big fight to look forward to.

On the day of reckoning, we all went up to the big field. Hutchy showed up in a pair of worn-out jeans and an old, ripped t-shirt. He hadn't shaved for three days and looked like a wild man. Lionel, on the other hand, showed up dressed to the nines in his usual outfit - hacking jacket, beautiful creased slacks, a white shirt, and the ever-present yellow tie with horse head pattern. I've never seen anyone so well-dressed for a fight in my life.

With perfect nonchalance, he said to Harry, "Well, I see you're ready for the fray."

"Ya bet yur arse I am!" Hutchy answered, swinging at the cold morning air. "Get yur coat off, or I'll bate it off ya!"

He was apparently hoping to avoid the fight by wearing his good clothes, but when he got there, twenty or so of us were standing around waiting to watch the brawl, and he realized he wasn't going to get off so easy. He took his jacket off, folded it, set it down neatly to one side and squared up with Hutchy like an old time fighter. Without a moment's hesitation, Harry just walked in and stuck one right on his chin. Lionel went down like a sack of potatoes. I picked him up. His eyes were rolling around in his head. I shook him until his eyes cleared and reluctantly threw him back into the circle. He made a couple of ineffectual jabs. Harry threw another hook, again connecting squarely with Lionel's chin. Down he went again. This continued for about five minutes. Lionel never laid a hand on Hutchy and was up and down about twenty times. We kept picking him up and throwing him back. The peculiar thing about it, though, was that he would never allow his good slacks to touch the turf when he fell. Even half-conscious and taking a severe thrashing, he was concerned about the condition of his clothes. I kept thinking poor Lionel was probably the first man ever to be beaten up for farting in church.

Finally, Hyndsie said, "I think he's had enough."

I said, "Aye, right enough. I think he's learned his lesson."

Lionel kept struggling valiantly to his feet, but I finally turned him away from Hutchy and said, "Okay, the fight's over."

With that, Lionel brushed himself off, put on his jacket, walked over to Hutchy, composed himself and said, "Well, the best man won. Congratulations."

Then he walked away, completely undismayed, no tail between the legs. Hutchy stood with his hands on his hips watching him, confused. Lionel's jaw must have been hurting because he took some tremendous thumps, but nothing seemed to bother him at all, not even a thorough thrashing in front of all his closest friends. Like everything else, he took it all in stride. He was as cool as cool gets. Lionel may have been beat, but he would not grovel or show any shame or embarrassment. This gracious acceptance of defeat robbed Hutchy of his feeling of victory. Again, Lionel got the last word. There was no way to win with him.

Lionel went to the pictures once and saw an actor with a shaved head playing some kind of an assassin. He decided he would try it. (Shaving his head, that is, not being an assassin, though that wouldn't have surprised me, either.) A lot of us were getting crew cuts, which were very popular then. It was a style that came over from America, and we all loved everything American. But Lionel decided to save the money and shave his own head. He was shaving a way up one side of his head when he suddenly changed his mind. He showed up the next day with one side shaved and one side regular length. This time, however, it was a perfect half and half, long hair on one side, bald as a jaybird on the other.

We said, "Fer fuck's sake, Frosty, did ye get gum stuck in your hair again?"

"No," he said, "I was gonna shave my head but I changed my mind."

I said, "Jasus, Lionel, you look like an idiot!"

He said, "Ah, it'll grow back. Don't worry about it." As usual, he didn't care at all about what anyone thought.

Lionel Frost, John Hynds and Harry Rankin

As you may have noticed by now, something that could not be added to a list of Lionel's finer qualities was his treatment of women. I suppose his good looks spoiled him and made him unappreciative. The prime example of this was when he decided he no longer wanted to see a girl he had been dating for about six months. He just went off her all of a sudden the same way he had gone off becoming a demon bowler or weightlifter. I asked if he was intending to break up with her. He said, "She'll find out how I feel about her the next time she has a shite."

Confused, I asked what he meant. He told me he couldn't bring himself to tell her how he felt face-to-face so he wrote her a goodbye note on toilet paper in the bathroom of her flat. I couldn't believe my ears. I was not one to preach about manners but that was just too much.

"You wrote her a goodbye note on toilet paper?" I said. "That's bloody awful."

"Hey, now just hold on a minute," he argued. "It was top quality toilet paper. Two ply!"

I looked at him like I was sniffing a turd.

"What difference does it make?" he said. "She was gonna find out one way or another."

I just shook my head. There was no point in arguing. In some ways, Lionel was just oblivious.

When Lionel got a bit older, the inevitable happened. He got a girl pregnant. He announced proudly to us that he was going to be a father and would stand by the girl and marry her, which he did, but he couldn't stand the baby screaming and keeping him up at night, so he went back home to live with his mother for about six or eight months until the baby had gotten past the colicky stage. He lived with the girl until another baby arrived, then took off again to let her raise the infant alone while he slept peacefully at his ma's. This pattern repeated three times with Lionel staying away longer each time. Finally, the girl got wise and dumped him.

Lionel later decided he wanted to go to England, probably to get even further away from any fun-squelching obligations. He had mentioned wanting to move there many times before he got married but at that time going to England was a big step. I would make the journey later, but at this point it was too much of a separation from the known for me to consider it. But Lionel's tickets were bought and his mind was made up, so we all took him down to the bar and had a few drinks.

I figured the trip had been well-planned and he had been saving for a long time, but during his send-off, taking advantage of my overflowing emotions, he tapped me for a quid. As usual, he was going to England without a penny or a plan, just winging it like everything else he did. He promised to pay me back as soon as he found work. We solemnly shook hands at the gangplank, overcome by Guinness and melancholy, and bade farewell for what we thought might be the last time we would ever see each other. He got on the boat and we all said, "Ach, big Lionel's gone. We'll never see him again." It was very dramatic and poignant. It was like he died.

This send-off was on a Tuesday night. Two nights later, I was standing at the window having a shave in my bathroom, which overlooked the street below. The window was always open because I liked to keep an eye on the neighborhood and the girls passing by on the sidewalk. But more importantly, a girl named Shirley who lived across the street would sometimes do a strip tease for my benefit, knowing I was watching her. She was only about sixteen but very well put together, and she knew I would be having a scrape about this time every other evening. Anyway, I was lathering away when I saw someone marching up the street who looked remarkably like Lionel. I thought it was a mirage. As the figure drew closer, sure enough it was Big Lionel, all dressed up, heading out on some cavort.

I yelled, "Lionel! What the hell? You're not here! You're in England!"

He just shrugged his shoulders and said, "Ah, I didn't like it."

I said, "Whaddya mean ya didn't like it? You only left Tuesday. You didn't give it a chance, eejit!"

"Nah. I saw enough. Didn't like it."

So he went over Tuesday night, came back Wednesday night, and Thursday night he was back to his old tricks.

I demanded that he stop and tell me what went wrong, but he only smiled and said, "I'll tell ya about it later. I've got a date with a 'good thing' (a girl who dispenses favors freely) at the Plaza." And off he sauntered, shoulder blades meeting, nostrils flaring, dispensing the soot of England from his lungs and replacing it with the good, damp County Antrim air.

A few months later, he decided he wanted to go to America. He had some relatives or friends in Rockaway Beach, New York, so off he went again. This time we all thought, "Well, he definitely won't be coming back tomorrow night this time because he's traveling three thousand miles away. We won't see him for a long, long time."

As it turned out, he was only there about a week when he started saving up to come back to Belfast. He couldn't stand the States, either. But this time it took him about six months to pay his way home. We all eagerly awaited his return until finally we heard he would be arriving the next day. Everyone in the neighborhood, young and old, waited with gleeful anticipation for his triumphant return and the latest word on his exploits. There was a noticeable stir throughout the street when news reached us that he had boarded a taxi at the airport and was on his way.

We had all missed him the past six months, and life had been considerably duller without him. With mounting excitement, the old ladies gathered around their front gates clucking with each other in speculation about how he might look and what he might have done in America. He was supposed to arrive around four o'clock that day. Finally, the taxi came around the corner with Lionel hanging out the window, magnificently tanned, waving a wide-brim cowboy hat like Gene Autry and yelling with a brazenly phony western accent, "I'm back, folks! God dammit, I'm back!"

We thought we were prepared for anything.

We were wrong.

"Ah, Jesus," I said. "Would ya look at him."

When he got out of the taxi, he paid the driver from a wad of American bills. He was wearing a two-tone, very American-style jacket which immediately became the envy of us all. As he came closer, I saw that he had a big ring on his finger with a gaudy, oversized, purple stone. It looked very expensive but I later learned he had acquired it in a box of frosted flakes. He swaggered around like one of the movie cowboys we had all grown up watching at the matinees.

Despite the rather obvious airs he was putting on, we all went out for a few drinks, excited to hear about his adventures in America. The American accent persisted for about two weeks, as did his wearing of the cowboy hat. I think he slept with it on. During this time, he succeeded in embarrassing us terribly everywhere we went. Suntans were a rarity in Belfast, so he was quite a sight. In six months, he had become a different creature entirely and no longer blended in. A green space alien couldn't have attracted more attention. Finally, we all decided we couldn't put up with the accent anymore. We were out having a pint when I interrupted him mid-sentence.

"Lionel, either the accent goes or you do. We can't take it anymore."

He dropped it just like that and returned to normal. I guess even he knew he was overdoing it.

I asked him one day why he left New York. It seemed so much more exciting than Belfast. He answered, "Because this is the best place in the world. New York is bloody awful."

I later learned that he had gotten himself into a little trouble at Jones Beach in New York for picking up and necking with a black girl he had met there. Some of the locals were not quite ready for such a public display of interracial relations and had told him so in no uncertain terms. I asked him how he handled it. He said, "I told 'em to fuck off. What do you think I did?"

Something was simultaneously lacking and appealing about Lionel. He was always good for a laugh, always outspoken and outlandish. It's a shame that his mental energy wasn't nurtured by the Belfast school system, or that his parents couldn't afford to send him to some institute of higher learning where his energies could have been channeled positively. In a more inspiring environment, he might have become a Renaissance man of some kind. Then again, he might have later on. I'll never know because Lionel and I lost touch with each other over the years. The last rumor I heard about him was that he had been arrested for passing bad checks and had moved to the Channel Islands where he married a rich lady and was running a whorehouse. While I have no proof this was true, with Lionel, anything was possible.

- The **North Irish Horse** is a yeomanry unit of the British Territorial Army raised in the northern counties of Ireland in the aftermath of the Second Boer War. Raised and patronized by the nobility from their inception to the present day, they were the first non-regular unit to be deployed to France and the Low Counties with the British Expeditionary Force in 1914 and fought with distinction both as mounted troops and later as a Cyclist Regiment, achieving 18 battle honors. They were reduced to a single man in the inter war years and re-raised for World War 2 where they achieved their greatest distinctions in the North African and Italian campaigns. Reduced again after the Cold War, the regiment is now at squadron strength and forms part of the Queen's Own Yeomanry. (Wikipedia)

CHAPTER 33

THE GRAND DISILLUSION

"Disappointment is the nurse of wisdom."
~ Bayle Roche

I think every child believes that his parents are somehow special. Despite the gloomy picture I have drawn so far, that was how I felt about my parents as a child. It was not until I reached my teens that I came to the conclusion that they were not only not special, but that they were vastly inferior in many ways. Not having any other experience to draw upon, I had always assumed the conditions in my house were normal. However, just as I had realized our house was not as nice as some of my friend's homes were, once I had met enough of my friends' parents and saw how well they got along, I began to realize that mine did not measure up as a couple or as individuals in many ways, either. The moment of this realization was so devastating to me that I cried for a full day, and it took me months afterward to adjust to this new perception of them.

Every now and then, I would run across a house that was in even worse shape than ours or couples who always seemed to be on the verge of killing each other, and I counted my blessings. However, the fact that other people were worse off didn't give me any real consolation. I've never been one for backward blessings. The void still existed, and the longings were still unfulfilled.

In my teen years, I started thinking about how I was going to leave home and get away from my parents to salvage what was left of my spirit. I stopped trying to share my life with either of them and stopped caring very much if they were interested. The house became nothing more than a launching pad for my adventures and a place to sleep and eat. I had a grand time exploring the world around me and enjoying romance and friendship without their involvement. I wished then and still wish today that it could have been different, but it wasn't so I made the most of things.

While I experienced the dynamic emotions and changes inherent to adolescence, my parents remained predictably, irrevocably changeless. Their problems together never worsened or improved. Instead, a benign tolerance settled into their relationship as the demons of youth aged along with them. My own demons, however, were tugging me in every direction at once. Strangely, I didn't feel any animosity toward my parents, only sorrow for the incurable differences between them and frustration with my complete inability to do anything to help. Perhaps I was giving them too much credit. Perhaps they deserved to be hated, but I just couldn't do it. In fact, their inability to show love for me only endeared them to me more. I felt no resentment toward them because

I knew, after I had truly realized the depth of their suffering, that they couldn't help being the way they were.

One night, when I was about thirteen years old, I was lying in my bed reading when my parents starting arguing in the kitchen downstairs. Usually, their arguments only lasted a few minutes, but this one lasted longer than usual. I couldn't sleep over the racket so I stood at the top of the stairs and listened. I kept hearing a word I wasn't familiar with – miscarriage. Whatever it was, my mother kept reminding my father that she'd had two of them before Olga was born. The next day, I asked my friends around the neighborhood if they knew what that word meant, but no one did. There was an older boy down the street trimming a hedge. He had always been friendly to me so I walked over and asked him.

"A miscarriage is when a lady loses a baby that hasn't been born yet," he said.

"How does that happen?" I asked. In my youthful naiveté, I thought he meant the baby was misplaced.

"Sometimes things just go wrong, and the baby dies inside the mommy," he said.

The horror of this knowledge made me feel like ice water had just been injected into my heart.

I said, "oh . . . thanks" and walked away feeling numb and sorry that I had asked. Still, it took years for me to realize how hard this must have been for my mother, and it was this that I most often thought of when she was harsh with me. My father, too, for they were his babies as well. I wondered what other wounds there were in my parents' hearts that I knew nothing of.

Because of this, the tears I cried on the day of my later epiphany about my parents were mixed with equal parts pain and sympathy. Though I was devastated to realize they weren't the all-knowing and perfect beings I had always imagined them to be, this same knowledge only made me love them more. I also cried for myself, for through the mire of all these tangled emotions, one feeling emerged - that I was alone. It was abundantly clear that I couldn't depend on them for anything. This acceptance of reality was as difficult as it was liberating because it hardened me in a place and time when I needed to be hard.

Freud defined "neurotic" as a clinging to adolescent mental postures when life is demanding us to abandon them in order to move to a more mature plain of existence. In that light, the independence and inner strength fired from that first grand disillusionment were my salvation, and my doorway to adulthood.

CHAPTER 34

HERBIE HANSEN, PART 1

"I was a little afraid of him; not the boy himself, but of what he seemed to be: the victim of the world."
~ William Saroyan

In a neighborhood near mine called silverstream, there was a kid named Herbie Hansen. All through our school years, Herbie was the kind of kid one could easily overlook. As young boys, there was a lot of skirmishing and testing of each other, pushing and shoving, and occasionally a bona-fide punch up. A typical conversation between two competing boys might go something like this:

"See you? See me? See your da? See my da? My da can whip your da."
"Who are you kiddin'? Your da's a big puddin', so he is!"
"Right, that does it. You just name the time and place, ya buck eejit ya!"
"How about right now and right here, ya big girl!"

Like boys everywhere, we were trying to find out who we were and what we were made of. The boy who rose to the top and became known a the "toughest" was an important distinction. The fact that many of our adult male role models made the same distinction didn't help us behave in a more civilized manner. Herbie, on the other hand, was very mild-tempered. He never got involved in the scuffles or tests of strength.

For instance, Herbie and I got into an argument one day. I don't remember why. I pushed him but he just fell down on the grass and started laughing. He refused to participate in the process. He did the same thing when other boys tested him. As a result, he became an easy target for the bullies around school. The other boys would knock the books out of his hands, trip him, bump into him, call him names; the usual. I noticed that over the years, Herbie stopped laughing about this treatment and started stoically accepting it, but he never did anything to defend himself. I guess he just felt he was too small and weak and that the teasing and bullying was preferable to a beating. Witnessing this constant abuse, I always felt sorry for him and never insulted him again after that first argument. I even extended myself to him a few times in conversation but he had turned inward and I couldn't seem to draw him out. I eventually stopped trying and assumed that he counted me among his enemies because of the argument we had gotten into.

Most of us quit school at around fourteen and started working. While we were busy with our new jobs, Herbie underwent what can only be described as a Jekyll and Hyde transformation, physically and mentally. It was nothing short of a metamorphosis. He grew into an enormous hulk seemingly *overnight*. Not only that, but stories were circulating all over town about how he had single-handedly clobbered three or four guys on more than one occasion. His reputation was growing in leaps and bounds. My mates who had known "Wee Herbie" at school were bumping into him around town and each would come back with stories about what a monster he had become. Since most of them had offended Herbie in some way during their school years, they avoided him at all cost. The stories of his exploits were so outrageous that everyone thought he'd gone completely round the bend. Over the years, his resentment over being bullied had mounted. Emboldened by his sudden growth spurt and newfound strength, he decided to exact revenge on everyone who had hurt him. He even made a list of offenders and put their names in order from those he hated most to those he hated least. He then made it known that he intended to beat the hell out of everyone on it. He was busily working his way down the list with the efficiency of a door-to-door salesman, scratching off the names of each person he destroyed.

I knew my name had to be on the list somewhere because of our disagreement years earlier. The thought of what might happen when Herbie got to me became a growing source of anxiety until I was constantly looking over my shoulder. As well as sheer hatred, I think he also composed the list on the basis of those he figured were easy for him to overcome, progressing toward the more difficult ones at the end, almost like fighting for the heavyweight championship.

Belfast devoured good stories, and due to the well known ability of the Irish to embellish stories to make them more interesting, nobody knew what the truth was anymore. Tall tales about Herbie's street fights grew more and more outlandish every time they were told. First, he had beaten up three guys at a time, then four, then five. Even if it were just one guy or two, though, one thing was certain - Herbie never lost. With each new victory, his confidence grew, and the beatings got worse. People were hospitalized. He was a wrecking machine.

We heard he felt no pain or he enjoyed it, and many who previously thought of themselves as hardcases discovered quickly and harshly that they weren't quite so hard after all. The most fearsome characters around town would punch themselves out trying to put Herbie away only to realize that, as the fight developed, he only became stronger. They were all falling like dominoes under his clubbing, lunchbox-sized fists.

I personally witnessed Herbie destroying a notorious hard man from Silverstream who was previously believed to be unbeatable. There were a lot of American servicemen in Belfast at this time. Herbie would go downtown, deliberately pick a fight with two or three G.I.'s at a time and knock the hell out of them just for practice. He quickly entered into the realm of "living legend." It was only a matter of time before my number came up. I practiced my boxing in the back yard every day in anticipation, not because I wanted to beat Herbie up. I knew that was next to impossible. I was training to stay alive.

CHAPTER 35

DOROTHY

When you meet a man, you judge him by his clothes: When you leave, you judge him by his heart."
~ Russian proverb

I had been dating an Irish-Jewish girl named Dorothy Levin. Her family lived nearby and operated a vegetable and fruit shop near Oldpark Road, which meant they were wealthy compared to us. That was impressive to me but what attracted me to Dorothy most was that she was physically different from most of the girls around town. She had an olive complexion, brown eyes, and curly, brown-black hair which grew very low on her forehead in little swirls. This description may sound odd but she was quite attractive and exotic. Her sister Mildred was an attractive girl, too. Her brother Joe was a funny, wee guy who agreed with everything anyone said to him. Everyone got along great with him as a result. The Irish can start an argument in an empty house, so his agreeable nature set him apart, too. In retrospect, his was a very good philosophy. I heard a story told once of a man who sold everything he owned and hiked into the Himalayas in search of a legendary wise man. He finally found him and asked him the meaning of life. The wise man said, "Never argue. Just agree with everything anyone says to you." The man was furious.

"What?" he said, "After all I've gone through to find you, that's all you have to tell me! That's the most ridiculous philosophy I've ever heard!"
The wise man answered, "You're right."

One time, Dorothy and I were having a heavy petting session, just necking, nothing serious, and she said, "Oh, I'm being raped! I'm being raped!" I was shocked because her hands were just as busy as mine. I thought she was just being dramatic and we both continued. The affair between Dorothy and me never really went anywhere, just a lot of hand-holding and the occasional gubsucking (smooching) session. She was also the first girl to introduce me to the glorious joy of breast-fondling.

There wasn't much to do on the winter nights unless we had money to go to the pictures, so Dorothy and I and our other friends got into the habit of meeting at a construction site where an old night watchman had a brazier, or coal fire, in a big metal drum with holes punched in it so the heat could escape. The name for us then was "corner boys." The watchman was very gregarious, and it was fun and cheerful to stand around on cold, wet winter nights, warming our

172

hands, everyone's faces lit by the glow of the orange flames, listening to the old night watchman tell greatly exaggerated stories of his younger days. His job was a lonely one, and he seemed to appreciate the company.

Belfast kids sharing the watchman's fire

At the time, I was short of clothing and money and every other bloody thing. I got tired of wearing the same old clothes when I went out with Dorothy and started to consider my options. My father and I were getting to be about the same size, and he had an outfit I absolutely coveted, a tweed jacket with gray, flannel pants with cuffs at the end. He had owned it for about fifteen years but it was still in pristine condition because of the way he doted over it. It was the only decent suit of clothes he had. He always hung it carefully behind his bedroom door when he was done wearing it and covered it with newspaper to keep the dust off it.

My father spent ninety-nine percent of his time in his railway uniform. He would come home from work and take his collar and tie off, then sit in his railway pants and shirt listening to the radio, so I hoped he wouldn't mind if I wore his prized suit. I labored over ways to approach him about borrowing it but couldn't think of anything important enough in my life to warrant it. I thought about lying about some major event I needed it for but I knew he wouldn't believe it. I could just hear his response -

"Major event? You? Gimme a break! What is it? Has the other ball descended?"

I finally decided to try to impress upon him the fact that it was not getting enough wear, and that he should let me *share* it with him. It was hardly a convincing argument, particularly since the outfit was already about as old as I was, and he quickly declined my generous offer to help him "break it in."

However, after a lot of hinting and shameless whining, he finally got tired of listening to me and let me wear it on the condition that I took good care of it and only used it on special occasions. I was elated and made plans to wear it the next time I got together with Dorothy. After all, his definition of a special occasion and mine weren't necessarily the same. Little did I know at the time that my special occasion with Dorothy was going to be crashed by Herbie.

CHAPTER 36

HERBIE THE HATE BUG RETURNS

Oppose not rage while rage is in its force;
but give it way a while and let it waste.
~ William Shakespeare

I saw Herbie around town a few more times. He had always sort of looked beyond me before, but he was now starting to eye me and size me up. I tried to walk past him casually but felt his eyes burning holes in my face like Superman's laser beams, trying to get me to make eye contact with him. On one occasions, he swerved toward me at the last second and bumped shoulders, hoping I would say something and start things off. I just pretended it didn't happen. It was downright primitive, like the nature reels I had watched at the movies about gorillas sniffing around each other until they finally got into an all-out war for territory.

I knew my turn was coming with Herbie and I was not looking forward to it. However, I also knew that he respected abilities in me that he had gathered from rumors and speculation, abilities I had not really proven and was not even sure myself that I possessed. I had been in a couple of scraps with inferior opponents and these accounts had been embellished upon by the neighborhood pundits. Maybe it was my attitude or demeanor, but he was hesitant around me, as if testing the waters. Otherwise, he just would have clobbered me and been done with it. I had been able to intimidate Herbie on that one occasion when we were kids, but we had never actually fought. Half of the battle is intimidating and weakening the resolve of the opponent *before* the fight, as Mohammed Ali demonstrated so well. I had learned early on that an overwhelming display of bravado was usually sufficient to intimidate all but the most hard-bitten opponents.

Some of the other boys and I would often go by the construction site during the day, too. The sheer scale of the site was interesting to us because cranes and other heavy machinery were being used. We would have rock-throwing contests, hitting tin cans and so forth, or weightlifting contests with bricks or lead pipes. We were in the midst of one of these contests when Herbie showed up with his ever-present sidekick, Raymond. They were classic characters - the hulking brute with the sneaky, little rat pulling his strings. Though only about five feet tall and skinny as a rifle pull-through, Raymond was constantly mouthing off, knowing that he had Herbie to protect him. He would instigate the fights while standing behind Herbie, then get well out of the way when the punches started flying, his pointed, yellow teeth grinding together and his eyes widening with sadistic glee in direct proportion to the pain Herbie meted out.

Raymond and Herbie stood and observed the competition for a few minutes. I struggled to lift a pipe and managed to get it over my head. Herbie finally said, "That's nothing! I could lift twice that!"

"Go ahead," I said. "Have a go."

It was quickly and painfully obvious that Herbie was much stronger than I was because he hoisted the pipe effortlessly. Everything about him was thick and powerful-- his back, his neck, his hands, even his face. I expected him to start the fight after he threw the pipe on the ground but he just gave me a dirty look, grumbled something and walked away, looking over his shoulder a few times to scowl. I got the feeling that he still had some measure of doubt somewhere inside of himself, and that this had been just another attempt to size me up before the big event. Because he had come out on top on this day, he had more courage to give me my beating and scratch my name off his list. His only task now was to find a way to make it happen.

A few nights later, Dorothy and I went to the movies and decided to take a walk afterward. We ended up walking past the construction site to see who was hanging around the watchman's fire. I was wearing my father's outfit for the first time and feeling like quite the dapper gentleman. I could tell Dorothy felt a little more proud to be on my arm as well. Clothes make the man, as they say. (Or the awkward adolescent, in this case.) Some of our friends were there so we joined in and were having a good laugh when who should come along again but Herbie and Raymond the Rat. When I saw them approaching, my heart sank because I knew this had to be it. D-Day.

Herbie knew that Dorothy and I had something going so he started messing around with her. Bumping the person next to Dorothy out of the way, he squeezed in beside her and whispered, "How about a wee kiss, love?"

Blissfully unaware of the drama unfolding, she laughed and said, "Ach, away with ya."

But Herbie put his arm around her and said, "Ah, come on! Just one wee kiss!"

My face was growing hotter by the minute, knowing that the moment of truth had finally arrived. Herbie kept looking up at me, gauging my reactions. He wasn't actually hurting her so I didn't say anything. Then Herbie turned up the heat by twisting her arm behind her back.

"What's wrong? You too good for me?"
Dorothy looked at me now for support, realizing that this guy was bad news. I swallowed the lump in my throat with the remaining spittle I was able to muster and said, "Herbie!"
Herbie kept breathing down her neck, ignoring me.

"Herbie!"

He looked up at me with the same look in his eye that the gorilla in the nature film had.

"Yeah?" he said.

"Knock it off. You're out of line."

A silence descended over the group. That was all the excuse he needed. He stepped away from her, stood toe-to-toe with me and glared at me. Five or six inches doesn't look like much on a ruler, but they make a hell of a difference when standing face to face.

"Are ya askin' me or tellin' me?" he growled.

"Take it any way you like. Just knock it off," I answered.

"Right. That's it." He started taking off his jacket.

I knew then that it was battle stations. Instead of taking off my jacket as he was expecting me to, I seized the opportunity for a surprise attack and punched him between the eyes as hard as I could before he could get his jacket off. I wouldn't say this had no effect whatsoever, but it was sort of like shooting a rhino in the forehead with a BB gun. It might notice, but it wouldn't make much of an impression on the rhino, except perhaps to annoy it slightly. Herbie just staggered backward a little, shook his head, and fixed his eyes on me again. And they glowed red. I swear. They glowed red.

I'd given him the best shot I could possibly deliver, and it hadn't even phased him. I was in trouble. He then charged me with his arms spread out. I didn't have time to do anything except hold on for the ride. I sprawled my legs so he couldn't pick me up and grappled with him until I succeeded in getting him in a headlock. I struggled to get my forearm under his chin. Once I did, I hung on like grim death. He was rearing like a bull, trying to lift me, shaking his head and punching viciously at my legs. Fortunately, he was more brawn than brains. If he calmed down for a second, he would have realized that all he really had to do was grab me by the berries or hit me a good thump in that general area, and I would have had to let go, but all he did was fight to free himself and punch my legs like a mindless animal. I had such a stranglehold on him that he couldn't get free. But the blows he did manage to land rocked me to the tips of my toes. He even tried to bite me a few times; anything to break free. I held on grimly because I knew that if he got free, death and dismemberment would surely follow. The inevitable finally happened; we hit the ground, rolling around in the dirt, mud and oil from the construction site. This went on for what seemed like hours but was probably only a few minutes.

We were both getting exhausted when my friend Harry Rankin came along. He watched for a few minutes before he jumped in and separated us, saying, "Okay, that's enough, for God's sake!"

I stood up, ecstatic to find myself still in one piece. We were both completely knackered. Herbie wiped the mud from his face and said, "We'll let it go for now, but next time I see you, we'll finish it."

"Aye, alright," I replied.

I was now a hero in Dorothy's eyes and my stock soared. She was exceptionally affectionate after I defended her honor, but I was in no condition to continue the evening. I was walking home feeling lucky not to be permanently altered when it dawned on me that my father's suit was not so fortunate. The knees and elbows were missing and I was covered with grime from head to toe.

My pride in being Dorothy's white knight was tempered by the terror of wondering what my da's response would be when he saw the condition of his best clothes. My mind searched feverishly for adequate excuses such as being mugged, knocked over by a bus, charged by a herd of runaway buffalo, etc., but I didn't think I could pull any of them off with a straight face. I've never been a good liar. I finally decided the truth was the best option.

My da was home when I arrived. I gathered up my courage and walked into the house. He was behind his newspaper, as usual. He glanced up at me as I walked in, went back to reading his paper, realized what he had seen, lowered the paper again and turned a red which deepened more and more by the moment until he finally arrived at a light shade of purple. He them emitted a sound that wasn't a scream or a sob but more of an anguished, guttural moan, the kind of sound that sends chills up one's spine when heard while camping in the woods.

"Awwrrrhhh! For fuck's sake! What have ya done to muh clothes?" he asked.

I was sure he was about to finish the job for Herbie, but I think he must have felt pity for me because as I explained to him what happened, his face started to soften and return to its normal pinkish hue. He seemed to understand that there wasn't much I could have done to avoid it. He said, "Ach well, they're just clothes. Never you mind, son. You couldn't help it. Away upstairs. Have a hot bath and get some sleep."

There was no possibility of returning the suit to its original condition. The beautiful tweed jacket and flannel pants he had carefully preserved every day for fifteen years ended up in the trash bin.

Little moments like that are what I remember when I think of my da. Despite his shortcomings and the troubles in his life, he wasn't all that bad. A lesser man would not have been so forgiving toward his son for ruining his best and only outfit, the first time wearing it no less. This was yet another example of his disproportionate discipline.

A few months later, my da gathered up enough money to get himself another outfit at Spackman's, a very popular store in Belfast at the time, much like Woolworth's was in America around the same time. It was so popular, in fact, that there was a well-known rhyme around town about it.

When I was a lad, I went with my dad
And we all got clad at Spackman's.
Now I'm a dad and I go with my lad
And we all get clad at Spackman's.

I don't know if an ad man came up with this jingle or if it came from the street but whoever originally penned it should have been paid because it became part of the local folklore and did much for Spackman's business.

I ran into Lionel the day after the infamous construction site wrestling match and told him the whole story. Lionel had been in a blue funk since he found out he was on Herbie's list, too. When he heard that Herbie had gotten to me, he was absolutely sure he was next since he was a friend of mine. He started ranting and raving that Herbie was going to slaughter him, that he wouldn't be as lucky as I was, that his days were numbered, and other such confidence-building affirmations. Amused by his discomfort, I said to him, "Yeah, I think you're next, Lionel. I sure wouldn't want to be in your shoes." He looked at me with an expression of pure terror. Valor was not Lionel's strongpoint.

This was amply demonstrated after he and I went to see a horror film called *The Smiling Ghost* at the Park Picture House. For months afterward, when we were walking around town at night, I would secretly fall behind and let him walk ahead alone. He would dander along talking away to himself, and then suddenly realize I was no longer there. He would look back to see me standing next to a streetlamp, my face illuminated, smiling maniacally.

"What're ya doin'?" he would ask nervously, the fear mounting.

I would answer, "The smiling ghost has come for you, Lionel!"

That's all it took. He would break into a sprint down the street, pleading with me to relent.

"Stop it, ya bastard! That's not funny!"

I would pursue him relentlessly, grinning and howling like a ghost until he practically wet himself.

The next day, Lionel told me he was moving back to England. He didn't admit that it was because of Herbie, but I'm sure it factored into his decision. He was as aware as anyone was of Herbie's reputation and had been living in fear long enough. Though I had survived the first bout, I was wondering if I would be as lucky the next time around. If the stories about him beating up entire groups of soldiers were true, what chance would I have? He would surely be a little smarter next time we mixed it up.

Then Lionel and I got a reprieve. In those days, crime was practically unheard of. The gas company didn't trust people with a bill back then so they had to feed change into a meter when they wanted gas. If they didn't have any money, they didn't get any gas and couldn't cook. So stealing change from gas meters or an occasional incident of vandalism were the main crimes at the time. There was also the occasional burglary and the ever-present street brawls, but serious crimes were almost unheard of. I remember reading about one murder in a different part of town, but this kind of thing was so rare then, it completely rocked all of Belfast. I wish it were still as rare.

As Lionel and I were wondering which one of us would run into Herbie next, we heard that he had been arrested. No longer satisfied with just pulverizing people, he and Raymond decided to rob the local market, Maggie Moore's Sweet Shop. The shop was owned by Mr. and Mrs. Moore, a couple in their eighties who had been running the shop for as long as any of us could remember. It was located on the Ballysillan Road in a very remote corner of our neighborhood. They sold cigarettes, candy, magazines, newspapers, and basic grocery items. The beauty of their operation was they were open every day until nine or ten o'clock at night, so if somebody needed an essential item, they could always run over to "Maggie Moore's". It was our 7-11. The shop looked like a wooden shack and there was always a pungent smell inside; a mixture of lavender, cigarettes, bread, candy and something which I thought of at the time as "old people", a sweet scent they seemed to produce. I actually found this scent to be strangely comforting, perhaps because it reminded me of my country grandmother. My mother often sent me there to pick up groceries. The Moore's were very friendly, and everyone liked them. However, like the rest of us, they barely eked out an existence, and there was probably no more than a few pounds in the till at any one time.

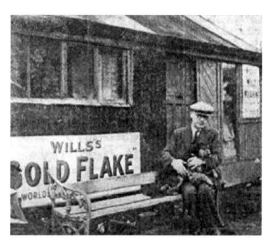

Maggie Moore's Sweet Shop, Ballysillan Road

Herbie's decision to rob the place was a prime example of the madness which had overtaken him; not only robbing a store but robbing one so close to home where he could be easily identified. He didn't even wear a mask. He and Raymond just walked in and demanded money. Apparently, they wouldn't tell him where the money was hidden so Herbie slapped wee Mr. Moore around a little. He even slapped Mrs. Moore a few times. Finally, they gave him the two or three pounds they had and Herbie and Raymond ran off into the night. Mr. Moore called the police. They were picked up by the police a few hours later. The police were very effective back then. They knew who to talk to and what questions to ask. They didn't waste any time rounding people up. Of course, it was a smaller and more manageable population then.

A wave of shock washed over the entire neighborhood when news of the event spread. The Moore's were badly bruised but they recovered completely. Herbie had to go to court. Despite all his brawling, this was probably his first time in a courtroom. Being the main perpetrator of the robbery, Herbie was immediately convicted. The judge said, "You've got two choices, Mr. Hansen. You can go to Borstal, or you can join the navy where you won't have a criminal record. I'm giving you the opportunity to mend your ways and you better appreciate it."

Borstal was the facility for juvenile delinquents, a place everyone was terrified of, where the real hardened criminals were sent. Things went on there that were unspeakable, or so it was said. Herbie elected to join the British Navy. He was only about seventeen and off he went to sea with grown men. There was not much sympathy around town for him. In fact, we all breathed a sigh of relief that at least he was out of our way for a while, and we could all relax again. Actually, half the neighborhood relaxed because so many were worried about getting caught up in Herbie's path of destruction.

A story about Herbie wafted back to us from wherever he was, but no one knew the origin. Since Belfast was a city of rumors, I didn't believe it at first. I had learned not to put too much stock in the ridiculous rumors that flew around town after being absolutely devastated by one about a British heavyweight champion I idolized called Bruce Woodcock. When I was boxing, he was the one I emulated. He fought an American fighter called Joe Baksi. Baksi was considered a tenth-rate fighter, but he broke Woodcock's jaw and put him in hospital. I was upset enough about the defeat of my hero already when I heard that Woodcock had died during the night. I cried for hours. I woke up the next morning and found out he wasn't dead at all. Somebody started the rumor and it spread all through the city like wildfire. I cried so much, I could have used a saline injection, and it was all for nothing.

The rumor about Herbie, however, turned out to be true but nobody seemed to know the whole story. Apparently, Herbie was still carrying on the way he had before, only now he was dealing with sailors who had been around the world and were serious hardcases themselves. Most of them had come from the mean streets themselves. The navy was the best option for a lot of people from hard circumstances. That is still true today. Apparently, Herbie was talking when he should have been listening, and he got himself thrown over the side of the boat into the Irish Sea in the middle of the night. The Irish Sea is cold in the summertime. In the winter, anyone who lands in it wouldn't last more than a few minutes. His body was never recovered.

I hate to admit it, but even though we were all shocked by the news, there was a sense of relief that we didn't have to contend with Herbie any longer. Our lives had been considerably more stressful wondering when it was going to be our turn to get a good plastering so the common response was feigned sadness immediately followed by relief. i.e., "Ah, that's too bad. Poor Herbie . . . thank God."

I wondered what his little friend Raymond would do now, floundering around in the world alone, surrounded by all the enemies he had made laughing and cheering while Herbie beat them senseless. I never found out because he never came back from wherever he went, either. He probably moved to Timbuktu, knowing what awaited him in Belfast if he returned.

Herbie's transformation, exploits, and untimely end all took place within a few months. I don't know what caused such explosive rage to appear in him the way it did. I didn't know his parents. I didn't even know if he had brothers or sisters. I just knew him at first as a quiet, unassuming kid in school who bore no resemblance to the maniac he became. Though he had been picked on a bit more than the rest of us, nothing could explain the level of rage bordering on madness that he had within him, the rage which ultimately cost him his life.

I tell this story with sadness because I remember so well the timid, gentle-spirited boy Herbie was. I tell it with shame because I made it onto his list, though for a minor offense. The only thing that makes me feel any better is the fact that I tried to talk to him about why he was fighting so much. About two months before Herbie and I got into the fight at the construction site, when his reputation was just beginning to grow, before he had really gone over the edge, I was standing near him outside a store downtown. I hadn't even heard about his list at this point, but I could sense something about him had changed. This was the last time I ever saw him normal and sane. He was civil and introspective during this conversation but he never gave me an answer as to where his anger was coming from. Maybe he didn't even understand it himself. Then again, it's not that complex. When someone feels that their pride and dignity have been damaged, they want to punish those who damaged it. Sometimes the wounds are just too deep to forgive and forget.

I can't help thinking about the tragedy at Columbine High School in Colorado as I tell this story. It seems the same dynamic that caused those kids to snap was at work in Herbie. There's at least one in every group - the kid who is picked on because he's different in some way. Most just carry their wounds into adult life and, with any luck, manage to forget about or rise above them. Every now and then, though, there's one who lacks the mental resiliency to let it go and makes a calculated decision to strike back at those who wronged him. I'm just glad that guns were not as available to us back then as they are to children today.

CHAPTER 37

THE EXCREMENT CONTACTS
THE ROTATING OSCILLATOR

"I slept under a roof my father owned, in a bed my father bought. Nothing was mine except my heart, and my fears, and my growing knowledge that not every road was gonna lead home anymore."
~ Narrator, *The Wonder Years*

When I got into my teenage years and wanted to stay out a little later, my father insisted that I be home by 10:30 P.M. If I happened to be going to a movie, this was completely impossible. I tried to explain to him that I couldn't watch the whole movie if I had to come home that early. My father responded, "I'm not interested. Be home at 10:30." I could never pull myself away from the movie and would arrive home at about a quarter past eleven, the house in total darkness. I would feel along the top of the windowsill for the key and slowly insert it into the front door a notch at a time, then tip-toe through the house, trying not to make the floorboards in the front entry creak. Once I had made it across the minefield of the entry floor, there were the stairs to contend with. They were the creakiest, squeakiest stairs on earth. It would have been easier to break into Buckingham Palace than to get up those stairs without waking my father. Usually, however, I would not have to worry about them because my father would be standing in the shadows of the hallway waiting to deliver a resounding smack to the side of my head from out of the darkness, roundly chastising me as he did so. I would run up to my room, punch the pillow a few times in frustration and fall asleep with a ringing ear. Being well into my teens, I felt very aggravated at having to come home so early when my friends were still out enjoying themselves. I had grown quite a bit in recent years so I wasn't feeling so helpless physically anymore and was growing less and less tolerant of the smacks my father gave me. It was a formula for disaster.

The situation came to a head one night when my sister Olga was about six years old, and I was attempting to write a letter. She was bothering me by grabbing the notepaper. In exasperation, I slapped her lightly on the behind and told her to stop. My father was assembling a broom at the time. Making use of what was at hand, he smacked me on the funny bone with the broom handle. The electric shock traveled up and down my arm. I jumped up and heard myself yell, "I'm getting fed up with this bloody nonsense!"

Shocked, my father responded, "This is my house and you'll do as I say!"

I answered, "I live here, too, and I have rights!"

"The bloody hell you do! Get out!" he yelled.

"Why don't you try to put me out!" I answered challengingly.

The next thing I knew, my father had chinned me with a half punch, half slap. Without thinking, I reacted and punched him back. It was purely reflex on my part. To my horror, he hit the floor. Fearing his temper and potential reprisal, I jumped on him and held him until he promised to calm down.

All the excitement made his asthma kick in and he began to wheeze. I let him up but left the house before he had a chance to recover. I stayed away for several hours, wandering the streets in a daze, full of anger and sorrow. When I finally returned, he glared at me over the newspaper but made no comment. We both had fat lips so I figured we were even.

I was completely aghast that I had hit my da, but it was a turning point in our relationship. Perhaps it was a rite of passage for me in some way. From that point forward, I was my own man and could come and go as I pleased. No grudges were held by either of us. If anything, our relationship improved. I had won my freedom, and it was great to be able to come home whenever I wanted to. I immediately started staying out until all hours.

I came home at two in the morning one night after the pub had closed and arrived home in a taxi. My father was waiting for me, but rather than giving me a red ear like he used to, he merely said, "Jasus, it must be great to afford to ride around in a taxi!"

I dismissed his remark with a blasé, "Well, we all have to live a little now and then, don't we?" Now that I was able to stop fearing him, I began to think that he had tried so hard to take my freedom away because he had none left himself. Perhaps I represented everything he had lost or never had to begin with. There are few things in this world sadder than a father who is jealous of his own son. Yet as necessary and unavoidable as it felt at the time, and as liberating as it turned out to be, striking my father is and always has been one of the greatest regrets of my life.

CHAPTER 38

BOBBY EWART

Warm summer sun, shine kindly here;
Warm southern wind, blow softly here;
Green sod above, lie light, lie light.
Good-night, dear heart,
Good-night, good-night.

~ Mark Twain, for his daughter's gravestone.

Bobby Ewart wasn't one of my regular chums because he lived five or six blocks away, which was a long distance for us then. Most of my close friends lived within a block or two of my house. I usually only saw him at school or at the weekend soccer games. He was a brilliant soccer player. He could make a ball sing. We were all sure that if any of us went professional, it would be Bobby. He was magic to watch and made most of us look like we were standing still on the soccer field. We might have been jealous if he wasn't so nice and so quick with a laugh and a friendly word. He was also a great listener when the rest of us were just great talkers. When he asked how I was doing, he always looked right at me with keen interest and asked questions about my stories.

One day Bobby and I and some other guys went out to the orchard to steal some apples and pears. We felt justified in doing so because the fruit never seemed to be harvested by anyone. We always saw rotten fruit on the ground and thought it was a terrible waste, so we would go over there at night and collect as much fruit as we could carry in our pockets and shirt. One night, a middle-aged man ran out of the house yelling at us. We all took off like jackrabbits. Bobby was the fastest of us so he got out ahead of me instantly. We were all running down a narrow path with high hedges on each side. There was only room for one person to go through at a time. Bobby started to slow down, apparently thinking the man had stopped chasing us, but I could hear him panting behind me. In my panic and desperation to pass him, I accidentally knocked Bobby down. I couldn't stop myself, so I just jumped over him and kept running. I felt bad, but it was an "every man for himself" situation. Bobby called me every name in the book as he scrambled back up to his feet. We all got away. When we had reached a safe distance, he said, "That was a terrible thing you done on me."

I just said, "Well, you were in the way, Bobby. You weren't movin' fast enough."

Though I felt slightly ashamed, we just laughed it off, including Bobby. He wasn't the kind to hold a grudge.

One weekend, Bobby didn't show up for the soccer game. We just assumed he had something else to do, but he didn't show up for the next one, either. When he didn't show three weeks in a row, we all went round to his house to inquire about him. His mother was a friendly, soft-spoken, down to earth, country woman we all liked very much. That day, she came to the door looking pale and tired and told us only that Bobby was sick and couldn't come out. We all kept hoping Bobby would get better and show up at the field again, but he never did. His mysterious illness became a source of speculation among us all. Finally, one of us asked our parents if they knew what was wrong with him, and we found out that he had a disease called polio.

We didn't understand the nature of the disease because it was still pretty rare at the time. In fact, Bobby was the only person I ever knew who had it. I asked my ma to tell me about it. Probably trying to shelter me from harsh realities, she told me he would be fine. I didn't know that the polio vaccine had not been discovered yet and that few children survived it. Bobby's father had died many years earlier of a heart attack, which left his mother alone to take care of Bobby and his younger sister.

Another month or so went by, and we finally heard that Bobby had died. He was only nineteen years old. We were completely dumbfounded. Since none of us really knew what polio was, and no one our own age had ever died, we had all been expecting and hoping that Bobby would get better.

Lionel, Hyndsie, Harry Rankin and I were in a state of shock at the funeral. We were all trying to understand how this could have happened to Bobby. He had always been so strong and full of life. He was our age, and we were fine. We couldn't grasp that it was really him lying in that box. Surely it had to be a joke, or he was only sleeping. As we listened to the minister speak, the immensity of what had happened to Bobby took hold of us, and we began to weep. We would never cry in front of each other under normal circumstances, but somehow all the usual rules were suspended here. We were only children, after all, confronting man's oldest enemy too soon.

A few days later, we went to the cemetery where they laid Bobby to rest and said our goodbyes to him privately. We were all angry with ourselves for not insisting that his mother let us come into the house and visit him when he was sick, but we took some consolation in the fact that there was no way we could have known he would never get better.

I went back to the cemetery a week later and kneeled at Bobby's grave. There was a rectangular mound of dirt surrounded by grass and a white headstone with Bobby's name on it. I couldn't believe that the fastest and strongest of us was lying still under that earth. I wanted to dig him up and wish him back to life. I wanted to watch him fly down a soccer field again. I put my hands and face on the earth and cried. When I was cried out, I sat there for a long time, remembering everything I could about Bobby – his laugh, his easy-going manner, his bright-eyed enthusiasm - and it dawned on me that the onset of his polio was probably the reason he had fallen in the orchard. After all, he could always outrun me before.

I touched his cold headstone and said goodbye. I promised I would live the rest of my life for him, too. I apologized for running past him in the orchard, and told him that if I had it to do over, I would have stopped to help him up.

CHAPTER 39

HARRY RANKIN

"The best of men cannot suspend their fate:
The good die early, and the bad die late."
~ Daniel Defoe

The only person who could keep up with Bobby Ewart on the soccer field was Harry Rankin. We all knew he was going to be a pro someday. There was no doubt about it. He ate, drank and slept soccer. But Harry was superior to us in other ways, too. He was tall, good-looking, slow to anger, and didn't swear, smoke, drink or chase after girls. He was very disciplined and didn't squander his time and money like the rest of us did.

For instance, on Saturdays, we all couldn't wait to spend all our earnings at the movies or on food and frivolous amusements at the seaside, but Harry would take home all his pay and give it to his mother. I was with him one day during one of these exchanges. Harry's ma was a very thin, birdlike wee woman.

"Now Harry, do you have enough money?" she asked, looking up at Harry lovingly.

"Aye, I think so, ma," he answered.

She hugged him and said, "Well, here's another half a crown just in case."

He was babied by his mother a bit too much, probably because he was the first born of three.

One of the odd things about his family was that they never drank tea, which is a national staple, but they always had about a dozen bottles of lemonade in the pantry, which they drank at every meal.

Harry was a deadly center-half. He used to practice jumping because center-half's need to head the ball a lot. We would try to jump and reach the cross bar of the goal with our heads. Harry could jump above it and hit the top part of the bar. He had legs like steel springs.

There was a guy on a team from out of town by the name of Butcher Lindy. His nickname was Butcher because he worked as a butcher's helper delivering meat around the neighborhood. This nickname may have contributed to his desire to be perceived as a tough guy. Start calling a guy "Butcher" and it's bound to go to his head.

A lot of scrappy guys came from the inner city to work in our neighborhood. The locals were a bit rough around the edges too but not quite as rough as the people from the inner city where living conditions were even worse. Scrapping and squabbling was just part of an ordinary day for them. Butcher Lindy was from the mean streets. One way he showed this was with a constant and mild belligerence. He was always mouthing off. The other way was how he played soccer. For example, a sliding tackle in soccer is permissible if the player slides with one leg and goes for the ball, but a two-footed sliding tackle is illegal. If he goes for the legs instead of the ball, it's doubly illegal. It just takes the legs right out from under the other player and a leg can easily be broken.

Harry did something on the soccer field one day that simply amazed me. Harry was on the ball and Butcher came in with two feet, going for Harry's ankles. Harry saw him coming and jumped up in the air, avoiding the tackle and possible serious injury. Then he paused, gave Butcher two clean smacks across the face, and went on playing. It was a forehand and a backhand, the kind gentlemen in Victorian England did before challenging someone to a duel. The ultimate disrespect. He didn't say a word to Butcher. Just smack-smack and on with the game. Butcher sat there in shock, trying to decide what to do about it. Wisely, he finished the game without retaliating. As the old saying goes, "Discretion is the better part of valor." Butcher probably knew he was in the wrong, but he also knew he couldn't take Harry in a fair fight.

The double-smack incident perfectly encapsulated Harry's character. He never threatened anyone but he knew how to end things quickly and cleanly if someone threatened him. No hesitation but no gratuitousness, either. He was a class act.

One Saturday, I went over to Harry's house and was waiting for him outside. I was kicking a ball around in the street to amuse myself when I accidentally kicked the ball over a fence into someone's front yard. I hopped over the fence, picked up the ball, hopped back out and started kicking the ball around again when a man in his forties came charging out of the house – a big, heavy-set shipyard worker type. He stood toe-to-toe with me, screaming at the top of his lungs and cursing me for hopping over his fence. I was shocked because he was so much older than me. Just as I was beginning to worry about him taking a swing at me, Harry came bounding out of his house. He stepped in between us and stared at the guy. The man just continued on yelling at Harry the way he had at me. Harry was standing his ground when the man suddenly drew back and punched Harry in the face. Harry staggered back but recovered and started taking off his jacket. The man fixed his eyes on Harry, apparently disappointed with the almost complete lack of effect his best punch had on him. Enraged at seeing Harry attacked for no reason, I stepped between them and stuck one on his chin. He went down hard and bounced right up the pathway but got back on his feet quickly. I expected him to retaliate but he just ignored me, fixating on Harry. I realized there must be bad blood between them over some previous disagreement. He and Harry then proceeded to box their way up and down the street. Harry was up on his toes like Sugar Ray Robinson, all left jabs. The older man just flailed away with wild roundhouse swings, no skill whatsoever. Harry peppered him with stiff jabs to the nose and lips and every so often, a vicious right hook.

Inside of three minutes, the man's face looked like the window display of a butcher shop. Harry's ma finally came running out of the house, and as if the man needed any more punishment, began slapping him up the face and neck and yelling, "Whuddya hittin' my wee son fer?"

Harry had a swollen eye from the first sucker punch but was otherwise unscathed. The man took this opportunity to escape and charged back into his house, cursing and yelling all the way. He was so frustrated from the pasting he had just received that he tried to kick his front door open, but the door didn't budge and he only succeeded in severely injuring his big toe. He let out a loud, tortured moan and hobbled into the house as we both laughed with glee, yelling after him, "Ah, go on, ya silly big shite!" and "Away and fock yarself, ya great puddin'!"

A few days later, we saw him walking around with a crutch, his face swollen up like a bap and a cast on his foot. We laughed again, but he pretended not to hear.

"Serves him bloody rightly," I said to Harry, "trying to beat up helpless, wee kids like us."

"Aye, right y'are," Harry answered with a wink.

In contrast to Harry's looks and confidence around other boys, he was hopelessly shy around girls. As soon as one appeared, he would become tongue-tied and awkward. This was remarkable to me because he seemed to have everything going for him.

One night, a hard rain was falling so we ducked into the Park Picture House. In the lobby, big Harry asked me, "How do you talk to girls? How do you start a conversation with them?"

Though I was no Casanova myself, I did have the gift of the gab and never had much trouble striking up conversations with girls.

I told him, "Harry, the first thing you've got to remember is women *want* to talk to boys, especially the pretty ones, because everyone is afraid to approach them. You can find out soon enough whether or not they want to talk to you by the signals. Guys are expected to make the first move. Don't make such a big deal out of it. Just be yourself."

We sat down in the theater and were watching the movie when two girls came in and sat right next to Harry. I gave them the once-over when the theater was more illuminated by one of the brighter scenes of the movie. They were big, tough-looking girls probably from the Chapel Fields area. They just seemed to grow them bigger over there. They were a couple of real hard chaws. For a laugh, I leaned over and whispered to Harry, "Now ya see those two there? I can tell by looking at 'em that they're good things. (Easy women.) It'll be easy. Go ahead and make your move."

Harry became nervous immediately at the prospect of actually talking to a real, live girl. With panic in his eyes, he whispered, "What should I do?"

I told him, "Feel her leg and see what happens. Nothing ventured, nothing gained."

For five minutes, I watched Harry's trembling hand inching toward the thigh of the girl closest to him. I was equal parts curious and frightened about what she might do. It was riveting.

I had tried the very same thing a few times and it had turned out quite well. Since Harry was better looking than me, I thought he had a very good chance of repeating my success. But the second he made contact with her leg, she stood up and delivered a profanity-laced tirade.

"Whaddya think yar doin', ya darty fockin' bastard! Are you some kind of fly mon? I'll git my brother down to give ya a hidin', so I will! Who d'ya think y'ar?"

Everyone in the theater had turned around to see what all the commotion was about. Harry was as red as a fire truck. He pleaded with the girl, "It was an accident! I-I-I didn't meant to! It was an accident!"

The audience had now taken a greater interest in the unfolding drama between Harry and the girl than in the movie. We walked as fast as we could without actually running to the emergency exit as the offended girl continued her rant. It was a relief to get out into the relative peace and quiet of the busy street and thunderstorm.

This incident did nothing to help Harry's confidence with girls. It was the first time in his entire life that he tried anything untoward with a girl and it had traumatized him. He receded further into his shell and probably always held a grudge toward me for my lousy advice. The finger of fate truly is fickle. If the girl had actually been a good thing rather than just looking like one, Harry might have had the time of his life that night and became quite a lady's man later on.

Harry and I were at the glens with the rest of the gang one day. A tree had fallen over the river. Harry was walking across the tree when he lost his footing and fell about eight feet onto the rocks. He screamed in agony. We knew right away that he was badly hurt. Afraid to move him, I ran for help while the others stayed with him. An ambulance came and he was carried away on a gurney. He was in the hospital for three weeks, his back badly injured. After he was released, he had to wear a corset to support his discs. We all thought it was temporary but he ended up having to wear it permanently. He had resigned himself to living with it when, ten years later, his back miraculously recovered almost overnight. It was as if whatever was broken had suddenly righted itself. He started playing soccer again but he was twenty-seven by that time and his chance for a soccer career was over. Most pros were at the height of their careers in their early twenties. A few lasted into their thirties, but not many.

Harry ended up becoming a police officer. He met a nice-looking girl and got married. On a trip home recently, I heard that she ran off with someone else when they were in their forties. I suppose she just got bored and needed someone more edgy and exciting. Harry was probably just too good for his own good.

The last I heard of Harry was the he died of dementia ten years or so after the divorce. I only hope he found another woman who appreciated his kind nature, and that he experienced some happiness in his final years. He was a good soul, and after such a difficult life, he deserved a little joy.

CHAPTER 40

BOXING

"I was called "Rembrandt" Hope in my boxing days because I spent so much time on the canvas."
~ Bob Hope

There was a young fighter named Randy Turpin from Leamington Spa in England. He had a white mother and a black father. This was after the first wave of Jamaicans came to England, so there were some mixed marriages. The first time I heard of him, he was fighting the Dutch champion, Piette Van Damme. Our radio wasn't working so I went to the YMCA to listen to the fight on theirs. Everybody I knew was there. They brought the radio into the lounge and put it on the table. I ran into the other room to get a chair and had barely sat down when, boom, the fight was over. Turpin just walked over, hit Van Damme right on the chin and cold-cocked him. We knew right away that he was someone to watch.

Around the same time, Sugar Ray Robinson was the world middleweight champion. He was in the middle of a European tour and beating everybody. He went to France, Germany and Italy and demolished the local heroes. Then he came to England to fight Randy Turpin, but Randy beat him on points and beat him well. I think Sugar Ray underrated the quality of this kid and lost the title as a result. British titleholders were few and far between, so I was completely captivated by Randy Turpin.

RANDOLPH TURPIN

Randy Turpin

The film of the fight was being shown on a monitor at the Great Northern Railway every day at lunchtime. I must have watched it twenty times. That fight was my inspiration to try my hand at boxing. I asked around to see where there was a good club and found one called The Crown Entry named after a famous lane in Belfast; kind of a long, narrow alley between tall buildings. It dates back to the last century and is very medieval looking.

The Crown Boxing Club was right in the middle of the block. I didn't realize it at the time, but in retrospect it was the epitome of what a boxing club should be - dank and musty, with the smell of sweat and resin in the air, boxers working bags of all kinds, a full-sized ring, and pipes leaking overhead. A real dungeon. Resin isn't used much anymore, but we used to rub it on the soles of our shoes in the old days to keep from sliding. In old fights or movies, one will sometimes see fighters stepping into a box full of resin and shuffling around. The shoes had leather soles back then, and the sweat made the floor of the ring slippery. The resin was gritty, so it helped the fighter keep his footing.

I stepped into the Crown Boxing Club trying to act like a seasoned fighter. I was about seventeen at the time. Prior to that, I'd done a bit of sparring at the YMCA near where I lived, but I knew that this was another arena, a higher plateau. I felt intimidated and excited at the same time, the way a young gladiator might have felt stepping into the coliseum for the first time and watching the other slaves training for battle.

I expected to see a few of the guys from the neighborhood with the fierce reputations, the ones we all thought were real tough, but those kind of guys never got into a boxing ring. They would come down and watch but they'd never even spar around, even if they were invited. They'd just stand to the side with contemptuous looks as if it was beneath them to put on a pair of gloves. Eventually, it dawned on me that they were afraid to fight in a ring where there were rules of conduct, where it was man against man with no friends to back them up if their opponent happened to get the upper hand. There was also no kicking, head-butting, or eye-gouging, which eliminated most of their tactics. Harry, Lionel, Hyndsie and I would get into the ring and blatter away at each other with oversized gloves that were more like big pillows. It was impossible to seriously hurt each other, but if one of us connected right, we felt it well enough.

I remember sparring with Hyndsie one day. Hyndsie was about a hundred and thirty-five pounds, and I was about a hundred and fifty-five pounds, so I was kind of cocky. I stuck my chin out and dropped my hands, playing around, like he couldn't hit me, and it wouldn't hurt even if he did. He took full advantage of my stupidity and stuck one right on my chin. Hyndsie had one of the best right hooks I've ever seen. My legs buckled and I could feel myself starting to fall. Fortunately, I regained my senses before I hit the floor. It served me right. A big ego is a big target.

Everyone called the trainer at the Crown Boxing Club "Wee Arthur". He was in his seventies and a typical trainer, just like Mickey in the Rocky movies - raspy voice, hypercritical, feared by all, and very much in charge of the whole place. But we all knew it was part of the act and in our best interest, just as a drill sergeant has the best interests of his troops in mind as he breaks their bodies and childish minds so he can rebuild them into fighting men.

In Belfast and Northern Ireland in general, most of the good professional fighters were Catholics from the tough, lower class neighborhoods where it was very difficult to find work. There were a few good Protestant fighters too, though. In fact, the Protestant champion in the middleweight division was Tommy Johnson from the Shankill Road. He was a tall, rangy guy, thin with wide shoulders, like a fighter should be built. All speed and power. No heavy muscle, just sinew.

We trained a lot at the Crown and Wee Arthur brought us up to speed quickly. I hadn't really decided what I wanted to do, but I liked the training and fighting under controlled circumstances with someone there to save me in case something went wrong, or I was getting my head handed to me.

There was one guy at the club who took boxing more seriously than any of us. We called him "Big Eggo" after a comic character at the time - a big, dumb ostrich who was always getting himself into ridiculous situations. He didn't appreciate the nickname, but that name stuck until nobody remembered what his actual name was.

Big Eggo

That's how it was all over town, particularly if the nickname really fitted. For instance, there was a guy whose head tilted to the left a little because of some neck problem. We called him "Ten Past Six." Another guy had a similar problem but his head tilted to the right and, as if to compensate, his right leg stuck out a little when he walked. Everyone called him "Capital K." He didn't appreciate it either, but a nickname in those days was like a brand on a horse. The nicknames were cruel because they were usually inspired by a physical abnormality that was probably the result of some kind of poverty-induced vitamin deficiency. But little boys don't think about such things. Everything was fodder for jokes. That may be one of the reasons so many great entertainers came from Ireland. An audience couldn't say anything worse to them then their friends already did.

My friend Joe McGlade knew a tomboy in his neighborhood who received the most unflattering nickname of all of us. Her family was very poor and could not afford underwear for her but her mother made her wear dresses all the time, probably in an attempt to develop feminine instincts in her. She would engage in all the usual rough and tumble with the boys and her skirt would occasionally fly up, giving all present a full view of her bare bum. This earned her the nickname "No Knickers".

This nickname, like all the others, followed this poor girl throughout her entire childhood. She could have left the country for decades and come back to the neighborhood a mature, distinguished woman and someone somewhere would say, "Hey, No Knickers! How are ya?"

So it was with Big Eggo. Perhaps his anger at being addressed as a comic book ostrich added to his motivation to give us all a good thumping in the ring. When he was sparring, he would expel air with every blow, which isn't uncommon. However, his were great and mighty gusts that could be heard around the gym and down the block outside. It was quite a distraction to the other fighters trying to train. The guys working the speed bags couldn't concentrate, and their rhythm would be thrown off. But despite their groans and protestations, Big Eggo would just keep puffing away, oblivious to everyone. He was always very stern and serious, and he was constantly begging wee Arthur to get him a professional fight. Arthur always refused because he hadn't even had any amateur fights yet. But Big Eggo was so convinced of his own greatness and potential that he wanted to step right into the professional ranks. He could hit pretty hard and sparred well, but Arthur was not sure about how he would stand up against the pros.

One night, wee Arthur pulled me to one side and said, "This guy's getting on my nerves. I want you to get into the ring with him and beat the shite out of him. He's not ready for a professional fight, but he thinks he is, and he won't stop pestering me."

I said, "That's hardly fair. I'm about twenty pounds heavier."

"It doesn't matter," wee Arthur replied, "Get into the ring and give him a good thumping. I'd rather see him hurt a little bit by you now when I can control it than hurt bad in the ring when I can't."

I agreed, though I wasn't sure if I could beat Big Eggo. When we got into the ring, he was overly excited, going through all his usual gesticulations, squaring off, circling around and snorting like a bull. I kind of plodded around, acting slower and more cumbersome than I really was. He danced and shuffled around me, exhaling with every jab, snapping out-of-range punches in my face. He was like Shemp of the Three Stooges. He finally came within range and swung an ineffectual hook. I ducked and buried a vicious right into his ribs on the way back up - a real gut punch, and down he went, retching loudly in an effort to force air into his collapsed lungs. I put my hand on his shoulder and asked if he was okay, but he brushed it away, staggered out of the ring and left the gym. A couple of weeks went by, and he never came back. Growing more and more concerned, I saw one of his friends one day and asked what happened to him.

He said, "Oh, that thump you gave him was enough to convince him that he wasn't really made for boxing. Up to that point, he was only thinkin' about how he was gonna dish it out. He never really thought he was gonna get hit back."

So, obviously, Big Eggo's heart wasn't truly in it. I like to think I did him a favor. After all, as wee Arthur had predicted, he might have gotten into the ring with someone much stronger and nastier than me.

Tommy Johnson and I were the only two middleweights in the gym. There was one light-heavyweight. The rest were featherweights and lightweights. One day, Tommy said to me, "I need somebody bigger to spar with. Would you mind working out with me?"

I said, "Yeah, I wouldn't mind workin' out with ya, Tommy, but you're much better than I am. I don't like the idea of being your punchin' bag!"

He said, "Don't worry. I won't hit ya too hard."

So I worked out with him, but even when he was pulling them, I could feel the power of a professional punch. It was actually kind of mysterious. I felt like I hit the same way he did and even tried to emulate him as we sparred, but my body punches had little to no effect on him while his sent shock waves right through me. Every time we finished sparring, my ribs and arms ached from absorbing his punches, but I managed to survive without major injury. I did my best to give him some competition but he was so far ahead of me, it was very humbling. I felt he was in another league entirely and possessed secrets I had no knowledge of. Wee Arthur, on the other hand, was convinced that I had a future in boxing. He said, "You've got a great left hand, kid. Love your left hand. Let me fix ya up with a fight."

I told him, "Listen, Arthur. I haven't really decided if I want to be a boxer. I enjoy comin' down and working out, but I don't know if I want to take it that far."

He said, "Ach no, you've got to get in the ring and have a real scrap. This sparrin' around is not the real thing. Let me fix ya up. We're havin' a tournament this Saturday at the Lower Shankill Boy's Club. Why don't you let me put your name in?"

I said, "To tell ya the truth, Arthur, I play soccer Saturdays."

Much to my relief, Arthur stopped pressing, and I got out of it. Saturday rolled around and I went down to the field to play but the game was rained out. So there I was with nothing to do at one o'clock in the afternoon. I walked over to the club to watch a few of the fights. As soon as I walked in the door, Arthur grabbed me and said, "I'm glad you showed up. You're up next."

"What?" I said, "I told you I didn't want to fight."

He said, "Ach, go on ahead. You're already here. Ya might as well."

I said, "Alright, alright. Who am I supposed to be boxing?"

He said, "That guy over there."

He pointed to a guy who looked like Frankenstein's monster. He was about 6'4 with shoulders as wide as a small aircraft. Despite his height, he was about the same weight as me, but he was a hell of a lot tougher-looking. He really looked like he'd been through the ringer - flat nose, cauliflower ears, the whole bit - the kind of guy that can scare the hell out of someone without even trying. Noticing my rapidly waning courage, Arthur rushed me into the locker room and handed me some gear.

A few minutes later, I found myself stepping into the ring with a heart full of dread. The bell rang and the monster stood up and lumbered around the ring, very professional looking. My sphincter was in full cinch mode. I decided the best plan was to keep my distance and keep moving. It's typical in the first round of a fight for fighters to feel each other out, but we felt each other out for most of the first round, making only the suggestion of the possibility of a punch once in a while. Finally, the referee called us to the middle and said, "Are you guys gonna start fightin' someday?"

It dawned on me then that this guy was as apprehensive as I was. Fortunately for me, I realized it before he did. So I got stuck into him in the second round, and the fight was stopped. I knocked him right out of the ring at one point. I thought, "Oh, shit. That was easy." My boxing career was off to a flying start.

For the next few days, everyone at the club called me Rocky (after Rocky Graziano.) I felt like a real big shot. Growing more and more cocky, I decided to enter the YMCA championships. I put my name in the light-middleweight division. Because of the shortage of fighters, only two of us entered. We went right through to the final. There were three or four elimination heats, but I was automatically shoved into the finals, which were held in a little town just outside Belfast called Carrickfergus. They bussed all of us into town. I was still high from my big knockout and felt more confident. Hyndsie entered, too. Big Harry showed up as our second, but he didn't enter because he was still wearing the back brace from the fall he took while we were hiking.

My turn came up and I got into the ring. I didn't know who the guy was ahead of time, but inside about thirty seconds, I knew I was outclassed. He was fast and tough, throwing punches from every angle with lightning speed. I never even saw them coming. Next thing I knew, I was lying flat on my face on the canvas, and the ref was shouting, "Six! Seven!" I remember thinking, "What happened to one through five?" I dragged myself up again out of pride and bang, I was kissing the canvas again. After the second round, Big Harry said to me, "This guy's making a complete mug outta you! You haven't even touched him!" There's nothing like the support of your friends.

I thought, "I wish somebody would stop this. I'm gettin' a hidin' (beating) here." But I was too stupid or dazed to stay down. I was up and down like a yo-yo. I kept hoping the ref would take pity on me and halt the slaughter but he didn't. The last round came and Harry said, "For God's sake, do something. Get stuck in!"

I had to get at least one good thump in to redeem myself a little, anything to save face, literally and figuratively. So as soon as the bell rang, I shot out of my corner like a rocket right across the ring and met him getting off his stool. I was in such a stupor from getting pummeled during the first round, I stumbled and ran into him headfirst. Our heads knocked together like two coconuts. He went down hard, bleeding badly above one eye. I was beside myself with a mixture of every undesirable emotion known to man. They wrapped a white towel around his head, and it went completely crimson in a matter of seconds. I must have opened some blood vessel or artery in his forehead. The crowd went berserk. Everyone thought it was a deliberate head butt on my part, and it probably appeared to be from ringside. To make matters worse, it turned out that this guy was the local hero.

The crowd screamed, "Dirty pig!"

"Get him!"

"Fuck you, ya Belfast bastard!"

In an attempt to discourage anyone from making good on their threats, I acted like a wild man, taunted them from the ropes and yelled, "Fuck you, too! Get into the ring!" I was scared out of my wits, so I put on a front of bravado and challenged the entire arena to fight, but before they could get into the ring, my friends and every available handler whisked me away into the locker room. The door was hastily bolted and locked as the men converged on the other side. The crowd gradually dispersed, and we all thought that was the end of it, but just as we were about to leave, a guy came in and said to me, "There's about thirty guys outside waitin' for ya. They think you're a dirty fighter. They're gonna give you a hidin' when you go out to the bus."

We all sat back down, not knowing what to do.

I said, "Maybe they'll go away if we stay in here long enough."

We waited for an hour, and they still hadn't left. We could hear them yelling "Send that prick out here!" Everyone else was waiting on the bus and the driver was anxious to go. Somebody came up with the idea of hiding me at the bottom of a wicker basket the janitor used to carry all the sweaty jock straps, shorts, socks and so forth. Seeing no other way out of this mess, I climbed into it, held my breath and closed my eyes as the janitor dumped the laundry on me and closed the lid. Then he and a few other guys carried me right past the mob to the bus. They must have wondered why it took three men to carry one basket of laundry. I was unable to hold my breath for the entire journey from the gym to the bus, and as I got a whiff of someone's sweaty jockstrap in direct contact with my nose and lips, I began to wonder if being crushed by an angry mob might not have been a better option. Once I was safely stowed away on the bus, heard the engine charging and the yells of the crowd dying in the distance, I jumped out of the basket and breathed again. Thus, I was smuggled out of Carrickfergus and returned safely to the breast of my beloved Belfast.

That event marked the end of my boxing career. I discovered, much like Big Eggo, that I didn't really have the heart for it. I guess I felt like I had better options than getting my head dented for a living.

Another incident a few years later also served to solidify my feelings against a boxing career. I was walking around the City Hall when I saw Tommy Johnson standing alone. I hadn't seen him since we were sparring partners at the Crown. I walked over to him and said, "Hey, Tommy! How ya doin'?"

He didn't even recognize me. He looked at me but beyond me at the same time and said, "Fourth round. I'll get 'im in the fourth."

Shocked, I said, "Okay, Tommy. I'm sure you will," and walked away. He was completely out of it. Twenty-eight years old and his brain was already scrambled. He'd been through some tremendous fights. In the years since we sparred together, he had even traveled to England to fight the English champion, Johnny Sullivan. The crowd had thrown money into the ring in appreciation of how tough the fighters were. The two of them picked more money up off the floor of the ring that night than they were paid, which was only about two hundred pounds.

Despite my short-lived career, I've always retained an interest in boxing because I think it's truly a sport where the best man wins, a battle of wills between two people with only the third man in the ring to keep things safe. But as much as I loved the sport and strategy of it, I didn't think it was worth ruining my health over. I wasn't that desperate for adulation or money. But I did succeed in finding out what boxing was like firsthand, and I've always had respect for anyone with the courage to risk life and limb climbing into a ring.

All sports contain great metaphors for life, but one of the best is from boxing - "When life knocks you down, you've got to get back up again." The fact that it has become a cliché takes nothing away from its wisdom. It takes a warrior to get into a ring and get back up with his head ringing, seeing two or three of everything he looks at, when all he really wants to do is lay there until the stadium empties and the crowd goes home. It also takes a warrior to keep getting up again after absorbing the beatings life inevitably gives us all.

CHAPTER 41

THE IRISH AND BRAWLING

"The old Irish, when immersing a babe at baptism, left out the right arm so that it would remain pagan for good fighting."
~ Anonymous

Since we're on the subject of boxing, it might be a good time to discuss a few common stereotypes about the Irish - namely, their love of boozing and fighting. Like all stereotypes, they are part myth and part reality. Neither of these vices is unique to Ireland. Both flourish in places where men have very little else to brag about. Most men in Belfast in those days didn't have occupations which gave them a feeling of importance or purpose. They didn't own their own homes. They were working for wages which barely covered expenses. If they had several children, there was always a shortage of money and food, as there was in my home. Halfway through the week, families had to eat bread and jam, bread and sugar, or bread and HP sauce sandwiches. There was no meat on the table. It was just survival, no joy. So the only way some men could build up their self-esteem was by becoming the toughest guy in the neighborhood. Idle hands really are the devil's workshop.

The latest street fights were always the first topic of discussion at the pubs and at work on Monday morning. Every fight was described in detail. All writers know that conflict is the essence of drama. Unfortunately, this is true of human affairs as well and may be one of the reasons peace never lasts very long on a small or large scale. Most men need to test their steel one way or another. A typical pub conversation might go like this:

"Did you hear about Jimmy?

"No, what happened?"

"He got plastered Saturday night at Mooney's and got into a fight."

"Who with?"

"I don't know, but the cops came down, and it took three of them to take him in!"

"I wouldn't be surprised. Jimmy's a bloody headcase, so he is."

Now Jimmy, who was just another poor slob on Saturday morning, was revered all over town as a hard man on Sunday morning. He had elevated himself above the crowd. The women had to put up with all this macho nonsense, as they do all over the world. In *The Ballad of the White Horse*, G.K. Chesterton wrote a verse about the Irish that's very fitting.

'For the great Gaels of Ireland
Are the men that God made mad,
For all their wars are merry,
And all their songs are sad.

There was probably not much more brawling going on in Belfast then than there was in Liverpool, Manchester or any other British city with a lot of working class people struggling to survive. The nature of life was different then. Belfast at that time probably had a third of a million people. It was like an overgrown village. There were only two newspapers. Like all small towns, everyone knew what was going on with everyone else. If a guy got into a fight at a dance with a complete stranger, he could find out who he was and where he lived just by asking a few people. He would then usually show up at his house the next day looking for a rematch. Fights were rarely lost gracefully and were almost always followed by a vendetta. If the person was outmatched and didn't have much confidence in winning a rematch, he would employ more treacherous methods, such as a bottle across the back of the head in an alley. If they didn't get their revenge that day, they'd get it a week later from behind. Each neighborhood had its own top guns; hardmen who seemingly couldn't be beaten. The city was filled with stories about them and their exploits.

Growing up in that environment, it was as if I had no choice but to become part of it. The problem was I hated fighting. I hated the idea of hurting someone as much as the idea of getting hurt myself. Any brawls I was involved in were always more fun to talk about later than they were when they were actually happening. I was just thrust into things and felt like I had to follow the rules or suffer severe consequences. I always felt that the most important attribute for a hardcase was stupidity, and the second, callousness. Stupidity to be oblivious to the dangers inherent in even a small scuffle, and callousness to be able to punish or even maim the other guy enough to make him quit. One punch in the right spot and one could end up dead or a vegetable. It always seemed more intelligent to me to avoid confrontations entirely, if at all possible. After all, boxing wasn't the first form of self-defense; running was. So I had these two conflicting thoughts working inside me. I couldn't and wouldn't let myself back down from trouble because of the social ridicule that would surely follow, but I knew that it was the height of ignorance at the same time.

There were brawls constantly at the Plaza Dance Hall, mainly because it was attended by both Protestant and Catholics. Differences in religion, excessive consumption of alcohol, and competition for girls are never a good mixture. Some of the guys would get tanked up and go into the dance for the sole purpose of starting a fight. Saturday night was not complete without at least one good punch-up.

In the bathroom at the Plaza, all the guys crowded in front of the mirror combing their hair. Back then, everybody had Tony Curtis style haircuts, piled high on top with a D.A. (Duck's ass) in the back. If someone made the fatal offense of looking at someone else's reflection in the mirror for too long, that was all that was needed for an argument to start, something like, "Wudder you loogin' at? Do I owe you money or somethin'?" Then all hell would break loose.

I liked getting along with people and making friends. Most of my friends were this way, too. Not everybody our age was a troublemaker, but there were always plenty of them around and we did our best to avoid them and the neighborhoods where trouble seemed to flourish.

One night, when I was about eighteen, my friend Hyndsie and I went to the Park Picture House to see a movie with a couple of girls we'd met earlier that day. We were both nicely dressed. Dressing nicely immediately marked us as a couple of sissies in the eyes of the hardcases. We had our nice jackets and pants on, shoes shined, and our plastic raincoats under our arms in case it rained.

We met our dates and had a nice time with them at the movie. When we came out, we were walking up toward the fish and chip shop when we heard a commotion across the street. Four guys were coming out of a pub, obviously drunk, shouting "Up the IRA!" I looked over out of curiosity to see what the noise was. As usual, this was taken as a challenge and one of them yelled over the standard and always original, "Wudder you loogin' at?"

I gave the obligatory answer, "Not much."

A few more insults were batted back and forth. In retrospect, I should have kept my mouth shut instead of allowing myself to get sucked into it, but I was young and with girls I wanted to impress. One of the guys sprinted across the street and before I knew it, he launched himself at me, hitting me with his head, boot, and fist simultaneously. I went down like a bag of spuds. Before I knew it, I was on my back with my arms pinned down as he straddled my chest and pounded my face. My boxing experience was completely worthless against the ferocity of this attack from an obviously hardened street brawler who was older and more experienced than me. He really knew how to club and proceeded to knock the shite out of me in short order. I didn't even have time to throw a punch. Several times, he yelled, "Have you had enough yet?"

Being too proud or stupid to submit, I answered no every time, so he blattered me some more. I knew I was getting badly beaten but my pride wouldn't let me beg him to stop. Then I noticed that he was starting to get tired, so I seized the opportunity to break free. I pulled my arms out from under him and grabbed his wrists. I felt a surge of elation run through me because I knew I would have a chance to get my own back. I threw him off, sat on him the way he had sat on me and said, "Now it's your turn." I got four or five good licks in before one of his friends came over and pulled me off of him by the hair. Hyndsie tried to intervene at this point but immediately got hit right up the nose with a bottle. He was bleeding profusely but kept swinging and kicking wildly at the assailant's friends. He was tenacious. I was able to stick a few good ones on my attacker, but I knew I was hurt much worse than he was.

A crowd had gathered to watch this but nobody did anything to stop it, which was typical. It was like the John Wayne movie *The Quiet Man*. Everybody just had a good time watching the fight. However, unlike the dishonest violence of movies where people can punch each other all day without drawing a drop of blood, we were actually getting hurt; particularly me. We were now fighting with all four of them, and I was really starting to get worried about getting hurt worse than I already had, perhaps even killed. Just then I saw two big cops ambling down the street, just sauntering along like they had all day to get there. When they got close enough, somebody shouted, "Here come the cops!" The four guys took off across the Bog Meadows. I took off after them because I still felt that I'd been humiliated by four ignorant louts, and they'd gotten away with it because the cops didn't bother to chase them. They just watched them traipsing away across the meadow. I caught up to them halfway across the field. The one who had first attacked me was lagging behind. They all stopped and turned around. My opponent reached into the lapel of his jacket and pulled out a bicycle chain and started swinging it around. I could see the chain had been sharpened at the edges. This was something the hardcases used to do. Getting hit with a chain was bad enough, but a sharpened chain would cut through clothes and flesh. I was smart enough to realize that I couldn't win so after delivering a few choice words, I walked back to where my friends and the cops were still standing. The cops wanted to get information on the four assailants. I was livid.

"I have no idea who they were and I don't want to talk to you two about it." I said. "You're too fuckin' lazy to move yourself to stop the fight or to chase them but now you want information on them? I think it's a bit too fuckin' late to start pretending you care, don't you?"

The two cops said "suit yourself" and continued on their beat.

This was typical for the cops in those days. They would let people practically kill each other then stroll over and pick up the remains. I suppose brawls were so common, they just got tired of risking their own necks to break them up. They may have also felt that fights were usually the result of some kind of mutual stupidity with no clear victim, which they usually were, so it wasn't like an actual crime was being committed. This wasn't always the case, however, so I resented their casual attitude toward the pasting I had just received. The usual question the cops asked was, "Who threw the first blow?" Whoever struck first was the one they would arrest, if they arrested anybody. Overall, though, they seemed completely bored and disinterested.

The worst thing about all this was that I was due to leave on a weekend holiday at the Isle of Man two days later and my face was badly cut and swelling more and more by the minute. I went up to the doctor's house to see if he could make me more presentable. The doctor lived in our neighborhood and had an office in his own home. It was about eleven o'clock at night when I knocked on his door. He came to the door and almost passed out when he saw my face. I looked like a walking horror movie.

"My God, son. What happened?"

"I got into a bit of a scuffle," I replied.

"Looks like a bit of a train wreck to me."

He took me in and checked me over. Most of my wounds were superficial. One eye was completely shut and one was half-shut so I was able to see just enough to move around. My lips were split, every tooth in my head felt loose, and I had bruises over every part of my body. My hair was coming out in tufts from the guy yanking on it.

The doctor said, "Well, there are no broken bones anyway. I would suggest you go home and get into bed for about a week."

I said, "Well, unfortunately, I'm going on vacation the day after tomorrow."

He sent me home but not before giving me a lecture on the dangers and evils of fighting. Talk about preaching to the choir!

My family was all sleeping when I got home. I collapsed into bed and promptly passed out. My sister knew I liked a glass of cold milk in the morning, especially when I'd been drinking the night before. She came into my bedroom about nine o'clock the next morning and saw me lying there with my face all swollen. She dropped the milk and screamed. She didn't even recognize me. However, youth overcomes everything. I recovered quickly and was back to normal in about four or five days, but my eye remained bloodshot for about three months. As luck would have it, it was the same eye that had almost been gouged out by the sadistic paperboy when I was twelve.

The thing that angered me the most was the completely unnecessary nature of what took place. I hadn't done anything to deserve a beating like that. I was basically a decent kid. Hyndsie was, too. They were just four drunk wasters looking to beat somebody up. We both were seething with a desire to get even. We decided to find them and return the favor when we got back from our holiday.

While at the Isle of Man, I had trouble eating and drinking just about everything for about a week because my lips were still hurting, but we enjoyed our holiday nevertheless. We figured these guys lived in a Catholic neighborhood called Ardoyne only because they were heading in that direction when they ran away. It was hot I.R.A. territory. For years, police wouldn't even go into that neighborhood. We armed ourselves with wooden sticks we could conceal in our pockets. We searched the neighborhood every day for about a week, but we never found them. Honor was never restored, and our pride had to be swallowed. Perhaps it's just as well we didn't find them because we might have ended up in jail for doing something we couldn't justify. It was the worst thumping I ever received in my life, in or out of the ring.

It dawns on me as I tell these stories that this chapter will do nothing to alleviate the stereotype of the Irish being drunken, half-mad brawlers. The only apology I can offer is that I considered this environment to be normal since I knew no other way. I absorbed the ethos of the people. Life was basically happy and fun, but there was always an undercurrent of violence in Belfast then. Since my goal is to capture the Belfast I knew warts and all, this book will have the same undercurrent. And bad as it was, violence in those days bore no resemblance to the kind of violence that took place in Belfast when the real troubles began, or even in the inner cities of America today. Today, one is lucky if he only gets punched.

Except for the roughnecks and hardcases, the people of Belfast were and are basically kind. The average young Irishman may be quick to anger, but he is just as quick to extend a hand in friendship if one is extended to him. And once trust is earned, an Irishman is as fierce a friend as he is a fighter.

CHAPTER 42

THE PARK PICTURE HOUSE

"Life isn't like it is in the movies. Life is harder."
~ Alfredo, *Cinema Paradiso*

The Park Picture House was like a cathedral; I always felt a sense of wonder as I walked into it. The walls were adorned with yellow lanterns and statuary that gave it an other-worldly air. It was also a great place for picking up girls and communing with mates.

All of the attendants were female and they all had tidy, well-fitting uniforms that drove all the boys mad. They came around with cigarettes and candy in a box held up with a strap around their necks, just like the girls in the old movies. About five girls worked there, and I dated every one of them at one time or another. I was like a bee in a flower patch. My friendships with all of them went very well, except one.

I didn't smoke yet in those days, but this particular girl was constantly sucking away on Woodbine cigarettes, the cheapest cigarettes one could buy at the time, made with raw tobacco and no filter. They stunk to high heaven. I was trying to kiss this girl one night, and the tobacco odor coming off her almost knocked me over. It took a lot to put me off when it came to girls, but that did it.

The great thing about the Park Picture House was that the movies were changed every other day. There were always double-features, yet another thing of the past. They were usually B-movies from Hollywood like *Boston Blacky, Hopalong Cassidy, and Roy Rogers,* and cartoons or *The Three Stooges* during intermissions. We always looked forward to the new *Dead End Kids* movie (or *Bowery Boys* as they were also called.) The first movie my future wife Rosaleen and I saw together was *That Midnight Kiss,* Mario Lanza's first film in 1949. The second was *The Sunny Side of the Street*, a great musical with Frankie Lane.

For that movie, I took her to a Picture House called the Lyceum on the Antrim Road. We called it The Flea Pit. It was full of every kind of bug imaginable because it was on the outskirts of an estate where the residents weren't able to clean themselves, their bedding or their garments regularly because there were no indoor toilets or bathrooms. Within minutes of sitting down, we were infested and scratched ourselves silly while watching the movie. We didn't usually go to the Lyceum for this reason and because we always ended up sitting beside people who hadn't bathed in a day (or twelve.) We weren't exactly slaves to hygiene but they were in a whole other league. The fleas would hop off them to us looking for fresh blood. Variety is the spice of life, as they say.

The Park Picture House was positioned near a Catholic neighborhood known as the "Chapel Fields". Further away was the Ardoyne where it was rumored I.R.A. men lived. At the end of the evening shows, the Park always played "The Queen," Britain's national anthem. The Catholics would try to escape the theater before it was played; whereas we, as staunch Protestants, would stand until the last bars were played out. We stood in the aisles by the doors to prevent the Catholics from leaving. Stymied, the Catholics would then begrudgingly cross their arms and stand for "The Queen" like the rest of us.

One night, I went down to the Park Picture House on my own. They were playing an *Abbott and Costello* movie. I was laughing and a girl beside me was laughing away, too, when she started slapping me on the leg in the middle of her laughter. This was a bit strange even by Belfast standards, but she kept slapping me on the leg and laughing like hell so I looked at her out of the corner of my eye. She didn't look too bad in the half light so I decided to have a go. I used the usual technique - pretending to stretch and letting the arm fall around her on the way down. Much to my delight, she slipped right under my arm as naturally as could be. She looked over and we started kissing. It became more and more soulful and impassioned until we were engaged in a raucous match of tonsil hockey. People around us were changing seats. After thirty minutes or so, the lights went up for intermission and I looked at her. Not only was she unattractive but she looked slightly demented. Front tooth missing and everything.

Stifling a scream, I stammered, "I, uh, I . . . gottagonow" and got up to leave.

"See ya here next week?" she said, holding on to my arm.

"Uh, yeah, sure" I said, pulling away.

"Same seat?"

"Aye, right, the same seat."

Being a teenager, profound sensitivity was not my strong suit and I had no plans of ever seeing her again. I never sat in that seat or even that area of the theater again and did my best to forget all about her. She almost put me off kissing for life.

About a month later, I went to the doctors up on the Ballysillan Road. I had a boil or a carbuncle on my arse. I wasn't quite sure what it was, but the pain was excruciating. I had three boils in my life, and all three of them occurred in the same year. Boils were quite common in those days because we weren't able to shower regularly. Usually, they went away or popped by themselves but this one was growing and growing to the point that I feared geologists might descend on my rear end with measuring instruments. I finally went to the doctor to have it lanced. I knocked on the door of the doctor's office, and who opened the door but the same girl from the theater. She was the doctor's maid. The shock of seeing her again rendered me momentarily speechless.

She said, "Where'd ya get tay? Ya never showed up. Have ya come round to see muh agayin?"

I was stunned. I couldn't think of what to say so I just turned and ran away, forgetting the pain of the boil and abandoning treatment for the sake of escape. I still feel guilty about it to this day. I console myself with the possibility that she thought I was the demented one, which I suppose I was, come to think of it.

But, alas, that was not to be my last encounter with her. About a month later, I was coming home on the bus at about eleven o'clock at night. My bus passed right by the doctor's office. Back in those days, doctors used to work out of their own homes. They would actually perform surgeries there. There were two Doctor Harvey's, Harold and Cecil, living in the same house with their mother. They had posh accents and appeared somewhat on the effeminate side. They tended to the medical needs of our entire neighborhood, my family included.

I looked out the window of the bus and saw a bunch of guys standing on the sidewalk looking up at the doctor's house. Albert McClanahan was with them; a big, lanky guy I knew. I got curious about what they were all looking at. This was not a usual hang-out spot, like fish and chip shops, candy stores, pubs and so on, so I got off the bus and asked Albert, "What's goin' on?"

Nobody looked at me. They were transfixed. Albert pointed up at the second floor window of the doctor's house, and there she was again, the doctors' maid, parading around without a stitch on, stopping now and then to examine her breasts in the mirror. She could be seen plain as day and must have known it. The room was completely lit up and the curtains were wide open. She had a great set of knockers, probably because she was a chubby girl to begin with. They were her saving grace. She kept lifting them up and shoving them together. The guys were saying, "Ah Jasus, look at that!" This went on for about half an hour, then the light went off, and they all went home sporting glass cutters. I, on the other hand, couldn't stop thinking about that all-pro spitting gap where her front tooth was supposed to be.

In those days, I could buy a movie ticket in the morning and stay for the show over and over again. When a particularly good double feature was playing, that's exactly what I did. I watched *The Jolson Story* about thirty times. *Robin Hood* was a close second. I only watched it about twenty times.

Sadly, the Park Picture House is no more. During a trip home in the late 70's, I stopped and stood in front of it. It had been gutted by a fire several years earlier and was ready for demolition. I passed by the spot where I had been beaten up by the I.R.A. supporters. I sighed again, after all these years, at the injustice of it all, but this unpleasant recollection was quickly whisked away by the memory of the girls I had kissed in the flickering light of the Picture House, the friends I had laughed with, and the movies made in a magical place called Hollywood; movies which were nothing less to me than flying carpets carrying me away from the often dismal weather of Belfast and my childhood worries to sunny, exotic lands and wondrous adventures. I tried on many different roles in the safe, dark womb of the theater, wondering what I might be when I became a man. Cowboy, pirate, detective, spy. The possibilities were endless, or at least the movies made it seem so. If magic exists anywhere in the world, it is in a Picture House.

This is yet another aspect of modern life that pales in comparison to yesteryear. The day of the movie palace is gone. Where one enormous, festooned screen used to be, there are now multiplexes with many small screens in generically mass-produced theaters with no craftsmanship or individuality. A few of the old style theaters can still be found, but most are in disrepair and filled with ghosts, or closed down entirely, as was the Park the day I stood outside it, forty years older, looking at her tattered, empty shell with love and remembering all she had given me.

CHAPTER 43

WORKING

"Work is the curse of the drinking classes."
~ Oscar Wilde

For my friends and me, our formal schooling ended at age fourteen and it was time to look for a job. The middle and upper class parents saw to it that their children had the advantage of a secondary school education. College was generally restricted to those with aspirations of a professional career. I didn't envy them. I was happy with the prospect of starting work. I had always found school boring, and I couldn't wait to get it over with.

Since Belfast was primarily an industrial city, most of my contemporaries were looking for an apprenticeship in the Belfast shipyards or in the aircraft or linen factories. My mother, however, decided that oily overalls and dirt under the fingernails were not for her son and somehow landed me a job in a linen exporting company called Richardson, Sons and Owden on Murray Street in central Belfast. I was not sure how she did it and assumed she had employed her posh British accent to impress the manager.

The company had a spinning factory in Bessbrook, County Armaugh, and sold linen products - sheets, pillowcases, tea cloths, tea towels, and damask tablecloths - all over Britain and around the world.

I started at the princely sum of seventeen shillings and sixpence a week, about a buck and a half at today's rate of exchange. During the five years I spent in the linen warehouse, starting in 1947, I graduated through the various departments, serving my apprenticeship in each one. My monthly salary increased each year to a maximum of five pounds ten shillings at the end of the fifth year. The wage was still small, but the extra few shillings were welcome as a supplement to my father's wages. I got to keep a couple of bob for myself every week, which lasted for a couple of nights at the pictures and a bag of candy. When I worked late, which was frequent, I was allowed three shillings and sixpence "tea money," as I was staff and theoretically not entitled to overtime pay.

The staffs' wages were paid monthly, a lingering Dickensian custom, so I was usually broke the last three weeks of the month. In Belfast terms, however, I was now a member of the white-collar working class, and what I lacked in income I was supposed to make up in prestige. I could theoretically look down my nose at the unwashed hordes that left the shipyards each day and with whom I stood beside in line at the bus stop at City Hall. This information did me no good, however, because I was completely unaware of this distinction at the time, and all I knew was that they were making two to three times my salary and were being paid every Friday, not once a month. Indeed, if it had not been for my shipyard friends, I would have spent most Friday and Saturday nights at home for want of money. They were always glad to see me right with a few bob at crucial times.

One major benefit of my office position was access to the secretarial girls who would not be seen dead with a working man. These young ladies plied their wares among the company directors' sons, the rugby-playing crowd at Ophir and the other meeting places of the upper classes. Not for them the grimy fingernails of the riveters and stagers or the weekly excursions to the Plaza Dance Hall.

The class divisions were particularly acute among the female population, and the event that made them feel the divides most acutely was the annual Miss Belfast beauty contest. Then the little mill doffers, habitual frequenters of the Plaza every week, would rub shoulders with their more advantaged sisters from Malone and Cherryvalley in the pageant, all vying to become Belfast's most beautiful girl. The wealthy girls would arrive with their mothers for protection and leave directly after the contest was over, while the mill girls would get back into their C&A dresses and resume their dancing. (C&A was the store in Belfast where the working class shopped, while Goorwitches and Robinson and Cleaver catered to the wealthy set.)

The social lines were clearly drawn and each side knew which side they belonged on. I met and dated both kinds of girls and had friends from both sides. While the wealthier girls may have been more refined and intelligent due to their classical educations, there was always something bloodless about them to me, and it was among the working people that I found the noblest character, strongest emotion and greatest inner beauty. I also found in some of them the worst aspects of Ulster life, but they were alive, and it made me feel alive to be with them.

Despite the poor wages, I couldn't wait to get into work every day. The place was filled with characters, and I kept up with the gossip of the city listening to their tales. I'm sure some of them were certifiable lunatics. As we used to say, "There are wiser one's up in Purdysburn." (The local insane asylum.) One such lunatic was Jimmy McDougal. He was a perpetually disheveled man with a thin body but huge potbelly, a nose shaped like an old boot, and wispy black and gray hair which shot out in every direction like a poorly stuffed muppet. Jimmy's defining characteristic, however, was hunger. He was constantly famished. At least three times a day, he said, "I could eat a child's arse through a wicker chair." Everyone was sure he had a tapeworm. Every day he would polish off his lunch in short order then eye mine like a hungry mutt waiting for me to offer him scraps.

If my eating slowed in the slightest, he would ask, "Are ya gonna eat all that?" hoping I was full. I usually gave him half a sandwich just to shut him up and get his eyes off me. However, Big Bob Mackenzie, a man of about fifty, an ex-regimental sergeant major and heavyweight boxing champion with the British Army, was fed up with Jimmy and his mooching.

"One of these days I'm gonna sicken that wee shite," he said.

Due to his background and size, I was worried he was going to murder wee Jimmy, but Bob had something much sneakier in mind. True to his word, Bob brought in a bap one day, a large dinner style roll, which he then cut in half and placed lettuce and tomato in. He then went outside and scraped pigeon droppings off the window sill and added it to the sandwich. He then scraped the contents of his pipe into it as well and covered the entire mess with several rows of ham.

"What are you doing?" I exclaimed. "You're gonna kill him!"

"Ach," he said, "He's got a stomach like a cement mixer."

During lunch, Jimmy saw the sandwich and asked, as usual, "Are you gonna eat all that, Bob?"

"No," Bob replied cordially, "I think I had too much for breakfast this morning already. You take it, Jimmy, and good health to ya!"

We both watched in horrified fascination as Jimmy polished off the roll, making not the slightest whimper about the pigeon excrement or tobacco shavings. Bob was clearly disappointed. Jimmy thanked Bob again and returned to work.

"What do I have to do to sicken that git!" he blasted.

A couple of weeks later, Bob pulled out what appeared to be a little package of "sweeties" (candies) from his pocket, which immediately got Jimmy's attention.

Right on cue, Jimmy asked, "What's that you're eating, Bob?"

"Ach, it's that old black Swiss chocolate," Bob replied. I can't stand the taste of it."

"Well, give 'em to me. I'll eat 'em!" Jimmy said, grabbing the bag from Bob's hand.

Jimmy didn't show up for work again for a week. During his absence, Bob had confessed to me that what he had given Jimmy were not sweets at all but chocolate-flavored Ex-Lax, and that Jimmy had eaten approximately one hundred times the suggested dosage. When Jimmy finally came back, he looked very pale and weak and was about ten pounds lighter.

"Where were you, Jimmy?" Bob asked innocently. "We all thought you'd died!"

"I don't know what came over me," Jimmy said, "but I haven't stopped keekin' for the past seven days. I was worried I was gettin' rid of something I still needed!"

Bob and I were splitting our sides trying not to laugh. It was hilarious at the time, but in retrospect, poor old Jimmy might actually have been killed. Even this didn't cure him, though. He still begged shamelessly from all of us. I did notice, however, that he showed no interest whatsoever in Bob's lunch thereafter.

One of my duties was receiving the incoming parcels, which consisted mostly of returned jute sacking from our customers to whom we sent bales of linen goods. The sacking was carefully taken off and returned for reuse. One day, I spotted a big parcel with a bunch of American stamps on it. Everyone was out for lunch at the time except me and the managing director, Mr. McDowell. He came around the corner as I was admiring the stamps on the parcel.

"What's that you've got there, boy?" he asked.

"Looks like a food parcel from America, sir." I answered.

"Take it into my office and leave it on my desk," he ordered, which I did.

That was the last I saw of the food parcel, which I noticed had been addressed to the employees of the company and was a gift from a generous customer in some place called Chicago.

"Right, that does it, you old blert," I said to myself, "What's good for the goose is good for the gander."

I wired the postman, "The next time you get a parcel from America, buzz me from downstairs and I'll save you carrying it up the steps."

The postman, an old geezer, was happy not to trudge up the steps carrying heavy parcels and agreed. The next time I heard the buzzer sound, I bounded down the stairs to the front gate, retrieved the parcel from America and hid it behind some boxes in the supply room, to which I had a key. I had brought my dad's raglan overcoat to work to conceal the package.

That night, as we were leaving, I shoved the parcel under the coat and went out the back door as usual. It was summertime and much too warm for such a big coat so old Jock, the security man at the gate, eyed me suspiciously.

"What's that you've got up your coat?" he said, reaching forward with his hand.

"Touch me and I'll brain you!" I said. "I've nothing up my coat except me arms!"

Jock obviously didn't believe me, but I looked like I meant business so he decided against frisking me. I knew he was watching me as I walked down the street carrying the forty pound parcel under one arm and trying to keep upright at the same time.

When I got home and opened the package, we were treated to canned peaches, pears, soaps and other delights that were in short supply. I shared the spoils with the postman to keep him quiet. Things were probably just as tough at his house. He was no dummy and kept his mouth shut.

Mr. McDowell could never figure out why the parcels stopped coming from America. It was stealing, but I managed to overcome my guilt every time I thought of the managing director's shameless greed and imagined him stuffing his fat gub with the treats that were meant for the entire firm. Besides, judging by his prosperous belly, it was obvious he wasn't hurting for food like the rest of us were. I also felt okay about it because I never took any linen out of the warehouse, as some of the other workers did.

I would often meet my co-workers in the public restrooms down the street and share the contents of the packages from America. We all enjoyed the delicacies and exotic foods the parcels contained. Food rationing was still in effect at this time and none of us had seen a banana or orange for years. Butter was restricted to two ounces per person per week. An egg a week was a big luxury for us, so digging into this bounty was pure rapture. The postman and his family enjoyed some fine Florida preserves that summer as well!

I was constantly assured by Mr. McDowell that my wages were so low because I was receiving a valuable education in the linen business from my new employers. Part of this education consisted in delivering letters around the city of Belfast and assisting others in the general office with minor tasks. I was also sent to the nearby Technical Institute, where I learned how a loom operated and how flax was converted into linen thread, knowledge I had no interest in acquiring and felt did not compensate in the slightest for my paupers' wages.

After a brief stint in the office, I was moved into the warehouse where the linen products were assembled, packaged, and shipped to the firm's customers. My responsibility was to see that the orders got out on schedule. Most of the warehouse work force was female with male department heads and a few other male workers scattered throughout.

When I entered that environment, I was as green as green could be. I can't recall receiving any instructions from my parents on anything of importance, sex included. All I ever recall hearing from my ma was "Eat" or "Put on your coat" and from my da, "Be quiet!"

In my new environment, I was exposed to professional types from the middle and upper classes, along with working class people from Belfast's Catholic and Protestant enclaves. Prior to this time, my exposure to these varying elements had been greatly restricted.

It was my exposure to the workers in the ware rooms over the course of the next five years which provided me with an education much more significant than anything I learned about the linen trade. I learned the lesson of class and how the advantaged took care of their own. I saw the snobbery of the rich and the resignation of the poor and disadvantaged, who were determined by conditioning not to aspire to more than the position they found themselves in through the accident of birth. To make matters worse, those few courageous souls who did try to break free of the confines of their impoverished circumstances were admonished by their peers with comments like "Who d'ya think y'are?" or "What're ya like?" or "I bet ya think you're too good fer us now, don't ya?"

For myself, I had no coherent thought as to where I would be next year, five years later, or ever. I was merely in a job, which was an advantage in itself. And though the wages were small, I was employed; a man. Deep down, though, I hoped that if I worked diligently and showed up every day, there would be some kind of reward at the end of it all, and I might be promoted to head clerk or even assistant manager in one of the departments.

As it turned out, I grossly misjudged those who were in a position to do me some good for as time went by, I saw the promotions going not to those who worked the hardest but to those who were well connected. The plum positions were reserved for the idiot cousins, nephews and other relatives of those who ran the show. When a position became vacant, someone was brought in from the outside. My hopes were dashed over and over and whatever nascent expectations I might have had gradually evaporated.

It wasn't all bad, though. There was always something going on within the company, even a company soccer team. There were parties or bus trips – and it was a great place to socialize. There were a lot of girls my age working in the warehouse. Because it was rarely too busy, I wandered around there all day chatting them up. Me and the other boys used to play Ha' Penny, which consisted of making a miniature soccer field on top of a table with two tacks at each end representing goal posts. Then, using a half penny as the ball, we would flick the coins toward the other goal trying to score. I was caught a few times and lectured by the boss not to fritter away their valuable time and money. I laughed recently when I saw two boys in a Bob's Big Boy restaurant playing a modern version of the same game, but with a piece of paper rolled into the shape of a triangle rather than a coin. As they say, "The more things change, the more they stay the same."

My immediate superior was Willie McBratten. He was middle-aged then and had worked for the company for most of his life. He was a small, nervous man with a severe case of eczema which would become aggravated in proportion to his stress level. Unfortunately, he was not a calm person even at the best of times. The higher the degree of stress, the more feverish his itching became. It was not a pleasant spectacle to witness. To make matters worse, the room was poorly ventilated and almost always too warm, a perfect breeding ground for bacteria. My mother's obsessive fear of germs must have had an effect on me because when the sun cut through the window and I could see the dust floating around the room, I would imagine it was Willie's dislodged skin particles and keep my breathing shallow so as not to ingest too many of them. It was always a relief when he sent me on errands, and I was able to get out into the cool, fresh air and take a deep breath again.

Occasionally, the managing director or members of the board popped in to see how their money was doing. When any of these luminaries were present, Willie would go into fits of worrying, pacing around nervously, muttering to himself and scratching his red, inflamed hands furiously. To create the impression of great industry, he would send me off on unnecessary jobs. I always thought that scratching and worrying was a hell of a way to spend one's life. He was a kindly wee man, though, and I liked him. His favorite expressions if some product wasn't quite up to snuff were, "Ach, well, it's not a *mile* off" or "A blind man on a galloping horse wouldn't notice it" or "You can't make a silk purse out of a pig's lug." (Ear)

Our American sales representative was Robert Redpath. His job was to travel to North America and secure orders from the big stores, Marshall-Fields of Chicago, Sears Roebuck, Macy's, and the T. Eaton Company in Canada. He was a tall, broad-shouldered man and impeccably dressed with suits purchased in the United States. His hair was like patent leather and had a blue sheen to it, slicked back from his forehead in George Raft fashion. He looked like a gangster, an impression reinforced by his penchant for chewing bubble gum. I was very impressed with him at first, as he was the epitome of everything I admired – an urbane, well-dressed and confident figure with an enviable job which brought him six months of the year to the United States and Canada, magical places to us at home in Belfast. He was fond of the drink, and as I delivered mail around town I would often see him knocking back pints of Guinness in the nearby Crown Bar on Great Victoria Street, watching sporting events on television.

When he had the drink on him, he was apt to be very nasty with those of us who had to fill the orders he placed. God help those who missed a shipping schedule. The worse time to meet him was after lunch and after he had consumed four or five pints.

I was responsible for entire orders in the fancy goods department, from manufacture to final packaging, and meeting the deadline for delivery to the docks. On many occasions, I worked feverishly in the packing room assisting the packers in getting the last horse and cart to deliver the shipment.

One day, we were frantically trying to complete one of Redpath's consignments. At the last minute, it was discovered that some of the tablecloths were slightly flawed. They were roundly rejected by our quality control woman, a nasty old lady by the name of Mrs. McGoldrick. She delighted in finding things wrong even if the flaws she pointed out were either infinitesimally small or completely unnoticeable, which was usually the case. She would fold her arms, set her chin firmly, and declare through tightly pursed lips, "This cannot be passed!" She seemed to get added joy from this when she knew I was behind and desperately needed to complete an order. It was all I could do to keep myself from ringing her boney neck. Gritting my teeth, I would take the offending piece of material away, wait a moment, then bring the same piece back to her, sometimes several times, folding it differently each time, until she passed it, unaware that she was looking at the same item over and over again.

She finally got me one day when I slipped an order past her but was still one piece short and substituted a similar item. The department head, Billy Chambers, approved my decision but Mrs. McGoldrick became incensed and gleefully informed Redpath of the horrible sin I had committed. Redpath immediately came storming over to confront me with the discovery.

"You horrible little git!" he bellowed. "What do you mean by screwing up my order?"

I decided to be honest with Redpath and explained to him what had happened. Unfortunately, this was just after one of his lunchtime booze-ups and he was in no mood for excuses. His face darkened.

"You stupid bastards," he thundered to Billy Chambers and I, "If I had my own way, I'd fire the both of you!"

Calling someone a bastard in Belfast was probably the worst name one could use at that time. Since Billy was my boss, I turned to him for leadership or a response of any kind. To my surprise, he dropped his eyes to the floor and shuffled uncomfortably. I snapped and said, "For fuck's sake, dry up! Who wants to listen to you shootin' off your big bake?"

Redpath's face contorted in a mixture of rage and disbelief.

"Why, you little shitehawk!" he exclaimed, grabbing me by the throat. "What you need is a bloody good thumping!"

I lashed out almost involuntarily and caught him right on the lips, drawing blood. I was immediately shocked at what I had done. This was an unforgivable offense, and I knew I had just lost my job. Redpath dabbed his lip in shock.

"Now you're really gonna get it," he hissed. "I'm gonna teach you a damn good lesson!"

We both squared off, my heart thumping with the tension of the battle to come and the enormity of what I had already done. I was sure I would get sacked anyway and decided that since the worst had already happened, I might as well be hanged for a lion as a lamb. Fortunately for both Redpath and I, Billy finally emerged from his shell and stepped between us.

"Come on now, lads," he pleaded, "This has gone far enough!"

The blow seemed to have brought Redpath to his senses. After a few mumbled threats, he departed. Before I could be fired, however, I dashed downstairs to the general manager's office and announced, "I quit!" I must have been a sight. The G.M. looked at me and said, "Calm down and tell me what happened."

"Well," I answered, "I've just gubbed Robert Redpath, and I'm handing in my notice."

The G.M. persisted and finally got the whole story out of me, including what had led up to the scuffle. He said, "Go back to your office and do nothing until you hear from me." As I was leaving, I thought I saw a slight smile tugging at the corners of his mouth.

I heard nothing further from anyone. The news finally filtered down to me through the company grapevine that Redpath had been roundly chewed out and ordered to stay out of the Crown Bar during work hours. Apparently, others had complained about his behavior, especially when he had been drinking. To my great relief, I got off scott-free, and the fact that Redpath had made the first move had helped exonerate me.

Redpath and I avoided each other after this incident. If he needed to ask me about the progress of an order, he would ask my manager, who would in turn ask me. I would then answer the manager, the conduit between us.

A few months later, Redpath was preparing for his regular trip to North America and was making his rounds with the department heads, shaking hands with everyone. I felt his presence behind me and turned around. He looked at me for a few seconds, then smiled and held out his hand.

"Put her there!" he said.

I stood and shook his hand, still somewhat distrustful. There is a dirty street-fighting trick where one offers to shake hands then holds on tight while clobbering the person with the other hand. So I shook his hand but got ready to duck just in case. No punch came, though. I sat back down and thought that was the end of it when he pulled up a chair, sat down beside me and said, "I know I can be a bit of an arsehole," he said, "and everyone is used to putting up with my bullshit, but so far you have been the only one with guts enough to do anything about it. Don't feel badly about what happened between us. It's all forgotten."

I didn't know what to say. He then went on, "How would you like to take over my job for the next three months while I'm gone?"

I couldn't believe what I was hearing. I hardly felt qualified. Somehow or other, I babbled out an affirmative response, and he promised to speak to the directors about my promotion, which I found out later he did. However, nothing further was heard. Redpath went off on his trip, and a few weeks later I checked with the G.M. to see what had happened to his recommendation.

"Things are a bit tight now," he explained. "There will be no promotions for a while yet, but we will keep you in mind."

I waited and waited, but nothing happened. Eventually, one of the misfit cousins was brought in from the outside and placed in the job I had been promised. I knew then that my future was not with this company; nor, indeed, with this country. Shortly thereafter, I packed it in with Richardson Sons and Owden.

Eleven years later, I returned to Belfast from my home in California and decided to drop in at the old place to see what was happening. The linen trade had gone into recession with the advent of man-made fabrics, rayons and nylons, which were much cheaper or more desirable to the public at large. The existing staff was only about twenty-five percent of what it had been when I worked there. There was a smell of death and decline in the air. All of the people I knew were gone. I asked about Robert Redpath. I was told he had absconded with a customer's wife in New York several years before and had not been heard of since. Like vines grown over a garden wall, this place and all the memories it contained had been swallowed up by time.

CHAPTER 44

ERNIE PATTERSON

"We become composites of everyone we have ever loved."
~ Anonymous

My duties at Richardson Sons and Owden continued to be "general dog's body." That is, whatever was asked of me, including delivering mail around the city to save on postage. As far as I could see, no consideration was given to my tramping through heavy rainfall to save a few pennies on stamps, but that was part of my responsibility and duty in "learning the business." The company directors would also send me on other errands when they saw fit. On one such occasion, the managing director, an elderly gentleman of probably unsound mind, sent me round to the local railway station to pick up a radio. I naturally assumed that the radio would be a table model I could carry easily. After all, who in their right mind would send one person to pick up and carry a heavy piece of furniture almost a mile without a dolly or any other form of conveyance? The item turned out to be a floor model weighing at least seventy-five pounds. The lack of handles added to the difficulty. After struggling with it for several minutes, a couple of railway workers took pity on me and strapped the cumbersome object to my back. Navigating a drunken path through pedestrians in the shopping district, I staggered the half-mile or so back to the office, finally delivering it to the managing director. For this, I was given the princely sum of sixpence, a truly miserly amount. I seethed for about an hour, regretting that I had not set it down on the managing director's foot.

The grand total of my weekly earnings was about seventeen shillings and sixpence a week, not enough to sustain a cat, much less a human being. I was expected to get next to nothing and like it for the "valuable education" they never failed to mention they were providing for me. They even tried to convince me that they were doing all this at great personal sacrifice.

Adequate clothing for the office was a constant problem. I had one good suit, a green serge my grandmother had bought for me for my birthday after I left school. The remainder of my wardrobe was a scattering of cast-offs and other mismatched items. As a result, I resembled a rag-picker more than what was expected of me by my employers.

I wore the green suit only sparingly, trying to save it for important occasions. John Anderson, who was one of my superiors at the office and who possessed a wardrobe of fine suits, often asked me why I didn't wear the green suit more often. When I gave him the reason, he suggested that I go out and buy more clothing. I answered, "Fine. Why don't you see about getting me a raise and I'll do that." The response to this request, of course, was conspicuous silence.

I was eventually shifted to every department throughout the building where I was given instruction on various linen commodities. When in H department, which specialized in fancy linens, I made my first real friend inside the building, Ernie Patterson. Ernie ended up becoming a mentor to me in my formative years when I sorely needed one. He guided me toward maturity in a number of ways.

My actual boss in H department was a Mr. Trotter, a pensive man of about forty who had a perpetual, worried frown. Like many of the other bosses in the building, he "knew somebody" and his job was handed to him. He obviously hadn't earned it through any display of creativity or brainpower. I put the worried expression down to efforts on his part to look intelligent or to suggest that he was pondering immense issues.

Mr. Trotter was "staff", as was I, which gave us a leg up over the ordinary workers. As far as I could tell, the bosses, including Mr. Trotter, were nothing more than glorified overseers, glancing up occasionally from their newspapers to make sure there was not too much talking going on, and that work wasn't being ignored. I spent several hours a day playing "shove ha' penny" with my pals, only diverting my attention to work when Trotter or another boss glanced in my direction.

If I had stayed out a bit too late the night before, I would sometimes sneak a nap under the warehouse tables where the girls worked, resting on bolts of cloth. The added benefit was that I also had a grand view of some remarkable legs!

Ernie Patterson generally ran everything of any value within H department and was responsible for making sure the products were shipped properly and on time to our various customers domestically and abroad. Ernie was about thirty-five, medium height and powerfully built. He told me he had been a boxer in his earlier years and had had quite a few bouts, including several at the main venue in Belfast, The Ulster Hall, and his face left no doubt that this was true. His nose was partially flattened and bent to one side. He had some scar tissue around his eyes, and his knuckles were thickly welted.

Aside from his duties, Ernie spent half the day ducking in and out of the "bog" (the washroom) to smoke his Woodbine cigarettes. Smoking was not allowed in the warehouse itself because the odor would get into the linen. Ernie would light up a cigarette, have a few draws, extinguish it and place the remains in his vest pocket. Because he was in there so frequently, he would habitually check to see who was in the men's restroom before lighting up. This meant looking under the six-inch aperture at the bottom of the door. Since I hid out in the toilet myself from time to time to read or just escape work, I would also check under the door to see who was inside. A fine pair of shoes denoted somebody on staff. A rough pair always belonged to one of the workers.

Ernie and I realized at about the same time that often no shoes were visible under the door even when we were sure that Mr. Trotter was still in there.

It was quite a mystery. We were starting to wonder if he was levitating above the toilet swami-style. We finally determined that Mr. Trotter, being a fastidious and hygienic wee man, was squatting like a vulture to avoid placing his rear end on a toilet seat used by commoners. As a sidenote in our investigation of Mr. Trotter's toilet habits, we also noticed that he was using copious amounts of toilet paper. This too was a mystery until we deduced that he was using the paper to deaden the splash caused by standing on the seat and keeking from approximately two feet above water level.

Ernie was on his hands and knees one day doing his usual check under the door when Mr. Trotter came darting out. He fell over Ernie and hit his head on the sink, which rendered him momentarily unconscious. Horrified, Ernie bolted for his workstation.

Ernie blurted out to me what had happened and I went inside to find Mr. Trotter on his feet but somewhat dazed. He didn't seem to know what had happened and apparently had not even noticed Ernie kneeling on the floor. I was relieved that Ernie wasn't going to catch hell but more relieved that wee Mr. Trotter was not seriously injured.

Northern Ireland is the Bible belt of Britain, and there are numerous fundamentalists and others around preaching the gospel day and night. Most of them are on the deranged side but there are a few honest Christians among them. I was a regular churchgoer on Sunday nights, not out of any particular desire to better myself but because we had nothing better to do. I had no interest in the hereafter at that stage in my life.

An American evangelist named Dr. Cook came to Belfast and appeared in the Ulster Hall. I went to listen to him out of boredom and a little curiosity. He turned out to be a marvelous preacher. I was enraptured. Toward the end of his sermon, he exhorted any and all of us to come forward and declare our allegiance to Jesus. I was so overwhelmed by the power his words, I took the plunge and bolted down the aisle to the front of the stage full of religious fervor. Dr. Cook grasped each of us potential converts by the head and demanded us to cast out the devil and accept Jesus Christ as our personal savior, which we all agreed to do. I was completely overcome by the emotion of the night and floated home feeling reborn. When someone is grabbing your head with both hands, you don't argue.

Ulster Hall

At work the next day, Ernie started in with his usual vulgar jokes and scandalous remarks. Being that I was now above such lowly behavior, I didn't laugh and offer one of my own as I normally would. Ernie asked if I was feeling alright. Feeling Jesus standing behind me to see if I would pull a Judas or proudly announce that I was saved, I decided to announce my new commitment.

"I am a Christian now," I declared. "Please don't use that kind of language around me anymore."

Ernie laughed, assuming I was joking. A co-worker, Kenneth, a lad from the country who spent most of his day with a Bible under his arm, looking toward the heavens, congratulated me enthusiastically and welcomed me into the fold with all of the other decent people. The rest of the workers took my announcement pretty much in stride. Ernie, now aware that I wasn't kidding, regarded me with a scornful expression.

"Does this mean you can't say 'fuck' anymore?" he asked.

"Ernie," I answered, "I'm asking you again. Please don't use words like that around me from now on."

"Oh, okay. Sorry . . . how about 'shite' then? Is 'shite' okay?"

"That one, too!" I responded.

"Well," answered Ernie, "I suppose 'arse' and 'keek' are also out of the question?"

Ernie's workstation was about six feet away from mine. For the next several days, he whispered to me, "Rickyyyyyy! Come baaaaack to us! Don't leave us, Rickyyyyyyyy! Come baaaaaaaaack!"

After several days of intensive reprogramming, I eventually gave up my new commitment and succumbed to Ernie's pleading to return to my old ways. I was obviously not a suitable recruit or else I would have held out longer despite his persistence. I was quite relieved to abandon the entire process and return to

my normal behavior. Ernie welcomed me back, giving me his own secular
blessing as he did so.

"It's good to have you back, Sidney! You gave us quite a scare there!"

By "us", I assumed he meant all the heathens of the world collectively.
A week or so later, I was walking home from work when Kenneth caught up to
me and asked, "Are you still looking up, Sidney?"

I looked up, wondering what he meant.

"At what?" I asked.

"God!" he said.

Somewhat embarrassed that my conversion had lasted less than a week,
I mumbled in the affirmative and got away from him as quickly as possible.

Ernie always took a great deal of interest in my youthful escapades,
especially when I told him about a date I'd had with a new girl. He always gave
me advice about how to handle myself and eagerly asked me how the date went
the morning after, demanding every detail. If I indicated any further lack of
interest in that particular girl, he would usually say something like, "What
happened? Did she let a fart?" or "Did she show up with a pimple on her nose?"
or some similar remark. Even though these were exaggerated and outlandish
questions, he seemed to sense how easily a teenager like myself could be "put
off" a girl by what would be minor violations by adult standards.

I was able to ask Ernie questions I wouldn't dare ask my parents or in-
laws, particularly in matters involving sex. In many ways, Ernie's attitude and
shocking comments reminded me of my Uncle Alfie. For example, he gave me
careful instruction on how women reacted to certain circumstances. He told me a
story of the time he had taken a girl for a walk up Cave Hill. It was a beautiful,
sunny day, and he and his new girlfriend were relaxing in the heather. Before
long, heavy petting began to take place, and as the passion intensified, the girl
suddenly "fainted". Not to be put off, Ernie said that he proceeded to hoist up her
skirt, remove her knickers, and complete the act. Throughout it all, the girl
responded to each thrust with a thrust of her own, sneaking peeks at him
occasionally while pretending to be unconscious. When it was all over, Ernie
dutifully replaced her knickers and straightened her skirt. She then "came to" and
innocently asked, "I hope nothing happened after I fainted!" Ernie assured her
that absolutely nothing had happened, and they were both satisfied. Honor had
been maintained on her part and Ernie "got his hole", as he would put it. This is
perhaps the crudest expression in the Belfast vernacular but one which perfectly
illustrates Ernie's character.

Often, I would be telling Ernie about a date I had been on, rambling on
about how pretty she was, how wonderful she smelled, how nice she was to talk
to and so forth, only to be impatiently interrupted by, "Did ya get your hole or
didn't ya?" Ernie was not the most romantic fellow.

Ernie loved to tell stories of his younger days and experiences he had
with women. Having no other source of information, I always listened with keen

interest. These were valuable lessons to me as a callow youth sexually inexperienced and unwise to the wiles of women.

Ernie and I didn't get along all the time. There's one thing I've noticed about Belfast people. They can be having a wonderful time one minute and thumping each other the next, or vice versa. I've seen it in my own family. After a horrible row with insults hurled in all directions someone will say, "Who wants a cup of tea?" and everything is forgotten. It's almost as if they become ashamed of themselves but don't really know how to apologize. So it was with Ernie and me. On several occasions, we had a difference of opinion. Ernie had a rough side to him and a quick temper. We never came to blows, though. We liked each other too much to throw punches, and we always ended up mending the fence.

I learned a lot about life from Ernie. He may not have been the most educated or philosophical person I've ever known, but he had an infectious exuberance; and he knew how to laugh and enjoy himself despite the hardships in his life. That was where his wisdom lay.

CHAPTER 45

HARD MEN

"In the struggle for survival, the fittest win out at the expense of their rivals because they succeed in adapting themselves best to their environment."
~ Charles Darwin

Although a fairly large city, Belfast was more realistically a collection of small villages. We all stayed within our enclaves. Parts of the city were almost exclusively Catholic or Protestant. Though Protestants stayed away from the Falls Road, which was IRA territory, and Catholics avoided the Shankill Road, the Protestant stronghold, numerous specialty shops on the Shankill attracted people from everywhere on a Saturday afternoon. Both groups had all they needed in their own neighborhoods - their own schools, shops and playing fields. The City Center was where they would all blend together for shopping or the occasional movie or dance.

Each neighborhood had its own leading "hard man" and numerous other roughnecks with their eye on the title. In fact, all the neighborhoods around Belfast had their retinue of tough guys whose fame had spread all over the city. The stories of their exploits were legendary.

The three hardest men in Belfast at the time were Silver McKee, Stormy Weatherall, and Buck Alec. Silver was the hardest Taig (Catholic), Stormy was the hardest Prod (Protestant), and Buck was in a league all his own.

Silver was not very large, only five-foot eight or so, but he was built like a carnival strongman and, of course, was very proficient with his mitts. He got his nickname because his hair was a silvery-blonde color. Silver made his money collecting on bad debts for bookies, who at that time were almost always Catholics.

Silver McKee (left)

Bookmaking was legal, and there were booking shops around where the working class men could go in and place bets. If someone got too deeply in debt and was not coming up with the money, they would call Silver. The story was he would go as far as England to hunt down a defaulter if the money was good enough. I heard his usual line was, "Either pay up or I've got to break your arm. Take your pick." It wasn't an idle threat.

Folklore has it that Silver overstepped himself in a London nightclub one night and was unceremoniously tossed down a flight of concrete steps by two English bouncers who had not heard of his reputation. Though one of his arms was broken, Silver went back about an hour later swinging a club with his good arm. He destroyed the bar and sent the two bouncers to the hospital.

When back in Ireland, his good luck ran out, and he was sentenced to six months in the Crumlin Road Jail for extortion. One of his pals went up to meet him when he got out. As they were walking along Royal Avenue, he said to Silver, "I hate to tell you this Silver, but nobody knows who you are anymore. A couple of new guys have taken over your spot."

"Well," he answered, "I suppose I'd better remind everyone then!"

Without hesitation, he turned and jumped headfirst through a plate glass store window. This was before the days of safety glass, incidentally. He then jumped back out, brushed the shards of glass from his clothes and casually returned to his stroll along Royal Avenue. It wasn't long before word spread around that Silver was back in town. The challengers to the throne who had been talking a big show when Silver was in jail were nowhere to be found.

The Prod's head tough guy was Stormy Weatherall. His real name was Jim. The nickname "Stormy" was derived from his last name. He was a commando in the British Army, served in World War II and took part in the European invasion by the Brits. The most common story about Stormy was how he had tied one on one night and single-handedly destroyed an entire village in France. According to legend, it took about fifteen MP's to get him under control.

Stormy was over six feet tall with a huge back and shoulders. To meet him personally, he was the most inoffensive person imaginable, but in a street brawl he was an awesome spectacle to behold. He used every part of his body - fists, knees, elbows, head, anything to annihilate his opponent. He could demolish someone before he had a chance to get his hands up. However, he only employed fighting when provoked.

I've heard tales that Stormy and Silver inevitably met in battle, and that Stormy came out on top, proving that a tough, large man will usually win out over an equally tough but smaller man.

The most famous of all the hard men was Buck Alec. He was quite small at about five-foot six, but he was built like a gnarled oak tree. I don't think it's a coincidence that the most feared men throughout history have been short of stature. (Napoleon, Mussolini, Hitler, etc.) I suppose this has always been true, in Belfast or anywhere else, and the reason is no mystery. To be taken seriously, a smaller man must simply be nastier than the other guy. While a large man's strength and skill is rarely tested because of his imposing physical presence, a small man must defend himself constantly. Thus, the bag of dirty tricks, tolerance for pain and killer instinct are developed.

Buck Alec

Buck's real name was Alec Robinson. He lived off York Street, one of Belfast's toughest, most hard-bitten neighborhoods. When referring to that part of town, people often used to say, "They eat their young over there, you know."

York Street ranked with Shankill Road, Falls Road and the Ardoyne as neighborhoods to be avoided.

Each morning at six o'clock, Buck would ride his bicycle from his home down to the Belfast Lough and go for a swim, winter or summer. This was remarkable because the Lough was freezing in the wintertime. This toughened him up and did wonders for his reputation as a hard man.

Belfast Lough

Local folklore held that "The Buck" went to Chicago in the 1930's and became a hit man for gangsters, but Belfast was such a rumor mill, it was hard to know what was true and what was made up by someone at a pub to add excitement to whatever tale they were spinning. The city was full of natural storytellers who loved to make up wild, bold-faced lies and elaborate shamelessly on rumors. All anyone really knew for sure was that Buck Alec came back from Chicago with a lot of money and a lot of mystery connected to how he had obtained it. His past dalliances in America were the subject of endless, whispered speculation.

Something else that added to Buck's mystique was a mysterious rumor that he kept a menagerie of exotic animals in his back yard. The only "pets" I was ever able to verify he owned were three lions. The story goes that he bought the lions from a circus which was about to put them down because they were old and no longer useful for performing. I never did find out where Buck Alec lived so I could see for myself what other animals he had, but the gossip mongers and tale spinners of Belfast claimed to have seen or heard about all sorts of strange and wonderful creatures strolling around in his yard. This was very exciting to me because the only other place I had ever heard lions roaring was in Tarzan movies. I would lie in my bed at night imagining giraffes strolling casually around the yard and monkeys swinging in the trees.

I also heard that Buck would sometimes take one of the lions around the streets in a cage drawn by a horse and cart and, for a few pennies from the children, would get into the cage and wrestle with it. He wasn't doing it for the money, though, just the show. He would sometimes walk them around town on a chain, too. This didn't hurt his reputation as a tough guy. He was our Tarzan.

The Belfast City Council wasn't too crazy about Buck's lions and the threat they posed to the general public if they should escape, but there was nothing in the city charter at that time that said anything about owning wild animals. Buck's show became so well-known that when Laurel and Hardy visited Belfast, they insisted on going up to meet Buck at his little house on York Street.

Buck had been a professional boxer at one point and retired undefeated. He was never known to have lost a street fight, either, even into his sixties. The most common story was how he had battled five and six policemen at once and came out on top. I don't know if this was a common occurrence or if it had only happened once, but at that time in Belfast the main measure of one's manhood was how many cops it took to bring him in. As far as I could see, however, the cops were always respectful toward Buck, nodding at him as he passed.

"How ya doin' today, Buck?" they would ask.

"Just fine, Constable!" he would bellow.

As Buck got into his later years, he was constantly being challenged by young guys trying to dethrone him, like young gunslingers coming into the western town to test their speed and skill against the aging legend. Buck Alec's son-in-law told me a story about one such occasion when he was having a quiet pint of Guinness with Buck in a bar off York Street. Buck was around sixty-four at the time. A man in his twenties approached their table.

"Are you Buck Alec?" the younger man asked.

Without looking up, Buck answered, "I am that."

"You don't look that hard to me," he said, obviously looking for a row.

"Ach, go away and stop botherin' me," Buck said. "Can't you see I'm having a pint?"

The hardcase persisted and called Buck a name. Unfortunately for him, Buck had forgotten more about fighting than the younger man had yet learned. Buck spun around on his stool and delivered a wicked upper cut to his jaw. The rough went down like a brick chimney, unconscious before he hit the floor. Buck then got off his stool and booted him across the floor out the front door and onto the sidewalk outside. A cop was walking past.

"This parcel of shite is annoying me, Constable," Buck said. "I wish you'd take him away."

Though it was obvious the man had already been taken care of, the cop answered, "It's no trouble, Buck." He then summoned a Black Maria, or paddy wagon, which arrived about ten minutes later. He was still unconscious as the cops loaded him in.

It's hard for me to guess if even Mike Tyson would have been a match for Buck Alec in his prime. In the Belfast Public Library, there is a section devoted to Buck Alec to this day. There's talk of a movie and a book about him. He is a true legend of Belfast and just about everyone there still knows his name and can tell a story or two about him.

I have the privilege of knowing a bit more than the average person does about Buck Alec because my wife and I have been friends with his daughter, Sally, for decades. Despite all the rumors, she refers to her father as a "free spirit" and remembers him as a dedicated family man, a faithful friend, and a loving father. Apparently, the hands that crushed all foes were equally gentle when rocking his babies.

Despite these characters and the chance we all ran of receiving a bloody good thumping from one of them, the worst that could happen was a day or two in the hospital. Murder was unheard of. Shooting and knifing were out of the question. Crimes against women and children were strictly forbidden. Anyone who tampered with a woman or child could be sure of swift justice on the street or inside Belfast's city jail. There was a code of ethics in Belfast at that time in spite of the squalor and viciousness. Someone who beat up someone else was just as likely to buy him a pint and send him home in a taxi afterwards. Nobody wanted to kill anyone, although they might have come close to it sometimes. The brawls were usually over politics, religion, or women and almost always fueled by alcohol.

The hard men, however, are no more. With the advent of "the troubles" since the sixties with the I.R.A.*, the U.D.A.*, and the U.V.F.* organizations, a hard man in Belfast became a fifteen year-old with a handgun. Whereas in the past they used their fists, heads, and feet in a fight, today its baseball bats, knives, and with increasing frequency, guns. Ireland has become much more serious, as has most of the world. Even fighting isn't as carefree as it once was. It was almost a game to us, but it certainly is not that anymore, as the death tolls constantly demonstrate.

A case from the late 1990's comes to mind of two Australian tourists, young men, walking through Belfast who were set upon by a group of about twenty street punks who were marauding around the neighborhood, attacking anyone who got in their way. They were both beaten savagely. One of them lost an ear. I was disgusted when I read that article and wondered how anyone could take honor or pride in such a cowardly act. I felt an odd kinship with the boys because the story reminded me of the beating Hyndsie and I took from the four I.R.A. supporters outside the Park Picture House. To the credit of the people of Belfast, however, when the story hit the news, donations and gifts flooded in for the two Australian boys. Their hospital bills were paid for and then some. The story ended with the boys saying they were very touched by the kindness of the people of Belfast and would gladly come back. Goodness had overcome evil once again.

I am providing the following descriptions of the I.R.A., Provisional I.R.A., U.D.A. and U.V.F. for anyone interested in the history and definitions of these groups, taken from Wikipedia and other sources.

I.R.A. –

The **Irish Republican Army** (**IRA**) (Irish: *Óglaigh na hÉireann*) was an Irish republican revolutionary military organization. It was descended from the Irish Volunteers, an organisation established on 25 November 1913 that staged the Easter Rising in April 1916. In 1919, the Irish Republic that had been proclaimed during the Easter Rising was formally established by an elected assembly (Dáil Éireann), and the Irish Volunteers were recognized by Dáil Éireann as its legitimate army. Thereafter, the IRA waged a guerilla campaign against British rule in Ireland in the 1919-21 Irish War of Independence.

Following the signing in 1921 of the Anglo-Irish Treaty, which ended the War of Independence, a split occurred within the IRA. Members who supported the treaty formed the nucleus of the Irish National Army founded by IRA leader Michael Collins. However, much of the IRA was opposed to the treaty. The anti-treaty IRA fought a civil war with their former comrades in 1922-23, with the intention of creating a fully independent all-Ireland republic. Having lost the civil war, this group remained in existence, with the intention of overthrowing both the Irish Free State and Northern Ireland and achieving the Irish Republic proclaimed in 1916.

The **Provisional Irish Republican Army** (**IRA**) is an Irish republican paramilitary organisation whose aim was to remove Northern Ireland from the United Kingdom and bring about a United Ireland by force of arms and political persuasion. It emerged out of the December 1969 split of the Irish Republican Army due to differences over ideology and over how to respond to violence against the nationalist community. This violence had followed the community's demands for civil rights in 1968 and 1969, which met with resistance from the unionist community and from the authorities, and culminated in the 1969 Northern Ireland riots. The IRA conducted an armed campaign, primarily in Northern Ireland but also in England, over the course of which is believed to have been responsible for the deaths of approximately 1,800 people. The dead included around 1,100 members of the British security forces, and about 630 civilians. The IRA itself lost 275 – 300 members of an estimated 10,000 total over the thirty-year period. The Provisional Irish Republican Army is also referred to as the **PIRA**, the **Provos**, or by its supporters as the **Army** or the **'RA**; its constitution establishes it as *Óglaigh na hÉireann* ("The Irish Volunteers") in the Irish language.

The IRA's initial strategy was to use force to cause the collapse of the Northern Ireland administration and to inflict enough casualties on the British forces that the British government would be forced by public opinion to withdraw from the region. This policy involved recruitment of volunteers, increasing after Bloody Sunday, and launching attacks against British military and economic targets. The campaign was supported by arms and funding from Libya and from some groups in the United States. The IRA agreed to a ceasefire in February 1975, which lasted nearly a year before the IRA concluded that the British were drawing them into politics without offering any guarantees in relation to the IRA's goals, and hopes of a quick victory receded. As a result, the IRA launched a new strategy known as "the Long War". This saw them conduct a war of attrition against the British and increase emphasis on political activity, via Sinn Féin.

The success of the 1981 Irish hunger strike in mobilising support and winning elections led to the Armalite and ballot box strategy with more time and resources devoted to political activity. The abortive attempt at an escalation of the military part of that strategy led republican leaders increasingly to look for a political compromise to end the conflict, with a broadening dissociation of Sinn Féin from the IRA. Following negotiations with the SDLP and secret talks with British civil servants, the IRA ultimately called a ceasefire in 1994 on the understanding that Sinn Féin would be included in political talks for a settlement. When this did not happen, the IRA called off its ceasefire from February 1996 until July 1997, carrying out several bombing and shooting attacks. These included the Docklands bombing and the Manchester bombing, which together caused around £500 million in damage. After the ceasefire was reinstated, Sinn Féin was admitted into all-party talks, which produced the Belfast Agreement of 1998.

On 28 July 2005, the IRA Army Council announced an end to its armed campaign, stating that it would work to achieve its aims using "purely political and democratic programmes through exclusively peaceful means", and shortly afterwards completed decommissioning. In September 2008, the nineteenth report of the Independent Monitoring Commission stated that the IRA was "committed to the political path" and no longer represented "a threat to peace or to democratic politics", and that the IRA's Army Council was "no longer operational or functional". The organisation remains classified as a proscribed terrorist group in the UK and as an illegal organisation in the Republic of Ireland. Two small groups split from the Provisional IRA, first in 1986 (Continuity IRA) and then in 1997 (Real IRA). Both reject the Belfast Agreement and continue to engage in violence.

U.D.A. –

The **Ulster Defence Association (UDA)** is a loyalist paramilitary group in Northern Ireland. It was formed in September 1971 and undertook an armed campaign of almost twenty-four years during "The Troubles". Most UDA attacks were carried out using the name **Ulster Freedom Fighters (UFF)**. It is classified as a terrorist group in the United Kingdom.

The UDA's declared goal was to defend unionist areas from attack and to counter Irish republican paramilitaries. However, about 80% of its 259 known victims were civilians. The majority of these were Catholics killed in what the group called retaliation for attacks on Protestants. High-profile attacks carried out by the group include the "Milltown Massacre", the Castlerock Killings", and the Greysteel Massacre." The UDA declared a ceasefire in 1994, although sporadic attacks continued until it officially ended its armed campaign in November 2007.

U.V.F. –

The **Ulster Volunteer Force (UVF)** is a loyalist paramilitary group in Northern Ireland. The current incarnation was formed in May 1966 and named after the Ulster Volunteers of 1912, although there is no direct link between the two. The group undertook an armed campaign of almost thirty years during "The Troubles". It declared a ceasefire in 1994, although sporadic attacks continued until it officially ended its armed campaign in May 2007.

The UVF's declared goal was to destroy Irish republican paramilitary groups. However, the vast majority (more than two-thirds) of its 481 known victims were Catholic civilians. During the conflict, its deadliest attack in Northern Ireland was the "McGurk's Bar bombing", which killed 15 civilians. The group also carried out a handful of attacks in the Republic of Ireland, the most deadly of which was the "Dublin and Monaghan bombings" - this killed 33 civilians, the highest number of deaths in a single day during the conflict.

The group is a proscribed organisation in the Republic of Ireland and a designated terrorist organisation in the United Kingdom.

CHAPTER 46

THE BELFAST SHIPYARD

"When I started here there were 24,000. We're down to a handful now. It's like a dead city down here where it used to be a teeming city. You get the impression from the men that it would be a relief to be over because it's been hanging over them for the last couple of years."

~ Bill Alexander, CEO of The Belfast Shipyard, on its closing. BBC, 1/13/03.

As a lad, I was constantly hearing stories about the famous Belfast shipyard. I thought it must be a marvelous place. I had developed a love of ships and the ocean from high sea adventure movies and books. I must have read *Treasure Island* a dozen times. I always imagined men hanging from ropes and scaffolds working and singing old sea shanty's in perfect unison like in movie musicals.

Belfast Shipyard, circa 1900

I was never fortunate enough to work at the shipyard when I came of age, but many of my mates did. It employed about 12,000 people in the early 1950's - boiler makers, platers, riveters, electricians, carpenters, red leaders and the like. The Belfast shipyard has the dubious distinction of having built the *Titanic* which, as everyone knows, went down on its maiden voyage after striking an iceberg. I often thought that was typical of Belfast and its bad luck. It's a wonder that the myth of "the luck of the Irish" lasted another day after that.

There is a rumor that the serial numbers of the ship when held up to a mirror read "No Pope Here" leading some to believe that the sinking was some kind of divine retribution.

The shipyard men used to take trams from their tiny row houses in East Belfast and around the dock areas. The trams, electrically propelled with trolleys, were often overburdened with men hanging on from every projection on the outside. The drivers and conductors knew better than to complain and tolerated the overcrowding with good humor.

One day, an English conductor, unschooled in Belfast ways, refused to move the tram until half the hangers-on got off. The tram sat for twenty minutes, and nobody budged. The conductor refused to give the signal to start. At that point, somebody yelled, "Can anyone drive this tram?" A ruddy shipyard worker replied, "I can!" whereupon the driver and conductor were unceremoniously ejected from the tram. With its new driver, the tram was driven down the road at full throttle to the hooting and hollering of all the workers, as pedestrians scrambled for their lives in every direction. That particular conductor was never seen or heard from again. He probably went back to England the same day.

There were people employed at the shipyard whose only job was to collect and place bets with bookies. The management closed its eyes to this practice because it was better to have a few runners working in the shipyard than to have everyone going out to place their bets. However, some of the workers did take advantage of this leniency and would sit in the bathroom stalls all day to avoid working. As a result, management decided to have what was known affectionately as "shithouse clerks" to man the toilets. They would check each man in and, after an appropriate time, perhaps ten minutes, would go down and tap on the glass window of the toilet door and say, "Your time is up." A story went that one guy answered, "But I'm not finished yet." To which the clerk responded, "You're not even trying. Your face isn't red!"

The bosses were known as "hats" because of their distinctive derbies. The hats were hated and feared since they had the power to end one's shipyard career on a whim. One hat in particular was extremely disliked. He was a big man with a prominent stomach who walked slowly around and, with cold eyes, surveyed those who were not moving fast enough. One winter, several feet of snow settled in Belfast, covering not only the streets but the decks of the ships under construction. A couple of the lads made a snowball on the deck of a ship that was taller than a man when they finished it. One of them saw the hat walking by about fifty feet below. With one mind, the lads gently pushed the enormous snowball off the side of the ship, scoring a direct hit on the hat. The men fell all over the deck with laughter. He never quite regained his full authority after that and he quit in disgust a few weeks later.

Many fine ships came out of the shipyard. Sadly, the shipyard today is but a ghost of its former self. Once bustling with industry, it is now eerily quiet as if still mourning the souls lost on the *Titanic*.

CHAPTER 47

THE B-MEN

"I have never seen a situation so dismal that a policeman couldn't make it worse."
~ Brendan Behan

I was about eighteen when I joined the B-Specials, a reserve police force in Belfast. We weren't paid much for our service – maybe ten pounds a year - but we were there in case of an uprising by the Catholics or an assault by the I.R.A. In those days, there were stories of a Captain Black (what else?) amassing an army south of the border, preparing to march on Northern Ireland and wrest it back from the crown, driving the Protestants into the sea as they did so.

We were trained very minimally in police duties and were taught how to fire a rifle and a handgun. Our main purpose was to patrol the city on Saturday nights to make sure the peace was kept.

Little was known about the B-Specials before Northern Ireland made world headlines in the civil unrest which commenced in 1969 and they were disbanded by the British Government for alleged over-reaction to Catholic demonstrations. We were the equivalent of police reservists in the States. We all held regular jobs during the week but would don police uniforms and weapons on weekends to assist in basic policing – collecting drunks and breaking up brawls - so that the actual cops could concentrate on more important matters.

Even then, over twenty years before the troubles officially began, everyone in Northern Ireland knew that sooner or later there was going to be a showdown between the Protestants and the Catholics over the existence of the state. I never knew what the official qualifications were for membership in the the B-Specials but from some of the characters I knew in it, it seemed as long as you were alive, male, and Protestant, you were in.

I decided to join because I was considering a career as a constable, not because of any grand calling, but because I liked the look of the uniform and wanted to carry a gun like the old west sheriff's I had seen in American movies. So I went to the Queen Street police barracks and filled out the application. After a cursory screening, I was told to report to Dee Street police building for training. I was eighteen, fit and raring to go. There were several other young men like myself, but some of the other recruits were in their thirties and older.

The first few nights, we were drilled and marched around the building. Finally, rifles were produced and we were told we would be given instruction in weapon handling and shooting after we learned how to march. I was pretty good at walking, and I had mastered turning left and right years ago, so I thought,

"This is gonna be easy!" I'd also had a little practice shooting rats with my uncle's .22 rifle (well, one rat and a few trees) so I was confident I'd do well in that area, too.

During the drill instruction, one individual attracted my attention because of his peculiar mannerisms. He looked very old for a recruit, was shabbily dressed, and had a generally disheveled look as if he needed a good meal and a month of rest. While doing a marching drill one morning, the Drill Sergeant called out the instruction but before he had completed the command, this recruit started quivering uncontrollably, trying to anticipate whether he would be asked to turn right or left. I had formed a friendship with another recruit named Billy McKeown from a tough Protestant neighborhood known as Sandy Row. He noticed the antics of our nervous comrade, also.

"Look at that silly shite," he whispered to me out of the corner of his mouth. "He's keekin' himself."

The twitchy, wee man was a humorous, almost slapstick character. Charlie Chaplin or Buster Keaton couldn't have done a better job of playing the nervous buffoon. The combination of my worry for the poor sod and Billy's remarks had me sweating and biting my lip, desperately trying to hold in laughter as the Drill Sergeant glared at us suspiciously. I was about to bust a blood vessel but Billy was relentless. I began to wonder if he was trying to get me thrown out of the group.

"Look at him!" he said, "It's touchin' cloth!" (This is another colorful Irish colloquialism which, in the name of decency, I will refrain from defining. Suffice to say the "cloth" is that of one's underwear.) When the Sergeant looked over, Billy appeared beyond reproach, his face completely expressionless; while I choked red-faced knowing I would catch hell if I busted out laughing.

Miraculously, our unstable friend made it through the drill classes and we found ourselves holding rifles uncomfortably close to him, ready to try our hands on the firing range. The instructor stepped clearly out of the line of fire as we lay down on our stomachs and aimed at the targets at the end of the hall. A few of the lads had parked their bicycles at the side of the hall even further out of the line of fire. The sergeant bellowed, "Get set! Aim! F-!" but we were all over-excited about firing off our first round and pulled our triggers before he could finish the command. All the gunfire pushed Old Shaky, as we had now christened him, right over the edge. He started shaking even more violently, his rifle spasming in all directions. Most of us did fairly well for beginners, but when Old Shaky pulled the trigger, the rifle became a living thing in his hands, pulling him in every direction. He squeezed off a round that missed the sergeant by about a foot. The sergeant dove out of the way, and the bullet hit one of the bicycles hanging on the wall. The front tire fell off and rolled across the floor.

"In the name of Jasus, stop shootin'!" the sergeant bellowed, horrified by his brush with death. After this accident, it was decided that Old Shaky represented a greater threat to the Protestants than the I.R.A. did, and he was given his walking papers, much to our relief. Turning him loose on the streets of

Belfast was more than the city deserved. Hopefully, he found work more agreeable with his nervous system.

After six weeks of training, we were considered safe enough to release on an unsuspecting public and were issued the black uniform of the force. We were given black leather belts and instructed on their care and polishing. Our truncheons were lead-filled black mahogany. A blow from one of them could paralyze a man's shoulder for a month. We were told never to hit anybody on the head as it would probably be lethal. We were not allowed to take our weapons home but picked them up at the start of duty each day. We were issued 45's - large, clumsy weapons which were ridiculously heavy and had a kick like a mule. The idea of any of us developing a "quick-draw" like we had seen in the Hollywood westerns was completely out of the question. As we left to go on duty each time, we were ceremoniously issued five bullets, which we solemnly loaded into our weapons, leaving the chamber next to the hammer empty to save us from blowing a toe off, or worse, shooting a civilian because of an accidental discharge. I wondered if the I.R.A. men we were supposed to be protecting Belfast from also kept the hammer chamber empty. At the end of the tour of duty, we had to give the bullets back and turn in our guns, as we could not be trusted to bring them home. We couldn't wait to get started and most of us put on our uniforms as soon as we got home and strutted proudly in front of our admiring families.

B-Specials rifle training exercise

The first night out, I walked up our street, very conscious of my new uniform, which fit me fairly well. I was fortunate in this respect because the uniforms were "one size fits all." Some of the larger boys were splitting the seams of their uniforms while the smaller boys were lost in theirs, looking like kids playing in their father's clothes.

As I came up the street in my new uniform, Mrs. McCallister, the matriarch of the only Catholic family in the neighborhood, was in her usual position at her front gate, keeping an eye on the comings and goings of her neighbors and chatting to each one that passed. She was never too fond of me, especially since I had bounced half a brick off the head of her dog Rex, the vicious hell-beast mentioned earlier. Her resentment toward me over the brick incident was not improved by the sight of me in the uniform of the force most Catholics despised. A look of deep loathing spread across her face as I passed.

"In the name of Jasus, wud ye luk at him!" she said to Gutsy Perky, the neighborhood slander specialist who happened to be standing there.

"God help Ulster with the likes of that defendin' it!" she continued.

She was about to say something else when I turned. Her jaw stopped mid-flap. Having noticed the effect my father's comment had on her years before, I decided to say it again just in case she had forgotten it.

"Hell will never be full till you're in it, Mrs. McCallister."

Again, she turned brilliant red, and I continued on my way, feeling a bit better but still smarting from her comments. It was not exactly an encouraging critique of my appearance in my new uniform. The fact that her assessment was the first was not helpful, either.

My decision to join the B-Specials had no meaningful impact on either my mother or my father, as far as I could tell. They remained as blasé as ever. No fuss was made and no photographs were ever taken of me in uniform.

We had a sergeant from the south of Ireland, probably a Catholic, who came up to the north looking for work and found himself in the police department. We always got a bit of a lecture before we went out for a Saturday night prowl. We were given assigned streets or areas to cover, but I used to wander all over the place looking for action.

My closest friends didn't take me at all seriously in my uniform, either. In fact, they yelled very disrespectful comments as I walked by trying to look the part.

"Ach, would ya look at her!"

"Big, good thing!"

"Aye, big fifty dollar ride!"

"Thinks he's marvelous, so he does!"

Any pedestrians nearby would burst out laughing at my expense. Finally, I would take out my nightstick and chase them all down the street while they whistled the Keystone Cops theme.

My friend Jimmy was the worst offender of all. Every time he saw me on patrol, he would sneak up behind me, dig his hand up the crack of my arse, and run me down the street for as far as he could while I struggled to dislodge his hand. This didn't help elevate public perception of me as an authoritative lawman.

I was assigned to patrol the central area of Belfast, including Wellington Place, the City Hall, Donegal Square, Fisherwick Place, and College Square. Nothing much happened in these areas, so after the first few nights, I started wandering farther away over to Dublin Road and the infamous Amelia Street where prostitutes and a plethora of undesirable types sought out each other's company.

Amelia Street was a sight to see. It was only about a hundred feet long and ran parallel to the Great Northern Railway. It contained a pub at each of its two corners, warehouses at the bottom end, and old row houses in between which had been built around the turn of the century. Several of these houses had biblical tracts in the windows, but every one of them was a house of ill-repute. The girls stood in the doorways or walked along the front of the railway station looking for customers. (I call them "girls" out of a generous impulse, for not one of them looked younger than forty.) They would pick up men, take them to the back alleyways and have a quick kerfuffle for half a crown, five bob, or whatever the going rate was at the time. They only dealt with working class guys, shipyard workers and other men who hung around the bars.

The girls made no effort to conceal themselves when I came along and would often proposition me as well, doing their best to embarrass me and take advantage of my naïve sensibilities. They made comments like, "Hey, Maggie! Here's a big peeler comin' to lift ya!" The term "peeler" was used to describe the police officers in Britain because of Sir Robert Peel, who introduced a police force in London some two hundred years ago.

As I walked by one evening, I spied an acquaintance from my neighborhood, Dessie Burns, who was slightly challenged mentally and notoriously girl crazy. He was about thirty but had the mind of a ten year old. Dessie was fascinated with the hookers on Amelia Street and chased after them constantly. Whether or not he actually had anything to do with them I never knew. I was amusedly watching his futile attempts to create some magic with one of the girls one night when one of them approached me.

"That fella is botherin' us!" she complained, pointing toward Dessie, who was peering across from the opposite side of the street, doing his best to be invisible.

"What do you mean, bothering you?" I asked. "Have ya no home to go to?"

She gave me a dirty look and stormed off. Dessie came scooting across the street.

"What'd she say about me?" he demanded. "Did she say I was doing anything wrong?"

Dessie was harmless and I could not get upset with him. I said, "Dessie, your ma told me to tell ya that if I caught ya hangin' around down here, I was to run ya in."

All the color ran out of his face.

"You're not gonna take me in, are ya, Ricky?" he pleaded. "Sure I wasn't doin' nothin'!"

"Away home with ya, Dessie," I said, "or I'll tell yer ma you were bein' a bad boy!"

Dessie said no more but scuttled off in the direction of City Hall. A feeling of sadness washed over me as I watched him run around the corner and I sighed to myself. If I ran in every harmless kook in Belfast in Pied Piper fashion, there wouldn't be any room left in the jail for the real criminals.

The sergeant was giving us our instructions one night, pacing in front of our line and eyeing us one at a time to make sure we were all listening.

I thought, "Oh, my God. It's a crime wave! The I.R.A. is on the march from Dublin! Al Capone is in town! Gangsters have arrived in Belfast! There'll be pandemonium in the streets! Finally, we're gonna see some action!"

The sergeant continued, "Some of the shopkeepers on Castle Street . . . (the suspense was killing me) . . . have been complaining about fellas . . . (Yes? Yes?) . . . coming out of Maxims Bar . . . (Maxims Bar? So that's the hideout the gangsters and the IRA are going to use to launch their attack!) . . . and pissing in doorways."

Pissing in doorways? My heart sank. My hope for some excitement and possibly saving Belfast from invading hordes was dashed.

"Anybody you find pissin' in shop doorways, arrest 'em on the spot! We have to make an example of these fellas."

Maxims was a dance hall that was popular with the rugby crowd at the time. I had often seen young guys coming out of the dances at the City Centre and pissing in shop doorways, much to the dismay of the shopkeepers who would open up on Monday morning and find trails of urine leading from their door to the street, which was not very hygienic or pleasant to smell.

Searching for people relieving themselves was not exactly the kind of action I expected when I joined the B-Specials. Later that night, however, eager to prove myself an obedient soldier, I prowled around the city after the bars and dance halls emptied, shining my torch (flashlight) into doorways and alleys for phantom pissers. I spotted two young guys walking into a shop doorway on Donegal Place, but they didn't see me. Shortly thereafter, I heard a familiar and unmistakable splashing sound.

Donegal Place, Belfast

I walked up quietly and when I got to them, they were both pissing away unashamedly. I shone the torch on them. The hissing stopped abruptly as they frantically attempted to cover themselves.

"Jasus, what's that?" one of them yelled.

"There's no point in rushing now," I said. "You might as well finish. Then you can come with me."

They emerged from the shadows of the doorway, wide-eyed and white as ghosts. I grabbed each of them by the arm.

"Whudda ya doin'?" they asked in unison.

I said, "What am I doing? I'm arrestin' ya. Ya broke about six different laws."

I rattled off as many infractions as I could think of as I marched them down Queen Street: "Public urination, indecent exposure, spoiling of private property, sexual aberration, committing a lewd sexual act, contaminating a public thoroughfare . . ."

The two of them were struck with horror.

"Oh, please, let us go, let us go."

A variety of excuses then started flowing such as, "We were caught short!" and "We couldn't help it!" and "We had too much to drink!" and "We have overactive bladders!"

One of them said, "Oh, God. I'm a student and I'm gonna become a doctor. My parents'll never forgive me and I'll be kicked outta school. A police record'll ruin me for the rest of m'life."

"Ya, my da will kill me if he hears about this! Please, mister. Give us a break!" the other said.

"Well," I said, "you should have thought of that before you pissed in somebody else's doorway!"

One of them was becoming more and more panic-stricken over his impending crime record. I was doing my best to keep from laughing and maintain my stern expression. After all, I was only a year or two older than them myself but since this was my first time running in desperate criminals, I maintained my steely expression. I got them as far as the entrance to the Queen Street station when I stopped and very imperiously said, "Okay, I'm gonna give you guys a break. But I'll tell ya right now, if I catch either one of you pulling another stunt like you pulled tonight, you won't be so lucky. I'll throw the book at ya. On your way!"

They were so delighted to be let free; they were falling over themselves to thank me, nearly shaking my arm off. I thought one of them was going to kiss my hand. They promised it would never happen again and sped off like a couple of greyhounds in case I had a change of heart. I was finally able to have a good laugh. That incident was the closest I ever came to arresting anyone in the two years I spent with the B-Specials. I knew all along that I wasn't going to turn them in. They were just harmless college boys, and I didn't want to damage their futures for something so trivial. I enjoyed giving them a good scare but I could scarcely arrest someone for the very same offense I myself had committed too many times to count.

I didn't learn much in the B-Specials, but I did come to understand how the public perceived a police officer. All I had to do was look at someone to cause them discomfort, wondering why I was looking at them or what law they had broken.

One night, while on patrol in Belfast, I rounded a corner and was suddenly confronted by eight or nine tough-looking characters having a conversation. It was late at night and they had probably been drinking earlier on. I tensed up, wondering if I might be assaulted, which was not uncommon. The police uniform appeared to have a civilizing effect on them, though. Once they saw me, they exchanged goodnights and went their separate ways, even giving me a cheery, "Goodnight, Constable!"

Fortunately, I was tall enough to be taken for a regular police officer. Many of the B-Specials were treated disrespectfully because they were shorter and easily identified as reservists by the public. The Catholics didn't like the police because they were representatives of the state they despised. There was little love lost with the Protestants, either, even though they supported the police force in principal. For ourselves, we made no distinction between Catholic and Protestant in making our rounds and tried to base our dealings with people on their behavior, not their religion or other personal factors. I had entertained the idea of a police career before joining the B-Specials, but the terrible boredom of night patrols convinced me that it was not the career I wanted.

Another night, I was walking down Royal Avenue near midnight. The streets were deserted. I saw a figure approaching, staggering back and forth from one side of the sidewalk to the other. As he drew closer, I recognized him as Silver McKee, who I introduced you to earlier, reputedly the toughest Catholic in Belfast. Silver had a terrible reputation which I was all-too aware of. I had also heard that he was even meaner when he was loaded, as he now obviously was. As we were walking toward each other, he stopped in the middle of the sidewalk and gave me the once over. I knew that some of the tough guys around town would actually assault peace officers and try to get their guns, probably for the I.R.A., and here was none other than Silver McKee himself looking at me, a lanky eighteen year-old. I could see the thought racing through his mind, wondering if he should have a go. I kind of disarmed him by saying, "How ya doin', Silver?" He seemed to relax, quickly said, "Oh, just fine, Constable" and went along his way. By saying his name, I had shown that I knew who he was and could identify him later if he tried something. I don't know what he was thinking when he was leering at me but I was relieved that, whatever it was, he thought twice about it. I wouldn't have known what to do if had he gone for me, even if I had used my gun. After all, I had one empty chamber and only five bullets. I don't think five bullets would have been enough to stop Silver.

After two or three weeks in the Specials, we were all starting to get a little bored with the lack of real action. None of us had made an arrest attempt except Billy McKeown, who arrived back at the station one night shepherding a bevy of six or seven whores he had rounded up between Amelia Street and the City Hall. We had all been instructed by our Sergeant to leave the "hooers" alone as this was the job of the detectives who would round them up at periodic and pre-arranged intervals. Billy had either forgotten about or ignored this command. The girls he had picked up were chattering like mad and were obviously upset with Billy, who ignored the slurs being directed at him. We had nowhere to put them at the station, the cells being filled with the usual Saturday night drunks and punch-up artists, so after taking all their names, the Sergeant let them leave. The sergeant commended Billy for his initiative but reiterated his demand to leave the whores to their business. Obviously, they were not a priority for him.

While on patrol another night, I was checking out the display in the window of a sporting goods store when out of the corner of my eye, I sensed a huge figure trundling toward me along Wellington Place. I turned and recognized him immediately as "Pig" Minelly, a cop with the Royal Ulster Constabulary (R.U.C.) from Brown's Square Barracks. Pig was about six-four and weighed at least two hundred and fifty pounds. He was an imposing sight in his black R.U.C. uniform and greatcoat with a Webley strapped to his side and a truncheon at his hip.

Pig Meneely

Pig's fame was widespread in Belfast. He was given his nickname long before it was fashionable to call policemen by that name. It was said that one of his favorite practices was to sneak up on courting couples having a "knee trembler". When close enough, he would quickly bring his truncheon down hard between the mating pair, causing severe trauma to the appendage that connected them. Obviously, the effects on the man were most devastating and any further efforts at sexual activity were out of the question for weeks. I often wondered why someone who had received an attack of such an incredibly personal nature didn't complain about him or clobber him with a board when he wasn't looking. Perhaps somebody did and I didn't hear about it.

On the day I first met Pig, even though our uniforms were very similar, he recognized me as a B-Special immediately. It was getting late in the evening, and the pub crawlers were starting their usual Saturday night antics.

To that point in my police career, the most dramatic moment I had experienced had been the aforementioned incident during training when one of my fellow recruits had accidentally discharged his revolver, succeeding in mortally wounding a bicycle. But that was about to change.

The regular cops didn't like us at all. We were considered weekend cowboys, unpaid, untrained, and unsophisticated. Though we performed the same duties as the real cops, we didn't get paid a dime. I didn't know what Pig's feelings were about B-men, so I was very nervous as he approached.

"Are you on duty?" he snarled, his face twisted with disgust.

I reluctantly admitted that I was.

"Well, follow me then!" he said, "A couple'a boys are going at it in the College Bar and the bartender's gettin' nervous. We hav'ta go and break 'em up."

This particular bar was frequented mostly by college students, thus the name, and the odd Belfast lay-about. As we approached it, the sounds of breaking glass, tumbling furniture and incoherent yells grew in intensity. I thought it sounded more like a few hundred people fighting than a few. We stood in front of the door for a moment. He looked at me with steely eyes and asked, "Are ya ready then?"

"I'm right behind you," I declared. (I sure wasn't going in first.)

As we reached for the bat-wing doors, they burst open and someone shouted, "Here come the peelers!" A mid-sized Belfast hardcase came through the door as if he'd been shot out of a cannon. With amazing reflexes and without even breaking stride, the rough drove his boot upward and into Pig's groin. Fortunately, Pig's thick greatcoat muffled the effect of the blow. These coats were made of horsehair material and designed to ward off the lethal dampness of an Ulster winter.

"Ya fockin' wee bastard!" Pig bellowed, simultaneously grabbing the lout by the ears, yanking him forward, and rubbing his face up and down vigorously over the rough material and brass buttons of his tunic, kicking him up the shins as he did so. The man yelled and struggled to get free but he was like a child in Pig's grip. He screamed as the buttons shaved pieces of skin from his nose, lips, and eyebrows. After about fifteen seconds of this, the hardcase looked as though he had stuck his face into a thresher. Pig whacked him around the ears a few times with his large, red hands, spun the thoroughly defeated man around, and planted a size fourteen police boot squarely in the center of his arse, driving him forward about ten feet. Holding his face in one hand and his backside in the other, he staggered away down Wellington Place. I had never seen anyone so thoroughly demolished in such a short period of time, or so creatively. Prior to this, I had never considered buttons to be a weapon.

"Do you want me to go after him and arrest him?" I asked.

"Arrest him?" he snarled, "D'ya think I wanna spend my day off in court testifyin' against that wee bastard? Let 'im go home 'n explain that face to his mates."

Then he looked at me and said, "That's your first lesson. With twats like that, ya kick the shite out of 'em. That's the only court appearance they deserve."

For the first time, I had seen Belfast street justice up close. Immediate and effective. There were no complaints of police brutality. The hooligan got what he deserved. He knew it and the cop knew it. After that, quelling the remaining disturbance in the bar was easy.

He stepped into the bar and everybody froze one by one as they noticed Pig standing there. When everyone had stopped swinging, he announced, "That's it. You're finished. Everybody out."

The place went dead silent. Everybody stood there in tableau for a moment, frozen in mid-swing, then they all dropped their fists, politely set down the chairs or bottles they were about to throw, and casually headed for the door as if a meeting had just adjourned. A few of them even stopped to straighten up the place a little before they left. It was the most impressive piece of policing I've ever seen in my life. Pig was like an adult talking to a room full of children. In ten seconds, the place was deserted except for all the broken furniture and one befuddled bartender. Pig walked over to the bar and sat down.

"Pour a pinta Guinness, Jimmy" he said to the bartender. "I've got a terrible drouth on me. And give the lad here one as well."

He proceeded to sink about three pints in quick succession while I struggled with my one.

"Well," he said, "did'ya learn anything tonight?"

"Indeed I did!" I said. "That was better than the six weeks training they gave me at Dee Street!"

"Is there anything else you would like to know about real police work?" he asked.

"Not really," I said, "but I would like to ask you a favor."

"What's that?"

"If you ever see me having a knee trembler behind the city hall," I said, "try not to notice me!"

His stern face broke into a grin for the first time. He raised his glass and said, "Aye, that I will!" Pig Minelli wasn't so bad, after all.

I never did have to make use of the lesson Pig Minelli taught me that night, which was just as well. I wasn't big or mean-looking enough to command the kind of respect he was given. Most of the cops in those days were gargantuan men from the country. Their mere size was enough to stop riots. When I look at the average size of the present crop of R.U.C. men in Belfast, I wonder how they manage to survive. Then again, one doesn't have to be the size of Pig Minelli to pull a trigger, as thugs on either side of the political divide have demonstrated.

They finally did away with the B-Specials in 1969, long after I had left them. Due to protests from Ulster's Roman Catholic minority, who found their methods objectionable, the force was disbanded. At that point, they were considered by many to be a thug-type force commissioned for no other purpose than to harass the Catholics. I can't speak for those who came after me, but I never treated anyone badly and no one else in the B-Specials did either as far as I knew. However, the B-Specials somehow developed a bad reputation over the years. Perhaps they became more aggressive as threats and attacks by the IRA grew in severity and frequency.

The IRA wasn't the only thing to worry about, though. Unprovoked attacks on B-Specials by tough, local Catholics, primarily around the border areas of Northern Ireland, became more common. A few B-Specials may have behaved badly as a result, making the entire force questionable. Of course, the hardcases who attacked them and made them feel the need to use more drastic measures to defend themselves weren't held to the same standard. Organizations are easy targets for crusaders and zealots with agendas to push, but scattered, disorganized groups of thugs with no standards cannot be monitored or disbanded.

Many years later, I met an I.R.A. supporter in California whom I christened "The Pride of the Provos." She was originally from Belfast and appeared on radio and television, pleading the I.R.A. cause in Southern California. I met her during a radio interview about the troubles, and she told me the police in Belfast had kicked the door of her house down and arrested her repeatedly. After hearing about some of her escapades, I told her, "Well, at least it wasn't a case of mistaken identity as far as you were concerned."

When she found out I had been a B-Special back in the early 1950's, she became elated. At last, she had the devil in front of her in a safe venue where she could unload. She called me every name in the book and maligned me at every opportunity to anyone who would listen as "one of those black-enameled bastards" who terrorized the poor Catholics. Not wanting to disappoint her, I lied and told her I had kicked in a few Catholic doors myself during raids up the Falls Road, where she came from. That was a complete falsehood, but I didn't want to ruin her preconceived notions.

I'm sure I would handle the situation more maturely now but at the time of this interview, I was young, proud and contemptuous toward people like her who did everything possible to make trouble, or encourage and support those who were doing so, then complain about the effects it had on their lives. I wasn't going to listen to her half-baked accusations. Though there were certainly a few roughnecks and wild cards in the B-Specials as there are in any police force anywhere, I tried not to let the uniform go to my head and never abused the small measure of authority it granted me. I knew that telling her this would either not be believed, make me look like I was trying to hide something, or fall on deaf ears, so I became the devil she expected me to be.

Anyway, the B-Specials exist no longer. The main policing agency in Northern Ireland, the Royal Ulster Constabulary, has been reformed and is now known as the Northern Ireland Police Authority. Ulster's Protestants decried these changes, but their protests were ignored.

On a trip home recently, I was talking to a postman. The postal authority is still known as the Royal Mail, and the red post office vehicles still show the British crown as its emblem. We were discussing the changes in the police force.

"I guess you guys are next!" I remarked. "That British Crown on your truck will have to go!"

His face darkened.

"I'm bloody sure it won't," he snapped. "There'll be no more changes!" That remains to be seen. The symbols of Ulster's Protestant, loyalist heritage are being slowly but surely dismantled to render the province more acceptable to the Catholic minority. The Ulster of my day is on the verge of vanishing altogether, along with the "B-Specials".

"A.T.T. RICKERBY, SPECIAL CONSTABLE - Ulster Special Constabulary - Killed by Irish Republican Army – On 28th May 1922, a party of Specials were on mobile patrol in the Belleek and Garrison area of Fermanagh when they were ambushed by gunmen. Special Constable Rickerby was driving the lead vehicle when he was shot and fatally injured."

(An entry from the annals of the B-Specials. Possibly a distant relative of mine I never knew.)

"During its fifty years of service, the B Specials came to occupy a unique place of mythic proportions within the unionist community. They were regarded as the embodiment of the Northern Ireland state's ability to protect itself from internal and external threat." -
(The Ulster Special Constabulary, The B Specials, The Facts, An Educational Pamphlet.)

CHAPTER 48

THE STARLET AND THE SMALL TOWN BOY

"Ships that pass in the night, and speak each other in passing: Only a signal shown, and a distant voice in the darkness; So on the ocean of life, we pass and speak one another, Only a look and a voice, then darkness again and a silence."
~ Henry Wadsworth Longfellow

Lita Roza circa 1950

When I was about 18 or 19 and working at the Irish linen factory, I would usually take the bus home for lunch because I couldn't afford to go out to eat every day. I was on the upper level of the bus looking out the window at Royal Avenue one day when I spotted two very statuesque girls looking into a store window. They were beautifully dressed and obviously not from Belfast. I looked closer and recognized one of them as Lita Roza, an internationally famous singer. She recorded dozens of popular songs on the Decca label. Her best known song was *How Much is That Doggy in the Window*? My friends and I were crazy about her. Bursting with excitement, I ran downstairs, jumped off the bus, bounded over to her like a dopey puppy dog, smiled widely and said, "Hi, Lita! I'm Sidney!"

Startled, she stepped back a little but quickly relaxed as I told her how much I enjoyed her singing. Her sister smiled benignly, obviously accustomed to these intrusions.

Lita said, "Well, thank you, Sidney! How would you like to come to the theater tonight and see the show?"

"Yeah, I'd love to!" I answered.

"Well, go around to the side door and tell the watchman I told him to let you in, okay?"

I thanked her and walked back to work on a cloud. I couldn't wait to tell everybody at work what happened. Some of them believed it and some didn't. I talked the boss into making up a gift box of fine linen handkerchiefs to give her as a gift. He graciously had a lady in the office prepare it for me.

Grand Opera House, Belfast

I arrived at the Grand Opera House around seven o'clock, went down the alley to the side door, knocked on the stage entrance and introduced myself to the watchman. It was just like a movie. The only thing missing was a slot in the door with someone looking out and asking for a password. Hoping she had remembered to put my name on the list, I said, "I'm Sidney Rickerby. Lita invited me",

The watchman said, "Oh, right. Come on in."

Lita was sitting in her dressing room in front of a mirror framed by bright lights. She looked radiant. Her sister was beside her. They both looked over and gave me a wave. I went in and we talked for a few minutes. The stage manager came crashing in and said, "You're on in five, Miss Rosa!" I felt like I was in a Bing Crosby musical. She got up and said, "I hope you enjoy the show, Sidney."

I walked her to the edge of the stage and she skipped onstage to deafening applause. An English comedian named Arthur (whose last name I can't recall) stood next to me as I watched Lita from the wings. He was her supporting act and couldn't have looked more bored. In fact, he was checking the football scores.

I said, "What are you doing? The pools?"

He answered, "Yeah, and if I win, I'm gonna go out there and give 'em the finger."

I hadn't seen his act but gathered that it didn't go well.

Lita sang her heart out, floated offstage, high from a flawless performance, and said, "I'll be right out, Sidney." She went into her dressing room and came out in a pink dress and white mink coat. I went outside with her. The cameras started popping and people swarmed around her, vying for autographs and interviews. Two guys rushed over who were connected to her or the opera house somehow. One of them said, "Come on, Miss Roza. We'll drive you home."

She got in the car. One of the two guys said, "Who's he?

I thought I was about to get dumped when she answered, "He's a friend of mine. Come on and get in the car, John."

We went up the Antrim Road to a bed and breakfast she was staying in. She told me she preferred them to hotels. It was a nice area with high class houses. I remember being impressed that she asked me questions about my life like any ordinary girl would. We tend to forget for some reason that celebrities are just people, too. Now that I was a B-Special, I said I was a reserve policeman. It sounded more impressive than "linen factory delivery boy." She seemed impressed so it had the desired effect. I left her at the door and said goodnight. She gave me a kiss on the cheek. Knowing this was my last chance, I turned and said, "How about a date?"

"How can we have a date when I'm working every night and you're working during the day?" she answered.

"How about Saturday afternoon?" I suggested. "I'm off and your show isn't until that night."

I was thrilled to hear her say, "Okay! Sure!"

She smiled and said goodnight. I couldn't contain myself. I had to tell someone, but it was almost midnight. I rushed over to Hyndsie's house, climbed up the trellis, went through his window and woke him up.

"Hey, Hyndsie! How would you like to have a date with Lita Roza's sister?"

"Have you been drinking?" he said groggily, rubbing his eyes.

"No, I'm sober as a judge."

I told him what happened. His eyes got wider and wider. He couldn't believe it, either.

I arrived at her bed and breakfast on Saturday afternoon at the appointed time and, as usual, her sister came out with her. She and Hyndsie hit it off immediately and we all went to the movies at the Mayfair Theater on Great Victoria Street. We watched John Wayne in The Fighting Kentuckian. His right-hand man in that movie was Oliver Hardy, if you can believe that combination. It was a magical night. Lita's sister was a smasher, too, so Hyndsie wasn't complaining. I spent half the movie looking at Lita Roza's face in the flickering light from the silver screen and wishing the night would never end. I wanted to put my arm around her but didn't want to be too forward and risk insulting her. It was excruciating just keeping my arm on the armrest. We took a taxi back to her bed and breakfast after the movie and I got another gleaming smile and another peck on the cheek as Hyndsie said goodnight to Lita's sister.

The next day, Lita was going to Dublin to perform. The night before, she had told me when her train was leaving so I met her at the station, handed her the linen handkerchiefs and saw her onto her train. She gave me a hug and turned her cheek for me to kiss. I decided to carpe the diem, pulled her close, held her face in one hand (gently but firmly), and planted a big one right on her lips.

She said, in a soft voice, "My goodness. Thank you."

She gave me one last hug and got on the train. She sat at the back of the car. The train slowly began to move. I waited to see her in the window. She looked out and waved, and then she was gone. It began to rain as the train rolled out of sight. Old Belfast seemed grayer and lonelier than ever.

CHAPTER 49

THE ISLE OF MAN

When the summer day is over
And the busy cares have flown,
Then I sit beneath the starlight
With a weary heart, alone.

And there rises like a vision,
Sparkling bright in nature's glee,
My own dear Ellan Vannin
With its green hills by the sea.

Then I hear the wavelets murmur
As they kiss the fairy shore,
Then beneath the em'rald waters
Sings the mermaid as of yore,

And the fair Isle shines with beauty
As in youth it dawned on me,
My own dear Ellan Vannin
With its green hills by the sea.

Then mem'ries sweet and tender
Come like music's plaintive flow,
Of someone in Ellan Vannin
That lov'd me long ago,

So I give with tears and blessings,
And my fondest thoughts to thee,
My own dear Ellan Vannin
With its green hills by the sea.

Ellan Vannin – by Eliza Craven Green, 1854.
(A poem and song about the Isle of Man made popular by The Bee Gee's)

Port Erin, Isle of Man

The Isle of Man is a small island midway between England and Ireland in the Irish Sea. Although it has some year-round residents, it is primarily a holiday resort catering to young people from all over the U.K. My pals and I heard from friends of ours that the Isle of Man was a great place to visit, with lots of girls, cheap booze and fun things to do like fishing, hiking and diving. Up to this point in my life, I had never had a proper vacation anywhere. Since I was now working and had a few shillings to spare, my friends and I decided to give the Isle of Man a try.

Our trip was made even more exciting by some peculiarities we heard the island had. For instance, it had its own legal system and courts and its laws differed from the mainland. Hooliganism and rambunctious activity of any kind were frowned upon. In extreme cases, transgressors were reputedly given the "cat of nine tails", a whip with eight separate lashes that lifted the skin off in strips. In this respect, the island was like going back in time to the Dark Ages when such punishments were commonplace throughout Great Britain. I suppose the island fathers felt this was the most appropriate way to keep the young people in check. Hooliganism is now epidemic in Britain, particularly during soccer games. Tony Blair has called it a national disgrace. One has to wonder how long the problem of hooliganism would continue if the cat of nine tails was still in use there today.

The four of us had booked our holiday months in advance but during this trip, Hyndsie and I were still recovering from the attack by the I.R.A. supporters outside the Park Picture House. The recuperative qualities of youth enabled us to heal quickly but my face was still festooned with cuts, multi-colored eyes and puffed lips. However, I was determined to not let my prize fighter appearance spoil my vacation so we went anyway, despite a doctor's orders to rest.

We arrived in the town of Douglas by ferryboat from Belfast after a couple of hours on the choppy Irish Sea. The trip passed without incident except for one of my less seafaring friends heaving all over someone's shoes, a nasty start to the vacation. Fortunately, the offended party had a good sense of humor.

We checked into our hotel agog with excitement and anxious to see what the island had to offer. While looking out the window, we spotted a couple of very beautiful girls, a blonde and a brunette, in the window of a building across the street and yelled hello to them. They leaned out of the window but the distance was too great so our conversation consisted of hand signals and shouts. We could only see their faces faintly. We managed to arrange a meeting with them in front of the building at 5:30 that evening. We couldn't believe our good luck. Barely on the island and already set up with two girls!

Hyndsie and I were waiting outside the hotel at the appointed time, spruced up and ready for the evening when I noticed two very, very small people walking toward us. As they drew closer, I recognized them as the two girls we had been signaling to earlier. I hoped it was a trick of the light or the perspective I was looking at them from and that they would become larger as they drew closer but it quickly became evident that they were both little people.

"Jasus," I said to Hyndsie, "Don't look now but I think this is our dates comin'!"

He immediately whipped around and looked at them very conspicuously. Like myself, he was shocked at the stature of the two young ladies.

"Oh, my God. What do we do now?"

"Don't look at them and don't say anything to them. Just keep talking and looking at me."

Out of the corner of my eye, I could see the two girls looking at us quite closely with questioning looks on their faces. Nevertheless, we attempted to ignore them and kept talking to each other and they eventually passed us by.

I tell this story with great shame because our behavior was obviously abominable. However, as teenagers, we were not equipped in any way to gracefully handle such a departure from the norm. We had rarely seen a little person prior to this day, much less dated one, so imagining the sight we would have made walking around the pier with two girls barely exceeding our belt buckles was just too much for us to handle. Our fear of public opinion was made even stronger by the fact that the Irish are notorious "slaggers". We would never have lived it down. With the passage of time, I now think they might have made much more interesting companions than the "normal" girls we ended up with, whom I have almost completely forgotten. Telling their stories would have made this chapter a lot more interesting, too. I have no defense other than immaturity.

This story does have a sequel, however. The following day, Hyndsie and I were down at the seaside and decided to rent a rowboat. The wind was very gusty and the waves were choppy. We struggled for about half an hour but could not get the rowboat to leave the shore and kept landing back on the beach. Neither one of us had been in a rowboat before and had no clue as to how to operate the oars. To make matters worse, I noticed the two little girls from the day before standing on the beach watching us. I wasn't sure if they recognized us as the two mugs who had stood them up the day before. Either way, they offered to help us row the boat out from the beach. Embarrassed but not wanting to insult them twice, we agreed. They climbed into the boat, then each took an oar and skillfully guided us out of the surf and off into the ocean. We felt like a couple of big ninny's for being rescued not only by women but by miniature women. Half the people on the beach witnessed the odd spectacle and were unguardedly laughing and pointing at us. Once we got far enough out to no longer hear the laughter and catcalls, we fell into conversation with the girls and had a wonderful time. They were very good-natured and full of personality. After a quick spin around the harbor, they delivered us safely back to shore. They cheerfully said goodbye and walked away, barely even giving us time to thank them for the help with the rowboat. They were so nice, I felt even more ashamed for being too image-conscious to keep our dates with them the day before.

Afterward, Hyndsie and I walked quietly along the beach toward the village. He was apparently feeling as bad as I was because he said to me, "We're a couple of shitehawks."

"Aye, that we are," I said.

We agreed to buy them a pint the next time we saw them but we never ran into them again. The last few days of our trip were spent sunning on the beach during the day and chasing women around the pubs at night. We had such a good time that we resolved to go back again the following year.

When the time for our return trip rolled around a year later, we decided to be a little more organized and booked into Howstrake Holiday Camp, a place we had heard of where a group of friends could rent a chalet. Again, we ferried over from Belfast, arriving late in the afternoon. We had a few beers and decided to have an early night and get up early the next day to enjoy the festivities.

We got up at about six the following morning. The cafeteria in the holiday camp had not yet opened. Someone produced a tennis ball and we started playing soccer in the quadrangle near our chalets. I was wearing a pair of shoes with thick, crepe soles, which were quite popular with young people at the time. The tennis ball skipped over a short wall which enclosed the area. I tried to hop on top of the wall but caught my toe and fell ass over tit right over the edge. The next thing I knew, I was hurtling headfirst towards the earth about fifteen feet below. The distance was so great that, as I was falling, I had time to casually note that the surface below was mostly grass. What I was unable to see, however, was a wide plank just below the surface which the grass had grown over. I made this discovery when my mouth and nose made contact with it. The pain was excruciating.

I emerged back onto the quadrangle and knew by the horrified gasps of my mates and the others that I had just received yet another beating with the ugly stick, or the ugly plank in this case. Dazed and disoriented, spitting up bits of grass and dirt, I staggered back to my chalet to examine the damage. My lips were split in several places and I could actually feel them puffing up like two balloons. As the day progressed, my nose and lips continued to swell and my eyes blackened up very nicely. I was a sight.

I couldn't believe my bad luck. The date of this accident coincided almost exactly with the severe thumping I had taken the year before from the

I.R.A. supporters. Even the same areas of my face were affected. During this trip, I met many of the same people I had met the year before when I also had a busted gub, who said things like, "My God! Haven't you healed yet?" and "What happened to you this time?" and "You should be wearing a helmet. You're a hazard to yourself!"

Youth triumphed once again and I survived but hot tea or coffee was off the menu. Salt was right out as well. I met a sympathetic girl who somehow found me attractive busted lips and all and discovered that kissing was another problem. I surmounted this obstacle by kissing her from a side angle with the undamaged portion of my one good lip.

We discovered upon our arrival at the holiday camp that roughly half the chalets were for women and the other half were for men. The area was patrolled at nighttime by security guards to keep the two sides from mingling with one another. I suppose they didn't want the island getting a bad reputation from young girls returning home impregnated.

Some girls we met in the village invited us over to their chalet for drinks and we had to devise a plan for getting past the security people. We reconnoitered the grounds to see if there might be a place to slip through undetected but there wasn't. After much deliberation, Hyndsie and I asked the girls to go to their chalet and bring back two scarves and the largest dresses they had. They brought them back to us and returned to their chalets. After dark, we got dressed up in the girls' clothing and sashayed across the wide lawn between the two sets of chalets, staying as far away from the security guards as possible. They looked at us suspiciously but, with a little girlish laughter on our part, we were able to pass by them and find our way to the party, which was especially enjoyable because we were the only boys there.

Because all the young people on the island were far from home, the English, Scotch and Irish tended to stick with their own. Occasionally, though, we would find ourselves in mixed company. One night, we were out with a group of Irish girls. Hyndsie had met an English girl earlier that day and we brought her along, too. She was a shy girl and being the only English one in the group didn't help bring her out. During the course of an otherwise pleasant conversation, one of the less cultivated Irish girls exclaimed, "What are you doing here? You're English!"

The young English girl was deeply wounded and dashed out of the bar. Hyndsie was too far gone to pursue her so I set off after her, hoping to persuade her to return. The girl must have been a long-distance runner because I chased her for about a mile before a finally caught up with her. She was still sobbing over the insulting remark.

I said, "Don't let one ignorant person spoil your entire evening. Come on back with me."

She thanked me but refused to return to the bar and walked off into the night alone. I hoped that, if nothing else, I had balanced out rudeness with kindness and improved her opinion of Irish people. After all, if nobody had gone after her to apologize for the uncouth one in our midst, she would have thought we all felt the same way. I went back to the bar and gave the big mouth a good tongue-lashing. I remember thinking what a shame it is that people assess one another by so many trivial things like nationality, religion and skin color rather than character. I guess some people are just too lazy to deal with others one at a time.

A few nights later, I saw the English girl sitting with a few other English girls. I sent her a drink over and she gave me a friendly wave. I was glad to see her enjoying herself.

A tragedy was narrowly avoided one night when Hyndsie and I were in a bar at the top of a steep hill. As usual, we got royally smashed. Hyndsie started to feel ill and leaned out the window to evacuate his system of some of the Guinness he had been drinking all evening. The relief of vomiting caused him to momentarily pass out. Out of the corner of my eye, I saw his body slipping forward through the windowsill. I sprinted across the ten feet or so to the window, sending several other patrons flying in the process. He was almost completely out the window by the time I reached him. I grabbed the back of his belt and yanked him back in. He thanked me but was too drunk to really understand what had just happened. I didn't think much of it either until I looked out the window and saw that there was a 200-foot drop straight down to the rocks and crashing surf below. It was a dumb place to put a bar and an even dumber place to put a window. Apparently, the building authorities did not anticipate drunken Irishmen puking out of windows when they constructed the property.

The Isle of Man was a happy place when I was there in the early 1950's, a place where young people, usually restricted by the desire to maintain a proper reputation in the towns and villages they came from, were able to run wild, stretch their youth and test their limits. I already knew I didn't want to stay in Belfast forever and that many hard choices awaited me when I returned. I was on an island in more ways than one.

Hyndsie and I enjoyed ourselves immensely. To that point in my life, I had never felt as carefree. We were young, and life, with all its promise and wonder, was still ahead of us. Even today, I firmly believe that if we had never left that island, Hyndsie and I would have stayed young forever, and we would still be there right now laughing on the beach in the sunlight shining through the mist above the Irish Sea.

Rosaleen (right) at the Isle of Man.

CHAPTER 50

WE LEAVE FOR ENGLAND

"The purpose of life, after all, is to live it, to taste experience to the utmost, to reach out eagerly and without fear for newer and richer experience."
~ Eleanor Roosevelt

One's life is measured by firsts and lasts, glorious moments that shine above the rest, terrible moments when our souls seem utterly crushed, and moments that mark major turning points. Ironically, it is usually the awful moments that change us the most. After all, when we're happy, there's no motivation to change anything. As the years pass, these highs and lows remain enshrined in the soul among the thousands of ordinary, forgotten days.

The most dramatic moment of my youth was the aforementioned day when I realized that my parents were not only imperfect but that they were not even average. The second biggest realization of my youth occurred immediately after the first. It was that, since my parents were so overwhelmed by their own problems, the only person I could depend on in life was me. Thus, I was left to figure out life alone. But I'm not complaining. Worse things than that can happen to a boy. However, I felt that I had to get out of that house for the sake of my own sanity. And aside from the problems with my parents, Belfast had been the scene of too many failures and disappointments for me. I felt like I had explored every inch of the city and knew every crack in every sidewalk. I needed to go somewhere new with new people and new places to see.

Looking at any map of the world will show that the British Isles are small and close together. To us at that time, however, England was a full night's boat journey away. It seemed like the other side of the world to us and it represented both a challenge and a new beginning. The world outside Belfast was so overwhelmingly large to us, the overnight boat trip to England was an adventure almost too heady to imagine.

The world has shrunken considerably since then and rampant commercialism has infiltrated even the most exotic cultures. The wilds of Africa are spotted with tour group vans and Club Med's. Savages who still think nothing of taking an enemy's head are smoking Camel's and wearing Nike tennis shoes. And what's left of the rainforests is littered with Coke cans. But the need for adventure and the desire to strike out for new lands is still a strong urge in the human soul. NASA's development of a commercial space shuttle for those who can afford the fare is ample evidence of this fact. I suppose there's nowhere left to go but up now that man has managed to upturn and plunder most of the planet. However, I made my trip to England at the tail end of travel's golden age when it was still extremely difficult to get from point A to point B. Thus, every trip abroad took on the proportions of a quest.

I suggested to Hyndsie that we go to England. He felt the same way I did. We felt stymied in Belfast and wanted to find virgin territory and greater opportunities. We both also agreed that we wanted to live there for a while, not just take a vacation. Belfast was safe and comfortable so the decision to go was fraught with foreboding. The comfort zone is a force to be reckoned with. Youthful courage won out over all our doubts and we made the decision to go. However, as the day of departure approached, the feeling of trepidation got stronger. We were separating ourselves from family and friends, had little in the way of a stake to tide us over when we got to England, and our prospects of finding employment were dubious. When I announced my plans to my father, he laconically remarked in his usual soul-destroying fashion, "You'll be back in a week." My mother cried a lot until I promised her that I would return the moment I couldn't feed myself adequately, and for holidays. I was touched with my mom's unbridled emotion. I guess Kahlil Gibran was right when he wrote, *"Ever has it been that love knows not its own depth until the hour of separation."*

We finished up a boozy last evening in Belfast, with our friends giving us the customary send-off. The nearest port was Liverpool. After saying good-bye to our sad and befuddled mates, we found ourselves boarding the boat with pounding hearts. We staggered up the gangplank with our cardboard suitcases held together with belts and tape, ready to put our heads down anywhere we could. We had not arranged for a berth and had purchased the cheapest tickets available - steerage.

The boat was crammed, a condition I was to find as normal, with soldiers going home on leave, young couples immigrating to England with their children, and laborers from the south of Ireland returning to their jobs. The bars on the boat were doing a lively trade and there were many inebriated youths (aside from ourselves) on board. We ordered a couple of pints at the bar and found two uncomfortable seats in the lounge where we planned to stay for the night. There were so many people on the boat, we felt lucky to have chairs at all and found the cold, hard chairs preferable to sitting on the floor, which was coated with spit, cigarette butts and all manner of filth.

The boat left its berth and we felt our stomachs tighten with anticipation for the adventures that lay ahead. We had no idea where we were going. Our "plan" was to figure it out when we got there.

When Big Lionel found out we were going to England, he told us he wanted to come with us and that we could all stay with his relatives in Liverpool. Typically, however, he disappeared at the last moment. I later found out he had decided not to go and, rather than facing the discomfort of admitting it to us, had just pulled a vanishing act.

Shortly after we boarded the ship, I lost Hyndsie in the crowd on deck. I went to look for him and ended up at the stern. I was surprised at how far we had already traveled. The Antrim Coast spread out wide, with sunlight dancing on the distant fields, and Cave Hill looming over old Belfast like a dark knight. It all seemed so small from this distance, it was hard to believe that I had spent my whole life there and that this little patch of land had been the stage for so many dramatic scenes of my life, events that felt so large and important to me when they were happening, but so small and insignificant now. I gazed around the deck at all the other travelers engaged in conversation, or reading their papers, or organizing their belongings, and thought about how unnatural it is for human beings to stay in one place forever. They say animals have no awareness of death. Maybe that's why they're content to graze in the same field their entire lives. But human beings are doing creatures. It is wired into us to seek adventure of some kind. Without it, we wilt and shrivel.

I left the stern and walked to the bow as the boat sliced through the briny Irish Sea. The cold spray invigorated and excited me. I had never felt more awake. What would we do without the glorious possibility of "there", whether a place or a station we hope to reach? The view from the stern was yesterday. The view from the bow was tomorrow. Tens of thousands of other souls before me had looked into other seas and other oceans dreaming of a better life waiting for them somewhere over the waves. This same horizon that had lured so many others toward great adventures, even the great travelers I had read about in my history books, now lured and seduced me. But it was my turn; my chance to find my own fortune in a new land. I could be anything I wanted to be there. The choices were truly endless.

A young woman was standing alone at the railing nearby, looking out to sea. I wasn't sure if she was crying or if the ocean wind was bothering her. I watched her secretly. I had found that the longer I watched someone, the more I could see into their souls, at least a little. This woman was exuding sadness. She looked over and I smiled. She smiled back. No words were needed. My smile asked if she was alright, and her smile answered she was. She was just caught up in the bittersweet emotions of leaving one place for another, as I was.

It started to get cold so I went into the bar. I found Hyndsie there. We drank ourselves stupid as usual and eventually made our way to the lounge. We were seated for a little while and I was just starting to doze off when I was awakened by the arrival of a very large man of about fifty wearing a black, turtleneck sweater. He was obviously twice as gassed as anyone else in the room. He stood in the doorway glaring at everyone one at a time as if trying to decide which of us to kill first. He had bad news written all over him so everyone was trying to avoid his gaze.

"Who wants to fight?" he bellowed.
We all ignored him and concentrated on our newspapers and magazines.
"Which one of you puff merchants wants to fight me?" he asked again, stalking into the lounge. Again receiving no answer, he then walked through the circle of people repeating his challenge and jabbing a meaty forefinger at each person he passed. Everyone acted like they didn't notice him, while watching

him in their peripheral vision so they could duck in case he decided to clobber them anyway. Finally, he stood in front of me.

"How about you, Curly. Fancy your chances?"

Without looking at him, I said, "Get lost before I hit you a dig in the gub." I was hoping my disinterested look would intimidate him. It didn't. The next thing I knew, the fight had commenced. I saw a large fist arcing toward my head. I pushed myself backward with my feet in a desperate attempt to get out of the way. He caught me on the retreat with a grazing blow to the neck. Both I and the chair ended up overturned. Out of the corner of my eye I saw Hyndsie, who was seated beside me, catapult out of his chair and deliver a crashing blow to the aggressor's chin, dropping him like a pole-axed steer. Bedlam then broke out and it seemed every man in the lounge was kicking and punching our unfortunate adversary, who quickly disappeared under a sea of thrashing bodies. I could hear him moaning under the pile as I righted myself. For a moment, I only watched, feeling that he had it coming. However, he had not really hurt me and I had no desire to see him murdered, which everyone seemed intent on doing, so I pulled the bodies apart and rescued him. As I pulled him free, he moaned, "My heart! My heart!"

As I walked him toward the door, I said, "The best thing you can do, Charlie, is take yourself outside before somebody kills you."

Everyone had returned to their seats by this time and the man stumbled off toward the door. Before he got there, however, he unbuttoned his fly, pulled out his willy for every man, woman, and child to see, and urinated on the carpeted floor of the lounge. A chorus of disgusted remarks filled the room.

"Ah, fer fuck's sake, man! Catch yourself on!"

"Ach, ya dirty bastard!"

"Piss off, ya big eejit!"

The big man turned and left, tossing a final "Fuck the lot of yuz!" over his shoulder as he walked out the door.

I wish I could say the story of this wretched soul ended here but there is a sequel. About a year later, I was back in Belfast on holiday (yep, we lasted more than a week in England!) and was in a bar off Royal Avenue ordering a pint when I noticed the same big oaf standing next to me. He was cold sober this time and it was obvious that he didn't recognize me. He was probably seeing two or three of me on the night of the altercation, which was fortunate for me because he had apparently tried to hit the wrong one.

"Hey! Charlie!" I said, "Remember me?"

"No, no, can't say as I do," he replied, turning away.

"Sure you do," I pressed. "Don't ya remember takin' a swing at me on the Liverpool boat last year?"

He looked as if he hoped the ground would open up and swallow him.

"That couldn't have been me," he said. "You must be mistaken."

I wasn't about to let him off the hook that easily. "It was you all right," I said. "I couldn't forget an ugly mug like yours in two lifetimes!"

Angered, he turned around and started to puff up like a frog. He held up his finger and was about to say something when a small woman next to him, who had been listening intently to our conversation, turned around and said, "What's this about you hittin' someone on the boat?"

He was squirming with embarrassment. He looked at her with a fearful expression and said, "This fella has me mixed up with somebody else, sweetheart."

"No, Missus," I said, "I'm not mistaken. The man I'm talking about had an anchor tattooed on his hand . . ."

I pulled his hand up, revealing the same tattoo.

"Do you know what else he did?" I said. "He took out his willy and peed all over the floor of the lounge in front of a room full of women and children!"

The wee woman turned bright red and erupted.

"So that's what ya get up too when ya go across the water!" she snapped. "Makin' a bloody fool o'yarself!"

She punctuated this comment by nearly taking his head off with her purse. She reached up, grabbed his collar, and marched him out of the bar like a six-year old, loudly berating him all the while. All he could get out were a few "but honey"s. I wanted to get him in trouble, but not that much. She obviously had the big lummox by the short hairs. But I did learn that day that one doesn't always need to damage one's knuckles to get even with an old adversary!

CHAPTER 51

ENGLISH HOSPITALITY

"To be honest, I live among the English and have always found them to be very honest in their business dealings. They are noble, hard-working and anxious to do the right thing. But joy eludes them; they lack the joy that the Irish have."
~ Fiona Shaw

The boat journey continued without incident. We dozed fitfully because of the throbbing turbines and chairs the Marquis de Sade would have envied. I finally fell asleep at about four in the morning and was awakened a few hours later by Hyndsie, who told me the boat had docked and the passengers were disembarking. My mouth felt like the bottom of a garbage pail. After leaving the ship, we found a dockside greasy spoon restaurant where we swilled down life-giving sweet tea and munched on bacon and egg sandwiches.

We had intended to look for work in Liverpool where the boats docked but a Belfast man we met on the boat told us Liverpool was "full of mad paddies" and we would be better off trying our luck in Manchester, which was a couple of hours away by train, figuring Liverpool didn't need us to add two more. We took his advice and landed in Manchester at midday.

The next order of business was to find a place to stay. I stopped a pedestrian in Piccadilly and asked if he could tell us where we could find digs.

"Are you Irish?" he asked.

I told him we had just arrived in England that day from Belfast.

He pointed to a bus stop across the road and said, "Catch that bus over there and ask the conductor to let you off at Moss Side."

We thanked him and got on the bus. The conductor looked at us strangely when we asked to be let off at Moss Side and asked us what we intended to find in that area. I told him it had been recommended to us as a good place to find lodging.

"Somebody's having you on, son. Just have a seat and relax. I'll tell you where to get off."

A few stops later, the conductor told us we were going through Moss Side. I looked out the window. I thought I was in central Africa! There wasn't a white face to be seen. I later learned the district had a high crime rate. Blacks weren't faring as well in England then as they are now. We wouldn't have lasted long there.

A couple of stops later, at the conductor's recommendation, we got off the bus in a district called Whalley Range. It seemed pleasant, with old Georgian houses along the main thoroughfare. In a shop window, we saw cards offering various services, including some peculiar offerings by French and Swedish ladies. Then we spotted a card which read:

DOUBLE BEDROOM
FOR TWO YOUNG IRISHMEN
APPLY 26 MANLEY ROAD, MANCHESTER
ASK FOR MRS. O'ROURKE

"Hyndsie," I said, "This must be providence. That card was meant for us."

After receiving directions from some passersby, we finally found ourselves at the home of Misses O'Rourke, a ferret-faced little woman from Dublin who kept a boarding house nearby. The house had seen better days and had probably belonged to a wealthy family many years before. Having seen her card advertising the rooms and wanting to match her expectations, we introduced ourselves as Irishmen. She was very suspicious, however, and demanded our identification as proof. Apparently, she was unfamiliar with the Belfast dialect. We produced our insurance cards, which gave our home address. Somewhat reluctantly, she allowed us to enter and view the available bedroom. It was small and cramped. I checked the bed sheets, which had been white at some time in the distant past but were now a disgusting shade of yellowish brown, or as Hyndsie crudely but succinctly whispered, were "full o' skid marks and cock hairs." I asked Misses O'Rourke if the sheets could be changed and she agreed to do so. She produced sheets and pillow cases from a nearby cupboard which were not white either but only a lighter shade of brown. Not wanting to press the issue further, we stoically accepted them.

There was a communal bathroom down the hall we would have to share with others at the house. We ensconced ourselves and paid the first week up front, two pound ten shillings for each of us. This price included breakfast and dinner.

We later found that there were about six other renters in the house, all construction workers from the Irish Free State, big country lads who worked for the mostly Irish construction companies who were building half of England at that time. One of the major companies was Wimpey's, which some wag said meant "We employ more paddies every year!"

One Sunday morning, after a breakfast of hard-boiled eggs and toast, we borrowed the local paper and started searching for employment. I searched the ads for clerical workers and circled a few prospects to check out the next day. Hyndsie was a house painter and there were many ads for his line of work but none for persons experienced in the manufacture and sale of Irish linen. I was reminded yet again that the five years I spent at the linen warehouse were a complete waste of time.

CHAPTER 52

ACTUALLY

"A man willing to work, and unable to find work, is perhaps the saddest sight that fortune's inequality exhibits under this sun."
~ Thomas Carlyle

Early the next morning, Hyndsie and I set about trying to find a job. Someone told us there was work to be found in the industrial district of Manchester known as Trafford Park. We tramped around there, stopping in at the various manufacturing plants and warehouses to offer our services. Everyone else was working so the streets were deserted.

Around midday, we encountered another job seeker who came wandering over a hill toward us. He certainly was an odd-looking character, dressed in an army overcoat, knitted seafarer's-type cap, and gloves with the fingers cut out. Every one of these garments was khaki material. He looked like the great white hunter. He was balding with long, yellow, prominent teeth he flashed in their entirety with every sentence he spoke. His name was Cedric but after an hour or two, we secretly christened him "Actually" because of his excessive use of that word.

"I say," he said, "are you chaps Australian?"
Apparently, he was unfamiliar with the Belfast accent as well. We told him where we were from.

"Oh!" he exclaimed, "You're Oirish! I never would have thought so, actually. I say, would you chaps mind if we joined forces and looked for work tagethah? I've been looking for several days now, actually, without much luck."

We welcomed him aboard and off we all went, trudging from plant to plant and applying for employment of any kind. We slowly realized that any chance we had of impressing anyone greatly diminished the moment we teamed up with Actually. He had devised a peculiar methodology of seeking employment. He would march up to the gatekeeper's window or front office and triumphantly declare, "We're here to save the firm!"

This comment was invariably met with frozen expressions on the faces of those he was attempting to impress. I could tell this was not a workable gambit on the first attempt but Actually kept saying it to everyone we met. This was getting embarrassing. I said to Hyndsie, "We better lose this guy or we're never gonna find a job today."

Hyndsie agreed. We said we were going to go have lunch, hoping he would go his own way, but he said, "Oh! That sounds lovely! I'm famished meself, actually!"

A half-hour later, we found ourselves at a café eating food we really didn't want to eat and listening to Actually's life story. I fell into a sort of trance and counted several hundred actually's during his half-hour monologue.

We continued on our way, stopping at a few more factories. Actually kept offering to save each of the firms we went to. Hyndsie and I were at our wit's end. When we got to the next factory, we found that the entrance was about a quarter mile from the front gate. Inspiration struck.

I said, "Listen, Act-, uh, Cedric, you have a better appearance than we do and you speak better than us so why don't you go up and check out the prospects and come back and let us know."

Actually cheerfully agreed and marched off purposefully toward the gate. Once he was safely away, Hyndsie and I took to our heels down the street in the other direction.

I know it was a lousy thing to do but we were young and desperate for work. We never saw Actually again. He's probably wandering around Trafford Park looking for a job to this day, or perhaps he became fabulously wealthy after delivering his line at a factory in trouble where, moments before his arrival, the owner's were wringing their hands with worry and saying, "I wish someone would show up right now and save the firm."

CHAPTER 53

MRS. O'ROURKE'S PECULIAR TALENT

"Travel is fatal to prejudice, bigotry, and narrow-mindedness, and many of our people need it sorely on these accounts. Broad, wholesome, charitable views of men and things cannot be acquired by vegetating in one little corner of the earth all one's lifetime."
~ Mark Twain

For the rest of that week, we scoured Manchester for jobs but found nothing, and we didn't even have Actually to blame for it. Friday came around and the rent was again due. Between the two of us, we had about three shillings and sixpence, not the five pounds needed.

At the end of each day, we would arrive home bedraggled and dirty, clean up, and eagerly await Misses O'Rourke's dinners, along with the other boarders, hoping she wouldn't bring up the rent. I'll never forget the first night we sat down at the table with them. Hyndsie and I came back from our day of job-hunting, went upstairs, got washed up, shaved, put on our best clothes and sat down at the table spanking clean. Hyndsie was particularly cherubic in appearance with pink cheeks, blue eyes, and corn-blonde hair. He added to this swanky image by wearing a white shirt, paisley scarf of the finest silk, gold ring, and (imitation) gold watch. To quote a Belfast expression, "He looked like a whore at a hockey match." The other lads were seated around the table covered with cement dust, dressed in their work clothes, looking like Neanderthals beside Hyndsie and I. We certainly made an odd set. I don't know what they thought of us. They probably thought we were gay.

One of the boys in particular, Danny, stared and stared but couldn't seem to figure us out. He weighed about sixteen stone, had fists the size of a baby's head, and had cement dust in his ears at all times, even Sundays. He seemed fascinated with Hyndsie and sat transfixed all through dinner while we tried our best to carry on a conversation with them. It was as if we were from outer space, though, and try as we did, we couldn't seem to develop a rapport with them until we were there almost a week and they had gotten used to us. I didn't realize at first how little we had in common with our fellow Irishmen from the south, especially from the rural areas of the west. We later met some lads from the City of Cork and Dublin and found we had much more in common with them, mainly our city heritage.

Dinner at the O'Rourke house was an experience in itself. Mrs. O'Rourke, whom we had begun to call Cissie, would burst out of the kitchen with steaming platters of mashed potatoes and cabbage and leave them on the table. The first night, the meat dish was bacon strewn over potatoes. We thought

272

these items were merely for garnish, but while we took our eyes away from the table momentarily waiting for the meat dish to appear, we noticed that the potatoes and cabbage were being snatched up wantonly. We realized immediately that it was every man for himself at this table and those who didn't grab didn't eat. We began to dive headlong into the food with the others as soon as it arrived.

Hyndsie and I had never known anyone from the Irish Republic on a personal basis. We found the lads quite likable but, being city slickers in comparison, we also found them somewhat naive and unsophisticated. The primary conversation at the dinner tables at nighttime was how many yards of concrete had been poured that day on the jobsite and how many pints of Guinness had been quaffed the night before at the local pub.

I'd heard that the Catholic Church dominated thinking in the Irish Free State and figured it must be true. These guys seemed to have no interest in girls at all whereas Hyndsie and I were completely obsessed with them.

At breakfast one morning, I asked Big Dermott, a strapping youth of about twenty-two, what he had done the night before. He said, "I went out and had fifteen pints, then I went into the cafe and had two pounds of steak, then I went back to the pub and had another seven pints." Twenty-two pints of Guinness in one night was incredible to me. Bear in mind, the English pint is larger than the U.S. pint. These guys had developed a tremendous capacity for Guinness built over many years' experience. What makes this even more incredible is that Guinness is one of the thickest beers made. If it were any thicker, one would need to eat it with a spoon. In those days, doctors recommended Guinness to pregnant women because of its rich iron content. (This was before fetal alcohol syndrome was discovered.)

An unpleasant situation developed during the first week at Misses O'Rourke's house. Our bedroom was positioned directly adjacent to a second floor bathroom, which was much larger than a normal bathroom because it had once been a bedroom. I was used to a cozier environment so sitting on the toilet at the corner of this gigantic bathroom was somewhat doleful. One night, I went into the bathroom to perform my ablutions and noticed a monstrous "floater" in the toilet bowl. I flushed the toilet several times but it kept bobbing back up into view. I noticed a piece of wood beside the toilet so I used it to break it into manageable pieces, then succeeded in flushing the remains down the toilet. I concluded that the piece of wood was there for that purpose.

Several times thereafter, I discovered new, fresh floaters of immense proportions bobbing around in the bowl and wondered which of the members of the household was responsible. My first bet was Big Paddy, a huge brute about six-foot-six inches tall and two hundred and fifty pounds. In Sherlock Holmes-ian fashion, I decided to keep an eye on the comings and goings in the bathroom, particularly Paddy's visits. However, he always left the bathroom neat and clean.

I eliminated the boarders one by one, leaving only one remaining suspect, Misses O'Rourke. She weighed less than a hundred pounds so it was hard for me to imagine that she could be responsible for the colossal jobs I had seen. Nevertheless, I checked her out as well and, lo and behold, she was the guilty party. I almost brought the subject up with her but wisely decided against it.

Misses O'Rourke loved to talk about her "operation." It was obviously the biggest event in her life. She talked about it endlessly and at great length, leaving out no detail, to anyone who was unfortunate enough to be in her presence. Since the dinner table gave her a captive audience, this was usually the time she would bring it up. It was all I could do to keep from regurgitating my dinner. One night, she even offered to show me the scars, which were located somewhere near her crotch. I didn't like what was already visible and had no desire to see what remained mercifully covered so I politely declined. Whatever her operation was, it hadn't interfered with her bowel movements. Every day there was a new floater. Some were so gargantuan, I half expected them to talk to me. I was also amazed at the buoyancy of them. It was like she was snacking on corks. In any case, as they would say in Belfast, her hole was in quare order.

CHAPTER 54

REVEREND SAM

That best portion of a good man's life; his little, nameless, unremembered acts of kindness and love."
~ William Wordsworth (1770–1850)

The second Sunday we stayed at Misses O'Rourke's house, Hyndsie and I decided to go to church, not for divine guidance but, as usual, hoping to meet some girls. I asked Misses O'Rourke if there was a Methodist church in the area. I realized immediately that I had asked the wrong question. She froze and asked, "Methodist Church? Are you Protestants?" She asked us this the same way one would ask, "Are you escaped convicts?"

I probably should have lied to preserve the peace but I didn't want God to punish me for denying my faith so I proudly said, "Yes, we are."

From that moment forward, Misses O'Rourke's attitude toward us changed drastically. The proof of this came the following Friday when we were in the position of not having the next week's rent. Toward the end of the week, we both had finally found jobs and were to start the following Monday, Hyndsie with a machinery moving firm and I with Massey Ferguson tractors in a clerical position. By this time, our slim funds had dwindled down to practically nothing and the rent again came due. The deadline was Saturday and we stayed out all day, purposely avoiding a confrontation with Cissie.

We went to church that day and heard a passionate sermon delivered by a one Reverend Sam. He was a small man with a cheery, round face, kind eyes, and a slight speech impediment caused by a cleft palate. He noticed the two new faces in his congregation and chatted with us at the door as we were leaving.

Hyndsie had plans to meet a girl in Manchester later that evening so he said to me, "You're a great talker, Rick. Away down and talk to Misses O'Rourke. Ask her if we can pay her at the end of next week." He then promptly left.

I explained our predicament to Misses O'Rourke. I told her we had a job to go to on Monday and would be able to pay her two weeks rent the following Friday. She wouldn't hear of it.

"No!" she said, "Ah need me money now! Whaddya think Ahm runnin' here, a free hotel? I 'ave me groceries to gid in!"

I was shocked by her reaction. I begged and pleaded with her to change her mind but she was adamant. In fact, she ordered us to leave the house immediately. I went upstairs and packed our bags, then decided to go around and see if I could borrow some money from Reverend Sam, the Methodist minister we had met the weekend before. He was the only one I could think of to turn to for help. I went round to the church, took his address from the bulletin board, and walked through the rain to the minister's house, not knowing what to expect. I was soaked to the skin by the time I reached the door. His wife ushered me inside in motherly fashion and sat me by the fire to warm up as I recounted my sad story to her and Reverend Sam.

"How much do you need, son?" he asked.

I told him the rent for both of us was five pounds. He didn't have five pounds in the house at the time but offered to write a check.

"If worst comes to worst," he said, "come back here and we'll work something out."

I went back to see Misses O'Rourke with the check but she refused it and told us we had to go so I set off downtown to look for Hyndsie. Even though Manchester is a large city, I miraculously managed to find him under a bus stop shelter with his new girlfriend. It was raining hard at the time. I was soaked to the skin and so were they. Hyndsie asked me how I got on with Misses O'Rourke. I told him we were homeless.

"What did you do with our stuff?" Hyndsie asked.

I told him our two bags were on the sidewalk waiting for us in front of Misses O'Rourke's. He bade his girlfriend a hasty farewell and we both went back by bus. The bags were still there. As we walked through the entry, we saw Misses O'Rourke sitting in the parlor. She didn't even look over at us. I was angry and insulted about her dismissive attitude. I thought we had been good tenants and deserved better. It was my first encounter with prejudice. I had always been on good terms with Roman Catholics at home in Belfast, so I never dreamed I would encounter this kind of negativity outside of Ireland. After all, we were all Irish over there. We weren't put off by her Catholic faith and made no mention of all the crucifixes she had hanging in every room of the house, except when Hyndsie, referring to the crucifix looming over the bed, had remarked, "Your man there looking down at me makes me nervous."

In disgust, before we left, I moved the tallboy and scrawled on the wall behind it, "King Billy slept here." King William was the patron saint of the Orangemen in Northern Ireland. I thought it would give the next guest in this room something to think about. I also liked the idea of the old cow moving it sometime in the future and discovering it. I said goodbye to her when we were leaving and thanked her sarcastically for her Irish hospitality. She glared at me as I went out the door.

In a way, I was glad I was going because Misses O'Rourke and her retellings of her operation story were beginning to depress me. I would also not miss having to cope with her total inability to flush the toilet after hatching her daily behemoths. She was a regular shit, in every sense of the expression.

We splashed back through the rain to Reverend Sam's house. When he answered my knock on the door, I said, "The worst has come to the worst."

He invited us in and his wife, Maureen, assured us we could stay with them as long as we wished. We thanked them profusely. She seemed to take to us a great deal and fed us like middleweight contenders. We spent long hours each evening discussing our plans and our future in England.

We had started in our new jobs and each morning Reverend Sam would get up and make our breakfasts for us. He seemed to enjoy our company as much as we did his. We talked about cricket and soccer scores and the latest movies over tea after breakfast. I was a little surprised that a man of the cloth showed such a keen interest in and knowledge of such mundane and earthly things, especially the pictures. In Ireland, Protestant ministers seemed to frown on movie-going. I never saw one entering a Picture House, though I saw many Catholic priests doing so.

At night, when we returned home, there was always an extravagant dinner followed by tea in their lush living room, the rich wood judge's paneling on every wall reflecting the glow from the fireplace.

I felt sure that sometime soon our conversations would turn to religion and the state of our souls. All week long, I was waiting for the minister to make his play to save us from ourselves. After three or four days, I couldn't take the suspense any longer and brought up the subject myself. I said to him, "I can't wait any longer. When is the pitch gonna start?"

"Pitch?" he asked, confused.

"The religion pitch," I said.

He laughed and said, "If you want to hear me talk about religion, come to my church on Sunday. Right now, you're a guest in my home and I wouldn't dream of trying to convert you."

His slight disfigurement, his cleft palate, only further endeared me to him. The fact that he had not pressed the issue of religion whatsoever while opening his home entirely to us during that week did more to convince me of the value of Christian spirit than any lecture could have done. After a week, though, we started to feel like we were taking advantage of their hospitality so we found another place to stay and let them know we would be leaving.

A solemn mood descended on the house as we packed our bags. As we said goodbye and gave them our thanks for the emergency accommodations, Maureen hugged us and I was very touched to see a small tear trickling down her face. Reverend Sam seemed a little choked up, too. Before we left, she said, "You know, you boys really livened up this household the past week. I feel like you are my sons."

I was very touched by this comment and as I left the house, I remember thinking Reverend "Sam" must stand for Samaritan. I knew I would miss them as well and vowed to visit regularly. Hyndsie and I sent them Christmas cards that year but, swept up in our new lives in England, we never visited again. I might have been more inclined to if I had perceived them as solitary people but they had a loving church family of hundreds. Still, I have always regretted not seeing them again and have thought of them countless times over the years, remembering their hospitality and their kind eyes as we told our youthful tales to them. They completely healed the injury done by the small-minded Mrs.

O'Rourke. As the years have passed, they have always stood out in my memory as one of the greatest examples of true goodness I have ever encountered.

They have surely earned their wings by now and in some blessed corner of heaven, even more blessed for their presence, I'm sure they have a home just as warm and welcoming as their earthly one was. And when I make it to heaven, as I someday hope to, their door will be among the first I search for.

CHAPTER 55

TOUCHIN' CLOTH

No fancy quote necessary or possible on this one. Just wanted to let you know that this is one of the chapters I thought about leaving out in the name of decency. You have been warned.
~ Mark Rickerby

Things went well for the first few days or so in England, when I developed a rather, uh, distracting problem. It suddenly dawned on me that I hadn't been to the toilet in about four days, a condition I had never been troubled with in the past. I put it down to the change in diet and the excitement over my new surroundings. I waited a few more days but nature did not take its course so I went to the chemist's, which was full of housewives filling prescriptions. The druggist saw me at the back of the store and called out to me, "There's a working lad, ladies! Let's take care of him!"

Somewhat embarrassed over my condition, I stepped forward and whispered the name of the product I wanted in his ear. To my chagrin, the druggist did what all druggists everywhere do when someone whispers an embarrassing product name to them. He yelled it to his assistant. A twitter ran through the ladies assembled there, causing me to redden to the ears.

Druggists must be trained to do this. I can imagine an instructor at pharmacist school saying, "Okay, class, don't forget - the more embarrassing the nature of the product, the louder you yell it. Got it?"

"There you are, lad!" said the druggist with a wink. "These will get the cogs churning again! Take a couple tonight and tomorrow your troubles will be over."

I hurriedly paid him for the pills (actually, they were more like tablets - the kind Moses brought down from the mountain) and walked out as fast as I could walk without actually running.

I took two pills before retiring that evening, as instructed. Just to be sure, I took a third and fell asleep. The following morning, I arose but felt no different. I re-read the directions. They suggested going to the bathroom immediately upon rising. I did so even though it was the furthest thing from my mind at that moment. After a few token efforts of contraction, I gave up, donned my coveralls and left for work.

A short while later, Hyndsie and I were on the upper section of the double-decker bus when it hit me - the most desperate urge to go to the bathroom imaginable. One eye actually crossed. The problem was I was still fifteen minutes away from the plant. A cold sweat broke on my forehead and I crossed my legs, trying to think of something else, anything else, to take my mind off the mounting pressure.

Einstein said, *"Put your hand on a hot stove for a minute, and it seems like an hour. Talk to that special girl for an hour, and it seems like a minute. That's relativity."* He should have said, "Take an overdose of laxatives and sit on a bus for fifteen minutes and it seems like a century" because a hot stove would have been preferable to the excruciating agony I was experiencing. Fearing the social mortification that would surely follow if I were to relax my sphincter for even a millisecond, I was on full cinch, grimacing and quivering with the exertion. Because I was doubled over, shaking, sweating and pallid, other passengers nearby began to take notice. Hyndsie finally noticed as well and said, "Jasus, you look terrible. What's wrong with ya?"

I couldn't answer. My entire body had become a fist and I feared that if I dared to even speak, the delicate balance would be disrupted. The bus hit every bump and pothole, caught every red light, and the driver seemed to be driving maddeningly slow. Finally, it was my stop and I hobbled down the stairs of the bus, twisted and contorted. The plant was a good quarter-mile from the bus stop but I am sure I broke the British, Empire, and perhaps world record as I sprinted there, which isn't easy with one's butt cheeks on full lock-down.

The men's washroom was a row of cubicles, about ten in all, with three-quarter doors on each. In desperation, I ran to the first door and found it locked. I checked every other door in quick succession but to my great horror, they were all occupied. The plant workers were having their final cigarettes before starting work and the usual crowd was seated inside picking out the winners of that day's races. I had just about reconciled myself to soiling my pants when, thank God and all things holy, a door in the middle began to creak open. I looked in through the opening and saw an old man with a pipe in his mouth lackadaisically buttoning his trousers. I said, "Could you hurry, please? I'm bustin'!"

"Wait your turn," he answered casually.

"Please, sir. It's touchin' cloth!"

"Wait your turn, I said! I can only deal with one shite at a time."

I couldn't believe he used the old Churchill line on me. That did it. I reached in and yanked him out of the stall, yelling, "You can smoke your bloody pipe outside, you oul' bugger!"

He yelled, "Why, you cheeky, wee blighter!" but I didn't have time to argue. I was on a mission.

I rushed inside, slammed the door in his face and started tearing off my coveralls. The buttons defied me and I snapped several off in my haste. Finally, I made it to the sanctuary of the toilet seat. The absolute ecstasy of what followed cannot be described in mere words. Suffice to say I made up for what I had missed for the past five days and then some. The first few minutes were sheer bliss but I was producing so much, I began to worry that I was keeking away something I still needed. I think I shat out the first breakfast I ever ate. Up until that moment, I had not experienced the ultimate act of love but I was quite sure it could not have surpassed this unadulterated bliss.

When I returned to my senses, I suddenly became aware that my neighbors in the adjoining stalls were evacuating as if a canister of tear gas had been dropped on the floor. There was a succession of doors opening and closing and when I finally arose to leave, I found myself completely alone in the usually crowded washroom with the exception of the janitor, a Jamaican, who was busy mopping up the place. He smiled a toothy smile and said, "Hey, mon! Ya sure needed that shit awright, eh? I never saw this place clear out so fast, 'cept maybe during the fire last year."

"Aye, that I did," I said. "But why didn't you clear out?"

"Nothing puts me off, mon," he said. "I'm the janitor."

As I was washing my hands and compared the smell of the room with the cross draft coming through the open door, it dawned on me that the entire room was engulfed by the most offensive odor imaginable. I could understand why everyone had fled for their lives. Even the flies had left, sick to their stomachs.

Later that day, while eating lunch, I was listening to the banter of the workers when someone said, "Some filthy bahstard came into the toilet this mo'ning and dropped a load that weren't human! He should see a blinkin' doctor, who-evah he was! Spoilt me whole bleedin' day, ee did! I can't get the smell outta me nose and I don't think I ever bloody will."

He continued to describe the incident in lurid detail but I buried my face in the newspaper, trying to avoid being detected as the culprit. Perhaps he noticed my discomfort and put two and two together because he kept looking over at me with a suspicious glare. I was expecting him to stand up and say, "There he is! He's the one! Get him!"

I have forgotten the name of the product which produced this violent reaction. I may have been the victim of an early incident of product tampering. The laxative I was supposed to have been given may have been switched with Drano. Whatever it was, it did its job because I haven't needed another laxative in the fifty years since.

CHAPTER 56

OLD FRENCHY AND THE MYSTERY SANDWICHES

"My wife's a lousy cook. I've got the only dog in town that begs for Alka-Seltzer."
~ Rodney Dangerfield

We found new digs on Manley Road in an area known as Whalley Range. The building and clientele were very "upper crust" compared to Misses O'Rourke's place. We wondered why they let us in.

There were six or eight tenants including Hyndsie and me. One of these was the editor of *Cheshire Life*. He was a large Robert Morley-type Englishman who wore tweed coats with leather cuffs and elbows. He was a great conversationalist. There were also two homosexual medical students, a civil servant named Mr. Trotter who was small and delicate and mumbled incoherently, a school teacher named Quimble we never saw without his briar clenched between his teeth, and a shady-looking salesman named Edwards with nicotine-stained fingers. We made an eclectic group at the dinner table each evening but I always enjoyed the conversations.

The head of the household was Mrs. French, who we nicknamed Old Frenchy, an elderly but hearty and stout-bodied woman with a kindly nature. The food was passable but none of us could ever really determine exactly what kind of meat Old Frenchy was serving. The editor, Mr. Teddington-Smythe, or "T.S." as we called him, would occupy pride of place at the head of the dining room table.

After we had been served and Mrs. French had left the room, T.S. would produce a tube of horseradish from the pocket of his jacket, which we would then hurriedly pass around in an attempt to give the meat some flavor. The best we could say of the food was that it was filling. Then again, one could say the same thing after ingesting a shoe.

The only one who cleared his plate regularly was our smallest member, Trotter, who mumbled all through the meal while slicing his meat into neat fragments. He continued to tuck it away well after we had all finished our after-dinner coffees.

Unlike Mrs. O'Rourke's table, Hyndsie and I felt like the simpletons here. Neither of us had the advantage of education that most of our fellow guests had and the topics discussed were often beyond our grasp. However, this did not deter us from rendering our opinions and T.S., God bless him, never put us down for our views. Indeed, he seemed sincerely interested.

Mrs. French also made our lunches each day, which she would pack in brown paper and hand to us at the breakfast table. We usually ate them in a hurry during lunch breaks without investigating them. However, they were more often than not ghastly both in taste and texture so I opened the sandwich up one day before I bit into it to see what Old Frenchy had concocted. To my utter disgust, the piece of meat it contained looked like a slice off the back of a hog, with all the bristles intact! I showed it to Hyndsie and we determined that she was probably collecting the butcher's discards to cut down on costs.

From then on, we still took the lunches but never ate them, buying sandwiches from a local cafe instead. Not wanting to insult her, we would put Old Frenchy's mystery sandwiches in our raincoat pockets every day and disposed of them later. However, we would often forget about them and discovered that they were still in our pockets when we were back at the room. As a result, we started filling up a suitcase with the discarded sandwiches, intending to get rid of them at the first opportunity. One month and sixty sandwiches later, I said to Hyndsie, "You know, this is probably some kind of a sin, wasting all this food." Repeating one of my and every other mother in the world's favorite lines, I added. "There are children starving in Africa."

Hyndsie's curt reply was, "If we sent this mess over to 'em, they'd still be starvin' because no one would eat it no matter how bloody hungry they were."

One night, we realized we had to do something immediately as the suitcase was filled to capacity and the contents were starting to writhe independently. We decided that at midnight that evening, I would reconnoiter the lobby area of the house and Hyndsie would stand at the head of the stairs with the suitcase waiting for the all-clear.

At the appointed time, I scouted the lobby. All quiet. I gently opened the door to the street and looked out. The street was deserted. I hissed to Hyndsie and gave him the signal to go. He came down the stairs three at a time, dashed across the carpeted lobby floor on his tip-toes and flew out through the front door into the street. I followed closely behind. We ran into the street and collided head-on with a large Manchester bobby (policeman). All three of us went sprockling onto the sidewalk in a pile.

Standing and dusting himself off, the bobby yelled, "Wot the bloody 'ell is going on 'eah?"

He grabbed Hyndsie by the collar and lifted him to his feet.

Squinting one eye and peering at us suspiciously with the other, certain he had just captured two burglars, he rumbled, "What are you two up to then?"

We tried to stammer out an explanation but the story seemed implausible even to us.

"Let's just take a walk back to the 'ouse." the bobby said. "We'll find out what's goin' on 'eah."

We resigned ourselves to the inevitable as we approached Old Frenchy's boarding house. We stood by the front door as the bobby placed a massive forefinger on the doorbell. He rang the bell for several minutes before Old Frenchy appeared in curlers and dressing gown, peering short-sightedly through the frosted glass window by the door. She saw us first, then her eyes widened as she saw the bobby. She opened the door. The bobby spoke first.

"These two lads claim they live 'ere, mum, but I caught 'em running out of the 'ouse with a suitcase. Thought they moit be buhglars or somefing."
Old Frenchy was flustered and upset by the whole affair but she assured the bobby we did live there. Needless to say, she was curious about the suitcase and its contents as I tried to explain it away.

"Someone we know wants to borrow our case," I explained, "and we were just on our way over when we accidentally ran into the constable here. It's all a mistake. Really!"

I could tell Old Frenchy was not completely satisfied but fortunately the policeman did not insist that we open the case. Immensely relieved, we apologized to Frenchy for causing her to have to get out of bed, then to the constable for running into him, and we all went our separate ways. When the coast was clear again, we took the suitcase to a nearby vacant lot and covertly dumped the contents there.

The next day, we realized that the pile of sandwiches was visible from the bus we rode to work each morning. The pile of sandwiches full of mystery meat sat there for months, gradually deteriorating and actually changing colors. Not even the hungriest stray mongrel would go near it. Finally, we were glad to see a construction grader level the lot, obliterating for all time the evidence of our dark deception, and possibly another Black Plague. God knows what organisms that pile was home to.

Now that work and lodging had been secured once again, Hyndsie and I were again able to turn our minds to our first priority - girls. At eighteen, I still had not yet experienced the ultimate act of love, nor had Hyndsie. In both our cases, it had not been for lack of effort, and both of us had come close on several occasions. In any case, here we were on the threshold of manhood with our ducks unbroken. But I was about to meet a girl who would change all that for me. Out of respect, I think I should interrupt this reverie and devote a chapter to her. Her name was Sheelagh.

CHAPTER 57

SHEELAGH

"It is regarded as normal to consecrate virginity in general and to lust for its destruction in particular."
~ Karl Kraus

Hyndsie and I had found that conditions in Ireland were not very conducive toward the consummation of a love affair. In most cases, single girls lived with their parents right up until the day they were married, which was also true for young men. Many continued to live at home after they were married, too.

Though massive amounts of gubsucking went on, the complete and total unavailability of proper conditions made it very difficult for most of us to go all the way. Very few of us owned cars, which could serve as an adequate trysting place in a pinch, and the thought of checking into the staid establishments which pass for hotels in Belfast with an unmarried female and without luggage was a daunting prospect in itself. We later learned that old-fashioned morality also had a much stronger grip on the young in Ireland than it did in England.

Up to this point in our lives, most of our romantic interludes had been conducted in drafty alleys, or "entries" as we called them, where we were under the constant surveillance of suspicious canines and subject to the unwelcome attentions of abusive drunks looking for a relief station. Nothing ruins the mood of a budding kerfuffle quite as well as someone urinating in the adjoining doorway. The Irish climate is not agreeable to anything except puddle-hopping, let alone love in the great outdoors. It took stentorian qualities for anyone, male or female, to bare oneself with rainwater trickling down the back of their neck. Some of our more determined friends claimed to have achieved success despite these obstacles, but Hyndsie and I hadn't.

In my first year or so of sexual exploration, I had innumerable knee tremblers in doorways all over Belfast but could never quite manage to complete the act. In fact, I couldn't even locate the entry point. Sexual education in school did not exist then, so we were all left to figure everything out for ourselves. I had always imagined that the woman's sexual part was located right up front just under the belly button like mine was. It took quite a bit of trial and error to discover that it was actually underneath.

I finally worked that problem out during a soiree in the doorway of a girl's home. I was well on my way and the girl seemed willing when I heard a bell tinkling above us. I looked up but could see nothing, so I continued my desperate efforts. The bell tinkled again, and again I did my best to ignore it. The passion mounted, and we were both on the verge of complete abandonment when the bell tinkled again more insistently than ever.

Concentration thoroughly broken, I asked, "What the hell is that?"

"It's my mother," the girl answered. "That's how she tells me to come in." The old doll shook the bell again as she explained this to me. I don't think I ever hated anyone as much as her mother at that moment. The ol' doll must have been up there listening to the tempo of the breathing and waiting until the last possible moment to declare an end to the festivities. Her apparent application of Pavlovian theory did the trick because her daughter obediently began to toddle off into the house at the sound of the more insistent ringings, signaling the official end of the mating ritual.

"Time to come in now, dear!" her mother said, as if the bell wasn't making that clear enough. She tried to leave. I held her arm. Driven mad by aimless, useless hormones, I pleaded, "Just a wee bit longer."

"I can't. I must go!" she said.

And off she went, leaving me in the cold night alone. I was so close!

As I walked home through the fog, I cursed the old woman, her bell, her impeccable timing, the weather, and everything else I could think of.

On at least a dozen other occasions, I had almost managed to overcome the obstacles of location, social mores, climatic conditions, and mothers with bells. Staggering homeward on rubbery legs which had been weakened by the excitement of the occasion and the difficulty of negotiating a coupling in an upright position (against a brick wall) with someone a foot shorter led me to conclude that the term "knee trembler" was very fitting. My frustration mounting, I concluded that it just wasn't worth all the effort and trusted that, one fine day, the ideal situation would present itself – namely a bed, four walls, a ceiling and a locking door.

One of our friends, Charlie Bingham, had an outstanding record of success with doorway sorties, and we were finally motivated enough to ask him how he managed the physical handicaps involved. His answer was simple.

"You don't try to get in from the front, you stupid eejits!" he said. "You bend them over caveman-style and attack from the rear!"

A few weeks later, I was walking home from the pictures at about midnight and was passing a cluster of shops. As I drew near, I saw a white object moving in and out of sight at the edge of one of the doorways. I gave the object a cautious berth as I approached, fearing that it might be some kind of wild animal. I was relieved when I heard Charlie's voice giving me a cheery greeting from the shadows. I drew closer and discovered that the gyrating object I had seen was Charlie's white arse. And there was Charlie pounding away merrily in doggy fashion from the rear. The object of his affection was bent forward from the waist, just as he had earlier described. She seemed undisturbed by my presence as she was busily engaged in devouring fish and chips wrapped in newspaper, which I later found represented the value of her favors. I was somewhat embarrassed for Charlie and his friend, but neither seemed to mind, nor did either of them pause in their activity as I stood there watching this demonstration of Charlie's technique.

Though I had sworn off the indignities of such doorway interludes, I found myself a few nights later once again overcome with desire for a girl I left the Plaza with and who lived at the top of the Shankill Road. The houses on the Shankill Road had doors that opened directly onto the sidewalk, and an inside door at the end of a short hall. We were inside the hall and her parents were in bed, or so I thought. After some furious necking in the hallway, I suddenly realized to my wild delight that my partner appeared willing to go ALL THE WAY!

It was difficult for me to maintain the masterful, worldly lover facade while absolutely ecstatic at the prospect of finally losing my virginity, which had actually acquired a physical weight over the years due to accumulated adolescent frustration. With Charlie's sage advice still in mind, I maneuvered myself into the suggested position of entry. Any remnant of romance the situation might have held immediately drained as I noticed that her head was jammed rather uncomfortably into the corner of the entry. However, youthful exuberance and an unreasonably impatient erection would not allow me to observe the finer points of sexual etiquette, even if I had known what they were. I directed my throbbing appendage into what I hoped was the correct latitude and longitude and thrust forward like a Norseman. There was a split second of absolute ecstasy, and then . . . her father opened the door to put out the milk bottles. We both collapsed forward onto the living room floor, the bottles clattering all around us. I panicked out of embarrassment and alarm and, without any attempt at explanation or concern for my unfortunate accomplice, pulled myself to my feet, yanked my pants up and dashed down the steps and up the street as fast as I could, her father's angry bellows following after me. I heard a milk bottle crash several feet behind me and decided that running was definitely the best decision I had made that day. I didn't stop until I was a good mile and a half down the Woodvale Road.

I ran into the girl again a few days later in the Plaza and tried to apologize, but she cut me dead. I didn't blame her. It undoubtedly would have been nobler to stay there and let her father bludgeon me to death with milk bottles. In any case, I had just missed it once again. The ultimate act of love was still a mystery to me, and it seemed the gods were conspiring to keep it that way.

Since we were apparently cursed in Belfast, Hyndsie and I hoped we would unravel a few of the mysteries of love in Manchester. We had discovered that the best place to meet girls was the Ritz Ballroom near the downtown area. It was Friday night. We washed, dressed and prepared ourselves for a night of "chasing", as girl-hunting was then called in Belfast. As we waited at the bus stop in Chorlton-Cum Hardy, along came an absolutely beautiful young thing about nineteen years old. She had incredible legs, a tiny waist, short, curly hair and an upturned nose.

I had always found it easier to strike up a conversation with a girl if there was someone else with me because I didn't have to speak directly to her, which might bring a rebuff, but could drop some exploratory comments which passed for romantic jousting at that time. Standard lines such as, "Isn't she lovely!" or "I think I'm in love!"

In this case, I was rewarded by a dazzling smile and a giggle from her. We boarded the bus together, sat beside her and paid her fare downtown. In due course, we formally introduced ourselves. We found out her name was Sheelagh, spelled in the Irish manner, and that she was intending to go dancing at the Plaza in Manchester. We tried to talk her into going to the Ritz with us as we preferred it to the Plaza, but she refused. We parted company when we got off the bus and headed our separate ways. A few minutes later, we heard the clatter of high heels on the pavement and turned around. There she was again.

"I've changed me mind," she said. "I've decided to come with you."

She took my arm, which signified to me that she had made her choice. Hyndsie understood, as we had a standing agreement between ourselves to back off if one of was on the verge of success.

I spent the entire evening with her, dancing every dance together. She had a very sexy way of pressing herself close during the slow dances. I was in heaven. We had a coffee together later then took the bus back to our neighborhood. It was always an advantage to find someone to take home who lived in the same general area, as an otherwise pleasant evening could be marred by the difficulty in finding transportation home afterwards.

We approached her front door, and she explained she lived alone in a flat. (Marvelous, I thought. She has her own place!) We entered, and I was surprised to find a young lad inside who turned out to be the babysitter for her one year-old child. I later found out she had been married at fifteen and separated at eighteen, although she told me she was fully divorced. Her former husband's name was Terry. I found out later from her mother that they were separated but still legally married.

Sheelagh and I went to the movies the next night. We got home at about eleven, and as we entered the babysitter said, "Terry was here, and he wanted to know who he was," pointing to me. Sheelagh seemed distressed at this. I didn't understand why since they were supposed to be separated. I assumed he had only stopped by to see the baby and could see nothing wrong with that.

The babysitter left, and we sat on her couch. She put her arms around me in a deep embrace. I felt her breast and discovered she was wearing "falsies." This slowed me down momentarily but didn't put me off much. We were getting into some very heavy petting and writhing around uncomfortably on the sofa when she pushed me away, sat up and said, "Just a minute. Let's do this right, shall we? There's no need to get our clothes all wrinkled, is there?"

I realized then that THE BIG MOMENT had arrived. The old duck was about to be shattered once and for all, and good riddance. She took me by the hand and led me into the adjoining bedroom, smiling coyly as she did so. I felt my mouth go dry at the prospect of what lay before me and started to tremble uncontrollably. With all my bragging among friends, posturing, and girl-chasing, I was still just a boy.

"Get a grip of yourself, eejit!" I whispered inwardly. "Don't screw up now, for Christ's sake. This is your big chance!"

We continued undressing in the pale light of the bedroom lamp. I became entranced with her as she removed her clothes. She slipped off her blouse and skirt and stood before me, wearing only soft pink panties. Her creamy skin was smooth and beautiful. I stood staring at her, transfixed. I suppose I had anticipated this moment for so long, I didn't want to rush. I took my time and savored the sight of her like one would a tropical beach, a sunset, a double rainbow or some other magnificent wonder of nature. She said, "Well, silly? Are you going to stand there gawking or are you coming to bed with me?"

I finished undressing, still in a bit of a daze, while she got into the bed and pulled the covers over her. It was cold in the bedroom, so I quickly finished undressing and slid in beside her. She came into my arms at once, and I felt the entire length of her warm body press against me. I hooked my fingers in the waistband of her panties, and she raised her back off the bed, allowing me to slide them over her legs. At this moment, my shyness left me, and I became very calm. I had anticipated this moment long enough, played it over and over in my mind, and knew what to do. I positioned myself between her legs, and she guided me inside her. All I remember after that is pure pleasure. It was as if my mind was exploding. All my fantasizing about this moment had not prepared me in the slightest, nor had the most vivid descriptions from more experienced friends. Nothing can prepare a boy on the fringe of manhood for the pleasure a woman can give him, especially the first time. The actual experience felt every bit as glorious as I dreamed it would in my youthful fantasies, times a thousand. God sure got that right.

We made love over and over again until the sun came up. I dressed and rose to get back home before her son woke up. We made arrangements to meet that same evening, and I left her in bed, a sleepy smile on her face. I could still smell her sweet scent all over me as I walked toward the bus station. I felt emptied and filled at the same time. The ideal situation had finally presented itself, and with an extraordinary beauty.

As much as I had wanted to lose my virginity, there was always a tinge of guilt in the back of my mind about it. This was undoubtedly implanted by the church, which discouraged premarital sex of any kind, or anything natural and pleasurable for that matter. But this didn't feel like the death of anything sacred. It felt like an expansion of myself, a discovery and celebration of one of life's most exhilarating experiences. So, completely guiltless and overflowing with joy, I floated all the way home, never touching the sidewalk, smiling at everyone I passed and knowing I would never be quite the same again.

Hyndsie was awake when I got home. I gave him the bare details, and he solemnly arose and extended his hand.

"Congratulations," he said. I suppose it's up to me now. You've really put the pressure on!"

I saw Sheelagh every night for the next month. I was completely in love with her. We made love at every opportunity, in every conceivable position, and in a variety of locations. She kept asking me not to pull out at the moment of climax and told me it was safe, but I felt I shouldn't take any chances. In retrospect, I was glad that I did because it soon became clear to me that she had an agenda.

I was at work when the boss came over and told me I was wanted on the telephone. I wondered who needed to talk to me so urgently and went into the office to take the call. It was Sheelagh's mother, and she was crying.

"You'd better come home right away," she said, sobbing. "Sheelagh's been hurt."

My heart fell like a stone.

"What do you mean, hurt? Has there been an accident?"

"It was Terry done it. Terry has nearly killed her!"

I told my foreman there was an emergency at home, and I had to leave. He took one look at my face and told me to go immediately. On the way out of the plant, I passed a bin full of trash. I pulled out a piece of lead pipe and stuck it in my pocket. I had no clear idea what I intended to do, but I was overcome with a deep feeling of revulsion and rage over what Sheelagh's mother had said. When I got to Sheelagh's flat, her mother met me at the door with a tear-streaked face and swollen eyes. There was a man there I didn't recognize. He was bending over Sheelagh and talking to her as she lay on the couch. Then I saw her face. She was completely unrecognizable. Her face was battered terribly and both her eyes were nearly swollen shut. There were several cuts around her mouth and eyes. My stomach lurched at the sight, and I wanted to drive my fist through the wall. I fell to my knees and cradled her in my arms.

"Why did he do it?" I asked her.

She seemed unable to answer and broke into tears, crying into my chest. I turned to her mother.

"Where does Terry live?" I asked.

"That won't do any good," her mother answered. "What are you going to do?"

I remembered I had seen Terry's address on a letter on the mantle and ran to get it. The letter was still there. I pushed the letter into my pocket and ran out the door. I was halfway down the street when I heard footsteps behind me and felt a hand on my shoulder. I whipped around, not knowing what to expect. It was the man from Sheelagh's flat.

"Just what the hell do you think you're doing?" he demanded.

"What do you think I'm doing?" I answered, pulling his hand from my arm. "I'm gonna find that bastard and kill him!"

"Now just a bloody minute!" he said. "I'm Miss Doyle's solicitor (lawyer), and before you go off half-cocked, I have some advice for you. What Terry did has given me the grounds for divorce that we needed. But if you go over there and get into it with him, you're going to ruin my case. Do you want to be the co-respondent in the divorce action?"

Though seething with rage, his comments made me take stock of what I was about to do. The term "co-respondent" was something I had gotten used to reading in the Sunday tabloids. It usually applied to a shifty character of some kind. The headline flashed in my mental sky:

"IRISH IMMIGRANT CO-RESPONDENT
WRECKS MARRIAGE.
DRIVES HUSBAND BERSERK!"

I could see policemen with notebooks and stubby pencils, courtrooms and white-wigged judges peering at me over their pince nez. I was stopped in my tracks.

"Okay, you win," I said. "I'll keep out of it."

"Now you're being smart, lad," the lawyer said. "Go on home now. I'll take care of Sheelagh."

I trudged home, sickened and disgusted at the turn of events. The sight of Sheelagh's battered face tormented me, and my stomach felt like I'd been hit with a wrecking ball. I lay on the bed until Hyndsie came home. I told him what happened. He listened intently but without much emotion. It struck me as odd that he didn't seem a bit disturbed about a woman being beaten. Finally, he leaned in to me, took a deep breath, and said, "I've been meaning to tell you, Rick, but you've been too twat-happy to listen. I've looked into it a bit because you're my friend. That whole family is no bloody good. Sheelagh's ma is screwing around with her husband's brother, the husband is nothing more than a glorified handyman in the house, her sister is knocked up from a married man, and Sheelagh seems to fit in real well with the rest of the family."

I couldn't believe what I was hearing. Blindly defending her, I jumped off the bed, grabbed Hyndsie by the shirt and raised my fist.

Without flinching, he said, "Go on and hit me if you want, but I'm tellin' you this for your own good. You've just been too blind to see it."

I dropped my fist, sat back down on the bed and with my face in my hands, said, "What should I do, Hyndsie?"

"Forget your woman Sheelagh," he answered. "Just put her out of your mind, Rick. Her troubles are of her own doing, you can be sure of that. And you're better off without her."

I spent the rest of the evening lying on the bed, trying to untangle my thoughts and feelings. I thought of the times Sheelagh and I were together, making love, how she felt sleeping in my arms, the way she laughed, how she linked her arm in mine when we went out walking, and the trusting, childlike way she looked up into my eyes. She had introduced me to some of her friends as her fiancé, which had given me a protective feeling for her. But then I thought of the times I saw her baby in dirty clothes, crawling over the stained floor of her flat. I remembered how I would pick up the baby's little socks from under the couch and laughingly chastise Sheelagh for not tidying up her apartment. I thought of the endless cigarettes she smoked even though the baby was always short of clothes. Finally, I began to see what Hyndsie had been trying to tell me and decided I had to end it after she had recovered from her injuries.

A week or so passed. I hardened myself and went to see her. She opened the door and threw her arms around me. She looked much better. The bruises around her eyes had begun to yellow.

"Where have you been?" she asked, "I missed you!"

"Thinking. Look, Sheelagh, I have something to tell you."

Her smile dropped. "What is it?"

"I don't want to see you anymore," I said with finality.

She immediately started to cry. "Why not? Don't you love me anymore?"

"I don't want to go into it," I said. "I just want to end it. Now."

She kept on at me until I finally poured out all the reasons. I made a point of mentioning the fact that I was giving her money for the baby while she wasted money on trivialities. I pointed to the cigarette dangling from her fingers for added emphasis.

"That's one of the reasons. All this bloody smoking when the child needs clothes and nappies!"

She tossed the cigarette on the porch, stepped on it and said, "That's my last one. I promise!"

I said I was sorry and turned to leave. She ran after me to the street, tugging at my arm, crying and pleading with me to stay, but I had made up my mind to go and ignored her. She stood on the sidewalk looking after me, but I didn't look back until I reached the corner. She was still standing where I had left her, with her hands over her face. I took the long way home. My heart was breaking for her, but I couldn't go back.

About a week later, the landlady came to my room and told me there was a phone call for me. I picked up the phone and a strange voice answered my hello.

"This is Terry. I understand you want to see me."

Until this moment, I had convinced myself that I was over the whole affair, but Sheelagh's beaten face flashed in my mind, and my anger rose to the surface again.

"You're fuckin' right I want to see you," I yelled. "Tell me where you are, and I'll meet you right now!"

"I'm calling from the railway station," he said, "and in about five minutes, I'll be getting on the train to Liverpool to catch the boat to America. I just wanted you to know something before I leave. You're welcome to Sheelagh if you want her."

"Oh, really? Well, first of all, I don't need your fuckin' permission. Second, why did you have to beat her up? That was a rotten thing to do."

The line was quiet for a moment.

"I went to see the baby," he said. I thought I heard his voice waver slightly. There was another long pause. "I couldn't care less who she sees," he continued. "Do you think I hit her because of you? Don't kid yourself, my friend.

I hit her because she said the baby wasn't mine . . . that it was a Yank's. I love that baby. When she said that, I couldn't stand it. That's why I hit her, and I kept on hitting her until she admitted it was a lie."

I didn't know what to say. I wanted to be mad at him. There's never a good excuse for attacking a woman. I still felt the impulse to do to him what he had done to her, but the gravity of his words had drained the rage out of me. I put the phone down slowly, my mind spinning, trying to blend this new information with everything else that had happened. There was something in the way he spoke which made me believe him. After all, if he were actually leaving for America, what reason would he have to lie to me, someone he doesn't even know? Some of it was vindictiveness toward her, I'm sure, but he was probably also trying to save me from the same mistake he had made.

I sighed and went back to my room. Hyndsie was sitting quietly, waiting for me. My heart heavy, I was glad to have him nearby. I felt the impulse to cry. He seemed to sense it. He put his hand on my shoulder and said, "Come on, Rick. Let's go out and have a few pints."

And we did.

CHAPTER 58

WORKING IN MANCHESTER

"The so-called rites of passage, which occupy such a prominent place in the life of a primitive society (ceremonials of birth, naming, puberty, marriage, burial, etc.) are distinguished by formal, and usually very severe, exercises of severance, whereby the mind is radically cut away from the attitudes, attachments, and life patterns of the stage being left behind."
~ Joseph Campbell

Hyndsie was working away at his machinery moving job and I at my clerical position in Trafford Park with Massey Harris. At the end of our first week, we compared our take-home wages. Hyndsie, who had worked some overtime, had twice as much as I did. I decided it was time to put the world of pencils behind me for a while and try my luck with physical labor. Hyndsie spoke with his boss and I was hired sight unseen to be a machine mover. I had no idea what the job entailed or if I could even handle it. I had no working clothes. Hyndsie had a second boiler suit but it was too small for me. I picked out the oldest set of clothes I owned but even then I felt conspicuous among the other men that first morning with their oil-stained denims and coveralls. But they were a friendly lot and the only difficulty I had with them was deciphering their Lancashire accent. They seemed to be having as much trouble with my Ulster brogue.

I was assisting a mechanic that first week and for the first several days, didn't understand a word he said. We ended up communicating by gestures and head movements as much as by speech. He might as well have spoken to me in Arabic for all I understood. I began to get the drift of the local idiom after a few weeks and even found myself using the odd Lancashire expression. For some reason, one usually learns the swear words first or the manner in which they are delivered. They say "bloody 'ell" a lot in Manchester. I found the various expressions quaint and easy on the tongue.

Among the crew, there was a twenty stone (280 pound) giant called, what else, "Buster." Although a man of monstrous proportions who growled when he spoke, I found him to be the most gentle and easy-going person I had met at work until then.

Others were not so pleasant. "Sam", for instance, was an old ogre with a vast repertoire of profanity. He could cuss someone out for twenty minutes without repeating himself once. His skin was pitted and his hair was always a mess. He was average sized but his hands were enormous and he had incredible strength. I used to think his hands looked like they belonged to somebody else, like some kind of grotesque cartoon character.

The lead man was Les, who was about thirty and a supreme con artist. He could double talk the plant engineers masterfully. He had the agility of a cat and was great for "high work." I saw him fall backward off an I-beam one day from a height of about twenty feet but somehow he twisted himself in mid-air and landed on all fours, rolling over and rising without apparent injury or the slightest distress. He probably could have been a world-class gymnast or high-diver if he'd had the opportunity.

The first day on the job, we were involved in some very heavy lifting and moving of large pieces of machinery. After several hours, my back was breaking from all the bending and lifting. Although I prided myself on my physical condition, I realized I was no match for those who had spent all their lives in jobs involving grueling manual labor. The lifting got easier as time passed and I soon realized that I had an ability to determine where the center of gravity was on any particular piece of machinery. I would then place wire slings in such a manner that the machine cleared the floor evenly on the first lift. The other men recognized this ability and I was given this duty from then on.

After a day's hard work and a hot bath, I found a great feeling of satisfaction I had never known before, except perhaps after a training session in the boxing club or a soccer game. My muscles felt pleasantly tired and I slept better than I had in years.

One day, we were on the third or fourth floor of a building relaxing after lunch with a bunch of the other guys when one of the men dared another to walk to the end of a beam which stuck out over thin air at the side of the building. The distance to the ground was over one hundred feet, which meant almost certain death if someone fell. The man who had been dared was young and inexperienced like me but he accepted the challenge. He walked about halfway but stopped and made the fatal error of looking down. The color suddenly ran out of his face and he began to tremble uncontrollably. A few of the men yelled very uninspiring remarks like "go on, ya big girl!" while others, fearing the worst, encouraged him to come back. After a few minutes, he went down to his knees and crawled back along the beam.

I found the terror that overcame him fascinating. He was fine until he thought about it so it was obviously his fear that had paralyzed him, not the height. Walking along a beam is no different from walking along a sidewalk as long as one stays calm and composed.

One of the older men said, "Lemme show ya how it's done, lad." He walked to the end of the beam effortlessly, did a little jig at the end, and walked back. Wanting to distinguish myself, I said, "I'll do ya one better!" I stepped out onto the beam, sat down on it, swung myself under, and walked hand over hand along the bottom edge. It wasn't difficult until I got to the end and had to turn around to come back. I began to feel the strength in my hands failing. Though I had just received a grand demonstration of the folly of looking down, the morbid desire to do so myself overcame me. The sight further sapped the strength in my hands and caused blind panic to set in. I inched along the beam back toward the building, the cheers of the men ringing in my ears, but my hands were spent and

I was forced to clutch the beam with my fingernails. To make matters worse, the beam was badly rusted and abrasive. There were less than ten feet between me and the building but it seemed like a mile. Lawrence of Arabia crossing the Sahara had nothing on me. I finally made it back and was helped up by the other men. They all slapped me on the back.

One of them said, "That was the bravest feat I've ever seen. Stupid, but brave."

The man who had walked out on the beam said, "I'm not outdone very often, lad. I'll buy ya a pint for that!"

Young as I was, the acceptance my peers, particularly the elders of the tribe, made nearly having my fingernails torn off well worth it.

CHAPTER 59

AT WORK AND PLAY IN LONDON

"You find no man, at all intellectual, who is willing to leave London. No, Sir, when a man is tired of London, he is tired of life; for there is in London all that life can afford."
~ Samuel Johnson

Me (back to camera) working at one of many jobs in Manchester, England

One of the nicest things about the jobs Hyndsie and I had with the machinery moving firm was that we never knew where we would be working next. We saw most of the towns around Lancashire and Yorkshire within the first few months, and I grew very fond of the down-to-earth people we stayed with and met during our travels. I found that the people in the north of England were much friendlier than those in the south. The north is working-class, industrial and ugly in certain areas, but I enjoyed Manchester and the way the shop girls and waitresses always called me "Love."

One day, the boss told us we would be heading down to London the following Monday to do a job at London University. Hyndsie and I were very excited as we both wanted to see the sights of one of the greatest cities in the world.

I had the feeling that the boss liked us because we worked hard and never refused an order. We had taken on some dangerous assignments that more experienced workers declined, including working in close proximity to high-voltage cables in a large plant the prior week. If we had refused, which was our right, the job would have been delayed until the day's end when the plant power could have been shut off. But we completed the installation, working within inches of the exposed power lines. I had a dreadful urge to touch the lines to see if they were really live, almost like the feeling one gets looking over the edge of a cliff. Thankfully, my curiosity and impetuousness had some limits.

We had also worked high on the exterior of the twelve-story Tootal Building, clambering up scaffolding with the other men looking up at us nervously and shaking their heads. They wouldn't risk their lives for any job, but it didn't bother us. We were too young and eager to win respect to recognize the hazards. Our employer reciprocated by giving us the best assignments. We could hardly contain ourselves over the weekend, thinking about the trip to London ahead of us. We had dreamed of seeing that city for so long it had taken on mythic proportions in our minds.

Bright and early Monday morning, we were at the station to catch the train. We met Sam and Buster on the platform. We selected a nice, clean carriage and settled in with our newspapers and magazines. To ensure we had the carriage to ourselves, Buster positioned his hulking frame in front of the window. When other passengers passed by on the platform looking for a compartment to sit in, he would twist his massive face into a ferocious and maniacal expression. If someone paused courageously at the door to think about entering in spite of this odd spectacle, he would shoot out his upper and lower dentures for added emphasis. That usually did the trick. I must say, Buster's technique was very effective because while every other carriage was packed to bursting, we all lounged comfortably in ours with room to spare.

About seven hours later, we pulled into St. Pancras in London. We stepped out of our carriage and walked into the street outside the station. Big, red, double-deck buses whizzed past in all directions with taxis negotiating in and out of the busy traffic. There were more people and traffic than I had ever seen in my life. The city was absolutely infused with happy, industrious energy. I felt like I was walking through a dream as I took it all in. It was just as I had always imagined it would be, with wet streets, red buses and phone boxes, beautiful statuary, glorious fountains, palatial buildings and cheerful people zipping around on bicycles under a pale blue sky spotted with cotton ball clouds.

St. Pancras Station, London

Our employer had supplied us with an address where we could find lodging while in London. We finally found our way there after asking a number of people for directions. It turned out to be a very disreputable rooming house with seedy bedrooms and flaking paint. Our crew foreman, who met us at the station, was an old fellow from the city of Newcastle. His name was Ned, and he took an instant dislike to Hyndsie and me when he heard we were from Ireland. We later discovered that he hated anyone from Ireland with a passion and lost no opportunity to give us the worst assignments he could find. There was little doubt he would have sacked us if he could have, but our good standing with his supervisor undoubtedly gave him pause to do so. Our relationship was not improved by the fact that I'd had a bit of a run-in with him a few weeks earlier in Bolton, where he was in charge. It was over a woman. Her name was Vera.

CHAPTER 60

VERA

"The best way to get over someone is to get under someone."
~ Anonymous

To get Sheelagh out of my mind, I had been seeing a young divorcee named Vera who worked in the plant with me. One night, I had arranged to stay at her house after our date rather than return to our home in Manchester. Ned owed me several days traveling money, and since I was short of cash for the date, I asked him about it. He tried to put me off by saying he had no money, but I knew he did and persisted. It was about five in the afternoon and we were preparing to leave the plant. Ned and the others were intending to head for the railway station. Ned stalked out of the plant as I was trying to tell him why I needed the money. Because I had been removing the machine oil from my hands and forearms, I was stripped to the waist. It was snowing outside, and I was shivering while I ran after him, trying to reason with him. He just kept on walking so I lost my temper, grabbed his shoulder, spun him around and pinned him to the side of the building.

"Stand still while I'm trying to speak to you, for Christ's sake!" I yelled. "I need my money now!"

Ned seemed to realize he had pushed me too far and reached for his wallet to pay me the back money I was due but added, "You're going to get sacked for this, lad. You can't go around grabbing people like that."

I said, "Do your worst" and walked away. I couldn't care less about his threats at that moment. My thoughts were more involved with the plans for the evening ahead.

I assumed we would be going to the pictures, but Vera suggested we go to a pub for a few drinks, which we did. I thought I could out-drink any woman, but Vera must have had a hollow leg because she put pints of Chester's Bitter away that night like a sailor. She seemed to know everyone in the pub, and they all sent pints over to our table during the course of the evening. It was about twenty minutes to closing time when I realized I had five pints of black and tan in front of me which I still had to beat down my neck somehow. I don't know how I did it, but I finished them all before we left. I felt a little funny but didn't think much of it until I got outside into the fresh air. The fresh surge of oxygen caused my legs to go limp and my head to spin. I crumpled to the sidewalk in a heap. The next sight I saw was Vera's face, looking down at me lovingly, lit from behind by a street lamp.

"What's the matter, luv?" she asked. "One too many?"

I'd had about six too many, I thought, but I was too sick to answer. With Vera's help, I got to my feet. My legs hadn't completely returned, however, so I draped my arm around her shoulder, too drunk to even be embarrassed for myself.

"Gimme a hand, Vera," I slurred. With her help, we finally made it to her house about half a mile away. I collapsed on a sofa in the living room while Vera took off her scarf and coat and went into the kitchen. I dozed off and she woke me a few minutes later holding a large plate of chips and pork chops in her hands.

"What you need, luv, is something in your stomach."

I decided she was right and dragged myself over to the table. Vera placed the plate in front of me. I got one chop and a handful of chips inside me when I was overcome with nausea and knew I was going to be violently ill. I groaned an apology and dashed out the kitchen door into the back yard. I barely made it out when I threw up over everything in sight. I heaved and retched uncontrollably for about five minutes until, at long last, spitting and eyes watering, I knew there was nothing left to disgorge. To my surprise, I actually felt good. My head cleared and my legs steadied. I went back inside, drank a glass of water and washed my hands and face in the kitchen sink, drying them on a cloth hanging on a nail beside the door.

"Feeling better now, are ya, luv?" Vera asked brightly.

"Much better," I answered. "Ready for anything."

"Well, I have to be up early in the morning," she said, "so if you don't mind, I think I should go to bed now."

I had assumed she would put me up for the night, although it hadn't been discussed.

"Well," I said, "I'm in no shape to get back to Manchester tonight."

"Oh, I wouldn't ask you to leave feeling the way you do, luv, and I do have a spare bed made up upstairs. You're welcome to stay the night."

We went upstairs, and Vera pointed to a small room.

"That's your room in there, luv. I hope you find the bed comfortable."

"Where are you sleeping?" I asked.

"In there," she replied, motioning toward another room at the far end of the hall.

Now that my head had cleared and I was confident that I was going to survive, my mind returned to its usual craftiness.

"Well, if you don't mind," I said, "I have a dreadful fear of sleeping alone in a strange place, and I would much rather sleep with you."

Obviously, I was taking advantage of her generous nature. You see, young men are evil. The devil's playthings. I was no different.

"Oh! My goodness," she exclaimed, "I hadn't planned on *that*!"

"Well, I bloody well did!" I said. I picked her up and carried her into the bedroom. She didn't need much convincing, and inside a few minutes we were both snugly tucked between the sheets and warming up as a soft snow fell outside the window. I didn't ask her how long she had been on her own, but it must have been quite a while because she came on like a lioness, gasping and panting with every touch, pelvis churning against me like a piston. She pulled me on top of her, whispering, "Put it in, put it in!" which I did as quickly as I could.

She awakened me five times during the night by throwing her thighs over me and pumping like crazy. I managed to get some sleep in between each frenzied encounter. To my surprise, I found myself beginning to lose interest, something which I had previously thought impossible. In fact, my emotions fluctuated between aggravation and fear for my physical safety. The alarm was set for seven A.M. so that I would get to the plant on time at eight. When the alarm sounded, sure enough, she threw the leg over me again.

"In the name of Jasus," I said, "Do you think I'm a bloody machine?" Give me a chance to draw a breath!"

I fell out of the bed and crawled away from her across the floor. It was freezing cold in the room, and I shivered as I put on my clothes. I went downstairs and into the kitchen looking for something to eat but couldn't find even the makings of a cup of tea. I put on my overcoat and staggered out into the snow. I didn't bother saying goodbye to Vera because I knew I would see her later at the plant. I was dreadfully hung over. My head felt like it had been used as a soccer ball in a grudge match. I knew if I didn't get some food and hot tea into me soon, I would not be long for this world.

I finally reached the plant and headed for the canteen, where I ordered a pint of hot tea and a fried bacon and egg butty (sandwich). The girls in the canteen somehow knew that I had been out with Vera the night before. I suppose she told them.

"Would you look at him!" one said, winking at the others. "Where d'ya think he's been to get into such a state?"

I had severe bedhead, my eyes were bloodshot, and my skin was a light green hue. I knew I looked like the Wreck of the Hesperus, but all I cared about was getting the hot tea and sandwich into me. The tea took effect almost immediately, and I began to feel a lot better. The canteen girls continued to joke about my sorry condition.

"Look at 'is eyes! Like pee holes in the snow, they are!"
I did my best to ignore them, and they finally left me alone to recuperate.

My relationship with Vera blossomed, and I was looking forward to many repeats of our first night together once I had recovered. When we got together, she again challenged and pushed my libido to its outermost regions. But Old Ned, may hell roast him, continued to complain about me and actually threatened to quit unless something was done. Finally, in an effort to keep the peace, the boss transferred me. Vera bade me a tearful farewell that day over lunch.

"You will come back and see me, won't you?" she asked, "I didn't expect we would be saying cheerio this soon!"

"Neither did I, luv," I answered, having adopted the local vernacular. "I'll get even with that old blert Ned over this, and I'll stop back this way soon and see you, too."

I firmly intended to see her again at the time but, as usual, I never did. There always seemed to be some new distraction, and I was tossed in other directions by one escapade after another. Such is youth. I didn't worry about her, though. Vera was too good a woman to be alone for long, unless she wanted it that way.

CHAPTER 61

CREEPY OLD NED

"It's not that the Irish are cynical. It's rather that they have a wonderful lack of respect for everything and everybody."
~ Brendan Behan

So here we were in London, back with Ned the old bastard, waiting outside the digs while he looked them over. He came outside.

"How do they look?" we asked.

"Perfect," he said. "She can take us all."

"Did you look at the rooms?" I asked.

"Of course I did," he snapped. "They're fine."

I wasn't satisfied and neither was Buster. He whispered to me, "Go on inside, Ricky. 'Ave a butcher's hook (look) at the rooms and see 'ow they are."

I went inside, met the landlady, and asked her if I could see where we would be sleeping. She took me up a narrow, winding staircase and showed me several tiny, filthy cubicles. I went inside to look at the beds and saw there were men sleeping in them.

"Who the hell are they?" I asked. "These rooms are taken!"

"They'll be gone by tonight," she answered. "They're truck drivers who work at night."

I had heard of such places before, where a room was rented to one tenant during the day and another at night. The beds never cooled off. I wasn't ready to rough it that much yet. I went back outside to where Ned and the others were waiting.

"Well?" Ned snapped. "Bloody well satisfied?"

"See you, Ned?" I answered. "You haven't a bloody clue. I wouldn't let my dog sleep in that kip house. Come on, Buster. Let's find somewhere decent to stay."

We marched off up the street, and the rest of the lads came walking after us, looking back guiltily at Old Ned. He hesitated and then came after us, too.

We found a nice place about a mile or two away, with clean, airy rooms and a cheery landlady with a ruddy face and a clean apron. We divided into pairs, and I selected the best room for Hyndsie and me. We gave old Ned a room to himself because no one wanted to share one with him. He slept with his cap on and his pipe in his mouth, drooling all over his pillow. No one wanted to live with that sight on a daily basis. In addition, it was rumored that Ned had a penchant, as some wag on the crew had described it, "not for wine, women, and song but for rum, bum, and gramophone records." He had spent about twenty years in the merchant marines, and the rumor was he had acquired a taste for male companionship in the most sordid sense of the word and would make advances regardless of whether or not his chosen target was of the same persuasion. No one wanted to test the validity of that theory, so we all gave him a wide berth after working hours.

The beds in the rooms were doubles, which was quite common. Since there were two to each room, we had to share the beds. It worked out quite well, as Ned was the odd man out (in more ways than one) and had a bed and room to himself. However, after the second week there, three members of the gang were transferred to another project, which meant we had to give one room up, and one unfortunate soul had to room with Old Ned. We tossed a coin, and much to my dismay, I lost. The prospect of sleeping next to Ned filled one with horror, and I had my mind made up that if he even looked at me funny, I would ram his foul-smelling pipe up his nose or any other orifice he dared display to me.

As bedtime arrived, I entered Ned's room filled with trepidation. He was already in bed sleeping, cloth cap on, pipe dangling from his lip, newspaper open in front of him, and drool trickling down his chin. It was a disturbing sight. I decided I could not face the grim prospect of sharing a bed with him and went back into Hyndsie's room where he was sharing a bed with a fellow named Bert from the city of Cork. Bert had been in the Royal Air Force and was very cordial usually, but he reacted very unpleasantly to the suggestion that we sleep three to a bed.

"What are you talking about?" he demanded. "We can't all three of us sleep in one bed, surely to God!"

"Well," I answered, "I'll be damned if I'm going to sleep with that old shite next door."

Over Bert's objections, I got into bed between them and pulled the blankets over me. Bert argued for a while, then seemed to give up the hope of persuading either of us to leave. Hyndsie laughed uproariously throughout the entire exchange. To our surprise, Old Ned appeared in the doorway.

"Who's sleeping with me?" he asked.

"Not me, you old fucker," I answered.
Hyndsie exploded again into paroxysms of laughter.

"What am I, an animal?" Ned asked.

"Bloody right! Y'are that!" I replied. "And a dirty old bastard, too!"

Hyndsie was laughing so hard, I thought he was going to mess himself. Ned stalked out of the room, cut to the quick. Bert sat upright.

"Are you getting out of this bed or not? We can't spend the night three in a bed. I won't get a wink!"

"Why don't *you* go sleep with old Ned then if it bothers you so much," I suggested, "because there is no way I will sleep in the same room, let alone the same bed, as that randy old swine!"

With an exasperated, "Jesus, Mary, and Joseph!" Bert hopped out of bed and started pulling on his pants.

Good, I thought, he's clearing off.

Bert stalked out of the room but returned a few minutes later with the landlady.

In a very deliberate tone, he said to her, "Would you kindly ask that fella to please get out of my bed?"

By this time, Hyndsie was howling with laughter, tears streaming down his face. He buried his face in the pillow, trying to muffle his peals of mirth. Ned then reappeared at the door, and the flustered landlady turned toward him.

"Mr. Thompson, would you mind telling me just what is going on with these three?"

"Nobody wants to sleep with me," answered Ned. "They think I'm an animal or something!"

Mrs. Brown seemed to realize what was bothering us and agreed to let us have another single bed, which solved the problem. Somewhat ashamed over calling in the landlady, Bert offered to take the single cot for himself. For weeks afterward, however, Hyndsie and I teased Bert mercilessly about his reaction that night, asking each other with mock ferocity, "Would you kindly ask that fella to please get out of my bed?"

CHAPTER 62

THE BOARDING HOUSE CAPER

"Live life fully while you're here. Experience everything. Take care of yourself and your friends. Have fun, be crazy, be weird! Go out and screw up! You're going to anyway, so you might as well enjoy the process."
~ Tony Robbins

I had the address of a couple of Belfast girls in London, and Hyndsie decided to look them up. We went over to their flat, which was in the Kensington area. They shared a bed-sitter on the second floor of an old home that had been converted into a boarding house. The girls didn't want to go anywhere for the evening, preferring to chat and exchange experiences about life in England.

Hyndsie and I decided to pick up some beer and booze. We borrowed a bag from the girls, went to the corner store and bought a variety of liquors. When we returned, the four of us got fairly well-oiled, and the time flew quickly. We suddenly realized we were going to miss the last subway train if we didn't make a move, so we wished the girls good night and dashed off. A light rain was falling. We were soaked to the skin by the time we reached the station. To our great dismay, we found it locked up with the last train already gone. We checked our funds and realized we had spent most of our money on the booze and didn't have enough left for a taxi.

"What the hell do we do now?" asked Hyndsie. "It's about ten bloody miles to where we live!"

"We've no choice," I answered, "the girls are going to have to put us up for the night."

We retraced our steps to the girls' boarding house. Fortunately, the street door was open. We went up to their room as quietly as we could. Rooming house landladies usually have a very strict policy against overnight guests and we didn't want to get the girls in any trouble. They were very upset at our arrival, and we had to do some fast talking to get them to let us in. They finally relented and told us to come in but to be quiet about it. They had two single beds and absolutely refused to allow us to share one with each of them, which of course was our first suggestion. Instead, they shared one bed and told us to make the best of the other. I set the alarm for six in the morning so we could be up and away before anyone else in the house was awake. We fell asleep almost immediately as it was late, and we were still feeling the effects of the earlier libations.

The alarm went off at six and I switched it off, planning to close my eyes again for a few minutes before arising, but I fell back into a deep sleep. I was awakened by a knock at the door. I sat up with a start and looked at the clock. To my horror, I saw it was almost eight A.M. Hyndsie was blissfully asleep, snoring up a storm. The door was starting to open so I looked around desperately for somewhere to hide, but there wasn't a thing to crawl under or behind. Our bed was behind the door, and when it finally opened we were partially shielded by it. It was the landlady; a chubby, little Scottish woman called Mrs. McLaren. The girls' bed was directly in front of the landlady as she opened the door.

"Hello, girls!" she trilled, "Ach, you're sleepin' together. Was it cold in here last night?"

I tried to make myself as inconspicuous as possible in the corner, but Hyndsie was still snoring away. I clapped my hand over his mouth and nose to muffle the sound, but it was no use. He was an abysmal sleeper. Mrs. McLaren turned, and her mouth fell open when she saw us there.

"What are you doin' here?" she demanded. "You have no right to be in this room!"

She ran over to the bed and grabbed the sheets and blankets, trying to pull them off us. I clutched them desperately at the other end, and we wrestled for possession of them for a few seconds. The girls lay still in their bed, petrified with embarrassment.

"I'm going to call the police," she yelled, running out of the room. Hyndsie was still snoring up a storm.

"Get your arse out of bed, for Jasus' sake!" I yelled at him, poking him in the ribs.

He sat upright with bleary eyes and his hair flattened on one side.

"Wassamadda?" he said. Hyndsie had apparently become an Italian overnight.

"The landlady knows we're here and she's calling the cops on us! That's wassamadda!" I yelled.

The girls were very upset and begged us to leave. We grabbed our clothes and ran down the stairs to the street, trying to dress as we did so. We passed Mrs. McLaren in the lobby as she was talking to the police on the phone. We didn't know whether this was a police matter, but we didn't intend to stick around to find out. We bolted through the door and landed on the sidewalk, startling a number of pedestrians standing at a bus stop. They appeared to be civil servants mostly, dressed in bowler hats, black jackets, and striped pants with brief cases and rolled-up umbrellas. They stared at us in amazement as we tried to get our remaining garments on and get off before the police arrived. One of the watchers heard our accents and turned to a friend.

"Bloody Irish swine! What can you expect?"

Hyndsie stopped and walked toward him saying, "I'll show you what you can expect, ya toffee-nosed, English puff merchant!"

I grabbed his arm and pulled him away saying, "Come on, Hyndsie! There's no time for that!"

Hyndsie contented himself with a glare and a "fuck you!" at our now panic-stricken critic, who was trying to use his open umbrella as a shield, and we both dashed off down the street, shirttails and shoelaces fluttering. Once around the corner, we slowed down and tucked in our shirts, trying to appear as normal as possible.

We didn't see any police cars, but found out later from the girls that they did respond. Mrs. McLaren asked the girls to leave, which they had to do a few days later. The girls had no hard feelings toward us. Fortunately, they had problems with Mrs. McLaren before and were planning to leave soon, anyway.

CHAPTER 63

LEAVING ENGLAND

"We are happier in many ways when we are old than when we were young. The young sow wild oats. The old grow sage."
~ Winston Churchill

London was like a giant playground to Hyndsie and me. We found that our usual antics had a much greater effect on the Londoners than they did on the Belfast crowd where we just blended in with all the other nuts. The fact that feathers were much more easily ruffled in London only made us appear worse. When returning home from the pubs late at night on empty, double-deck buses, Hyndsie's would go into his usual act – riding the second level of the bus and sticking his legs in the air, bucking madly and yelling "Yes! Yes!" in a soprano voice to make it appear that a woman was having wild sex. The English were even more shocked than the Irish had been.

Big Ben

Hyndsie and I were out dancing one night when I met a country girl from the Irish Republic working as a skivvy in a large home in Cheetham Hill, a wealthy district of the city. She wanted to know what I was doing in England. Not wanting to bore her with the truth, I told her I was an I.R.A. man on "a mission", which she swallowed whole-heartedly. She agreed to let me take her home, and we arrived at the mansion in Cheetham Hill around 11:30 P.M. We were having a knee trembler in the driveway of the house against the wall of the garage area.

In the middle of the exploration process, she appeared to go into what I can only describe as a comatose state. She froze, and her eyes went blank. I patted her cheek a few times but could not evoke a response. Remembering the story Ernie Patterson had told me about the girl pretending to faint while he made love to her, supposedly to maintain her chaste reputation, I removed her undergarments and was about to take the plunge when I suddenly realized why she had frozen. A large car had pulled into the driveway, obviously the owners of the mansion, and her employers. The lady in the car yelled out the window at me, "Hey, there! What do you think you're doing?"

I looked over my shoulder, blinded by the headlights, and said, "What does it look like I'm doing?"

The lady turned to her husband and said, "William, throw him off our property!"

I said, "William, take my advice and go on inside." They both did. Slightly unnerved, I abandoned any thoughts of further conquest and attempted to bring the young lady back into this world, but she remained in her catatonic state so I left her standing there in the driveway and beat a hasty retreat. This was becoming a tradition with me. I suppose I would have stayed if I had felt there was anything I could do for her, but when you're busted, you're busted.

While getting on the bus, I reached into my pocket for change to give the conductor and found that I had retained the panties. When I got home, my friend Hyndsie was in bed, snoring away with his mouth open. Seizing the opportunity, I draped the panties over his gaping maw. He awoke with a start, sniffed furiously, realized what was blocking his air passage, and called me a dirty bastard. Laughing, we threw the underwear on top of the armoire. After a week or so, we remembered what we had done and attempted to retrieve the evidence, but our landlady had apparently beaten us to it and had disposed of it without comment.

Hyndsie and I spent about two years in England. We came back to Belfast almost empty-handed because our entire purpose in going there was to sow our oats. We never actually said, "Let's go over to England and sow our oats." That's just how it worked out. As the saying goes, we spent ninety percent of our money on wine, women and song and spent the rest foolishly. Work's only purpose was to support the weekend's festivities. I had learned more from our cohorts at the pubs, the experienced men on the construction sites, and the women that Hyndsie and I had the good fortune to know and spend time with than I ever could have learned living at home in Belfast. It was the education of a lifetime. I left Belfast a boy and returned a man. I had proven to myself that I could make a living and pay my own way. I had broken the duck, fell in love in the process, and had my heart broken. Life is never as simple, or as easy, as we want it to be.

CHAPTER 64

ELEANOR

April flowers may conceal slugs.
~ William Shakespeare

When writing the story of one's life, it is hard to avoid the urge of telling the stories of the loves who have come and gone; the agonies and ecstasies of romance. At the time, I was too busy exploring and adoring women to realize that I would remember them forever, and it breaks my heart a little to tell the stories now because they were so long ago and the experiences, or at least the way they made me feel, are impossible to recapture, so entwined as they were with youth and innocence. But to omit them would be to leave the tale largely untold. Every lover we have forms who we are, even if we think it means nothing at the time.

I had been home for about a week when I developed a mad crush on a girl who lived in my neighborhood named Eleanor. The only problem was everybody else in the neighborhood had a crush on her as well. She had two sisters, Elizabeth and Karen. The mother was also an attractive woman and obviously the source of her daughters' beauty. My friends and I thought the two older daughters were astonishing but I was absolutely enchanted by Eleanor. She was the most gorgeous creature I had ever seen in my life next to Rosaleen. A lot of the local guys, and some from surrounding neighborhoods, would hang around her house just hoping for a sight of her or Elizabeth. The youngest sister was too young at the time for anyone to be interested in but it was obvious that even she was going to be a smasher when she got older.

Some of the guys hanging around were college boys wearing caps from the Belfast Royal Academy, the same kind of cap my mother made me wear as a child, though I had never attended. The blue and red, peaked caps set them apart from the rest of us as being of a higher class than us. I felt I definitely didn't fit into this group and there was no way on God's earth Eleanor would pick me over such a selection, so I just admired her from a distance and stayed away from the groups hanging around the house.

Wee Hyndsie lived across the street from Eleanor so he got to know the family quite well. When Hyndsie and I were running around Belfast, he would invite Eleanor to come along and sometimes she would. She never really attached herself to either one of us; she was more of a buddy than a girlfriend. She was a good laugh. She could take a drink and wasn't prudish.

Around this time, Hyndsie and I decided we were going to go back to England. After living in England for two years, Belfast had become boring to us. Eleanor said, "I'd like to go, too. I have an uncle in London."

"Well, come along then," I said.

And just like that the three of us planned to go over together. The idea was to take the boat to Liverpool then the train down to London.

Our decision to go back to England was a spontaneous one. Hyndsie and I were commiserating over the lack of opportunity in Belfast and the general ennui of being in the same place all our lives when we both said, almost in perfect unison, "I can't take it here anymore. I want to go back to England." This was a big deal because life wasn't exactly easy the first time we went there. In fact, it was much more difficult but also more full and exciting.

We were all set to go when Hyndsie changed his mind at the last minute. When I asked him why, all he said was, "I would miss my ma's cooking too much." Hyndsie was very attached to his mother and the thought of leaving her and her food again was too much for him to face. I wasn't very surprised to hear his reason for staying. The first time we had gone to England, he reminisced about her and her cooking incessantly. The rotten food we used to get when we lived in the boarding houses didn't help much. Even later, when he was married, Hyndsie would go to his mother's for dinner at least once a week. That's another funny thing about the guys back in Ireland - they call their mothers "mammy" and their fathers "daddy." It's kind of comical to hear these big, tough guys saying, "Hey mammy! When are we gonna have our tea? Daddy and I are starving!"

Eleanor and I were both reeling from the shock of Hyndsie backing out when I said to her, "Well, I'm still going. I suppose you're going to change your mind as well."

She said, "Oh, no. I'm still going, too."

A few days later, she and I were boarding the Liverpool boat together. I couldn't believe my good luck. Here I was all alone with Eleanor, the girl I had admired from a distance for years. We sat in the lounge downstairs. A few guys were playing poker and I joined them. Eleanor was sitting beside me, betting on my hands. As usual, the bar was overrun with drunks and roughnecks of all kinds. As if on cue, a big, completely plastered guy of about forty came stumbling in, not unlike the big eejit who had pissed on the floor of the lounge during my first trip to England a few years earlier. He wanted in on the game but we already had a full slate of players and couldn't let any more in so we all told him he would have to wait his turn. He started leaning over the table and throwing money down, forcing Eleanor to lean forward uncomfortably, spitting all over everyone and generally making a nuisance of himself. I pushed him back a few times but he kept leaning forward over Eleanor and forcing her forward. I stood up, pushed him harder, and told him to behave himself. Fortunately, he took the hint and disappeared. I sat down again and didn't think much of it until I saw Eleanor. She was looking at me with an expression I had never seen on her face before. It was obvious that she was turned on by violence or impending violence and, all of a sudden, I had changed from whatever she had perceived me as before into something infinitely more desirable.

This may be another reason men in Ireland are notorious for brawling. Many Irish women encouraged it, often subconsciously, as Eleanor was doing with me on this particular night. All I knew was, from that point forward, she became very loving toward me, hanging onto my arm and looking into my eyes. I was on top of the world. I was still a bit hesitant, though, because I couldn't quite buy the idea that Eleanor was really interested in me.

We got into England and caught the train to London. From there, we went over to her uncle's house. He was only a young guy of about thirty. His wife was in hospital having a baby so he said, "You and Eleanor can use our bed and I'll go into the spare room." He never even questioned whether or not we should be in the same bed. He just assumed that we were lovers.

We got into bed together. Still refusing to believe that Eleanor was attracted to me sexually, I turned onto my side and started to go to sleep. She hit me a big dig in the ribs and said, "Turn around and face me, eejit." So I turned around and we began to kiss. When things started to heat up a bit, she asked, "Have you got protection?"

I had never used condoms to this point and wasn't sure what she meant. She tutted with exasperation and got out of bed, picked up her purse and pulled out a Frenchy, which is what we called condoms in those days. The next thing I knew she was all over me. I was in the stratosphere.

We stayed there for a few days with her uncle. Then the wife was coming home from the hospital so we had to move out. We found a small flat nearby and moved in. Finding work was the next order of business so I set off early in the morning. For the first day or two, Eleanor walked around with me to various stores and businesses and anywhere else I could find that might be offering a job. We were on our feet for eight hours a day and she eventually couldn't take it anymore.

For the first week, I walked all day long every day but couldn't find a job anywhere. One night, I came in and said, "My feet are killing me. I walked all bloody day today and still haven't got a job." Without hesitation, Eleanor guided me to a chair and took my shoes and socks off. My feet must have been pretty rank because we didn't shower every day back then. She then got a pail of water, washed my feet and dried them.

I thought, "My God. One of the prettiest girls in Belfast is washing my feet." It was like something out of the Bible. I was getting attached to her very quickly.

One of the most bizarre coincidences of my life occurred while I was living with Eleanor. I had known another girl in Belfast named Margie Smith. I was attracted to Margie because she was a few years older. She was a little on the plump side, good-looking, and always dressed exquisitely. Great legs, too. She had lived in the states for a while and brought back a lot of clothing from there so she really stood out. She treated me in a kind of motherly, benign fashion but I think she really fancied me. Whether she did or not, I don't know, but we went out a few times. I got bored because I was attracted to her style more than I was to her as a person. It was kind of shallow of me at the time but that's the way I was then. I eventually told her I wasn't interested in seeing her anymore. She was a bit miffed but later told me she was going to go to London and gave me an address where she would be living. I was sitting with Eleanor later in the flat one night going through my wallet and I found the note Margie had given me. London is a huge city of eight million people, spread out over about four hundred square miles, but the address Margie had given me was right across the street! I could see it from the window. I thought, "Jesus, Margie will think I deliberately moved in here to spy on her."

Since she was right across the street, I couldn't very well not visit her so I walked over and knocked on the door. A huge Jamaican, black as coal, opened the door and eyed me suspiciously.

Somewhat surprised, I said, "Uh, does Margie Smith live here?"

He looked at me blankly and said, "Mahgie Smit?"

"Uh, yeah," I replied.

"Mahgie Smit?" he asked again, still no smile.

"Yeah, Margie Smith."

I was getting ready to duck when he smiled ear to ear and said, "Oh! Mahgie Smit! Yah, mon!"

He called up the hall and a white woman came out. I assumed it was his girlfriend. Margie came to the door next. I think she was a little embarrassed because back then there wasn't any mixing between black and white, at least not openly. She made all kinds of apologies about living there and said, "I came over to see my girlfriend but I didn't know she was living with Jamaican people."

I didn't think much about it. Jamaican's weren't any different from anybody else as far as I was concerned, just a different color. They were actually a refreshing change. I took Margie across the street to meet Eleanor. I saw Margie as an urbane world traveler I felt would be able to hold herself well in any situation, but when she met Eleanor, she was inarticulate and obviously uncomfortable. Eleanor was as cool and composed as could be. I was worried that Margie was going to think I was lording my relationship with Eleanor over her so I offered to walk her back to her door. We talked for a little while and I went back to my flat. That turned out to be the last time I ever saw Margie because circumstances would lead me to leave the flat soon thereafter.

The next Saturday, Eleanor and I went into another part of London to have a look around. I told her I'd be right back and went into one of the city toilets downstairs. I was only gone about five minutes. When I came back up, she was gone. I searched all around the neighborhood and couldn't find her anywhere. I began to panic because my parents used to talk about the white slave traffic in England, and how girls were snatched off the street, drugged and taken to Saudi Arabia or someplace. I thought, "My God, the white slavers have got her!" I walked around the general area, waited at the place I had last seen here for about an hour, then went home not knowing what else to do. She wasn't there either so I sat looking out the window all evening. It got later and later and there was still no sign of her. I gradually arrived at a state of complete and total panic. I couldn't control myself any longer so I went down to the local police station and talked to the old sergeant at the desk. I told him my story about my girlfriend disappearing and he said, "Did you have a row (fight) or something?"

I said, "No, we didn't have a row at all."

I told him exactly what happened.

He said, "Well, she'll probably show up. Don't worry about it."

I went back to the flat and got into bed. At about two o'clock in the morning, I heard the key in the lock and Eleanor trying to walk in without detection. I turned on the light and said, "In the name of Christ, where were you? I've been fuckin' worried sick!"

"Ach, I met a yank and went out for the evening. I got fed up with not having any money or anything else so I decided to let this guy take me out for dinner and dancing for a bit of a break."

"Well, what about me?" I demanded.

"Don't worry about it! That guy meant nothing to me."

"Well," I said, "What you did means a hell of a lot to me."

I felt so betrayed, the next morning, I got up, packed my suitcase and left. She didn't try to stop me. She just kind of resigned herself to it. That was the end of that romance.

The trouble with some beautiful women is that they have too many options. She was probably already scheming about who her next adventure would be with as I was walking out the door.

Many years later, out of curiosity, I tried to contact Eleanor by calling her mother's house. Her mother told me she was married and living in Florida. Her husband was very ill and Eleanor was almost a full-time nurse. I couldn't help thinking it was divine retribution for the way she had treated me and probably other men. I never tried to contact her and didn't pine over her for a moment because I knew a woman who would do what she did to me would have been nothing but trouble. Most of the misery in life stems from reality refusing to match fantasy. And often, regrettably, fantasies are just too good to be true.

CHAPTER 65

BACK IN LONDON

"I've always worked very, very hard, and the harder I worked, the luckier I got.
~ Alan Bond

As I walked away from the room I had shared with Eleanor, with all my worldly belongings stuffed into my suitcase, I went through the full gamut of emotions – anger, disappointment and disbelief that she would abandon me in the middle of London without a word and take off with a stranger she had met on the street. To make matters worse, it was a bloody Yank she had spent the evening with!

I had nothing against Americans but they had a reputation for being somewhat fast and loose with women. After all, very few of them had plans to live where they were stationed, particularly not Ireland with its abysmal weather. Thus any girl seen with one was written off as someone of low moral qualities. Few had much sympathy for the young American soldiers in Belfast for a few days before going off to war, perhaps never to return. That simply did not enter into the equation. The Yanks were considered to be "oversexed, overfed, and over here."

I'm not sure whether I would have been less affected by Eleanor's actions had she taken off with an Englishman or even someone from back home. The main problem was that she had deserted me.

For weeks, I tried to rationalize the event for my own sake. After all, we had only been together for a week and had reached no understanding at all about our relationship. Circumstances had merely thrust us together. However, Eleanor had always represented to me an impossible ideal, someone I could only admire from afar without any hope of a relationship. Her relationships with previous boyfriends included wealthy college boys, prominent athletes and others much more talented and successful than me. I was definitely the low man on the totem pole in that company. Yet there I was sharing my life with a girl I thought was something special, becoming lovers, discovering London together in a grand adventure, only to fizzle out ignominiously in a few short days. The disappointment was immense. I consoled myself with the thought that it was better to learn these things early than late. God knows what would have happened had we remained together. I probably would have ended up strangling her.

The more immediate concern was finding someplace new to stay. It was three o'clock in the morning and I was wandering around a strange city with no bed to look forward to. The thought that Eleanor was probably sleeping comfortably in a bed I had paid for did not help to improve my mood. The thought crossed my mind of returning and pitching her out into the gutter where she belonged. Instead, I spent most of the night in an all-night café drinking cup after cup of coffee and contemplating my future. I wished more than ever that Hyndsie would have come with me. Life's ups were always higher and the lows were always easier when he was around. I missed him, and Belfast. I never knew how alone being alone could feel until I sat in that café at four in the morning with no friends, no room, no job and very little money left in my pocket.

The following morning, after daybreak, I checked the window ads in the small stores, which listed rooms for rent and other such notices. I went to an address in the St. John's Wood District of London advertising a room to let. The landlady proved to be an eccentric, eighty-ish Londoner who had a room to let upstairs, above her own flat, available for a single person. However, she shared her accommodations with numerous cats, numbering about fifty (yes, 50!), all of which had free reign to the entire premises. The place stank to high heaven but I was in need of a room so desperately and my funds were so limited, I decided to rent the room anyway.

Fighting my way through an army of cats on the stairs, I reviewed the second-floor bedroom with its small stove and decided it would suffice. However, the old lady, who initially seemed so pleasant and welcoming, seemed to have second thoughts when she heard my Irish dialect. Apparently, she had rented the room to a previous Irishman who was constantly drunk and whom she finally evicted after discovering that he had messed the bed one night after coming home in a drunken stupor.

"I can assure you, miss," I said. "I have never wet the bed in my life and don't intend to start now."

"I only wish that was all he did!" she replied. "But he did the other thing as well! Number two!"

I was aghast. I didn't think it was possible for someone to actually have a bowel movement while sleeping without being aware of it. Now *that's* drunk! The wee woman's attitude was also a perfect example of the mental machinations of racism. Because one Irishman had a disorder of the bowels, she assumed that all Irishmen did, as if everyone in Ireland crapped in their beds every night. I said, "I can assure you that I'm not in the habit of drinking myself into oblivion, my bowels are in perfect order, and you don't have to worry about repeating the events of that terrible day."

She laughed and seemed to appreciate my sympathy. She returned to her light-hearted self and agreed to rent me the room.

After placing my few bits of clothing in the closet, I went down to the local hardware store, picked up a bucket, a scrub brush and a bottle of Jaye's Fluid, a disinfectant more popularly known in Belfast as Jaysus's (Jesus's) Fluid. I scrubbed the room thoroughly and the adjoining stairwell, which managed to eradicate most of the cat smell in my portion of the premises.

The next order of business was finding a job. After tramping the streets of London for a week, I had still not come up with anything and was becoming desperate as my funds were depleting rapidly. Through sheer luck, my first inquiry brought about a job offer at Lyon's Corner House on Coventry Street in Central London, just off Piccadilly Circus. Lyon's Corner House was a chain of restaurants within greater London and the Coventry Street location was the central distribution facility, which prepared food for the satellite stores. The money wasn't very good but there was an added advantage in that Lyon's provided food for their workers.

Lyons Corner House, Coventry Street, London

The job I landed was supervising a number of female food preparation employees and making sure that the orders from the satellite stores were filled on a timely basis. This gave me free access to the entire premises. I was on a health kick at the time. Each morning, I would whip up a half dozen raw eggs in a pint of milk and down it, to the horror and consternation of some of the ladies working in the kitchen. Actually, I got a laugh out of their reaction. This was a long time before eggs became the cholesterol culprit, when drinking raw eggs was recommended by boxing trainers and was considered by most to be a very healthy thing to do. Large roasts and shoulders of ham were also roasted in the kitchen at Lyon's daily and the rich aroma would permeate the premises. I thought nothing of tearing off a lump of roast in passing and wolfing it down.

The store operators provided a restaurant for the staff and we could eat as much as we wanted. The staff was made up of people from around the world, including the West Indies, the Indian sub-continent, Europe, and Africa. Each of the groups from these countries tended to share a table with their own people. Since there was no designated "Irish" group, and because I had a great interest in anyone from abroad, I decided to sit at a different table each day. I sat down with the West Indians the first day and was greeted with some suspicion on their part as a potential wise-ass but was accepted after they got to know me. The same held true for the Hindus and the Muslims from India and Pakistan. I made a number of friends in short order.

One of my new friends was a medical student who worked to pay his tuition fees at a local medical college. Fifty years later, his name still sticks in my mind – Suresh Shandra Shukla. He was tall, slender and quite handsome with a somewhat retiring demeanor. He spoke English with a thick Indian dialect. He had the most difficulty with English words of several syllables such as "vegetable", which he pronounced as veg-ee-tay-bul. In exchange for teaching him how to pronounce difficult words more correctly, along with some choice Irish swear words, he taught me some words in Hindustani. With his help, along with others at Lyon's Corner House, I was able to pick up girls of many ethnicities and get my face slapped in half a dozen languages!

Since the end of World War II, there had been a mass emigration of Jamaicans and East Indians into Britain. The influx of these dark-skinned people alarmed many of the Brits and brought out the worst in them. Enoch Powell, a politician of the day, publicly announced that they would be the ruination of the British style of life and that they should be shipped back to wherever they came from. Having been raised in a society where everyone looked alike and spoke the same language, the immigrants were a source of curiosity and exploration to me. This curiosity has extended through my lifetime and still exists in me today. Every person is a new adventure, a way of traveling without ever leaving the table you share with them.

The meager income I was receiving at Lyon's was sufficient to tide me over but I was determined to find a better-paying job. The hardest part about this decision was that it meant giving up all the free food and saying goodbye to my international array of new pals.

Every day after lunch, I wandered over to Piccadilly Circus and watched the multi-ethnic nature of those passing by. There were tall, bearded Sikh's in turbans; sloe-eyed Indian ladies in colorful sari's; huge, black-skinned Jamaicans and Trinidadians with bloodshot eyes and infectious, sing-song dialects, and natives of various African countries in colorful garb. After being in Belfast so long where everyone was a uniform, milk-bottle white, it was like switching from a black-and-white movie to a Technicolor one.

Piccadilly Circus

One day, as I walked along Coventry Street, I passed someone who looked familiar to me. He seemed to recognize me, too. We stopped and looked at each other.

"Don't I know you from the Plaza Dance Hall?" he said. I remembered seeing him there a few times, which was not difficult because he was a full six-foot-five inches tall and quite striking looking. Belfast guys averaged around five-foot-six during those years so he always stood out in the crowd.

He introduced himself as Terry and told me he was on his way to the St. Pancras Railway Station in London because he heard jobs were available there. I decided to go over with him and try my luck, too. We both landed jobs unloading goods from the freight trains. I packed in my job at Lyon's Corner House that day and started work at St. Pancras the following morning. We were given dollies and instructions on how to load them and move the goods from the freight trains to the waiting trucks. The work was a lot harder than the job at Lyon's but the wages were much better. Unfortunately, we were sacked two days later when Terry dropped a dolly loaded with bottles of Scotch, causing about three hundred pounds in damages.

By that time, the difficulty in finding work in London, along with the expensive digs, prompted me to look further afield. I had friends and contacts in Manchester in Northern England and both Terry and I decided to bail out of London and head north.

In my previous sojourn in Manchester, I had run into a young woman named Elsa and had met her family. She was only about seventeen at the time, much too young for me at twenty-one. Though I knew this, my attraction to her raced ahead of my common sense and we went out on a few dates. Even though she was an extremely attractive girl (an Elizabeth Taylor look-alike!), I felt she was too young for me and the relationship ended quickly.

When we arrived back in Manchester, I decided to drop in on Elsa and see if her family would put us up. Her mother and father, Billy and Les, greeted us warmly and readily offered to make a room available to us, which we took. Her mother's name was Billy. I never did ask what it was short for. While I was there, Elsa moved into her younger brother's bedroom and gave up her bedroom for Terry and I.

After a day of rest, Terry and I started prowling the construction sites of Manchester looking for work. Most of the sites were manned by immigrants from Ireland; primarily the Irish Republic.

I had made a friend at a construction site named Alan Taylor. It had been my practice to become friendly with the largest and toughest workers at the construction sites for the sake of protection as brawling among the workers was common. Alan was a big man of Jamaican descent, although born in Britain, with a strong Lancashire brogue. His job was a cement finisher, which meant wielding a heavy trowel eight hours a day. His biceps were like cannonballs.

I was working with Alan at a previous job a few years earlier on a particularly wet and miserable morning. The laborers were gathered in a small construction shack having their mid-morning tea. I was the last to arrive with a steaming cup of tea in one hand and a sandwich in the other. I was attempting to negotiate my way through legs, knees, and feet. I stumbled over someone's boot and accidentally spilled a few drops of tea on one of the laborers.

"What d'ya think yer doin', ya stupid Irish bastard!" he yelled. "Why don't ya watch where yer goin'!"

Since my spilling the tea was entirely accidental and it was such a small amount, I was surprised at the intensity of his outburst. I knew right away that the tea wasn't really the problem as much as the fact that I was Irish. I threw the rest of the tea in his face and said, "Well, fuck you, too!"

The man was utterly shocked. Rage filled his eyes. I prepared for the worst. Big Alan, who was seated nearby, stood up.

"Rick," he said, "Sit down in my spot." He gently guided me toward his place in the shack. He then turned around to my nemesis. "And you, bastard," he said. "You shut your mouth."

The Englishman mumbled to himself but did not pursue the argument further. Since he was a pretty tough-looking character, I was relieved that Alan had interceded on my behalf. He became my best friend at the site after that.

Alan later told me about his days in the British Marines and the various forms of prejudice he had encountered over his lifetime. He was so well-spoken and intelligent, I asked him what he was doing working on a construction site. He cocked his eye, looked at me and said, "Are you taking the piss?"

I assured him I wasn't and that I felt he was better qualified than to be laboring in construction. I learned that Alan's family was involved in boxing on either the amateur or professional levels. At that time, many of the British boxers were black fighters, including Alan Buxton and Randy Turpin, who were heroes of mine.

When Terry and I were looking for work at construction sites, I was hoping to run into Alan again when I spotted a man who looked very much like him but wasn't him. I asked him if he was related to Alan and he turned out to be his brother. Once he knew I was a friend of Alan's he said, "I'll fix you both up with a job. Don't worry." He spoke with the foreman of the site and we started work immediately.

As usual, my co-workers at the site were mostly Irishmen - giants from the farm country who had immigrated to England because they couldn't find suitable employment in Ireland. They had the habit of addressing others by their places of birth. Once they learned I was from Belfast, I was called "Belfast" ever after. On Thursday or Friday, when they had run down their cash reserves, they would ask, "Have you got a few shillings for a pint, Belfast?" They would rather have a pint of Guinness at lunchtime than a sandwich.

It was a novelty and a pleasure to be working with these men, most of whom were destined to be lifetime construction workers. It wasn't that they couldn't have gone on to better things. It was just that, as in small towns anywhere, some were following in the footsteps of their fathers and grandfathers who had spent their lives at the same or similar occupations. Others absolutely loved the work and the socializing that went along with it and had no desire to do anything else. Still others were master craftsmen. They were so skilled and efficient one just couldn't imagine them doing anything else. Even though many were somewhat simple and uneducated, they were not stupid. They took pride in their work and were dignified in their behavior toward others.

While living in England, I found out that the Irish were considered to be somewhat stupid, prone to drunkenness and brawling, some of which was true. The "Paddy" and "Mike" stories abounded, usually about feckless Irishmen with colorful speech. The Irish have always been able to laugh at themselves. It was no different then. They were not offended by the "dumb Irishman" jokes and would usually laugh along with the teller. Over the years, they have turned this form of self-deprecating humor into a national pastime. I found them straightforward and ruggedly honest. The work was often back-breaking but even the lowliest laborer had his own skills, which contributed to the sense of unity and even family.

I was digging trenches one day for the first time, blattering away crazily with my pick-ax and shovel and succeeding in getting absolutely nowhere. An older laborer in his mid-fifties was watching me.

"Hey, Belfast!" he said, "You're gonna kill yourself working at that pace. Just take smaller amounts of dirt on your shovel. You'll find that at the end of the day, your work product will be the same. Let me show you how it's done." I tried to emulate him but my impatience and desire to avoid being shown up by an older man made me forget occasionally and start blasting away at it again. By quitting time, his trench was longer, wider, and more precise than mine by a long shot. It was a re-enactment of the tortoise and the hare in a different setting, and another lesson to me that every man has something valuable to impart, even a ditch-digger. Nobody cut corners. Even the most common laborer took pride in their work.

Many of these men went on to operate their own construction companies. Others who were bound by tradition, lack of education or lack of business sense never advanced much further.

I had another near brush with death one day while working about six floors up on a building in the beginning stages of construction; mostly steel beams with plywood floors. The day's work had been made more difficult by a vicious storm and a persistent hangover from the previous night's debauch. I finished my work about an hour before quitting time and found a cubbyhole, curled up, and promptly fell asleep. I woke several hours later in total darkness. I stood up and looked around. All the other workers were gone. I went to the temporary workers lift and pushed the button. Nothing. The electricity had been turned off. It suddenly dawned on me that the other workers couldn't see me where I was sleeping and had assumed I had gone home. There was no other way down. To make matters worse, the rain had turned into snow and it was blowing in sideways. The coat that kept me warm enough during the day was almost entirely useless for the frigid weather now upon me. I walked around the plywood floor for half an hour looking for a way to climb down to the street, but there were no possibilities whatsoever.

Several times during my search, I passed a long chain hanging from a crane and thought about climbing down it like a rope but many considerations were sapping my courage to do so. For one thing, it was about six feet away from the perimeter beam and I would have had to jump from the edge of a wet beam to reach it. Second, it was a very thick chain used for lifting heavy objects and I wasn't sure I could get my hands around it. Third, I would be jumping against the wind, which was now blowing horizontally at about 50 miles per hour and carrying bits of pelting hail with it. The fourth and most important reservation I had was the distance to the ground should I miss the chain entirely.

I walked around for another half-hour becoming more and more frost-bitten and desperate but no other option presented itself. Hypothermia was setting in. I decided the chain was my only hope. I walked to the edge of the beam, gathered my courage for another five minutes, and jumped. To my great joy, I caught the chain and clung to it thankfully. However, as I started to climb down hand over hand, I discovered that much of the chain was heavily greased and the more I climbed, the more slippery my hands became. Eventually, I lost my grip entirely and began to slide down the chain at a speed not much slower than if I had been falling freely through the air. I managed to slow my descent a little by wrapping my entire body around the chain, including my face. The chain ended about ten feet from the ground and the next thing I knew, I was lying on my back in a puddle on glorious, wonderful earth, the wind knocked completely out of me, but alive.

My first plan was to lie there until the snow covered me, but as my lungs began to allow air in once again, I staggered to my feet and hobbled across town. I was covered with black grease, including half of my face, being that I had used my jawbone to increase friction with the chain and slow my fall. The hair on one side of my head was also sticking straight up. Pedestrians gave me a wide berth as I passed, assuming I was a vagrant and perhaps mad. In my wretched state, I was almost completely oblivious to their presence. I plodded toward home, thinking only of a hot shower and bed.

The next day, I told my mates at work about my plight the night before. After the usual hearty laugh at my expense, they all apologized for leaving without checking for me. I told them it was my fault for not letting them know I was sleeping in an obscure corner of the floor. I looked at the chain that had saved my life and couldn't believe I had actually been brave or stupid enough to jump for it. Neither could my mates. All's well that ends well, though, and we all had a good laugh about it. I was the talk of the site that day. The men were saying they wouldn't jump for that chain from that height for any amount of money. The survival instinct is a powerful thing.

Though my memories of this ragtag bunch are mostly happy, not all of them were a pleasure to know. One individual in particular stands out in my recollection. He was a huge man who reminded me of the actor Victor McLaglen. Every day, he would pick some poor slob as a new target for abuse. He would then flick small stones over the course of eight hours at his hapless victim, a slow form of mental and physical torture. He was so large and brutish, no one dared challenge him. Terry, however, was not impressed since he was about the same size.

"If that bastard starts in with me," he snorted, "I'll dent his fuckin' head with this shovel!"

A young, English chap of about seventeen standing nearby overheard this comment. It turned out he was the man's son. So much for "the luck of the Irish." He ran off, eager to give his dad a new target. The following Saturday, the beast showed up at the construction site tanked up on Guinness and looking for trouble. He approached me first.

"Belfast, are you the one who wants to thump me with a shovel?" Intimidated by his immense size and sociopathic tendencies, I told him he must have me confused with someone else. Not completely satisfied, he went on in his way.

That evening, I was thinking about my reaction and kicking myself for chickening out in the face of the challenge. The shame was eating me alive. I could barely stand myself. The following morning, I was ready for anything. Death before dishonor, as they say. I approached the brute and snapped at him, "Okay, big mouth, I'm ready for you now. Put up your mitts and let's go!"

I adopted a John L. Sullivan stance and danced around, flicking left jabs at him. To my complete and utter surprise, the big man backed down.

"Ach, Belfast," he said. "I've got a terrible head on me this morning with the drink and I'm in no condition for fightin'!"

I wasn't about to argue with him. My pride had forced me to return the behemoth's challenge but I didn't relish the thought of actually fighting him. Seizing the opportunity, I dismissed him with a curt, "Well, okay, but behave yourself in the future or you'll be in for a good skelpin'!"

I walked away counting my lucky stars. My honor had been restored. I could look in the mirror again.

Winter came and conditions at the construction sites deteriorated. We were out in the open, often soaking wet with inadequate clothing and little or no protective gear. We were the lowest of the low. Terry and I agreed that the experience was valuable but we held fast to the belief that we were meant for better things. We were city boys used to working with our heads, not our hands.

The final decision to quit the construction trade came about when we ran afoul of the payroll clerk, an Englishman who was responsible for doling out our wages on Friday afternoon. Someone remarked that this clerk had been fiddling the books and keeping some of the payroll for himself, which required underpaying the workers. We decided to keep close tabs on our time, including overtime we had earned. After receiving our pay and carefully doing the math, Terry and I realized that we were both short in our pay packets. We waited until the line cleared at the payroll shack window and approached the clerk with our complaint.

"I'm about ten bob short in my wages," I said.

Terry said, "And I'm about fifteen bob short in mine!"

An ugly look came over the clerk's face. With curling lip, he remarked, "You bloody Irishmen don't know how to count!"

"Well, let's see if you can count how many times I gub ya!" said Terry.

He reached through the small window, grabbed his lapel, and planted three rights on his chin before he was able to free himself.

Terry looked at me and said, "I think that was three. Wasn't it, John?"

"I don't know, Terry," I replied. "We can't count. Remember?"

It was obvious at that point that our careers at this particular site were at an end.

"Give us our cards!" snapped Terry. "We don't need to be robbed by the likes of you!"

He threw them to us from a distance because he didn't want to get within punching range again. We pretended to leave but waited by the back door. When he came out, Terry stuck another one on him. He landed on his back in a puddle of mud. We walked away laughing. Terry yelled back, "You can use the money you stole from us for iodine tonight!"

CHAPTER 66

EDDIE THOMAS

"A good character is the best tombstone. Those who loved you and were helped by you will remember you when forget-me-nots have withered. Carve your name on hearts, not on marble."
~ Charles H. Spurgeon

After a few days off to regain our composure, we went over to Beck and Pollitzer, a machinery moving firm in Trafford Park where I had worked during my previous trip to Manchester. We got lucky again and landed jobs starting immediately. Again, we got to travel all over Britain and see a lot of the countryside and all of our expenses were paid by the firm. A few weeks after we started, we were told that a job was opening up in South Wales in a small community called Cwm (pronounced Coom) near Ponty Pridd (pronounced Ponty Preeth). Six of us, including Terry and I, were assigned to this project. I had never been to Wales so I was very excited about it. We drove down the following Saturday and checked into our rooms, which had been prearranged.

That Saturday night, we got cleaned up and decided to go on a pub crawl around Cwm and Ponty Pridd. Our goal for the evening was to have a different drink in each bar we went to, and we went into eight or nine bars. This turned out to be one of the worst mistakes of my life. Before long, I was completely plastered and barely able to stand up. Noticing a dance hall nearby, we went inside hoping the dancing would sober us up a little. I had no sooner sat down than I started seeing three of everything and the entire hall started to swirl and pitch. From past experience, I knew I was going to be violently ill. I was always a polite drunk and did my best not to vomit publicly. I staggered off into the bathroom and proceeded to unload everything I had consumed over the last forty-eight hours. To this day, I've never been able to vomit without recalling some sage words from my Uncle Alfie on the subject. He said, "If you're boking and you feel something small and round in your mouth, don't swallow. It's your arsehole!" This was that type of boke session. It felt like my belly button was touching my spinal column. I was curled over a urinal, retching violently, when another chap entered the toilet. He slapped me hard on the back.

"Are ya sick, Paddy? What's the matter with ya?" he asked.

"No," I yelled, "the mirror was broken so I'm tryin' to see my reflection in the toilet water! Of course I'm sick, ya eejit!"

I returned to my boking. He laughed and slapped me on the back again.

"Well, at least ya haven't lost your sense of humor!" he replied, slapping me on the back a third time.

"Piss off and let me die in peace!" I pleaded.

He laughed harder and said, "Get it all up, lad! You'll feel better!"

The slapping on the back continued. I was getting very annoyed but was too wretchedly ill to think about standing up, let alone fighting. I just wanted him to leave me alone so I could continue my love affair with the toilet bowl. It was very disconcerting to vomit and wonder when I was going to get another slap at the same time. That was one too many things to concentrate on.

"Stop hittin' me, dammit! It's not making me feel any better!" I said.

"Now, now!" he said, "Sure I'm only tryin' to help ya!"

He punctuated this remark by smacking me on the back yet again. That did it.

"Well, help yourself to this, ya prick!"

I sprang to my feet and took a wild swing at him. He avoided the punch easily, slapping my hand away with little or no effort. Enraged, I swung again. Again, he swatted my fist away like it was a mosquito. Not having made the expected contact, I spun around and landed in a heap on the floor. Embarrassed and enraged, I jumped up again and took another swing at him and another and another but not one landed. It was like fighting a ghost. After falling down a few more times, the thought crossed my mind that I was doing all the work and beating myself up *for* him. After all, the elusive target had not thrown a single punch in return. I thought it very discourteous that he wouldn't stand still so I could hit him.

Through the mists of the alcohol I had consumed, the man's face came into focus for the first time. To my surprise, I recognized him from somewhere but I couldn't put my finger on it. Then it dawned on me.

"Hold on a minute," I said. "Don't tell me you're Eddie Thomas, the British Welterweight boxing champion!"

He smiled and answered, "Yes, I *am* Eddie Thomas, the British and *European* Welterweight champion!"

I swallowed hard and thanked God that he was merciful. (Eddie, not God.)

"Well, at least I can't be accused of picking on a piker!" I said.

"Think nothin' of it," he answered. "I've been there myself!"

He put his arm around me for support and we walked out to the bar. He bought me a bracing pint and we were friends for the remainder of the evening.

The following night, we went to the same dance hall and I saw Eddie there again. He was dancing around the floor with a pretty young thing. He saw me and said, "There's that crazy Irishman who tried to beat me up in the toilet last night!" We both had a good laugh and he sent another pint over to our table.

I have never forgotten Eddie Thomas since that incident. He could have given me a good thumping and no one would have been the wiser but he was a true gentleman. True power and confidence is having skill and not using it. Those who are truly dangerous don't seem to look for trouble as often as those who merely want to think of themselves as dangerous do. I suppose it has always been that way. The smallest dogs bark the loudest, as they say.

I learned that Eddie Thomas died of cancer recently at the age of 72, but not before becoming the mayor of Merthyr in Wales. He had a happy life and was loved by millions. He was a hero to the Welsh people, and to me.

Eddie Thomas

CHAPTER 67

LEAVING BELFAST FOR GOOD

"I showed my own appreciation of my native land in the usual Irish way, by getting out of it as soon as I possibly could."
~ George Bernard Shaw

After living in England for a total of about four years, I took a trip home to Belfast at Christmas in 1956. It didn't feel the same. I no longer seemed to fit in. Many of my friends had begun to disperse around the country and the world but most were still there, doing more or less the same thing. They were such a part of the place, I couldn't imagine them living anywhere else. But a deep restlessness had taken root in me that I couldn't shake or ignore.

My parents were happy to have me back. I had certainly shattered my dad's prediction that I wouldn't last longer than a week in England. They had more respect for me but were still difficult in their own ways. When I first arrived in England, I thought I would have so many stories to tell them if and when I came home again, but when I did come home, I had no desire to tell them. It was as if I had finally lost the need to impress them. I went my way and I left them to theirs. I suppose I had outgrown them, too, or at least who I was before I left. The old issues and grievances just didn't seem very important anymore.

I also felt that I had outgrown Belfast. I still loved it like a baby loves its mother's heartbeat, and I felt at home there, but I also felt that I could never make anything of my life if I stayed. It's a story as old as time.

Life in England had been hard but liberating. As the old saying goes, "Better beans and freedom than cake and slavery." I had learned a lot during my years abroad. Unfortunately, I also learned how to smoke, drink and swear excessively, which were standard behavior in the areas I was living in and with the company I kept, mostly laborers like myself, guys who were rough around the edges but very kind-hearted once you got to know them.

I was wandering around downtown Belfast trying to decide where I would go next when I passed a travel agency and as if by fate, spotted an advertisement in the window of snow-capped mountains standing majestically above a blue-green lake. The caption below stated that Canada was looking for new settlers and travel fares were slashed as a result. I went in only to inquire but walked out with the first payment made on a boat trip to Montreal the following May, five months away.

I told my mother and father of my plans. My father didn't tell me I would be back in a week this time, but he made no comment and offered no advice. My mother refused to accept the notion that I would be going so far away

330

to live, warning me that I was being too hasty and would certainly change my mind. They were used to not having me around by this time since I had been living in England for so long but they assumed and probably hoped that I was going to stay in Belfast for good. I'm sure they missed me but I'm sure they also missed the distraction I provided from the deficits in their marriage.

My parents came to see me off at the boat on the Belfast docks. I can still see my mother's face as I boarded the boat for the overnight trip to Liverpool, where I would board another boat to Montreal. She was totally bewildered and lost for words. My father, normally very stoic and unemotional, actually shed a tear. He knew I could make it on my own now, and I was going further away than I ever had before. I couldn't believe my eyes to see the old man displaying such blatant sentimentality. I think he felt that this might be the last time he would ever see me, or maybe he was regretting that he hadn't been closer to me in my younger years. The truth is I have no idea what was going through his mind. The man was a mystery to me.

Before I said goodbye, I waited a moment to see if he would say something but he didn't. He only said, "Take care of yourself, son."

I answered, "I will, da. You, too."

I hugged them both and told them I would come back to see them as soon as I could. I didn't know it at the time but it would be eleven years before I would be able to afford to return.

CHAPTER 68

CANADA

"Immigration is the sincerest form of flattery."
~ Jack Paar

The boat that took me to Montreal was called the "Empress of England". I celebrated my 24th birthday on the boat. The fare was fifty pounds, about two hundred U.S. dollars. A real bargain.

I wandered around the deck and found a small swimming pool surrounded by sunbathers and a few leggy beauties. The pool was empty so I decided to make a big entrance. I stripped to my shorts and made a running jump for the pool but as I was flying through the air, the boat tilted violently and I saw the water shift from one side to the other. I dove into about two feet of water, banging my forehead, elbows and knees against the bottom. The boat righted itself and the water filled up the vast wasteland I dove into, but the damage was done. I stayed underwater, casually swimming around and hoping nobody had noticed. I couldn't hold my breath any longer and had to surface. The sunbathers were all still looking at me with expressions of absolute horror, probably wondering if I was in a state of shock. Or perhaps they thought I was an employee of the cruise line; part of a death-defying circus act.

I got out of the pool and walked away as if nothing had happened, but when I was around the corner and out of sight, I crumpled to the ground, trying to hold my knees, elbows and forehead simultaneously. I looked at myself in a nearby window. It looked like someone had inserted a small tomato under the skin of my forehead. No wonder they were all staring at me.

I went to the bar to get some liquid pain-killer. I horrified everyone there with my bump, too, but it gradually receded. The resiliency of youth had once again restored my face to its original dimensions. The bartender laughed uproariously when I told him what I had done. I was angry at him for a moment but then laughed myself. After all, diving into an empty pool is pure comedy. And once again, I had managed to mangle my face on the first day of a vacation. That person on the Isle of Man was right – I did need to wear a helmet!

Five days and three thousand miles later, I was in Montreal and, a day after that, Toronto. Harry Hutchison was already living in Montreal and said he would meet me at the station but he never showed up. I had the address of another Belfast friend, Kathleen Wishart, and found my way to her door only to find that she had moved away. Her landlord, a Welsh man, offered to drive me to her new apartment on Quebec Avenue in West Toronto. Kathy was a tall, high-spirited girl, then twenty-two years old and living with a Scottish girl named

Margaret. They made me welcome and told me their roommate, Ernie, another Belfast guy, was out of town and that I could use his room.

Those first few days remain etched in my memory forever. The city was alive with youthful energy but it didn't have the element of danger that Belfast or Manchester did. The only similarity was the miserable weather. Canada was a new, growing country like America was fifty or so years before, filled with immigrants from all over the world. The only downside was that we were all considered to be "D.P.'s" (Displaced Persons) to the locals, who didn't appreciate the hordes of foreigners flooding into their city.

All these immigrants would gather to talk and play soccer at High Park. I would go down in the evening after work and watch the young men kicking the ball around, longing to play. Someone would usually kick the ball to me in way of invitation to join in. To establish my credentials, I would "trap" the ball under my knee, juggle it for a few seconds and kick it back, thus upping my worth as a teammate and starting a debate over which side I would play on. Some of the guys could speak little or no English but our love of soccer was a common language we all shared and that was all that was needed.

Me (holding five aces) with new friends
Joe McGlade and Bobby; Canada, 1957

Saying nothing, I mooched my way in as usual. They eyed me suspiciously at first, which is typical for Belfast people. But they realized I was one of them when they heard my accent and I was welcomed. People from other parts of the world would be welcomed eventually as well but not as readily and not until they had demonstrated a sense of humor and a fun-loving personality.

One of them was about my size but strongly muscled, obviously a weightlifter. He turned out to be the unofficial leader of the group and a wisecracker to boot. His name was Bill Cunningham. Bodybuilding was still somewhat unheard of at the time and I couldn't believe the size of his arms. It seemed like they were going to burst through his skin. When he saw me staring at them, he flexed a bicep and said, "Feel that!" I did and was very impressed.

"Where ya workin'?" he asked.

"In a dairy," I answered.

"A dairy? How much does it pay?"

"About fifty a week."

"Fifty what? Milk Bottles?"

We both had a good laugh, launching a friendship which has lasted over fifty years. We worked together one summer demonstrating exercise equipment in the window of a department store, but spent more time trying to talk with pretty girls through the glass. They were fun times. We can go months or even years without talking but when we do, we fall into the old rhythm and the old jokes, and it's as if not even a day has passed.

With Bill Cunningham (center)
and Bobbie Little (right.) Toronto, 1957

I felt I had sowed most of my oats in England and was not interested in repeating the life of excess I had led there in my new home in Canada, but a kind of auto-pilot kicked in when I met other young, unattached people like myself. Wanting to fit in and make friends, I found myself pub crawling again and getting into all manner of mischief. Inside me, though, something had changed. The empty flings didn't hold the same novelty they once did. In fact, a disquieting emptiness would often consume me afterward. I didn't understand what was happening at the time but I do now. I needed love; something real. There had been only one person with whom I had known this feeling consistently; only one person who had never let me down or done anything unseemly. She also happened to be the prettiest and sweetest one of the bunch. Her name was Rosaleen.

CHAPTER 69

ROSALEEN

"No, this trick won't work. How on earth are you ever going to explain in terms of chemistry and physics so important a biological phenomenon as first love?"
~ Albert Einstein

I wanted to "save the best for last" as they say so I hope you won't mind, dear reader, if I backtrack a little and tell you about the love of my life, my wife, Rosaleen.

I first saw Rosaleen in 1951. I was working away at my desk at Richardson Sons and Owden, the Irish linen company, when Billy McAllister came running over.

"You have to see the new girl in E Department!" he said.

"What about her?" I asked.

"She's an absolute wee smasher!" Billy said. "Just your type!"

This I had to see. Billy and I scurried down to E Department and he pointed out the new girl to me. She certainly looked pretty from the back, with a trim figure, dark hair, and great legs. She must have sensed we were looking at her and turned around, then turned back quickly. From the quick glimpse I got of her, the front side looked even better! She was indeed a wee smasher just as Billy had said. I looked around again and, seeing us gawking shamelessly, she blushed and again turned away.

She was exactly my ideal of what I liked in a girl. Pretty features, blue eyes, little nose, creamy complexion, and dark, soft hair. I was definitely a "face man" at this time in my sexual development (mainly because I had very little experience with any other areas of a woman at this point) and I do not exaggerate to say that her face deserved to be on a movie screen. She was the prettiest girl I had ever seen. The torch I had carried for Lita Roza since she came to town sputtered and went out in the first minute after I saw Rosaleen.

Worried that I might begin to frighten her by staring too long, I went back upstairs and resolved to try and meet her at the end of the workday. At quitting time, I darted downstairs and positioned myself as naturally as possible outside the front door. My heart was thumping with anticipation, worried she was going to tell me to buzz off. She appeared in the doorway. I went over and joined her. I could see that she was extremely shy but she raised no objections to my walking with her.

Due to my nervousness, I did most of the talking as we walked toward the bus stop by City Hall. She told me her name was Rosaleen and that she lived in east Belfast. She was 17 years old to my 18. She looked so Irish in her coloring I assumed she was Roman Catholic. As mentioned earlier, Belfast people swear they can tell a person's religion just by their physical characteristics. They say the Catholics have close-set eyes and that "the Pope is looking out" of them, though Rosaleen's eyes didn't look very close together to me or any more Papish than anyone else's. Before going further, I resolved to solve the mystery.

"Excuse me," I said. "Are you a Taig?"

Since Taig is a pejorative term used by Protestants for Catholics, I now realize I was very rude to address her in that fashion.

To my surprise, she answered, "What's a Taig?"

Now I knew she had to be a Catholic. Every Prod new what a Taig was, or so I thought.

"You don't know what a Taig is?" I asked in disbelief. She shook her head no, unapologetically.

Stupefied, I said, "A Taig is a Catholic! A Fenian! You must know what a Fenian is!"

"I'm not a Fen – a Catholic," she answered. "I'm a Protestant."

I was relieved. Though I knew many pretty Catholic girls, I didn't want to establish a long-term relationship with someone from "the other side" because of the difficulties such relationships could bring about.

Rosaleen's innocence in not even knowing a common slang term was very refreshing and appealing. In fact, this sweetness, along with her beauty, contributed to the feeling I was beginning to have that she was above it all but not in a conceited way. She floated in the ether while most of us wallowed in the muck.

I was hoping to stand and talk with her for a while before her bus arrived but as luck would have it, it came immediately. I gathered up my courage and asked her to go out with me the following week. To my great joy and surprise, she whispered, "Okay."

She turned and got on the bus. I yelled, "What night?"

She turned in the doorway of the bus, smiled and said, "Tuesday."

We parted there at the City Hall, her to the bus for east Belfast and me for the one to the north end of the city. If I hadn't been riding on a bus, I would have skipped all the way home. I thought the conversation had gone quite well and hoped I had made a good impression (except for asking if she was a Taig.)

The three options for dating at that time were the movies, a dance, or a walk if money was short. On Tuesday night, I met her at the City Hall as agreed and we went to a movie at the Park Picture House called *That Midnight Kiss* starring a new Italian-American singer named Mario Lanza. I always loved good male singers and had seen the movie trailer the week before. I was astounded by the quality and power of Lanza's voice. But every now and then, I stopped watching the movie and secretly looked at Rosaleen's perfect profile in the projector's light. She was by far the most gloriously beautiful girl I had ever seen. I couldn't get over my good luck that a creature so exquisite was interested in me.

When the movie was over, we took a long walk. She was a little quiet so I talked too much to try to make her feel at ease. But even when we weren't talking, there was no awkwardness between us as there usually was with other girls. I could already tell that she was a nice girl who wouldn't think poorly of me without good reason. That's what we all fear on first dates, after all.

I walked her back to her home and kissed her goodnight. Being a good girl, she pulled away. I couldn't contain myself any longer and pulled her closer. After some coaxing on my part, she kissed me a few more times but without losing control like I wanted her to. After that, we reserved every Tuesday and Saturday night for each other.

Like myself, Rosaleen was not rich growing up. She had lost her father and was working to support her family, including her mother and a younger brother and sister. However, despite her humble conditions, she always looked impeccable. She was always perfectly dressed and color coordinated. With her complexion and coloring, she didn't need much make-up but any that she did was used sparingly and only served to enhance her beauty. Unlike other girls, she never pressured me to go anywhere that required money. She always seemed content to go along with whatever I wanted to do, even if just a walk through the park.

Even after dating quite some time, she still exhibited a lot of shyness and innocence, which only endeared me further to her. My first few months with Rosaleen were a happy, uncomplicated time. We never discussed where our relationship might go. We were both too young to think about permanency. We became an item at the office and everyone quickly knew we were sweet on each other.

Rosaleen lived too far from me to walk to see her so I had to take the bus. We went out one night for dinner and a movie, then took a long walk and had a bit of a smooch in her doorway when I took her home. I checked my watch and saw that it was almost time for the last bus. I kissed her goodbye and ran toward the bus stop. As I approached, however, I saw the bus up the road, a dot in the distance. I had resigned myself to the long walk home when I saw a truck idling at a lighted intersection. Since a rain had begun to fall and I had no umbrella, I seized the opportunity to get home more quickly and jumped on a ladder at the rear corner of the truck. The driver took no notice and the truck lumbered along down the road.

I saw my street approaching and hoped that a streetlight would change to red so the driver would have to stop. He must have been timing the lights because he never stopped or slowed down enough for me to jump off. Before I knew it, we were leaving the city and heading into open country which stretched for miles and miles and had no streetlights to stop at. I knew that if I didn't get off somehow before the truck picked up more speed, the driver would discover me at his destination frozen to the ladder; an unfortunate human ice lolly.

I'd had a lot of practice jumping on and off buses while getting around town but they were moving much more slowly. Getting *on* the bus was easy enough, which involved running alongside it and grabbing a rail much the same way someone would be pulled onto a horse by another rider, but getting off was a bit more tricky. The technique most fare-dodgers used was launching oneself off the rear platform with a back-pedaling gate and trotting slowly to a stop. The perpetually wet streets made this practice quite death-defying, particularly if one was wearing leather-soled shoes. In such cases, the gradual stop usually included a long, Surfer-style slide.

With the vast countryside looming in the distance ahead and the truck steadily gaining speed, I pounded on the back of the truck hoping the driver would hear me and stop, but the road was so bad, it just blended in with all the other rattles and thumps. I decided I had no other choice but to attempt a dismount. I held the rail of the ladder nearest the corner of the truck with both hands and put my feet on the ground one at a time. The truck dragged me along, burning up the soles of my shoes.

For a moment, the trick horseback riders I had seen in old western movies came to mind. Unfortunately, I didn't have the option of leaping back onto a saddle. The road was too bumpy to consider a sliding stop so I began to prance, covering about ten feet with each stride. I hoped that I would be able to trot off to the side of the road when I released my grip on the ladder. I pictured myself doing this successfully several times. (This was a long time before the days of creative visualization, mind you.)

I managed to convince myself that I could pull it off but this certainty did not extend to my hands, which refused to release their grip on the ladder. I finally convinced the right hand to let go but the left was more stubborn and required further convincing. The truck was continuing to accelerate and my strides were now spanning about fifteen feet. With a quick but solemn prayer, I let go of the ladder completely and hit the ground like a snot, quickly discovering that God does not interfere with the laws of physics. I must have bounced along the road for another fifty yards before I came to a stop in a crumpled heap. I lay in the middle of the road like an Irish sausage for about ten minutes assessing the damages. As if God were punctuating his wrath, a hard rain began to fall on me. The only thing missing was getting struck by lightning.

I was thankful that my fingers and toes were still moving and I could turn my head but a searing pain began to mount in the area of my right elbow. It was fractured. This pain quickly took all my attention away from the myriad bumps, scrapes and bruises covering the remainder of my person.

Holding my bad arm with the good one, I hobbled back to the city and to the door of the first house I could find. I knocked with my foot and a kindly-looking, elderly couple came to the door. Seeing the state I was in, she rushed out, put her arm around my waist and said, "Ach, what's happened to ya, son?" I collapsed with relief and woke some time later on the floor of their living room with a woolen blanket over me and a pillow under my head. They propped me up and gave me a bracing cup of tea. I managed to tell them what had happened as well as my name and address. They called the hospital and a car was sent over to pick me up. I thanked them profusely, particularly the old woman whose compassionate, pale blue eyes I still remember to this day.

Fortunately, I had Sunday to recover a bit and get used to the cast on my arm. My father asked me, "What've ya done to yarself now, ya silly bugger?" He only rolled his eyes and shook his head with disdain when I told him what had happened. I spent most of the day in bed. My mother and sister doted on me, bringing me soup and tea. On Monday, I went into work and sickened everybody with my bruised and battered appearance. Because of my boxing, occasional street brawls, landing face-first on planks, diving into empty swimming pools, and the various other accidents I was prone to, nobody was terribly surprised.

Ernie Patterson had me laughing right away as usual. As I walked in, he looked at Rosaleen who was sitting at her station and said, "Rosaleen! Did Sidney chance his arm Friday night? I didn't think a wee girl like you could pack a wallop like that!"

The cast on my arm garnered much attention and sympathy from the women around the office and the neighborhood in general, so much so that a few of my mates started thinking about ways they might break their own arms. Like the dear old woman who rescued me, I was reminded that women are definitely the nurturers of the species. Thank God for them to balance out us smelly brutes. The only woman I wanted comfort from was Rosaleen and she didn't let me down. Perhaps she felt a little responsible since I missed the last bus because I was with her. Either way, she showered me with affection and I did nothing to discourage her.

Rosaleen and I (left) with friends.

Rosaleen and I dated casually for a year or so, both of us too young to consider marriage, when Rosaleen suddenly decided to move to England with her cousin. I was quite astounded at the time that this shy, quiet girl had the courage to leave home while still a teenager. It was during this time that I met Lita Roza. If Rosaleen were still in town, I probably wouldn't have noticed her. (And I'm not just saying that to stay out of trouble.)

When she came back I bumped into her at a coffee shop and we began seeing each other again until about one year later when I also decided to try my luck in England. This was the first trip with Hyndsie.

During my occasional trips home, I would sometimes bump into Rosaleen around town and we would go out together. After all this time, though, she and I had never done anything more than kiss. This was partly because of her shyness but mostly because I didn't want to offend her by trying anything too daring. Rosaleen was like a porcelain doll to me. I was usually quite bold with women, especially after going to England, but I was always afraid to touch her. She was dignified and I felt a little uncouth next to her, even though there was nothing particularly unusual about my experience compared to other boys. I worried that trying too much with her would put her off me. I was happy and proud just to be with her and thrilled just to be able to kiss her. It wasn't just me who saw Rosaleen this way. All my friends were envious of my relationship with her, too.

While living in Toronto, Canada, I was having a pint with Harry Hutchinson. (I had forgiven the eejit by this time for not showing up at the dock when I first arrived.) Harry was in the Canadian army and dating Rosaleen's cousin. I had been thinking about Rosaleen a lot but she had moved back to Belfast. I wasn't quite sure if she still had any serious feelings for me. I thought she might even be well on her way to forgetting about me entirely, figuring I was gone for good this time. So I was very pleased when Harry said, "Rosaleen was asking about you the last time I saw her. You should get in touch with her."

I played it cool and said, "Aye, maybe I will" but inside, I was doing a jig. She had been on my mind constantly and I now knew that I had been on hers. It was at that point that I started making serious plans about her. I couldn't think of anyone who would make a better wife and companion than she would. In fact, none of the other girls I had dated were even a consideration. Rosaleen had "ruined me for all other women" as the saying goes. I sat down and poured my heart out to her in a letter.

I checked my mailbox every day for a return letter from her. The mail was slow-going in those days and I started thinking she wasn't answering because she couldn't bring herself to tell me no. Then one day when I had just about given up, I opened the mailbox and there it was. I couldn't have been happier if there was a gold brick sitting there. After that, we began to correspond regularly. I asked her to come to Canada. Her letter in response to this one seemed to take the longest to arrive. When it finally did, I tore it open and saw a word that put me in a state of blinding, ecstatic bliss. It was the same word she had shyly whispered to me the first time I asked her out.

"Okay."

One year after that, we married.

The Big Day

Hamming it up for the camera at the wedding.
That's what a happy man looks like. Jackpot!

Rose and I with Paul, 1963

We didn't have much those first few years in Toronto, but when we were slow dancing in the kitchen late at night to *Chances Are* by Johnny Mathis, we couldn't think of a thing we really needed besides each other. We were struggling at menial jobs when she became pregnant. Our first son, Paul, was born in 1960.

Over fifty years have passed since then. Rosaleen and I are still together. The years have proven I could not have made a better choice. She is still the same girl I met back in 1951, still as beautiful and loving as ever. As a human being, she is infinitely better than I am, and more noble. Like my father, I can be a bit abrasive. Like my Uncle Alfie, I can be a bit crude. But Rosaleen is everything fine, good and true. Her patience and concern for others is endless and undying. Her love and compassion is not forced or contrived to please. It is intrinsic to her nature. Effortless.

Like everyone who lives long enough, Rosaleen and I have had our ups and downs. She lost her father as a teenager after he fell in the Belfast shipyard on Halloween night. It has been sixty years but at some time on Halloween day every year, I still inevitably see tears in her eyes, remembering. We have also both survived cancer and we lost a son. Thankfully, we have a second son who brings us great joy. My only regret is that the good things can't last forever. The only thing about life that remains changeless is the inevitability of change.

Men may bring strength to a marriage but women bring humanity. That may be an old-fashioned outlook but for Rosaleen and I, it has proven to be true. As the old saying goes, "She's the best thing that ever happened to a bum like me." It was true in 1951 and it's still true today.

Rosaleen in the Irish countryside, circa 1960

Rosaleen with our second son, Mark, 1968

CHAPTER 70

THE LAST TIME I SAW MY FATHER

"One father is more than a hundred schoolmasters."
~ George Herbert, *Outlandish Proverbs*, 1640

Rosaleen and I couldn't seem to make ends meet in Canada so we moved to New York for a year and then to Los Angeles where our second son, Mark, was born. Because of the difficulty of those years, I was thirty-five by the time I could afford to go home. Almost eleven years had passed since my parents said good-bye to me at the docks. My father was sixty-one.

As a boy, I had always admired his strength. So when I arrived at the house that day and he opened the door, I was startled to see how time had whittled him away. And after all that time, he was still working the same hours for roughly the same income. I later talked to my mother about his salary and learned that I was making more in a month than he was making in a year. This made my heart ache with sympathy for the old man. He was too old to still be toiling that way.

My mother put a pot of tea on for us. My father and I sat at the table. His newspaper was in front of him, as always. My sister, Olga, was twenty-three and still living at home, which wasn't unusual except that she rarely left the house. I worried that she might never leave and create a life for herself. My parents had given her as little love and guidance as they had me, but she was unable to escape as I had.

My mother was talkative and interested in my life in America but my father was still distant and morose. I tried to engage him in conversation but now more out of politeness than need. His answers were still monosyllabic, as they were when I was a child, and though I had made peace with who he was and had a firmer grasp of who I was, his disinterest still bothered me a little. After all those years, I could still feel the boy inside, still wanting him to say, "I'm proud of you, son." I spent two weeks with him on this trip but those words still never came.

Five or six years later, Rosaleen and I came to visit again. By this time, I had finally given up all hope of my father ever showing any interest in me. However, on this second trip home, to my amazement, he had transformed into a real gabshite. (Chatterbox) He asked me endless questions about what I was doing with my life. With my childhood and the last trip home still ensconced in my memory, I found myself thinking, "Where was all this interest when I needed it?"

Strangely, our roles had been reversed. Now he was trying to get my attention instead of the other way around, and I was the quiet one. As a kid, I would have loved to talk to him like this but literally never did. Now *he* wanted to talk and *I* was bored! The irony was profound. I answered his questions and listened to his stories but not with anywhere near the enthusiasm I would have had as a child. He waited too long and missed the boat. Just another one of life's little tragedies; the kind that don't make the newspapers.

I grew up thinking there was a high, thick wall between childhood and adulthood and that someday I would cross over it and never look back. But there is no wall. Childhood and adulthood intermingle throughout life, and the wounds inflicted on us as children shape us as adults. Though my father and I laughed and carried on as if there had never been any space between us, I felt no real satisfaction. The desire to connect with him had all but died long ago. Only a very small part of me still needed his approval; the little boy within that never really dies.

Despite it all, though, I loved my dad. I was never beaten, molested or starved. He did his best, even if his best wasn't good enough. He was more to be pitied than resented, for his pain and blindness had caused him to miss out on just as much as I had. Perhaps he realized that in the years since I left, and perhaps that realization had inspired him to make up for lost time. It was a relief to have a few moments of grace with him at last.

Attributes of the most significant people in our lives can be voluntarily emulated or unconsciously absorbed. I absorbed the crude sense of humor of my surrogate father, Alfie McKee, and from my mentor at work, Ernie Patterson, and also from that large segment of Ireland's population who revel in bathroom humor. I acquired a strong work ethic from my father. But as so often happens with fathers and sons, I also acquired some of his attitudes and repeated some of his mistakes.

I spent a lot of time with my sons and took them on trips all over America and the world, which my father was never able to do even if he wanted to, and I listened to their problems and did my best to guide them with the tools I was given, but I feel that I could have done more. I suppose every father feels that way to some extent but losing one of my sons magnified this feeling immensely.

I worked hard through my twenties, started my own business in my late thirties, and didn't retire until I was seventy-three. The demands of my career often occupied my mind. Unfortunately, we don't remember what the daily demands were as we look back over the great span of our lives, or what could have possibly been more important than simply spending time with loved ones. As Marley's ghost replied when Ebenezer Scrooge said he was always a good man of business - "Business? Business? Mankind was my business! The common welfare was my business; charity, mercy, forbearance, and benevolence, were, all, my business! The dealings of my trade were but a drop of water in the comprehensive ocean of my business!"

As a child, I wondered why "the dealings of his trade" were more important to my father than I seemed to be. Now, looking back, I wonder why I ever let the dealings of my trade distract me from my sons. As the old saying goes, nobody ever mentions how much time someone spent at the office when reading their eulogy.

I never had to worry about my son Mark as a kid, but Paul always seemed to find trouble. He was a real-life Dennis the Menace. But while childhood mischief is cute, adult mischief is usually illegal so the Dennis the Menace's of the world often become felons later on and live tragic lives. After many years of struggling with drug addiction, Paul died of a heroin overdose in 1998 at the age of thirty-eight.

Because of his death, there is an ebb and flow of regret in me. Unrealistic though it is, one minute I'll wish I had spent every minute of his childhood with him, anything to prevent the tragic end of his life. The next, I'll remind myself that one of the reasons I married such a good woman was so I could know my children were being taken care of at home when I was busy working. One minute, I'll be searching my mind for something I did or said wrong to him. The next, I'll remind myself that he had dozens of role models, not only me, and I worked so hard to make sure he had everything he needed. That was my way of showing my love for him. That was my father's way of showing his love for me, too. One minute I'll blame myself for everything bad that ever happened to him; the next I'll remind myself that my sons had defined characters since the day they were born, as if their personalities were predestined.

Perhaps another reason I worked so hard was the deeply imprinted memory of my mother and I hiding in that dark house when I was barely old enough to walk as the landlord banged on the door demanding the rent money. Or perhaps it was the psychic legacy of the empty promises made by the owners of Richardson Sons and Owden, the linen company I had worked so hard at only to see the higher paying position go to less qualified relatives. Or maybe it was all the lean years struggling to keep a roof over our heads and make Rosaleen proud of me. In fact, it was all of those things, along with the pride and competition that pollutes most men.

I thought all I had to do was work hard and provide all the essentials for my family and somehow my two sons would naturally or magically become who they were meant to be. Since I had managed to overcome my problems and become more successful than my dad, I assumed the natural result would be that my two sons would do better than I did; that there would be a gradual progression, with each generation doing better than the one before.

I never sat down and mapped out a course for myself. Life seemed to have some kind of pattern or map of its own and I just went along with it. Mark did not inherit this philosophy. He spent many years soul-searching and traveling the world. I often thought he intellectualized the good out of everything - work, love, marriage, even God. He was a gifted cynic who looked around, under and behind everything. I was worried about him but he is now married with a good career and a child on the way so I'm finally going to be a grandfather. He's a black belt martial artist, having apparently inherited my love of boxing. He's also a successful writer and poet, so all that soul-searching appears to have produced fruit.

Mark once told me that for Rosaleen and I to blame ourselves in any way over Paul's bad choices is like Mother Teresa wishing she would have applied one more bandage. One Father's Day, shortly after Paul's death, he gave me a list he wrote of happy memories from his childhood, hoping to show me that Paul's death was not my fault. There were thousands of memories there, page after page of little and big things that Rosaleen and I said or did which had made our sons' lives happy, most of which I had completely forgotten about. I cried.

Something else that stayed with me over the years is fear of embarrassment about having an untidy home, like mine was as a kid. I won't tolerate any disarray in or around my home to this day, much to the dismay of my wife and son who are always urging me to relax. It's a living hell for me in the fall when the leaves are falling faster than I can rake them up. Last October, Mark tried to convince me that I should not only not rake them up but learn to enjoy the multi-colored leaves on the lawn because "they make the house look autumn-ey." They probably do but I dismissed this observation by telling him, "That's just your lazy California attitude. Always finding excuses not to work."

He just shook his head in dismay and said to Rosaleen, "Mom, I'm afraid the situation is hopeless."

Mark has many of his mother's qualities, mainly sentimentality. If it were up to him, he would have kept every toy he ever had growing up. I, however, refused to tolerate having things laying around which he had outgrown or lost interest in and were "serving no useful purpose" (which Mark will tell you is my favorite expression.) He has complained several times that I threw away so many of his things over the years. I tell him if he saw the house I grew up in, he would understand my obsession with tidiness. He jokes, "It's been fifty years. Get over it." But some things, we never get over. One lifetime is not long enough.

Mark tells me it's a miracle that I'm even normal after the upbringing I had, but I never blamed my father for anything. I was never ashamed of him or felt that he should have been a better man than he was. He was what he was based upon his time, where he lived, and what had happened to him, and so am I.

So I'm afraid I have no sage words of advice for young parents. There is no foolproof formula for raising children. I did my best to provide a stable environment for my children to grow in, but their lives took courses I could not have predicted any more than my father could have predicted mine.

There is something intangible in us all that can't be controlled by outer circumstances; peculiarities and quirks given to us mystically or handed down to us genetically from some distant relative. So we each have our own private devils to deal with and control. If a man can manage to love and honor his parents, his wife and his children despite their failings, and his own, he's a success.

When my father struggled to connect with me on my second trip home, though it was too late, I appreciated it. I never did bring up any resentments or wounds of the past with him, and I'm glad now that I didn't. As I hugged him goodbye, I held him longer than I ever had before, trying to somehow let him know that it was okay, that I had finally begun to understand the source of his earlier blindness, and that I loved him in spite of it. What good would it have done either of us if I had yelled at him or called him names? I knew somehow that it would be the last time I would be able to hug him, and I was right.

My da at his Great Northern Railway retirement party

CHAPTER 71

RETURNING TO MANCHESTER

"The great secret that all old people share is that you really haven't changed in seventy or eighty years. Your body changes, but you don't change at all. And that, of course, causes great confusion."
~ Doris Lessing

Thirty years after I had lived and worked there, I went back to Manchester and revisited the areas of the city I had come to know so well in my youth. To my dismay, everything had changed. Urban decay had taken its toll. What had been genteel, middle-class neighborhoods now had the appearance of a slum. Fine old homes had been painted with gaudy colors by uncaring residents and trash was strewn everywhere. It bothered me so much, I haven't been back since.

My work in California regularly took me into bad neighborhoods, but to return to a place that was beautiful and vibrant in my youth only to find it in such a shambles depressed me terribly because it made me feel like the world had grown older along with me. We can't stop nature from taking its toll on our bodies. Time will beat us all up eventually. But surely we can preserve buildings.

My carefree days in Manchester in my early twenties seem like eons ago now, almost as if it never happened, or like a dream from some other lifetime. At other times, though, these accounts seem like yesterday and I feel twenty-one again on the inside. I can think of something that happened when I was a child or a young man and still feel remnants of the original emotion.

We inhabit so many different bodies in one lifetime – infant, child, adolescent, adult, old person - and with them, different lives, different hopes and different ways of seeing the world. I suppose a city has its stages as well, but seeing Manchester reduced to such a state made me feel, in that irrational place that exists in all of us, that if I had found Manchester to be just the way I had left it, I would be magically transformed, young once more. I could find one of the old bars Hyndsie and I used to frequent and find him still sitting there waiting for me, ready to buy me a pint and chase the girls again. Or, if Manchester hadn't changed so much, I might have at least been able to recapture the intoxicating feeling of being twenty-one again, with the world at my feet and plenty of time to explore it.

CHAPTER 72

MY PARENTS' FINAL YEARS

There is a tear for all who die,
a mourner o'er the humblest grave.
    ~ Lord Byron

In the fifty years since I left Belfast, I have returned perhaps a dozen times. My mother never reconciled herself with the fact that I was not coming back. No matter how many years had passed since she had last seen me, every time I returned for a vacation, she would ask over and over, "When are you coming home to stay, Sidney?" It made no difference how often I told her that America was my home or that I had two sons and a career there. She just asked the same question every time, right up until I boarded the plane for home.

They say human life is a circle from childhood to childhood. Elderly people can be like children in their inability to accept reality, and it is equally heartbreaking to see hope in their eyes that can never be fulfilled.

I have often wondered how my life would have been if I had stayed in Belfast. However, my imaginings have rarely been positive. America truly is the land of opportunity and I am certain I could not have advanced in my chosen career as quickly had I stayed in Belfast. The dead end jobs I had there and my father's lack of advancement despite his beloved "perfect attendance record" at the railroad were proof enough of that. But we all must make our own way in the world and I was no different. I just thank God that, like so many hundreds of thousands of immigrants searching for a better life, I had the courage to go to America.

Despite my happiness in California, I often had the feeling that I had somehow deserted my parents and sister. I would think about their lives in drizzly, old Belfast and mine in sunny Southern California, taking the kids to Disneyland every summer, building sandcastles on the beach, popping up to Vegas or Big Bear for the occasional fun-filled weekend, passing movie stars on the street, etc., and couldn't help but feel a twinge of guilt. I tried to make it up to them when I was home by taking them on road trips but the happiness felt during my short visits never completely obliterated the sadness I felt deep down for not being able to stay with them.

My da (left) chatting with Uncle Fred and Aunt Emily, 1978

My father died at the age of seventy-six the way he did everything else - efficiently and without fuss, just as my Grandma Tillie (his mother) had. I was surprised when my sister told me that my mother fell apart and mourned his death very deeply. As this account demonstrates, my recollection of their relationship was one of discord and perpetual frustration. It always seemed to me that if they weren't fighting, they were barely tolerating each other. It wasn't until after their deaths that I learned that I had been almost completely unaware of the tender moments between them. Even in the most troubled relationships, there are often moments of warmth and kindness, even joy, which usually come in the still of night, alone in bed, out of view of the children, when the day's aggravations and annoyances have begun to settle.

Because my father's death was so sudden, I was not able to get home in time for the funeral. As if my mother's life hadn't been hard enough, a few years later, she was knocked down by a bus near the City Centre. Nothing was broken but the physical and emotional jolt seemed to start a slide into an ever-deepening well of Alzheimer's Disease, which her own mother had. Finally, she became totally bedridden. She barely recognized me toward the end and would confuse me with other family members, some of which had been deceased for many years. My sister Olga took care of her until she died. She arranged the funeral through a small parlor on the Shankill Road in Belfast.

Thankfully, I was able to make it home for my mother's funeral. Olga and I drove to the funeral parlor together and I saw my mother lying in her coffin. As I kissed her forehead and felt her cold flesh, I felt the familiar regret carve into me again for moving away and leaving her alone for so many years. I knew that it was the best thing to do and that my guilt was irrational but my mind couldn't make peace with my heart over the feeling that I had abandoned her. I thought about her rattling around that old house in the years since my father died, perhaps looking now and then at the initials "S.R" I had written in the wet cement of the side porch, or the lines on the inside of the door jamb where I measured my height year after year, and felt sorry that I had not stayed in Belfast to take care of her and my da, or to at least stop by and visit once in a while. A phone call or letter can never replace the human touch.

But if I had stayed in Belfast, who knows if or when my father's discouraging attitude would have improved. If I didn't achieve at least as much in Belfast as I had in California, which was almost certain due to the lack of opportunity there, I'm sure it would have only served as more fodder for criticism of me, and that wouldn't have done anyone any good.

CHAPTER 73

MARRIAGE

"The three rings of marriage are the engagement ring, the wedding ring, and the suffering."
~ Anonymous

"Before marriage, a man declares that he would lay down his life to serve you; after marriage, he won't even lay down his newspaper to talk to you."
~ Helen Rowland

That my parents were separated only by death is not unusual for people of their generation from Northern Ireland. The tradition of staying together no matter what has carried over into my generation as well. Even in America, where divorce is commonplace, most of the Irish couples I know who came to America around the same time I did are still together after over fifty years. Belfast men might not be the most romantic husbands in the world but they are steadfast. For better or worse, they never leave.

A lot of American couples fall head over heels in love very easily, perhaps too easily. They're completely smitten with each other for a year or two until they suddenly announce they're getting divorced.

The average American today probably has everything too easy and is thus ill-equipped to deal with the ennui that inevitably slips into marriage, or the storms that beset it from time to time. Even in the most blessed unions, the intensity of the honeymoon eventually subsides and the couple becomes two people *actually* bound to the pretty vows spoken at the ceremony and to each other, for *life*. That's not easy for many people to get their minds around.

Marriage has also become one of the strongest symbols of youth's end in a nation obsessed with holding on to youth at any cost. For the first time, the number of divorces is greater than marriages as people hold on perpetually to the delicious irresponsibility of adolescence.

A recent study found that the institution of marriage would be obsolete in thirty years if current trends continue. If divorce wasn't such an acceptable option, people might be more motivated to solve their problems and attain greater happiness in the long run than they ever can searching for a perfect match that doesn't exist. There's a lot to be said for sticking together through thick and thin. As the old saying goes, the harder the climb, the better the view.

I hope all the unhappy years my parents spent together produced a few happy ones. After all, the in-laws who were so critical of them were all dead and gone, making their condemnation of my parents' marriage even more absurd. None of their agitations succeeded in separating them, nor did it affect the ultimate result of their lives together. All their hurtful comments ever accomplished were to add to their already heavy burdens while they were alive. Life flew by for them, as it does for us all. All the petty grievances, mostly rooted in conceit, have turned to dust along with them. My parents fulfilled their vows – for better or worse, in sickness and health, till death finally parted them – whether or not the insults had ever been spoken at all.

Perhaps it is unwise to tolerate a lifetime of anything but total happiness, but it is surely more unwise to quit too easily. It's easy to love someone when they're behaving and they haven't revealed all their demons, but loving someone means loving their faults, too, and relationships are strengthened in adversity. Everyone has heard stories of an old person complaining about his or her spouse's faults – snoring, for instance - only to say after they're gone that they would do anything to hcar their snoring again at night. Irish women in particular love to complain about their husbands, but no matter his transgressions, he is there every night when she goes to sleep, and he's there every morning, lying next to her, drooling on the pillow. I would consider this kind of dedication more valuable than all the wine and roses type of romance in the world. Rosaleen is my best friend today as well as the love of my life, and I know she feels the same way about me despite the problems we've had over the years. I hope the same was true for my parents in the end.

My parents in 1978, shortly before my father's passing.
Their apparently authentic happiness in this photo
heals me a little every time I look at it.

CHAPTER 74

SEEING UNCLE ALFIE AGAIN

"A person needs a little madness, or else they never dare cut the rope and be free."
~ Nikos Kazantzakis, *Zorba the Greek*

During my visit to Ireland in 1968, I went up to Coleraine and dropped in unannounced on Alfie, Flo and my cousins. Alfie opened the door and stood staring at me. It was obvious that he didn't recognize me. I decided to pull his leg a little.

In my best policeman's voice, I barked, "Are you Alfie McKee?"

"That I am," Alfie answered, "What is it you want?"

"I'm afraid I have to ask you to come with me to the station."

Alfie looked so discombobulated, I couldn't keep up the pretense any longer and started to laugh.

"It's me, Alfie!" I said, "Your nephew, Sidney!"

"In the name o' God, Sid," he gasped, "I would never have known you! How'd ya get so big?"

America had been good to me, and I had gained about fifty pounds. Alfie, on the other hand, had become much smaller since I had last seen him. It is common for everything from one's childhood to shrink as they get older - houses, schoolyards, streets, etc. However, this phenomenon is even more pronounced with people because they actually do become smaller. My Uncle Alfie was never a big man, but he was a giant to me. His personality made him larger than life. It was a shock to see him standing in the doorway, a wizened old man, and my heart overflowed with affection for him. Impulsively, I threw my arms around him. He patted my back and said, "It's good to have ya home again, Sid. Come on in."

He walked me into the house. Aunt Flo was as beautiful as ever, like a Spanish senora.

"Look who's here, Flo!" he said, "It's wee Sid, but he's not so wee anymore!"

Her eyes lit up and she rushed over. We hugged, sat down, and the three of us fell into conversation for hours. There was a lot of catching up to do.

I saw Alfie and Flo again on several subsequent visits. As always, Alfie was in great form and the house was filled with laughter. As he reached his seventies, though, his health deteriorated and his heart grew weak. Even in that condition, he made jokes about his "left ventricle" and other failing body parts.

My last memory of him was when Alfie and his daughter's husband, James, offered to drive me to the airport when I was leaving. Alfie came downstairs in his "simmet" (t-shirt) and trousers. The simmet was yellow from age and sweat.

"Ach," he said, "I think I'll have a shower."

I was confused because I knew there was no shower in the house. He picked up a can of underarm deodorant and gave himself a squirt under each arm.

"Ah, much better!" he said, "Ready for the road!"

What a character.

Alfie died before I got the chance to see him again. I was in Los Angeles at the time. I cried and cried, knowing that I would never see him again or enjoy his irrepressible wit. Coleraine would never be the same without him. Flo rejoined her Alfie a few years later in 2003. I'm sure that he's back to his old tricks in heaven and Flo is shaking her head with her usual mixture of dismay and affection. I can see Alfie either shocking the devil or giving God a good laugh with one of his stories. I hope it's the latter, because if Alfie's not in heaven, I don't want to go.

Alfie with his grandson, Darren, 1974

Note from the author's son:

I had a chance to meet Alfie on a trip to Ireland with my parents when I was fifteen. I liked him immediately. He had a seafaring air about him and spoke to me as if I were an old friend, not just some punk kid (which I was.) In other words, he gave me the same feeling of esteem about myself that he had given my father so many years earlier. I have often wished I could have met him again later in life. I knew even then that he had endless stories to tell and could surely tell them well. Alfie said to me, "Remember, Mark. You're Irish first and American second."

I had not been told the story at this point about how he had lost his eye and I didn't dare ask. But one day, while walking along a grassy trail on our way to see the Giant's Causeway, apparently reading my mind, he asked, "Do you want to know how I lost me eye?"

"Yeah!" I replied.

"Well," he said, "When I was a soldier, me and a few other boys got a weekend leave. We were staying at an old cabin in the woods. They were all going out for a few drinks, but I felt like staying in. I had been alone in the cabin for a few hours when I heard a knock on the door. I opened the door and nobody was there so I shut it again. A few minutes later, there was another knock. I was starting to think something fishy was going on, so I picked up the poker from the fire. When I opened the door, there was nobody there again, but I felt an ice cold wind brush past me that chilled me to the bone. I slammed the door and while I was rubbin' meself to warm up again I noticed it."

"What?" I asked, transfixed.

"A skull! Sittin' on the mantelpiece! Still covered with wee bits'a hair and gristle! I knew it wasn't there before. You notice things like that. I couldn't relax with it in the house so I took the poker I was holdin' and stuck it into one of the eye sockets, opened the door, flung the evil thing back outside and slammed the door. The next day, I lost the very same eye. It was . . . the skull's revenge!"

Thunder clapped overhead as he delivered this last line. I kid you not. I was completely aghast. It was the greatest ghost story I had ever heard, told masterfully.

Later that night, I mentioned the story to Flo. She said, "That's what he told you, eh? Well, it must be true!"

Maybe that experience was what made him want to become a medium.

Later, when I was saying goodbye to him for the last time, he whispered to me, "My greatest hope for you, son, is that you'll grow up to be as good a man as your da."

As I was getting into the rented car, he yelled, "Come back and see us again!" He and Flo stood smiling and waving until we were out of sight. I returned to California and, to my great loss, never saw Alfie again.

Having assisted my father with this book, it is obvious to me that Alfie was my father's main influence in life. His description of Alfie's personality is identical to my description of my father. My wife tells me that I'm exactly the same way, too. Many men say they're afraid of becoming their fathers. Personally, I can't think of a better fate. And if anyone ever tells me I remind them of Alfie, I'll consider that a supreme compliment, too.

Uncle Alfie with Rosaleen
Giant's Causeway, 1978

CHAPTER 75

ALONE IN BELFAST

"Other people have a nationality. The Irish and the Jews have a psychosis."
~ Brendan Behan

The last time I was in Belfast was nine years ago. I was 68. Both my parents had been gone for over ten years. My memories of my parents and Belfast were still so intertwined, it was hard for me to accept that they were really dead and that the city was rumbling along without them just as it always had when they were living and a part of it. Someone else was shunting at the railway station and worrying about his perfect attendance record.

I had always defined my life in relation to them so it was strange to be anywhere in the world when they no longer existed, but especially Belfast. Our parents define us whether we like it or not. When they're gone, a part of ourselves is gone, and we don't know who we are anymore.

As I walked around Belfast, I thought of how I had felt as a young man just before leaving for England. I remembered how eager I was to go someplace new and different. I was bored with Belfast, with the predictability of life and the same sights and people every day. And here I was, over forty years later, trying to find the very same things again.

Most of my friends had moved away or died. The Park Picture House was condemned. The Plaza had been converted to an office building. A highway ran through the spot where Maggie Moore's Sweet Shop used to stand. The old pubs, including Mooney's, my old favorite, had been replaced with glitzy department stores. Many of the pubs went out of business over the years because nobody wanted to go downtown for fear of I.R.A. bombings. The only pub that remains is the Crown, which is now a historical building.

As I wandered past the old buildings I had lived out my youth in, now overgrown with vines, a prophetic poem by Charles Kingsley called *Young and Old* crossed my mind:

When all the world is young, lad,
 And all the trees are green;
And every goose a swan, lad,
 And every lass a queen;
Then hey for boot and horse, lad,
 And round the world away;
Young blood must have its course, lad,
 And every dog his day.

When all the world is old, lad,
  And all the trees are brown;
And all the sport is stale, lad,
  And all the wheels run down:
Creep home and take your place there,
  The spent and maimed among:
God grant you find one face there,
  You loved when all was young.

I knocked on a few doors of people who knew my old friends. I learned that Harry Hutchison had moved to Canada, joined the Royal Canadian Dragoons, then dropped out of sight despite efforts by myself and others to contact him. Big Harry Rankin also fell victim to the dreaded Alzheimer's Disease in his later years. John Hynds ("Hyndsie") tragically lost his wife in a traffic accident but has since remarried. Being gifted with a grand singing voice, he can still be found making the rounds at the various social clubs in Belfast, entertaining the members. Big Lionel also left Belfast for parts unknown and without a trace. There are numerous rumors about his whereabouts, all equally outrageous, the most persistent being the aforementioned rumor that he was running a brothel somewhere in the Channel Islands. Decades after he had last been seen or heard from, Lionel was still the talk of the town, inspiring gossip and speculation.

Richardson Sons and Owden, my first employers, finally went out of business after one hundred years in the linen manufacturing business. Their grand, old building at 4 Murray Street in Belfast still stands but is occupied by a number of different tenants. On my last walk through Belfast, I stood at the front door and remembered waiting there for Rosaleen to come out when we were both teenagers - the best idea I ever had.

My son Mark accompanied my wife and me on our last trip home. We took many long drives through the countryside and he marveled at the way the pastures shone an almost blinding green in the sunlight. There is a reason Ireland is called "The Emerald Isle." One doesn't know what green is until he or she has seen the vast expanses of grass wet with newly fallen rain, illuminated and magnified in a sudden burst of sunlight unfiltered by smog or dust, with a double rainbow sparkling above it.

Mark has talked about how he felt strangely at home in Ireland despite his California upbringing and imagined how his life might have been had he grown up there rather than America. If his mother and I had made different choices, he might have been one of the ever-present, dirty-faced waifs running around the streets, shouting to each other with incomprehensible Belfast accents.

The troubles in Northern Ireland, and how such generally kind-spirited people can also be so stubborn and prejudiced toward each other was a mystery to Mark, as it is to most Americans. As the saying goes, "If you think you

understand the problems in Northern Ireland, you're not well-informed enough."
But despite the feuding and the politics, Mark was absolutely enchanted with
Belfast and with the Irish, north or south, Catholic or Protestant. In fact, he
became friends with people of both persuasions and went on numerous "pub
crawls" with them. (History repeating itself.) We were worried that he might say
the wrong thing to someone, but he insisted that everyone was as friendly as
could be and told us he had never had so many pints bought for him by complete
strangers in his entire life.

Mark also enjoyed the way strangers casually struck up conversations,
as if they were old friends of his. As friendly as Americans are, that just doesn't
happen as easily or as often in Los Angeles. For instance, Mark was walking
through the shopping district one day. An old man he had never met before said,
"Hey! How've ya been? I didn't recognize ya with your sunglasses on!"
Mark watched him after he walked away and saw him greeting everyone he
passed with similar comments. He was a delightful loon. Most just laughed and
said something equally ridiculous back.

Another time, we were going into a shop to repair a broken heel on one
of Rosaleen's shoes. The man behind the counter saw Mark standing behind us
and asked, "Who's that? Your minder?" (Bodyguard.) I jokingly replied, "Yeah,
so you just mind your manners!" He picked up his cobbler's hammer, smiled and
said, "Don't make me use this."

During the same trip, Mark was working out at Mike Bull's Gym in
Bangor in an attempt to burn off all the Ulster fries and pints of Guinness he had
been downing. Two men were working out together, one doing bench presses
and the other standing behind him as a spotter. The one lifting the weight was
singing Rod Stewart's "*If You Think I'm Sexy*" while pushing the heavily loaded
bar up and down, which was odd enough. The bar got stuck on his chest and he
yelled to his friend, "Get it off! Get it off!"

The "spotter" just stood there, looking idly around the gym.

"Get it off, eejit!" he yelled again, the bar squeezing the air out of
him. Mark yelled over to the spotter. He still didn't look down. His friend
continued to say "get it off" but with barely any volume since he couldn't get
a breath. Mark pointed frantically to his struggling friend. The daydreaming
man finally looked down and noticed his friend, now nearly unconscious, and
pulled the weight off his chest. The man sat up, rubbed his chest, paused with
perfect comedic timing and said, "What part of 'get it off' don't you
understand?"

"I thought you were still singing," his friend answered.

He said, "What song do you know that has the words "Get it off!" in it?

Mark laughed until he cried at this natural comedy team and suggested
they take their show on the road.

One of them answered, "Aye, maybe we will. You're not a talent agent,
are ya?"

As always, a snappy rejoinder was at the ready.

I was standing in line at the airport wearing a Hawaiian print shirt when a man leaned into me and as if passing some secret password to me, said, "I like yer shirt. Ya fit the part."
"What part is that?" I asked.
"Any part ya like," he answered. And off he went.

My friend Bill Cunningham told me he was standing outside a store in Belfast one day waiting for his wife, Kathy, to finish shopping. The street was buzzing with activity. A very agitated man walked up to him and said, "See him? See me? Right enough!" He then promptly walked away, apparently content that Bill knew exactly what he was talking about.

One summer day, I took a walk up to the local zoo. I was watching the lions when the male began to get amorous with one of the lionesses, mounting her from behind and gnawing on the back of her neck. A family was standing next to me at the fence and their wee lad asked, "What's that lion doin' to her, daddy?" Without hesitation, his father said, "He's clippin' her toenails. Come on." Then he led him away quickly before he could get a good look. No uncomfortable explanations or searching for the right words. The boy was satisfied and they went on to the next exhibit.
Later that day, while standing by the chimpanzee cage, a man stood beside me and whispered, "Checking out your ancestors?" The harassment is constant.

These exchanges stand out in my mind because they are somewhat bizarre but they are actually representative of the kind of thing that has always defined the Belfast character. There's almost no such thing as a stranger. Just say hello and you're old chums immediately. Ask for directions and you won't only be pointed in the right direction, you'll be escorted there personally and have a nice conversation along the way.
All this is very refreshing to tourists from big cities in America, where people seem to be more tentative about talking to each other. A great line comes to mind from one of the *Crocodile Dundee* movies. Nick Dundee was walking along a New York sidewalk for the first time. It was teeming with pedestrians, as usual, and he said, "That's incredible. Imagine seven million people all wanting to live together. Yeah, New York must be the friendliest place on earth."

Anyone who lives in a big city long enough knows that they tend to make people sick and suspicious. It's the small courtesies and friendly interactions that make a place a community. That was what impressed Mark most - the feeling that he was a part of something larger than himself for a change, giving and receiving smiles rather than being looked at like he's a potential mugger. Like any other metropolis, Los Angeles is an overwhelming place and neither Mark nor I have ever had any truly warm feelings about it. It's just too damn big.

In Mark's introduction to this book, he shared a bit of a poem he wrote with you. As he mentioned, his appreciation for all things Irish has increased as he's gotten older, which I'm happy to see. Here's the entire poem he wrote about our last trip home.

The Enchanted Isle

I was born and raised in the good ol' U.S. of A.
But my heart also belongs to a place far away,
An enchanted isle of leprechauns and banshees,
Of shining, green fields, craggy hills and bent trees.

Where ever-falling sunshowers light up the grass.
Their emerald beauty dazzles the eye as you pass.
The thatch-roofed cottages speak of simpler ways
And cause the mind to drift back to quieter days.

The beauty of the land stuns you into reverent silence
And makes you wonder how there could be any violence.
I wish every man on earth with an angry heart and mind
Could spend some time there to get them both realigned.

I could live there forever if I had my way and my choice.
The peaceful silence makes it easy to hear God's voice
It's in the whispering of the wind as it stirs the trees.
Your heart and soul are invigorated by every breeze.

A rainbow forming over a glade's babbling brook
Makes you abandon whatever you're doing to look.
The water's teeming with life and the bank is, too.
It's like a storybook, and the main character is you!

But you don't need to be Irish to love the "Emerald Isle"
For in the north or south, you'll receive a bright smile
From the kind-hearted folk, the nicest people on earth
Who've survived much adversity with humor and mirth.

In fact, the Irish have a greeting, unique to them alone.
I can't describe it. You would simply have to be shown.
It's a wee turn of the head and an impish wink of the eye
That seems to say, "Isn't it wonderful just to be alive?"

So come with me now, friend, to a simpler day
Just for a moment, 'fore you're back in the fray.
There are just a few people I'd like you to meet
Over that hill there and down the next street.
You might recognize them as family because
Half the world's Irish - and half wishes it was!

- Mark Rickerby

Irish gypsy caravan

Gypsy children. Poor but happy.

CHAPTER 76

BELFAST TODAY

"Home is a place you grow up wanting to leave, and grow old wanting to get back to."
~ John Ed Pearce

The city of Belfast was at the center of the war within Northern Ireland. The only thing worse than the destruction of the City Centre by I.R.A. bombers was the German blitzes in the early months of 1941. Yet despite everything, Belfast has survived. The shopping district buzzes with activity. There has been an influx of immigrants from around the world, particularly Asia. The City Centre has been reconditioned and rebuilt where necessary. A lot of people are making money and spending it. In my generation, most people could barely afford rent, much less the purchase of a home. Today, houses are selling for hundreds of thousands of dollars, and up to a million dollars for condominiums along the Lagan River. The city abounds with sidewalk cafes and restaurants offering cuisine of every nationality. The people are well dressed, driving their own cars and purchasing their own homes. The young people are taller, stronger, and more sophisticated than my generation.

On the adverse side, there is still a great deal to achieve with revitalization of what were once thriving residential neighborhoods such as the Shankill and Falls Roads. These neighborhoods are depressingly bleak, with the doors and windows of the old homes bricked over, awaiting demolition.

The weather, which no one but God can change but for some reason doesn't, remains miserable. Occasionally, though, the sun makes an appearance and the post card photographers rush out with their cameras.

I read a story once about a veteran in his elderly years who opened the Army trunk he had taken home after his discharge sixty years earlier. Among all the mementos he had kept of that tumultuous and dramatic time, he found his old combat boots. He turned one of them over and soil fell into his hand; soil from some long-ago battlefield where he fought and bled, screamed and prayed, and held comrades as they had breathed their last. This tangible evidence of that place and time overwhelmed him and he began to cry. Without thinking, he took a pinch of the soil, placed it on his tongue, held it there for a moment, and swallowed. Even he didn't know why.

People from the most war-torn and God forsaken places on earth usually feel the same way. Home is wherever one spent a significant portion of his or her life, the only life he or she will ever know. Their hometown is the stage where the drama of their life took place. The soil of that place is the same soil that caught all their blood, sweat and tears and the older they become, the dearer that soil becomes because of it.

I love California and the warmth is certainly kinder to my old bones but I still constantly miss the sights, sounds and smells of Belfast, the cold wind off the Lough; the view of Cave Hill, so mysterious to me as a child; being surrounded by others with the same Belfast brogue I have; and the feeling of familiar ground. I miss the smell of coal in the air. I miss seeing the streets teeming with kids at play because they had no televisions to watch. I miss the street venders yelling to the housewives and the women chatting over the hedges. I miss my friends, calling up to my window to come out and play.

In leaving Belfast so many years ago, I left behind my family, friends, neighbors and all the places I loved. But the human spirit is resilient and can adjust to just about any new environment. What I miss the most as the years pass is the chorus of friends and family who I shared my life with then. We're blessed if we can still phone them or send them a letter but more often they are either lost somewhere in the world, or dead and gone forever. "Homesick" is just another word for lonely, and loneliness is always worst when there's absolutely no way to soothe it.

My parents spent their entire lives in that old house, and except for those who have passed away, the neighbors remain the same to this day. Time has washed away most of the people and events of this tale. What remains is the cheerfulness of the Belfast people, their wry humor, their often blunt honesty, and the impish smile, nod and wink one can expect from passing strangers. The spirit of Belfast still thrives and can be easily accessed by anyone with an open heart. All the Belfast natives I know equally enjoy the visits home despite the weather, the political discord, and the gulf that still exists between the majority and minority populations.

Except for a bout with cancer when I was forty-five that almost took my life, two fights with breast cancer that almost took Rosaleen's, and the immense tragedy of my son's death, my life was and is a good and happy one. My sister Olga was not as fortunate and bears the scars of a dysfunctional family environment, a legacy she was unable to escape. Now that our parents are gone, I see her strength and independence finally growing, which gives me hope that she may find some peace, at last. Sadly, I had to leave Ireland to make something of myself and write this account from a distance in terms of both time and space.

Despite the dismal portrait some of these pages may paint of my early years, I was happy and content for the most part as a child. There was stability to life then which I have never felt as profoundly in America.

Rosaleen and I have thought about spending our golden years in Belfast many times but I don't think it's meant to be. America in general and California in particular has too much to offer and has been too good to us to leave now. But our memories of the happy, carefree years of our youth in Belfast and the warmth of the people we knew there will stay with us forever. And if heaven is everything they say it is, there will be a little patch of green up there somewhere where the Irish are getting along as God originally intended, their differences forgotten, where my friends are still laughing, where my parents are happy and I can hold them in my arms again.

EPILOGUE

The last time I was home, I dropped Mark and Rosaleen off at the city centre and went to see my sister. After visiting for a while, she left on some errands. The old house was as quiet as a tomb. Though they had been gone for twenty years, I still half expected to hear one of my parents call from another room. I walked upstairs to my old bedroom and looked out the window, remembering Lionel calling up to me from the street below, and thought, "Whatever became of you, my friend?"

Everything had changed; so much washed away. Sadness overwhelmed me. A lot of people would have had a good cry at that moment but, like most men, I don't always allow myself to feel uncomfortable emotions. It's easier to just bury them under some activity, so I went back downstairs and took myself out for a walk on the old street.

It was one of those days I used to love as a child, with the sun playing hide and seek behind the clouds and a soft, clean wind blowing up from the lough, the same wind that stirred my young spirit and made my heart ache for new adventures so many years ago. One side of the street was in bright sunlight and a light shower was falling on the other. A glorious rainbow shone over it all like a giant ribbon. Children were playing soccer in the street. I stopped to watch them and the ball rolled to my feet. I picked it up and held it in my hands. The familiar texture and the smell of leather awakened a long dormant memory of playing football for hours with my friends.

A wee lad ran over and said, "Can I have me ball, mister?"

I said, "Sorry, son. Here ya go."

I tossed it to him.

He said, "Thanks, mister" and ran off.

And it dawned on me that nothing had really changed. That I had grown older, but Ireland is what it always was, and Irish children were what they always were.

Seventy years is nothing at all.

Now sweetly lies old Ireland,
Emerald green beyond the foam,
Awakening sweet memories,
Calling the heart back home.

~ Irish Proverb

9 781456 836634